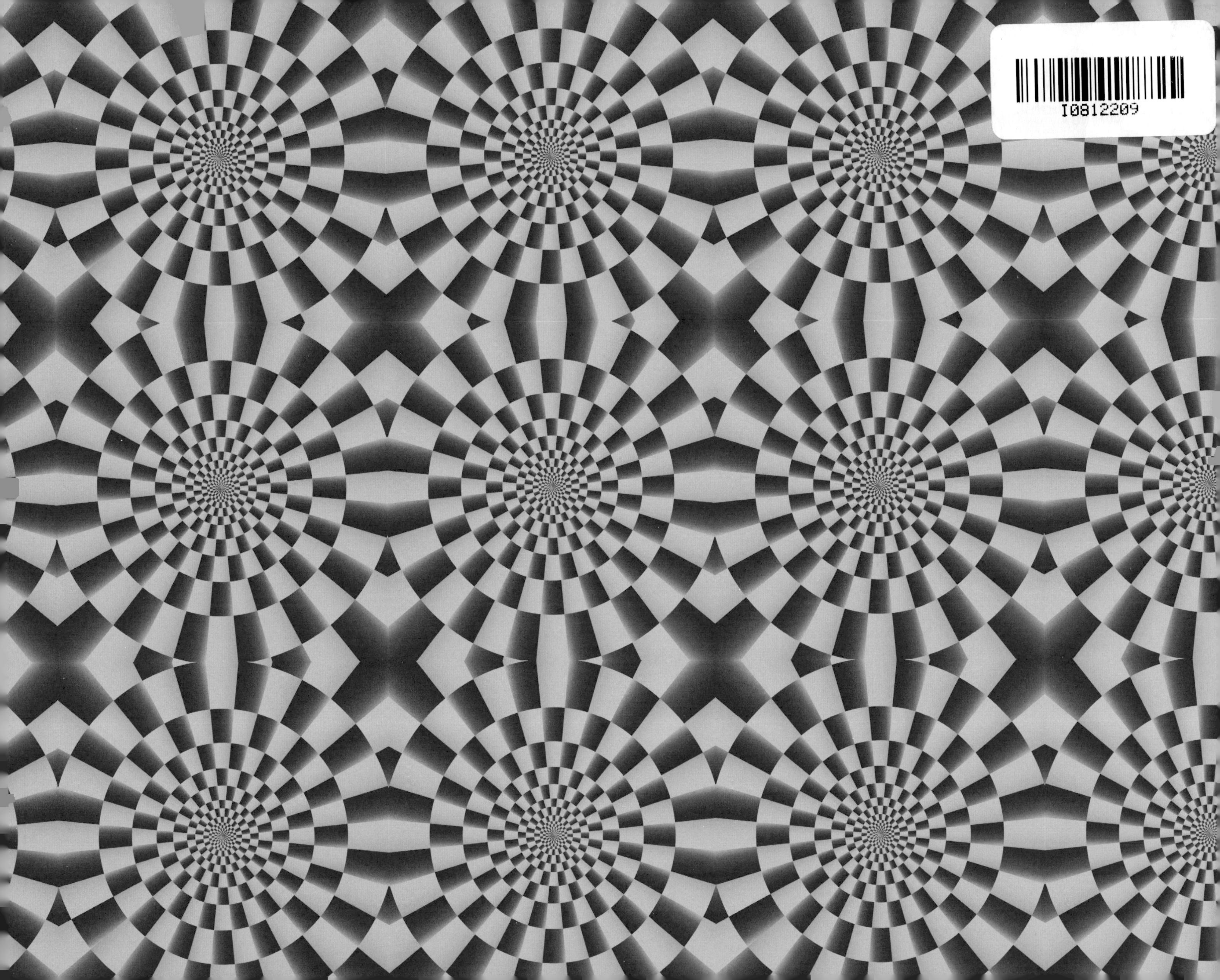

FREAKS OF SIDESHOW AND FILM

MARY BRETT &
STEVAN GOULD

Schiffer Publishing Ltd
4880 Lower Valley Road • Atglen, PA 19310

OTHER SCHIFFER BOOKS BY MARY BRETT

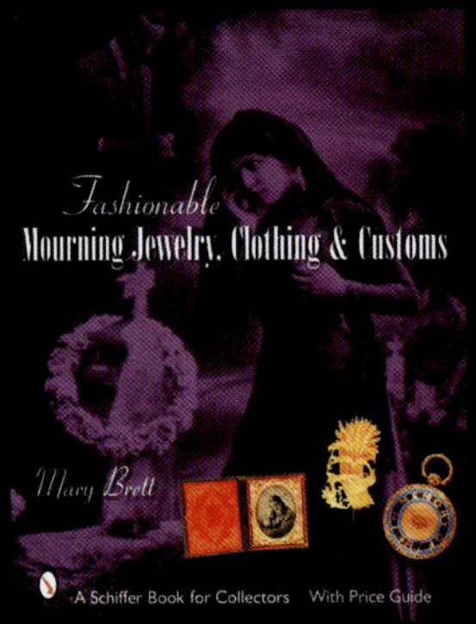

Fashionable Mourning Jewelry, Clothing, and Customs
978-0-7643-2446-8

OTHER SCHIFFER BOOKS ON RELATED SUBJECTS

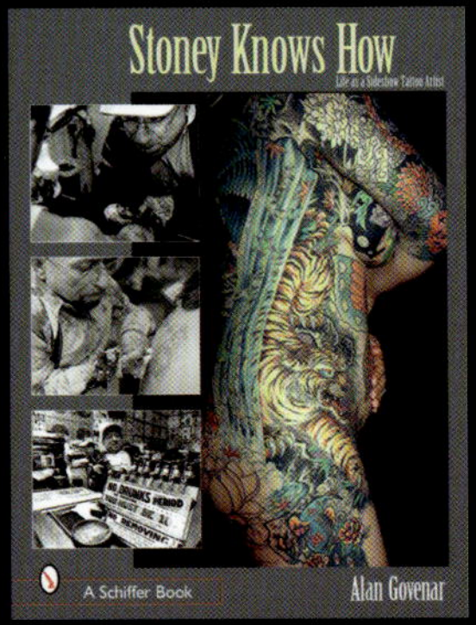

Stoney Knows How: Life as a Sideshow Tattoo Artist
by Alan Govenar
978-0-7643-1832-0

DEDICATION

This book is dedicated to Phyllis Gould—a most amazing woman and a descendant of William C. Coup, an early circus entrepreneur and business partner of P. T. Barnum—and to Brinkley, Tatum, William, Leah, Lily, and Addison, soon to become amazing people in their own right.

Library of Congress Control Number: 2015946791

Designed by Matt Goodman

Type set in Adobe Caslon, Engravers, URWWoodTypD, Egyptian505 BT, Rosewood STD & Tungsten.

ISBN: 978-0-7643-4845-7

Printed in China

Published by Schiffer Publishing, Ltd.
4880 Lower Valley Road
Atglen, PA 19310
Phone: (610) 593-1777; Fax: (610) 593-2002
E-mail: Info@schifferbooks.com

For our complete selection of fine books on this and related subjects, please visit our website at www.schifferbooks.com. You may also write for a free catalog.

This book may be purchased from the publisher. Please try your bookstore first.

We are always looking for people to write books on new and related subjects. If you have an idea for a book, please contact us at proposals@schifferbooks.com.

Schiffer Publishing's titles are available at special discounts for bulk purchases for sales promotions or premiums. Special editions, including personalized covers, corporate imprints, and excerpts can be created in large quantities for special needs. For more information, contact the publisher.

CONTENTS

PREFACE

This book is written to applaud the people whose lives are portrayed within these pages. Many endured harsh existences but most managed to overcome the limitations of birth and become comfortable in their own skins. Some became both rich and famous. A few even managed to find true happiness, a rarity in anyone's life. Before the advent of "politically correct" social behavior, people born "different" were often openly stared at, made fun of, shunned, cruelly ridiculed, or hidden from view by being locked away in attics, sheds, basements, or inadequate and vile institutions. In severe cases, they were killed. Many families believed that the birth of a "monster," a title bestowed upon the innocent babe by both the medical profession and polite society of the day, gave proof of God's wrath brought down upon that family for past sins. Traveling carnivals with the sideshow gave many of these social outcasts a chance to escape into a different world, a world that held the possibility of employment, excitement, travel, fame, and the chance to both be with and be accepted by people just like themselves.

Presented within these pages are the true biographies of the most amazing people that have ever lived. Their lives should be an inspiration to all of us, but please, no pity. An anonymous reporter summed it up well in a 1914 newspaper article when he wrote:

Freaks do not desire our pity, only our interest and the partial contents of our purses.

The facts presented in this book are, to the best of our knowledge, true. However, the times and quintessential showmen, such as P. T. Barnum, did not always let truth stand in the way of a good story, especially if that story sold tickets to shows or offered free advertisement captured in sensationalized newspaper stories. Whenever possible, we have talked to family members or obtained official birth, death, and marriage records. We have visited numerous graveyards to examine and record the engraved headstones, and we have pored over thousands of old newspaper clippings and advertisements to separate fact from fiction.

Herein are the fascinating biographies of incredible people who lived amazing lives, Celebrate the success of these amazing individuals who were born with every card in the deck stacked against them but were able to succeed against all odds, proving indeed, being born different is not so bad with the right attitude and a little luck! ♦

***Editor's note:** Readers will note that this book includes language that is no longer generally used to describe individuals, as it can be considered offensive. This language is used only in its historical context.*

ACKNOWLEDGMENTS

A very special "thank you" to these people who went out of their way to help furnish information that added to both the enjoyment and accuracy of this book: Mary Baldwin (the Otis Jordan story); Bound Brook Cemetery, Bound Brook, New Jersey (photo of grave for Zip, William Johnson); Armand Chevrette, president of Mountain Grove Cemetery, Bridgeport, Connecticut (photograph of Lavinia Warren's grave); Jackie Childs, director of Cedar Hill Cemetery, Philadelphia, PA (the Hannah Battersby story); Kyan Chuong, University of Pennsylvania (historical insight into Laloo); Carol Damon, Nemasket Hill Cemetery Association, East Taunton, MA (the Minnie Warren story); Stephanie Greer, Mount Royal Cemetery, Quebec (photo of J. T. Clark's burial site); Dan Hedberg, Oakland Cemetery, Sandusky, Ohio (the Fannie Mills story); Dianna Kinney, director of Schuyler County Library District, Lancaster, MO (the Bob Melvin story); Judith Lukas, (the Princess Beatrice story, the J. T. Clark story); Ann Poulos, Providence, Rhode Island Public Library (the Eugene Ferralto story); Jeff Richman, historian, Green-Wood Cemetery, Brooklyn, NY (historical insights); Anthony Salamone, director of Evergreen Cemetery, Brooklyn, New York (the Annie Price story, the Annie Jones story); and Bob Wainwright, Charlotte Eisenmann Wainwright, and family (the Charles Eisenmann story) ♦

1

THE HISTORY OF THE AMERICAN CIRCUS

CIRCUSES, MUCH LIKE THE ONES WE ARE FAMILIAR WITH TODAY, STARTED IN LONDON IN THE EARLY 1770S.

In 1793, an Englishman named John Bill Ricketts established America's first circus in Philadelphia. Ricketts was an outstanding rider so it is not surprising that his circus incorporated amazing equestrian feats along with theatrical performances. George Washington, a great admirer of good horsemanship, attended several performances.

In 1797, Ricketts had a permanent amphitheater built in New York City, but he also took his show on the road to Boston, Baltimore, Richmond, Virginia, and other major cities to increase his revenue. We were a young country that was still sparsely populated, even in our larger cities. He also ventured into Canada. Traveling was no easy feat for Ricketts since his road circus was shown in a large building that had to be torn down and rebuilt at each location.

By the early 1820s, numerous traveling circuses had sprung up. The early traveling circuses were often called "mud shows" in reference to the terrible roads they traveled throughout America and Canada. The "Big Tent Shows" would not surface until 1884 when the Ringling brothers from Baraboo, Wisconsin, introduced the well-designed tented circus that earned them the title of "The Kings of the Circus World." The sights of the circus enthralled and amazed a population whose social entertainment was usually limited to church and church socials, weddings, wakes, funerals, and public executions, all within a few miles of their birth. It was not unusual for some to walk all night to attend a traveling show performance that had come to town. The exotic sights and sounds of a circus probably seemed magical to most, and the shows were most likely remembered and talked about for a lifetime.

Not everyone approved of the circus as accepted entertainment for the masses. Most ministers denounced these performances as "devil's play," but that warning had little effect on the majority of the citizens. Indeed, that declaration may have even increased the local turnouts, especially among the male population. Sadly, Ricketts's circus was a financial failure and was defunct by 1799. However, he is still considered "The Father of the American Circus." Ringling Bros. and Barnum & Bailey, and other successful circus organizations owe their success, in part, to the pathway John Bill Ricketts forged for them. He introduced American and Canadian audiences to the circus spectacle that is still a well loved and well attended tradition today. In 1961, John Bill Ricketts was posthumously inducted into The Circus Hall of Fame in Sarasota, Florida. ♦

John Bill Ricketts, an Englishman, established America's first circus in Philadelphia in 1793 and is considered "The Father of the American Circus."

In 1797, Ricketts had a permanent amphitheater built in New York City but he also took his show on the road to Boston, Baltimore, Richmond, Virginia, and other major cities to increase his revenue.

2

P. T. BARNUM, "THE FATHER OF THE FREAK SHOW"

P. T. BARNUM NEVER UTTERED THE FAMOUS QUOTE THAT HAS BEEN ATTRIBUTED TO THIS GREAT SHOWMAN: "THERE'S A SUCKER BORN EVERY MINUTE."

That statement was fabricated long ago by an anonymous newspaper reporter trying to enhance his story. Barnum's feelings regarding the paying public were quite the contrary since he had both a deep-rooted love for and a pressing desire to please his audiences. He also possessed a driving need to be recognized. He actually stated once that he "preferred to be kicked to not being noticed at all." While that thought is not as colorful as the bogus quote, it does best reflect the mind and spirit of this legendary man. He wrote to a publisher in 1860, "I don't believe in duping the public, but I believe in first attracting and then pleasing them." Critics can cite numerous Barnum attractions that were, indeed, hoaxes but even they have to admit that he always delivered an amazing diversion to his paying audiences. Another Barnum quote: "Amusement (may not be) the great aim of life, but it gives zest to life and makes a grand improvement in human character." He is also famous for saying, "Every cloud has a silver lining," and he claimed he often thanked God that he had always been able to see the bright side of every situation.

Phineas Taylor Barnum was born in Bethel, Connecticut, on July 5, 1810, to the son of a poor father who tried many professions. Philo Barnum was a tailor, a farmer, a storekeeper, and a tavern keeper, all with scant success. Phineas seemed destined to follow in his father's footsteps. His first work venture was a storekeeper, heavily involved in the new lottery that was wildly popular nationally. After failing in that business, he started a weekly newspaper in 1829, *The Herald of Freedom*. Possibly due to the rashness of youth or his already developing flamboyant style, his writings offended enough readers to result in libel suits, prosecution, and a short jail sentence. In 1834, he fled to New

In his early years, P. T. Barnum started a weekly newspaper, but his rashness of youth and his flamboyant style offended enough readers to result in libel suits, prosecution, and a short jail sentence.

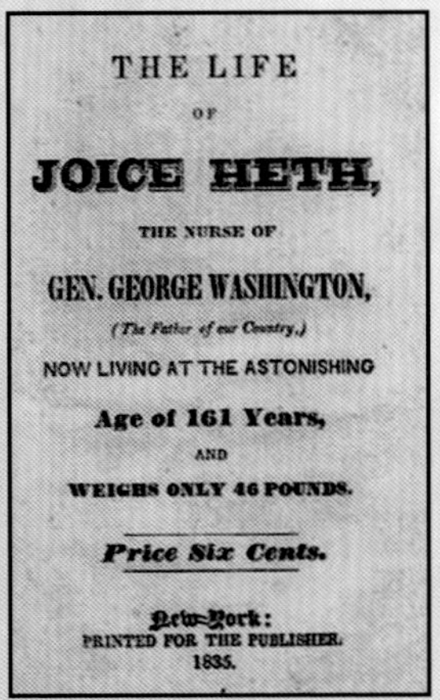

THE LIFE
OF
JOICE HETH,
THE NURSE OF
GEN. GEORGE WASHINGTON,
(The Father of our Country,)
NOW LIVING AT THE ASTONISHING
Age of 161 Years,
AND
WEIGHS ONLY 46 POUNDS.
Price Six Cents.
New-York:
PRINTED FOR THE PUBLISHER.
1835.

Barnum purchased an elderly black slave and exhibited her on profitable tours across America. His success came because of his ability to advertise and promote this hoax.

York City to escape his badly damaged reputation. In 1835, he embarked on the showman career that would be both his claim to fame and his avenue to great wealth. He purchased a blind and almost completely paralyzed black slave named Joice Heth for the reputed sum of $1,000 and exhibited her on profitable tours across America, traveling with a small company. His success came, for the most part, because of his ability to advertise and promote his deceptive show. Barnum claimed that Joice was over 160 years old and had been the nurse of George Washington. The public literally bought the sham. He continued to tour until 1839, even though Joice died in 1836. Her age at death was proved to be only around seventy to eighty years old.

After the hoax had been made public and his main attraction was dead and buried, Barnum had lean years that caused him almost complete financial ruin. He bounced back, however, and in 1841 he bought Scudder's American Museum on Broadway and Ann Street in New York City, renamed it The American Museum, and the rest is, as we say, history. It was open fifteen hours a day and was one of the top attractions of its day. These museums were called "dime museums" because of the fee charged to enter, and they were the forerunner of all museums in America to come, although the more sophisticated museums of today are, most likely, not particularly thrilled knowing this heritage. Barnum had learned first-hand from his tours with Joice Heth that the public is drawn to the different and to the spectacular. He augmented the conventional museum exhibits of stuffed animals and wax models with curiosities he collected from all over the world, both fake and real. His first big break came in 1842 when he exhibited the 25-inch tall Charles Stratton, whom he renamed General Tom Thumb. Many a businessman scratched his head and marveled that so much money could be made by simply exhibiting a midget dressed in costumes, singing, dancing, and telling jokes.

Barnum added the live and authentic original Siamese twins Chang and Eng to his exhibit and the dead and fake FeeJee Mermaid, supposedly a

In 1841, Barnum opened his very successful dime museum on Broadway in New York City named The American Museum. They were called "dime museums" because of the fee charged to enter, and these dime museums were the forerunner of all museums in America.

cross between a fish and a woman. His collection also included the Native American dancer, outrageously named Do-Hum-Me, to capitalize upon eastern America's fascination with the Wild West. Many of these live performers were housed on the top floor of the museum. He was not content to

Barnum's first big break came in 1842 when he discovered and exhibited the 25-inch tall Charles Stratton, whom he renamed General Tom Thumb.

just sell tickets to his shows. He realized the profit in having merchandise available for sale, and he was the first to put his picture on sale products, also fulfilling his need for public recognition. His beefy but good-natured likeness, with its bulbous nose and potbelly, were well known to the masses. At one time, he was called the most recognized man in America, and he was also one of America's first millionaires. As his success grew, so did the mag-

In 1850, Barnum engaged the world-famous soprano Jenny Lind, called "The Swedish Nightingale," to sing in America for the much publicized staggering salary of $150,000 for 150 concerts.

nitude of his publicity stunts. During 1844–1845, Barnum took Tom Thumb on a highly publicized European tour where they entertained the beloved Queen Victoria of England and her court. In 1850, Barnum engaged the world-famous soprano Jenny Lind, called "The Swedish Nightingale," to sing in America for the much publicized staggering salary of $150,000 for 150 concerts. Barnum also agreed to shoulder all expenses. He generated such a heightened degree of public excitement surrounding the anticipated event, actually bordering on

Barnum often put his face on advertisements and merchandise. At one time, he was called the most recognized man in America, and he was also one of America's first millionaires.

In 1871, Barnum established P. T. Barnum's Grand Traveling Museum, Menagerie, Caravan, and Hippodrome, which included a museum of freaks. It was this traveling show that introduced the concept of freak exhibitions to America and Europe.

Most of the famous freaks of the day toured with P. T. Barnum at some point in their career.

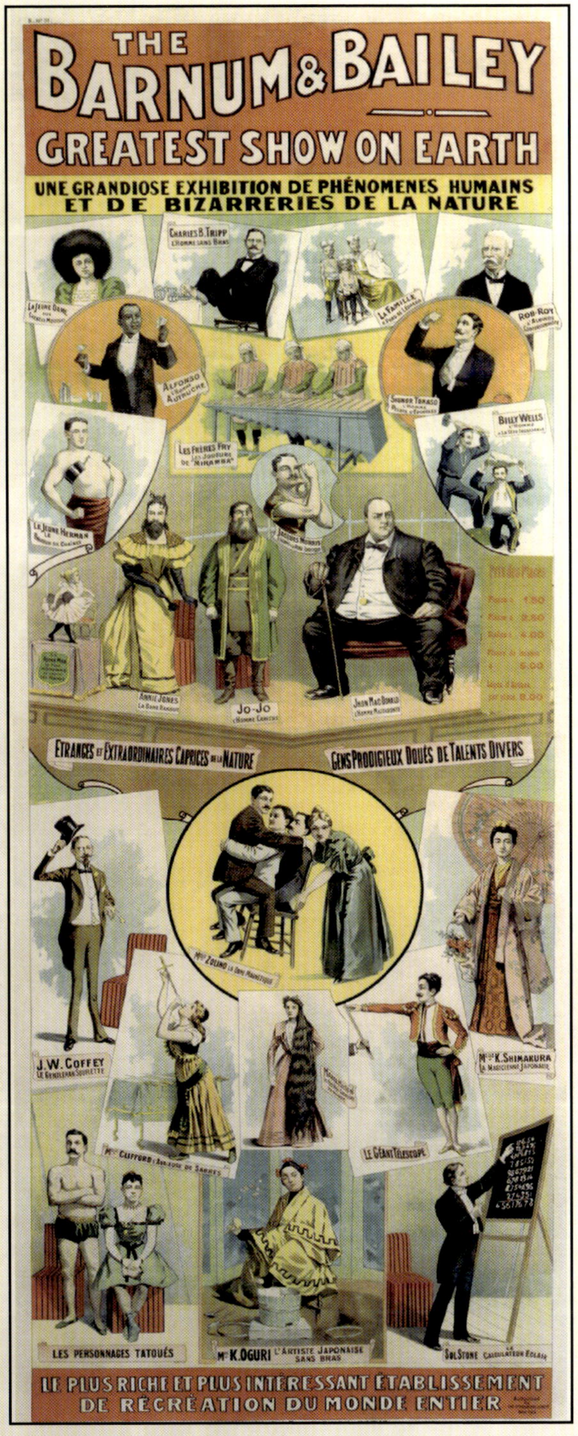

near frenzy in many towns, that he was able to book her with little or no difficulty. Men attending the concert outnumbered women ten to one, even though the devout and pious plain-looking Jenny abhorred makeup and preferred to appear on stage in a simple white dress rather than elaborate or revealing costumes. It is said her voice was the lure for the gentlemen. The less kind say it was P. T. Barnum's ability to advantageously publicize and market his product that made Jenny irresistible and the venture a success. In the end, Barnum had invested $187,000 but collected $700,000 in ticket sales.

Jenny Lind terminated the tour and contract after ninety-five performances, paying Barnum a financial penalty, but the two-year tour had been a money-maker and publicity boom for both singer and showman. Some speculate that while mon-

Barnum married his much younger second wife after the death of his first wife. Neither marriage brought the master showman much happiness.

Phineas Taylor Barnum died in his sleep on April 7, 1891, at the age of eighty. He is buried in Mountain Grove Cemetery in Bridgeport, Connecticut.

P. T. Barnum, aptly named "The Father of the Freak Show," was the quintessential showman but he never uttered the most famous quote attributed to him: "There's a sucker born every minute."

ey and fame were definite motivators for the showman, Barnum had also been trying to refine his image as a true patron of the arts by bringing Jenny Lind to the American stages. He retired from show business in 1855, but the need to settle with creditors, plus possibly boredom and the desire for continued excitement in his life, edged him back into the business in 1857. In 1865, his beloved museum caught fire and burned to the ground. Almost all was lost, including most of his live exhibited animals. The ones who managed to escape the fire were shot by policemen on the scene who were there to protect the public. He rebuilt the museum on the same spot, renaming it The New American Museum, but it too burned to the ground in 1868. He never rebuilt after the second fire. In 1871, he established P. T. Barnum's Grand Traveling Museum, Menagerie, Caravan, and Hippodrome that included a museum of freaks. This show of Barnum's shaped the future evolution of freak sideshows that sprang up all across America and Europe and remained wildly popular until the 1950s. Freak sideshows allowed people with severe deformities an honest vehicle by which to earn a living and an opportunity to live independently, not institutionalized as a ward of the state. It also afforded them an accepting social structure that was most likely missing in their lives up to that point. Most of the famous freaks of the day toured with P. T. Barnum at some point in their career.

P. T. Barnum did not introduce the circus to America or invent the modern three-ring circus prototype. In fact, he did not even apply himself to the American circus until he was over sixty years old. However, his name remains synonymous with "The Greatest Show on Earth," a lasting tribute to his ability to please his audience and be recognized. He married twice, taking a much younger second wife a few months after his first wife died. Sadly, neither marriage brought the man who gave pleasure to the world any true happiness. His first wife was a sickly woman who preferred her sickbed to life, and the second wife was said to have married only for monetary gain and comfort.

Phineas Taylor Barnum died in his sleep on April 7, 1891, at the age of eighty. He is buried in Mountain Grove Cemetery in Bridgeport, Connecticut. A comment by Barnum a few weeks before his death persuaded *The New York Sun* newspaper to print his obituary early so that he might be able to enjoy what was to be said of the great showman. ♦

3

THE FREAK SHOW IS BORN

THE EARLY DAYS OF OUR COUNTRY WERE HARSH FOR ITS PEOPLE IN THE BEST OF CIRCUMSTANCES.

Disease, war, poverty, poor sanitary conditions, archaic medical practices, and a shortage of nutritious foods readily available to the majority of citizens were all factors that contributed to the average life span being only fifty years. Imagine now that you were born physically very different from your peers. Life just got even harder. Much harder. Babies born with severe deformities were often killed at birth or left on their own, without care, to die a slow, torturous death. Superstitions abounded at this time. Many people full-heartedly believed that a deformed child was a sign from God that bad deeds had been committed by the parent(s) and punishment had been righteously dealt, or worse, that the cursed child was a spawn of the devil himself. If the child was allowed to live, he or she would most likely be institutionalized due to the antiquated belief that a deformed body also indicated intellectual disability. ♦

THE FREAK SHOW BECOMES A STAPLE IN AMERICAN & EUROPEAN ENTERTAINMENT

The financial success of the sideshow often hinged on the ability of the "barker" or "talker" to entice the public into purchasing a ticket to go behind the brightly illustrated tent banners.

A "freak show" is technically a show where human oddities and outlandish performing acts are presented for the awe, amazement, and enjoyment of the paying public. The term applies to both circuses and carnivals. While the term "freak" often offends us today, this was the term preferred by the performers. While the title seems harsh to us, let us remember both polite society

The "barker" would often use one or more performers to attract the buying public to the shows, always promising much more exotic sights once inside the tent.

Freak shows were most often a combination of working acts such as the sword-swallower, magician, fire-eater, and strong man, coupled with actual bizarre human oddities, and exhibited alongside the "created freaks," such as the traditional fat lady or tattooed people. They were generally referred to as "ten-in-one shows."

and the medical community of the day referred to these individuals as "monsters."

These shows were most often a combination of working acts such as the sword-swallower, magician, fire-eater, and strong man, coupled with actual bizarre human oddities, and exhibited alongside the "created freaks," such as the traditional fat lady or tattooed people. They were generally referred to as "ten-in-one shows." Since one sideshow was much like the last one to hit a town, the financial success of the production often hinged on the ability and talent of the well-paid "barker" or "talker," the industry term, whose job it was to entice the public into purchasing a show ticket to go behind the brightly illustrated tent curtains. Usually the barker would be aided by one or more of the show performers who paraded themselves outside the tent to heighten interest.

Once inside, there would be a "blow-off act," an industry term for a performer so spectacular or so hyped that the public would pay an additional fee to see, usually the price of the original ticket. Most ten-in-one shows had the usual line-up of created freaks such as the fat lady or tattooed man, the show performers such as the strong man, snake charmer, or sword-swallower, a few real or fake freaks, and the spectacular blow-off act.

Part of every good ten-in-one show was the scantily-clad sexy show girl.

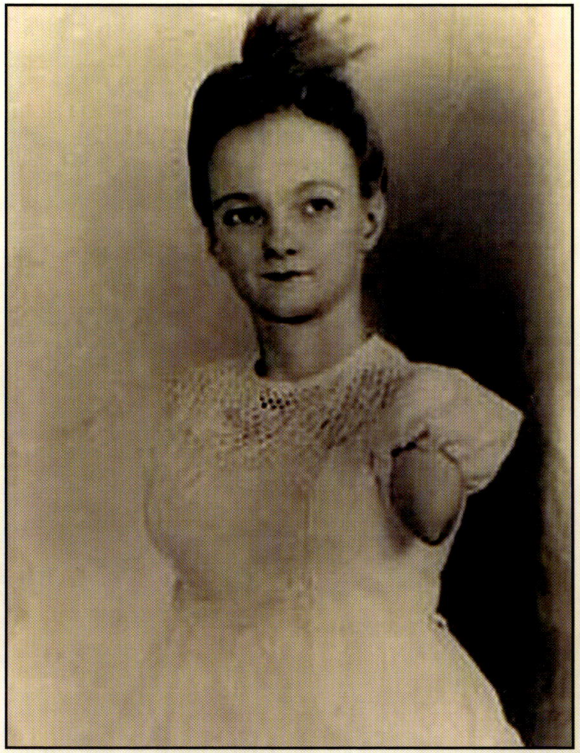

Once the paying public was enticed to go inside, there would be a "blow-off act," an industry term for a hidden performer so spectacular or so hyped that the public would pay an additional fee to see. (Shown: Freda Pushnik)

Soon circuses and carnivals were traveling all across America, into Canada, and to Europe, most adding a sideshow of freaks. This caused a high demand for the unique, the bizarre, and the very different, both real and fake. Now people formerly shunned by society had a way to make a lucrative salary, travel, gain fame, and add a quality to their lives that had been formerly impossible to attain. They signed contracts, negotiated salaries, and displayed themselves willfully. Many traveled from foreign countries to join successful American circuses and carnivals. The top freak performers even held audience with American and foreign aristocracy and dignitaries, as well as European royalty, and they usually retired financially secure with a lifetime of colorful stories to share. Freak shows also gave a nurturing social structure to people who had spent a vast majority of their lives shunned by mainstream society, many times including members of their own family. Collectively, they formed communities where many thrived. Some even found true love, married, and had children. Unfortunately, there were others who were not as fortunate. Many of these were, in essence, sold by their parents or guardians to the freak show at an age too young to comprehend the implications. Some were mentally challenged and thus often exploited by unscrupulous profiteers. Most had kind managers who protected them. P. T. Barnum, himself, had a sterling reputation in the industry and treated all his performers well and with respect. Sadly, there were exceptions to the rule. A few had managers who exploited the helpless and most of these performers led a miserable life, much akin to slavery. These few heartless managers kept all earnings and subjected their charges to beatings, isolation, and poor living conditions, then placed them in institutions when their earning potential ended. At various times during the history of the freak show, well-meaning but misled individuals and groups have protested what they consider the exploitation of these unique performers. However, the majority of freaks when asked will say: "Mind your own business and allow me to get back to my life and my pay check!" ♦

THE DECLINE OF THE FREAK SHOW

For over a hundred years, roughly 1840 through the mid-1940s, the freak show remained one of America's most popular forms of entertainment. During World War II, gasoline was rationed, making it difficult for traveling sideshows. After the war, it became less financially feasible to run a sideshow because America was suffering from inflated consumer costs on goods such as gas, food, and shelter. Amusement rides, games of chance, and eateries could occupy the space of the freak shows at a more profitable return. Also, salaries paid to the employees of the rides, games, and eateries were much less than the salaries paid to the stars of the freak sideshows.

Television shares the blame for the decline in demand for the sideshow. We now had a new entertainment vehicle that brought a vast variety of marvelous entertainment into the average household daily, and we did not even have to leave the comfort of home. Also, the Civil Rights Movement made us, as a world, more likely to see all people as human beings and not merely objects.

Today, only a handful of these freak sideshows still exist. Admittedly, audiences are more sophisticated today than in the heyday of the sideshow. We are also more politically correct with sensitive insights to those among us who are different. Unlike a monster to be feared, we actually view the

Before television and prior to World War II, traveling circuses and carnivals remained one of rural America's most popular forms of entertainment, amazing a population that seldom ventured more than a few miles from the place of their birth.

Brightly colored erotic banners heightened the public's interest in the performers who waited behind the tent's canvas walls, beckoning them to spend the money for a ticket.

disabled and different in a sympathetic manner. However, can we at least honestly admit a conflict of emotions generally plays through the modern viewer's senses when exposed to oddities? All said, let us confess that we can still be thrilled by the bawdy colors, sights, smells, and sounds of the time-honored American entertainment tradition of the freak show. Sophisticated and enlightened or not, we find it almost impossible to turn away from any lurid yet captivating image. ♦

4

SAMUEL W. GUMPERTZ & CONEY ISLAND

P. T. BARNUM IS UNDOUBTEDLY "THE FATHER OF THE FREAK SHOW" BUT SAMUEL W. GUMPERTZ IS THE MAN WHO BROUGHT THE "FREAKS" TO CONEY ISLAND.

Samuel, known as Sam, was born in Washington, DC, on September 6, 1865, to Herman Gumpertz, a German immigrant tailor, in the family's home at 407 W 6th St. (no document lists his mother's name). The 1870 US census records him, age four, living in St. Louis, Missouri, in a boarding house run by an aunt. No mention is made of his parents, most likely an oversight. The family was living in San Francisco, California, in the late 1870s. Circus lore claims that Samuel ran away from home at the age of nine and joined the Jackley family of acrobats in San Francisco. Truth be known, he was likely closer to the age of fifteen and went with his family's blessing, albeit a reserved and resigned blessing.

Samuel W. Gumpertz is the man who brought the freak show to Coney Island. True or not, legend claims he joined the circus when he was only nine-years-old. By 1904, he was a successful Missouri showman before being hired to build and manage Dreamland at Coney Island.

He was a rough rider in the Buffalo Bill Wild West Show and later managed a circuit of theaters in Chicago and New Orleans. He was once arrested and fined $100 for showing "a play too suggestive even for a New York police officer." That play, *Mrs. Warren's Profession*, was written by George Bernard Shaw. Samuel is credited for giving Flo Ziegfeld his start in the entertainment world by hiring him as a manager. Samuel also managed strongman Eugen Sandow and was the last manager of the famous Houdini. By 1904, he was a successful Missouri showman when he was hired by Senator William Reynolds to build and manage Dreamland, a new Coney Island attraction.

Coney Island, a five-mile stretch of beach at the entrance to New York harbor where Brooklyn meets the sea, started as a resort around 1882 with a hotel and a theater. It has always had a colorful reputation.

The first hotel was named The Elephant Hotel and quickly turned into an establishment frequented by prostitutes and their marks. "To see the elephant" was a humorous saying of the day that equated to visiting briefly with a lady of the evening.

In 1884, the first roller coaster in America was built at Coney Island. Then, the era of the big amusement parks began. In 1895, Sea Lion Park, the first enclosed amusement park, opened. Two years later, Steeplechase Park opened with the "Steeplechase Horse Ride" and by 1902 added a fantasy "Trip to the Moon" ride. In 1903, Luna Park opened, featuring hundreds of thousands of electric lights, a true technical advancement for the era, and then in 1904 Dreamland opened across the street.

In 1884, the first roller coaster in America was built at Coney Island.

Coney Island was comprised of three major theme parks: Steeplechase Park, Lunar Park, and Dreamland. Steeplechase was the last of the great theme parks to close in the 1960s.

Dreamland affected a higher tone than its competitors by presenting attractions with cultural and even biblical themes. A visitor could boat through "The Canals of Venice, dine at "A Japanese Teahouse," or ride a train through "The Snow-Covered Alps." The glowing beacon towers were visible from thirty miles out to sea.

Dreamland's main attraction when it opened, however, was the wildly popular miniature village Lilliputia, also called Midget World and Midget

In 1904, Gumpertz was a successful Missouri showman when he was hired to build and manage Dreamland, a new Coney Island attraction that was designed to compete with Lunar Park.

(Shown: "The Elephant Ride" at Coney Island) Coney Island was such a popular place to be that on many a Sunday afternoon, more people populated Coney Island than most towns in America.

City. It was built to resemble fifteenth-century Nuremberg, Germany, except that everything, including the inhabitants, was scaled down to midget size. The approximately 300 inhabitants were gathered from world fairs, expositions, and circuses around the globe. They had their own parliament, their own beach, their own theater, and their own fire department that regularly responded hit-or-miss to false alarms for the enjoyment of the crowd. To add to the spectacle, giants were occasionally hired to stroll good-naturedly through the city. By day, the midgets would entertain the paying public, but after the park closed, they enjoyed living together in this close-knit community designed just for them.

Unfortunately, they enjoyed living together in this created fantasy world a little too much. Reportedly, lewd and immoral behavior such as promiscuity, homosexuality, and nymphomania were widely practiced and eventually both encouraged and advertised by management as a means to attract early twentieth-century visitors breaking free of the confines of the Victorian era. The reports were probably correct given the number of marriages that ended quickly in divorce, plus the fact that almost eighty percent of babies born to the village inhabitants were illegitimate. The aristocratic titles loosely applied to any midget seeking such (Prince, Princess, Queen, Count, Countess, etc.) only added to this fantasy life that put personal pleasure and gratification above all else.

So much for the higher tone the developers were originally seeking for Dreamland. The continued success of early Dreamland is attributed to Samuel Gumpertz's keeping a sharp eye on profits as well as continually upgrading and changing many of the park's attractions and rides to keep Dreamland fresh and appealing to a fickle public. He also increased attendance by advertising Dreamland heavily in local papers and through fliers.

He hit pay dirt, however, when he introduced his freak show of human oddities and circus attraction to the Coney Island crowds.

Gumpertz personally explored Europe, Africa, the Philippines, Asia, and Egypt seeking out the strange and unusual. Among other things, he brought back to Dreamland fifty-one friendly tribesmen from the Philippines and advertised

Dreamland's main attraction when it opened to the public was the wildly popular miniature village, Lilliputia, also called Midget World and Midget City. They had their own parliament, their own beach, their own theater, and their own fire department that regularly responded hit-or-miss to false alarms for the enjoyment of the crowd.

By day, the 300 midget inhabitants of Lilliputia would entertain the paying public, but after the park closed, they enjoyed living together in this close-knit community designed just for them. They may have enjoyed their fantasy village too much. Lewd and immoral behavior became the norm resulting in almost eighty percent of the babies born to the village inhabitants being born illegitimate.

them as wild and dangerous poison dart–blowing head-hunters. He also brought back an entire Eskimo village. He exhibited people from all over the world to the delight and fascination of the paying public. Amazingly, he was always able to whisk his strange entourages through customs and past the eyes of the amazed and astonished port officials. Of course, it has been speculated that more than one port official received a monetary reward for relaxing standards.

Samuel Gumpertz hit pay dirt when he introduced his freak show of human oddities and circus attraction to the Coney Island crowds.

Samuel Gumpertz was so successful recruiting freaks because he genuinely liked and respected them. He was once quoted in a newspaper article as saying, "It might be imagined that freaks are temperamental but such is not the case. One of their most wonderful characteristics is that they feel no hurt in their condition. Those connected with them for any length of time know that they are unconscious of their deformities, as such, and are as happy on the whole as any living person."

He also lured away acts from circuses and traveling sideshows, and was especially appealing to those performers tired of being constantly on the road. He offered a more typical lifestyle and a secure paycheck. Other performers worked at Coney Island during the off-season, returning to the nomad life when a new circus season started. Retired performers often picked up additional income by performing for short periods of time at Coney Island.

Typical Sunday afternoon crowd at Dreamland's sideshow.

Dreamland, however, like its predecessor Sea Lion Park, which closed in the early 1900s, was relatively short lived. It burned down on May 27, 1911, on the park's opening day of the season and was never rebuilt. History recounts Senator Reynolds, a greedy and crooked politician, had built Dreamland so quickly that he did not follow city code for fire hydrants. The firemen responding to the blaze could only get a tiny trickle of water from their hoses. The New York Aquarium now stands on Dreamland's site, (Of the remaining original

Samuel personally explored Europe, Africa, the Philippines, Asia, and Egypt seeking out the strange and unusual. He guaranteed the success of Dreamland by frequently changing attractions to keep a fickle public happy.

A typical early American audience was so naïve that they even paid to see fat ladies.

Annoyed by obviously fake wild men exhibits, Gumpertz brought back to Dreamland fifty-one tribesmen from the Philippines and advertised them as wild and dangerous poison dart–blowing head-hunters.

great Coney Island parks, Luna Park survived until it was gutted by fire in 1944 and Steeplechase closed in the 1960s. (A new Luna Park opened in 2010, named after the original, at the former site of Astroland, an old amusement park.)

Gumpertz saw an opportunity in Dreamland's demise. He immediately organized The Dreamland Circus Sideshow in a tent on Surf Avenue. A newspaper of the day wrote, "The Dreamland Circus Sideshow opens while ruins are still smoking."

Gumpertz's freak show continued through the

(Shown: during and after the fire) Dreamland burned down May 27, 1911, on opening day of the 1911 season. History recounts that a crooked politician, William Reynolds, built Dreamland so quickly that he did not follow city code for fire hydrants. The firemen responding to the blaze could only get a tiny trickle of water from their hoses. Unfortunately, Dreamland Park was never rebuilt and The New York Aquarium now stands on Dreamland's site.

Today, the Coney Island freak show continues to amaze and thrill the public and is seeing a resurgence in popularity.

Gumpertz's freak show continued through the 1920s and kept Coney Island in business during World War I and after the public tired of the illusion rides. The success of the Dreamland Circus Sideshow led to many other rival sideshows also exhibiting the strange and unusual at Coney Island and elsewhere.

1920s and kept Coney Island in business during World War I and after the public tired of the illusion rides. The success of the freaks at Dreamland Circus Sideshow led to many other rival sideshows also exhibiting the strange and unusual at Coney Island and elsewhere in America. In 1929, Gumpertz left Coney Island and returned to circus life, eventually settling down in Sarasota. He became the vice president and general manager of the Ringling Brothers circus and made a fortune in various real estate adventures. An article in the *Herald-Tribune* published after his death at the age of eighty-four in 1952 noted that he was involved in various philanthropic causes, including having an addition built to Joseph Halton Hospital that was equipped for the care of indigent children. His vast land holdings on Siesta Key were donated to the Boy Scouts and became "Camp Gumpertz." Gumpertz was a charter member of the YMCA of Sarasota and also was on the park board of that city. He was married twice and survived both wives. He had no children. He was cremated, as were his spouses. Today, the Coney Island freak show continues to amaze and thrill the public and is seeing resurgence in popularity. ♦

5

CREATED FREAKS & SIDESHOW EROTICISM

Tattooed People, Fat Ladies & Men, Human Skeletons, Strongmen, & Circassian Beauties

MANY PEOPLE, FOR VARIOUS REASONS, YEARNED TO JOIN THE TRAVELING CIRCUSES AND SIDESHOWS THAT CAME THROUGH THEIR TOWNS.

Some worked lowly jobs with the show: laborers, cooks, drivers, animal maintenance work, and such. Women often sold themselves to the show, providing either visual or physical sex for the patrons and workers. Others yearned to be stars but had no talent or deformities to give them star power, so the more resourceful created physical differences that set them apart from mainstream America. Such a person in the business is called a "created freak." The tattooed lady and man were "created freaks" who also provided eroticism since they were scantily clad to show off their body art. The more tattoos, the less clothing worn. It was also not unheard of for tattooed women, performing to an all-male audience, to completely disrobe once behind the curtain and after the ticket fee had been collected. Sideshows hinted at the nudity that possibly would be exhibited behind the curtain to

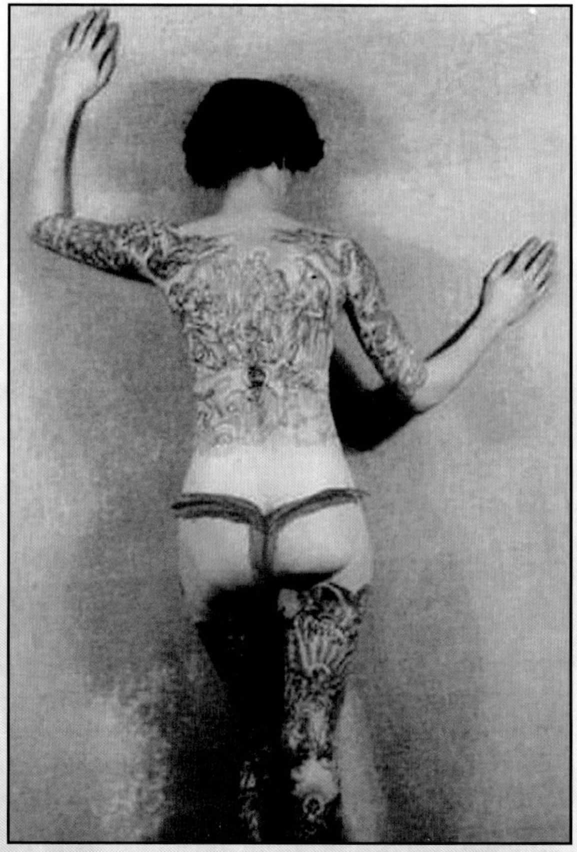

The tattooed lady was an example of a "created freak" who also provided eroticism. The more tattoos, the less clothing worn. It was also not unheard of for tattooed women, performing to an all-male audience, to completely disrobe once behind the curtain, and this possibility was coyly hinted at during ticket sales. (Shown: Jean Furella)

Women often sold themselves to the show, providing either visual or physical sex for the show patrons and show workers. Many had left home at an early age with no education and no talent, hoping to make a living with the circus or sideshow as best they could.

the paying public by flying large canvas art banners featuring women in erotic dress or erotic stances.

A "half and half," or a person physically having male and female sexual traits, was a very erotic attraction for the average person of the day. They were often the most popular act in a sideshow and even though the vast majority of these performers were fakes or "created freaks," they could still

Sideshows also hinted at the nudity that would possibly be exhibited behind the curtain by flying large canvas art banners featuring women in erotic dress or erotic stances. (Shown: Fred Johnson banner)

To the sheltered country fair attendee at the turn of the twentieth century, just the thought of a woman showing a bare ankle or knee was considered erotic and scandalous.

carry the entire show if able to visually display their bodies in a manner that would convincingly prove their claims. The circus fat lady was also seen as an erotic symbol for those men attracted to size and girth. Knowing this, it was not uncommon for the tattooed lady, the half and half, and the fat lady to engage audience members in good-natured flirting, guaranteeing that they would be returning for the next show. Women audiences were often visually excited by the show's strongman who flexed his muscles and showed off his bared body for their enjoyment. Many had never seen a man, with the exception of their husband, in such a state of undress and now, for the price of a ticket, they were able to openly stare, unquestioned and unchallenged, upon the half-nude man. The giant was also a sexual symbol since humanity equates strength with sexual prowess. Both the strongmen and giants played to the female and gay audiences by openly displaying their bodies performing acts of strength.

Prostitution among carnival ladies and male

patrons was not unheard of, especially among the low rung shows. This afforded a money-making opportunity for the carnivals that could not afford to attract and pay better-known performers and for female performers who, in essence, had hit the entertainment end of the line. Of course, to stay more than a few nights could be costly and dangerous to the carnival owners if the good folks of town got wind of the goings-on and brought in the law, or worse, took matters into their own hands and ran the troupe out of town on the preverbial rail. It was also not uncommon for immature and unsophisticated young rural men and women to become infatuated with the perceived excitement and sexual glamor of circus life and run away with the troupe when they left town. While a few succeeded in making a better life for themselves, most were ill-prepared for such a life and had no talent to add to the show. These unfortunates mostly ended up traveling down a road of ruin and desperation, with a very different outcome than the life imagined when they impetuously left home. ♦

Women audiences were often visually excited by the show's strongman who flexed his muscles and showed off his bared body for their enjoyment. Many had never seen a man, with the exception of their husbands, in such a state of undress and now, for the price of a ticket, they were able to openly stare, unquestioned and unchallenged, upon the almost-nude man.

TATTOOED PEOPLE

The word "tattoo" is said to have two major derivations: "ta" from the Polynesian word meaning "striking something," and "tatau" from the Tahitian word that means "to mark something." The history of tattoo began over 5,000 years ago and is as diverse as the people who wear them. Today, it is a popular craze that crosses all social and economic boundaries. This was not the case, however, during the heyday of the traveling sideshows that were touring the country, one small town at a time. Few people had seen a tattoo and even fewer were inked themselves. Getting tattooed was a way for a typically developed person to become a sideshow star and make a decent living when other avenues of employment were either not readily available or alluring. The first tattooed performers exhibited were so-called savages, but by the early 1800s, Europeans were also exhibiting themselves for profit and fame. American tattooed "created freaks" would follow suit in the early 1840s. Tattooed performers were paid very well due to their popularity, and each tattooed attraction strived to out-do the next. There are recorded histories of whole families of tattooed people performing on the sideshow circuit, as well as tattooed midgets and dwarfs, fat ladies, and even animals.

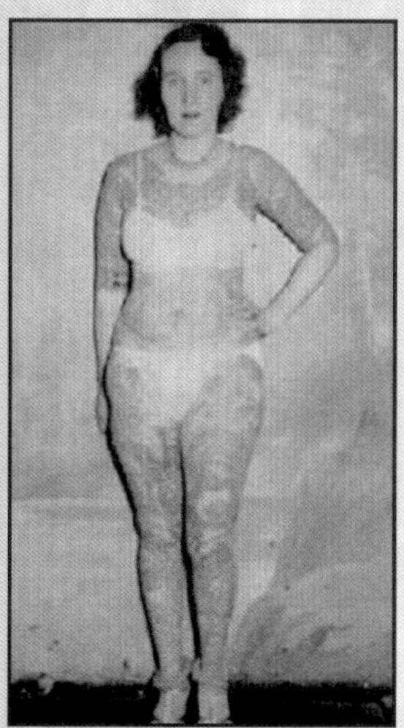

The show promoters often paraded tattoo ladies in front of the curtain in skimpy outfits to sell tickets. (Shown: Jean Furella)

While male tattooed performers were popular with early audiences, they were not nearly as popular nor sought after as were the female performers, and when tattooed women finally started to exhibit themselves in 1882, there was no longer much demand for men performers. It is interesting to note that the tattooed women were always referred to as tattooed "ladies" or billed under their stage names, even though they were often looked down on by the judgmental public. In an era when most women had few lucrative employment opportunities, often forcing them to marry or to depend on men for their very existence, tattooed ladies and other female sideshow exhibitors were able to support themselves. Many earned several hundred dollars a week. Financial independence meant that these women could choose to marry or remain single. Once married, they could divorce if the marriage was not to their liking. The first American tattoo studio opened in New York in 1870 and the invention of the first electric tattooing machine in 1891 significantly reduced the inflicted pain and time it took to execute a tattoo. This new device also required less artistic skill to operate. By 1900, every major American city had a tattoo parlor. Being tattooed was not impressive enough on its own anymore, even in the briefest of costumes, to entice the now more sophisticated paying public into purchasing a sideshow ticket. Most tattooed performers, except the rare ones who were exceptionally inked, were forced to expand their appeal and earning potential by reciting elaborate and fanciful stories in regards to their tattoos or by taking up a new skill such as knife throwing, sword-swallowing, fire-eating, or snake-handling. Many became tattoo artists themselves. ♦

Tattooed women were always referred to as "ladies" or billed under their stage names even though they were often looked down on by the public as hardly better than a street whore. The laugh may well have been on the judgmental public. In an era when most women had few lucrative employment opportunities, often forcing them to marry or to depend on men or families for their very existence, tattooed ladies and other female sideshow exhibitors were able to support themselves and many earned financial independence.

GIOLO ALIAS "PRINCE GIOLO"

Giolo was the first recorded human exhibited for profit as a tattooed performer; he made his debut in 1691 to a London audience.

Giolo was the first recorded human exhibited for profit as a tattooed performer. In 1691, William Dampier received Giolo, a slave, as settlement for a debt. He quickly happened upon a scheme to charge a fee to the London public for a chance to view this bizarre tattooed slave from the Philippines. Dampier created a frenzy over his new acquisition by heavily promoting Giolo. Among the many hyped claims, it was said that Giolo's extensive body tattoos provided him protection against poisonous snakes.

The masses clamored to see this remarkable primitive. Also among Giolo's audiences were the king and queen of England. Sadly, Giolo died of smallpox very soon after his arrival from the Philippines. His immune system was not adept at fending off Western diseases. The interest and fervor created, however, would set the stage for tattooed attractions and performers in the decades to come. ♦

OMAI

Omai was a tattooed islander from Huahine, near Tahiti, and he became the first South Sea Islander seen in Britain. He is sometimes referenced as Omiah in records of the day. Not much is known about his early history except that he was part of Captain James Cook's expedition led by Tobias Furneaux. Omai sailed to Portsmouth, England, as a crew member aboard the HMS *Adventure* on July 14, 1774. Omai was not as heavily tattooed as Giolo. His most notable tattoos were transverse lines on the back of his hands. However, he caused a minor fervor in England because of his regal demeanor. He was billed as a living example of a "noble savage," a popular romantic theme of the day. He was in his twenties at the time, and his sensual and exotic good looks made him immediately popular with the women who glimpsed this handsome man. Omai was discussed by scientists and philosophers, celebrated in all the best circles, and written about in everything from poetry to pornography. He was also painted by some of the best artists in Europe. He was even received by King George III and Queen Charlotte. Omai's grace, good manners, genteel behavior, and dignity impressed the royal couple. Once approved by the king and queen, Omai's place in England's society was assured. Reportedly, he was treated by all as an honored guest rather than an oddity or a spectacle even though many were disappointed that he did not convert to Christianity. He traveled across England extensively, but after a short time fickle society lost interest in Omai. It was decided that he should return home with Cook on his third voyage when the ships sailed in 1776. Nothing more is known about the life and death of this man. History credits Omai for creating the public clamor and demand for future exhibitions of tattooed people that were to come. ♦

Not much is known about Omai's early history except that he was part of Captain James Cook's expedition. He was not heavily tattooed and his most notable tattoos were transverse lines on the backs of his hands. Omai was promoted as a living example of a "noble savage," a popular theme of the day.

JEAN BAPTISTE CABRI

In 1804, Jean Baptiste Cabri was discovered by George H. Von Langsdorff, a Russian explorer. Cabri, a French military deserter, had been living in the Marquesas Islands for some years. He had willingly been tattooed extensively, per custom and in the style of the island natives. He had also taken a native wife. Cabri returned to Russia with Von Langsdorff. He initially enjoyed moderate success exhibiting himself in Russia and Europe. On stage, he invented tales for his audiences recounting his captivity with the wild and ungodly savages of the islands. Cabri is remembered in history as the first extensively tattooed European to exhibit himself. Prior to Cabri, tattooed exhibitions were comprised primarily of native people or sailors who returned with only small token tattoos from their journeys. He also set the standard for the tattooed stage act by telling exaggerated stories of his capture and forced tattooing. His career, however, declined quickly. He was uneducated and not very bright, so he was not adept at embellishing and alternating his tales to create a continued interest in his performances. Cabri died sometime between 1812 and 1818 and never returned to the islands. ♦

Cabri is remembered in history as the first extensively tattooed European to exhibit himself.

JOHN RUTHERFORD

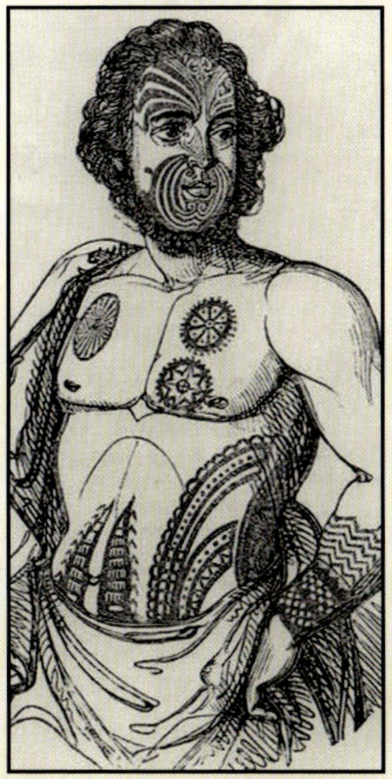

John Rutherford's career as an exhibiting tattooed man spanned from 1828 to 1830. His success and fame was due to his ability to manifest and change his fanciful stories to suit his audience.

John Rutherford has the distinction of being the second tattooed European and the first extensively tattooed Englishman to be exhibited. His career spanned from 1828 through 1830. Rutherford was heavily decorated with Maori tattooing. He far surpassed Cabri in his success and fame due to the fanciful tales he invented for his audiences. As with Cabri's stories, Rutherford's were greatly embellished and mostly fictional, but Rutherford seems to have possessed a talent for continually rec-reating himself and his stories to fit the tastes of his varying audiences. Common themes for those stories usually involved death-defying acts. He claimed his ship was lost at sea and all others on board perished. He told tales of captivity and enslavement by exotic tribes, painful forced tattooing, and eventual escape due to his ability to outwit savages. Often his stories would contain tales of his exploits as a chosen tribe leader and the taking of many beautiful island virgins as wives. In 1830, Rutherford disappeared from the stage, and it is speculated that he returned to New Zealand. Portions of his tales are recounted in *The New Zealanders* by George L. Craik. ♦

JAMES F. O'CONNEL

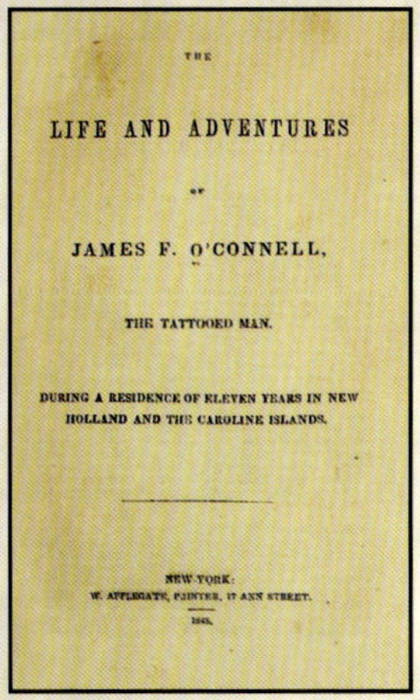

THE
LIFE AND ADVENTURES
OF
JAMES F. O'CONNELL,
THE TATTOOED MAN.
DURING A RESIDENCE OF ELEVEN YEARS IN NEW HOLLAND AND THE CAROLINE ISLANDS.
NEW-YORK:
W. APPLEGATE, PRINTER, 17 ANN STREET.
1845.

James F. O'Connel's "pitch book," first published in 1845, was sold at shows for additional income. As with all such booklets, truth was never the guiding force behind the writings.

The first tattooed person believed to have been exhibited in America was James F. O'Connel, who appeared on stage in 1840 at the Scudder's American Museum. He later exhibited with P. T. Barnum after Barnum bought Scudder's dime museum in 1842 and renamed it The American Museum. O'Connel basically came with the museum. Tattooed from head to toe, he fascinated the public by telling tales of abduction and forced tattooing by savages. These stories were similar in theme to those of Jean Baptiste Cabri and John Rutherford. He also published and sold copies of his adventures in a booklet, *The Life and Adventures of James F. O'Connel, The Tattooed Man, During A Residence Of Eleven Years In New Holland And The Caroline Islands,* that was first published in 1845. He did this as a means to earn additional income and was probably persuaded to do so by Barnum. Such a pamphlet was referred to in the business as a "pitch book." As with all such booklets, truth was never the guiding force behind the writings. It is often claimed that P. T. Barnum was the first American showman to exhibit a tattooed performer in America, but in actuality, it was Scudder. In 1873, O'Connel was succeeded by Prince Constantine in Barnum's show and nothing else is known of his life or death. ♦

GEORGE CONSTANTINE, "PRINCE CONSTANTINE," OR "CAPTAIN CONSTENTENUS"

George Constantine was born Alexandrinos Constentenus aka Djordgi Konstantinus in Greece but Americanized his name for his show business career. He chose "Constantine" as a sort of poetic justice since Emperor Constantine had banned tattooing in the Roman Empire in AD 325. He was billed as Prince Constantine or Captain Constentenus, The Greek Albanian, and he appeared as the tattooed man in Barnum's traveling show starting in 1873. On stage, he told the audiences a tale of capture and forcible tattooing reminiscent of the stories of those who came before

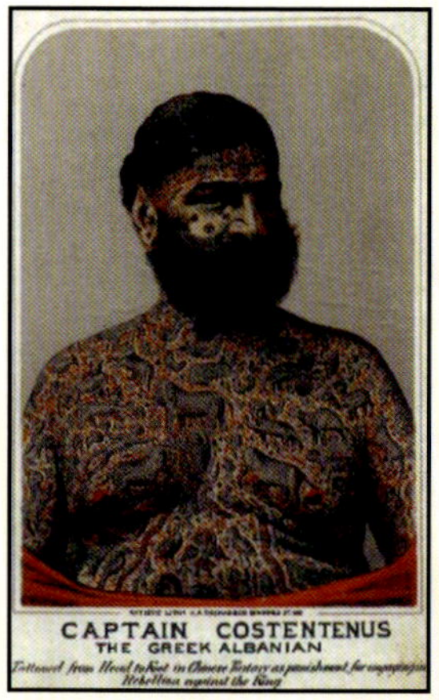

Constantine sported almost 400 tattoos that were closely entwined. They covered his entire body, including his face, eyelids, ears, and penis. He is considered the first person to decide consciously to get extensively tattooed as a means to enter the show business arena.

him. However, his tattooing was far more elaborate and extensive and experts of the time concluded his tattoos were done in the Burmese style, suggesting that Constantine had likely had the tattooing done while in Southeast Asia with the deliberate intention of becoming a tattoo exhibit. He sported almost 400 tattoos that were closely entwined, and they covered his entire body, including his face, eyelids, ears, and penis. Reportedly, the designs consisted of an array of exotic animals, fantasy animals, flowers, fruit, and human beings. Most were small but considered exceptional in their rendering and fine detail.

He later claimed his tattoos were done by Spanish and Italian tattoo artists who had learned the art while serving as sailors. It is impossible to discern the facts of his life since he changed his stories to suit his needs and the tastes of the ever-changing audiences. Regardless, Constantine is considered the first to consciously decide to get extensively tattooed as a means to enter the show business arena. He was also one of the most successful of all tattooed "created freaks." His salary with Barnum was a reported $1,000 a week, an incredible amount of money in the late 1800s. This success was due to his talent for spinning yarns that intrigued his audiences and for the visual beauty of his ink. True or not, legend has it that Charles Wagner, who would one day become a world-famous tattooist, was so inspired after seeing Constantine that he immediately set out to learn the art of tattooing, securing an apprenticeship with James O'Reilly, who patented the first electric tattoo machine. Irene Woodward, one of America's first tattooed lady exhibitioners, also cited Constantine as her inspiration. History loses contact with Constantine after he stopped exhibiting, and nothing more is known of his life or death. ♦

HORACE RIDLER, "THE GREAT OMI," OR "THE ZEBRA MAN"

Many myths, perpetrated by Horace Ridler himself, abound about this controversial performer's life. He was born in 1892 in Surrey, England. Reportedly, his parents were moderately wealthy and they expected great things from their son. He claims he attended Oxford University and was an officer in the British army who achieved the rank of major and was decorated for bravery. For whatever reason, he left the world of military life behind after World War I, and by 1922 he had spent his entire inheritance and was floundering, working the occasional odd job to scrape out a meager living. It was then he decided he wanted to join the sideshow circuit.

Horace claims he approached a Chinese tattooist, wanting to turn himself into a sideshow attraction. His first tattoos were very ordinary and crude, but he was still able to make a fairly decent living displaying himself to the public.

The need in the industry for tattooed performers to out-do one another, as well as the desire to keep the paying public interested and entertained, led him in 1927 to the world-famous London tattooist

In his desire to become the best, The Great Omi convinced renowned London tattoo artist George Burchett to tattoo bold, black, zebra-like stripes all over his body, including his head, face, and hands. To date, no one else has dared copy his design.

George "King of Tattoos" Burchett. He made it clear to the gifted ink artist that he wanted to be the greatest modern tattoo attraction in the entire world. He convinced Burchett to tattoo bold, black, zebra-like stripes all over his body, including his head, face, and hands. This procedure not only covered his old tattoos, but it was a design that, to date, no one else has dared copy. Horace was quoted as saying it took a total of 150 hours and approximately 500 sittings over the course of almost seven months to complete the painful and expensive transformation. The plan worked. The most famous circuses and shows all over the world were willing to pay top dollar to have "The Great Omi" perform for them. Gladys Ridler, Horace's wife, also worked with him. She became known as "Omette," introducing her husband to his audiences. She was not tattooed. An interesting note: George Burchett always claimed that he was never paid in full for his services. In addition to the very exotic tattoos, Horace also had his teeth filed to points and added stretched facial piercings. He embellished his act by citing wild stories of abduction in far-off countries and claimed that he had been captured and tortured via tattooing in New Guinea. As the years passed, The Great Omi's appearance became even more outrageous. He started wearing lipstick and nail polish. He signed publicity autographs with the words "Barbaric Beauty." This was most likely a show business stunt engineered to keep his act fresh and unique and to stay in high demand. To many people who study this era in sideshow tattoo exhibitors, Horace Ridler is considered the best and most popular showman of his time. He always insisted that, despite his tattoos, he was just an ordinary man. The Great Omi died in 1969 in Ripe, a small village near Sussex, England, where he and his wife had retired. He was seventy-seven. ♦

NORA HILDEBRANDT

Nora Hildebrandt was born Nora Keaton in Ireland in 1856 and was America's first professional exhibiting tattooed lady. She first exhibited on March 1, 1882, at the Bunnell's dime museum. She was twenty-six years old.

Nora was tattooed by Martin Hildebrandt, her common law husband. All of Nora's tattoos were done by hand. They would have been more painful and required much more time to execute than tattoos done after the electric tattoo needle was developed in 1891.

Nora Hildebrandt photographed with her tattoos covered and looking like the typical Victorian woman. She legally married at the age of thirty-three but died a few years later.

Nora Hildebrandt was born Nora Keatin in Ireland in 1856 to John Keatin and Mary Cochran Keatin. The family immigrated to the United States shortly after Nora's birth, settling in the Irish slums of New York City.

By most accounts, Nora Hildebrandt was America's first professional exhibiting tattooed lady. She was tattooed by her much older common law husband, German-born Martin Hildebrandt, who was an early professional tattoo artist with a shop in New York City. Martin had started out tattooing both Confederate and Union soldiers while a traveling artist during the Civil War. In New York, his usual customers were sailors or men with too much alcohol under their belts. Why Nora decided to embrace a career as a tattooed exhibitor can most likely be attributed to the fact that she would have been easily influenced by Martin, who was more than twenty years her senior. It is also possible that an uneducated and unsophisticated Nora may have

Early women tattoo performers followed the men's leads by also telling elaborate tales of being forcibly tattooed, usually by Wild West savages.

Nora claimed to have 365 tattoos, one for each day of the year. She is shown here later in her career. The amount of jewelry worn would indicate a successful career upon the stage.

This is the last known photograph taken of Nora Hildebrandt. The cause of her death, the exact date of passing, and the location of her burial site are not known.

merely been seeking a means to earn an income. All of Nora's tattoos were done by hand. They would have been more painful and required much more time to execute than tattoos done after the electric tattoo needle was developed in 1891. Nora first exhibited on March 1, 1882, at the Bunnell's Dime Museum (located at the corner of 9th and Broadway in New York City) a few weeks before Irene Woodward made her initial appearance. Borrowing from the male tattoo exhibitors, she made up fanciful stories to explain her tattoos. As with other performers, her stories had a few variations. She often claimed her father had forcibly tattooed her against her will, thus gaining sympathy from a possibly hostile and condemning prudish Victorian public. In another version, Nora stated that she and her father were both forcibly tattooed by savage American Indians. Still another and even

MYSTERY TO SOLVE

Why did Nora Hildebrandt die at such a young age? Where is she buried? What is the story behind "The Hildebrands, A Tattooed Married Couple" act?

more fanciful version claimed she had been captured by Sitting Bull, who held her family hostage. In her words, the only thing that saved them all from torture and certain death was her selfless willingness to allow her father to painfully tattoo her from head to foot while she was tied to a tree for an entire year, resulting in 365 tattoos that adorned her young body. All stories were fictional, but they made Nora seem more like a victim than a willing participant in the tattooing process. They also added an exotic and erotic element to her performance that fascinated the naïve paying public. The mostly male audience members were also quite appreciative of the skimpy costumes Nora wore to better show off her ink.

Nora exhibited at dime museums and toured primarily with Barnum & Bailey Circus throughout the 1890s until her untimely death in 1893 at the age of thirty-seven. The cause of her death, the exact date of passing, and the location of her burial site are not known.

She legally married Jacob Gunther on January 20, 1889, when she was thirty-three, but they had no children. (He remarried after her death.) In 1890–91, a man and woman exhibited as "The Hildebrands, A Tattooed Married Couple," so it is possible that her new husband was also a tattooed performer. It is also possible that Nora teamed up with a tattooed gentleman who was not her husband since truth in any sideshow advertisement was a rarity. Since the spelling of the last name is different, another tattooed couple may have innocently or purposely capitalized on Nora's fame or Nora may have slightly changed the name of her act after she was estranged from her common law husband, Martin Hildebrandt. So many questions, so few answers. ♦

IRENE WOODWARD, "LA BELLE," OR "LA BELLE IRENE"

Irene Woodward was born Ida Levina Lisk on August 24, 1857, in Philadelphia, Pennsylvania, to Joseph K. Lisk, a poor shoemaker, and Sarah Josephine Drew Lisk. The Lisks had six children but only Ida and a younger brother, John, lived to adulthood. She made her debut on March 21, 1882, at the Bunnell's Dime Museum at the age of twenty-five, although she was advertised as being only nineteen. Irene was met with great fanfare, including a story about the "illustrated woman" in *The New York Times*. After her introduction at Bunnell's, she worked at other dime museums and circuses throughout the US and successfully toured Europe where she was given the name "La Belle Irene." She also used the stage name "La Belle" and some today claim she also exhibited under "Mademoiselle Aimee," but that is not true. That performer came later and parroted a version of Nora Hildebrandt and Irene's fanciful stories. It is debated who was the first woman in America to exhibit as a tattooed lady, Irene or Nora. Most agree that Nora Hildebrandt first exhibited three weeks before Irene came on the scene, but that Irene was the more popular of the two performers both in the press and among the paying public. Both women, however, deserve to be credited with paving the way for other tattooed ladies to follow and tattooed women eventually became some of the highest paid performers in sideshows.

On stage, Irene's stories changed to suit the audience. She sometimes claimed to have been tattooed by her sailor father (mother missing) from the ages of six to twelve, but unlike Nora Hildebrandt, Irene always proudly proclaimed that she wanted to be tattooed and had the work done willingly. Other times she would add that she had been saved during an Indian raid that took her father's life because the tattoos he had applied to her body had frightened the savages and thus spared her life and the life of her brother. Still an earlier version claimed that she had spent most of her life living in a settler's wagon with her father and brothers: Her father tattooed a spool on her arm in order not to lose her; Though painful, she liked the result and urged him to tattoo her more, which he did during his spare time over a six-year period.

In truth, Irene had actually been tattooed by "Professor" William R. Davis, who was assisted by Martin Hildebrandt. The facts were either distorted to sensationalize her performances or in an effort to appease morality issues that would have arisen at the time if the public thought a woman had subjected her entire body to being tattooed by someone other than her father or legal husband.

Irene Woodward made her debut in New York in 1882 and later toured most of America and Europe, where she played to royalty and was given the name "La Belle Irene." She also used the stage name "La Belle."

Most likely, both scenarios fitted Irene's needs.

In an 1883 newspaper article, Irene's tattoos were described as "a Masonic emblem, then lover's knot, beasts, religious pieces, ships, and on each shoulder a sun, surrounded by stars, moons, and intersliced [sic] with these pieces are neat and artistic scroll work." The article was headlined: "A Tattoo Topic Mr. Sackett's Latest Addition to His Museum Miss Irene Woodward, The Original Tattooed Lady."

The reporter defined Irene as a "handsome young woman of medium stature" and "well-educated, refined, and very winning in her manners....She appears on the platform in bodice and trunks of embroidered white silk trimmed in lace; the arms, lower limbs and neck are covered with figures and emblems in blue and red, all joined by delicate tracery; the sight is an unusually beautiful one."

Another reporter described Irene as having a garland of flowers around her neck with butterflies flitting about, a beehive on her left arm with the inscription "Never Despair" above the hive and "Nothing without Labor" below, plus an American eagle on her right arm with the inscription "I Live and Die for Those I Love." On various parts of her body, he described colorful tattoos such as an Indian head, angels, swans, rabbits, figures representing faith, hope, and charity, a harp enclosed in a shamrock, the Goddess of Hope, a returning sailor, a wheat field, two ships in action, and two hands grasped in friendship, as well as others too numerous to report.

In a September 1915 deathbed interview, Irene claimed she had married her husband George E. Woodward, a printer, (who changed his surname to "Sterling" along the way) when she was only sixteen, and he introduced her to the circus life and acted as her manager. They had a son, George E. Jr., who was born in 1878. She went on to say that she had spent twenty years of her long career suc-

Early trade show booklet that is sometimes erroneously attributed to Irene Woodward exhibiting under the stage name Mlle. Aimee. Mlle. Aimee was an early tattooed lady who followed Nora Hildebrandt and Irene.

It is debated who was the first tattooed lady that exhibited in America. Both Nora and Irene, shown here, deserve credit for paving the way for other performing tattooed ladies and eventually the tattooed woman became one of the highest paid performers in the sideshow.

Trade booklet for Irene Woodward that was sold at exhibits, telling her fanciful story that she repeated on stage to her fascinated audiences.

Irene always claimed her inspiration to become tattooed came from having seen Captain Constantenus, The Greek, in person on stage. Most likely, her husband inspired her for financial gain.

cessfully touring Europe, even playing to crown heads and had traveled all the great circus routes in America. She also claimed that she had made a fortune, but she and her husband had spent it all and he abandoned her, leaving her destitute. Irene reported she was dying of stomach cancer and she blamed the ink from her tattoos for poisoning her. She died on October 9, 1915, at the age of fifty-eight in the Philadelphia General Hospital. The cause of her death was a carcinoma of the uterus, not stomach cancer and certainly not ink poisoning. Irene always claimed her inspiration to become tattooed came from having seen Captain Constantenus, The Greek, in person on stage. Most likely, her husband inspired her to get tattooed for fortune, fame, and travel and to save him from a tedious life as a printer. Irene was buried in a six dollar coffin in Monument Cemetery in Philadelphia. As ghastly as it sounds to us today, it was not unheard of for urban expansion and the need for city land to force the second internment of bodies to a more remote burial ground. Monument Cemetery's deceased were reburied in Lawnview Cemetery in Rockledge, Pennsylvania, sans many of the original headstones. Irene is buried in Lawnview Cemetery in an unmarked grave. ♦

Irene died on October 9, 1915, the age of fifty-eight in a hospital in Philadelphia, Pennsylvania. Even though she had earned a small fortune during her career, she died destitute and alone. She is buried in Lawnview Cemetery in Rockledge, Pennsylvania, in an unmarked grave. Shown here are the gates of the cemetery.

ANNIE HOWARD

Unfortunately, very little is known about the early life of Annie Howard, arguably one of the most beautiful Victorian tattooed women to exhibit in the sideshows. This is often the case when we do not know the maiden name of a married woman. Annie was married to another tattooed performer, Frank Howard, and usually performed under his surname while the marriage lasted.

Annie and her husband worked with P. T. Barnum in the early 1900s. As with most performers of that time, they created elaborate stories to enhance their act, thus guaranteeing more paying customers. The Howards, as many tattooed people before them, claimed they had been captured by savages who tattooed them against their will. At times, the savages were from some exotic land far away. Other stories claimed the savages were Indians from the wild western frontier. Annie was awarded more respectability by the viewing public than other tattooed ladies since she was a married woman, exhibiting with her husband.

The many tattoos on Anne and Frank's bodies represented a lucrative opportunity. Annie was very superstitious. Her most prominent tattoo was a good-luck horseshoe "necklace" inked around her neck.

Frank and Annie had one daughter, Ivy, who traveled with them on the sideshow circuit. Reportedly, the child started performing as a snake charmer at the early age of eight. A later portrait of Ivy shows her beautifully attired and looking the proper lady, a cornet soloist. It would not be much of a stretch to imagine that her parents wanted more

In her youth, Annie Howard was one of the most beautiful Victorian tattooed women to exhibit in the sideshows.

MYSTERY TO SOLVE

What happened to Annie Howard?
When did she die and where is she buried?

Early c. 1900s cigarette card showing "Some of Barnum's Freaks." With a giant and giantess is a moss-haired girl, bearded lady Annie Jones, and tattooed lady Annie Howard with husband Frank Howard. As was the custom among married women of the day, most if not all of Annie's tattoos were inked by her husband, who was a tattoo artist and fully tattooed, as well.

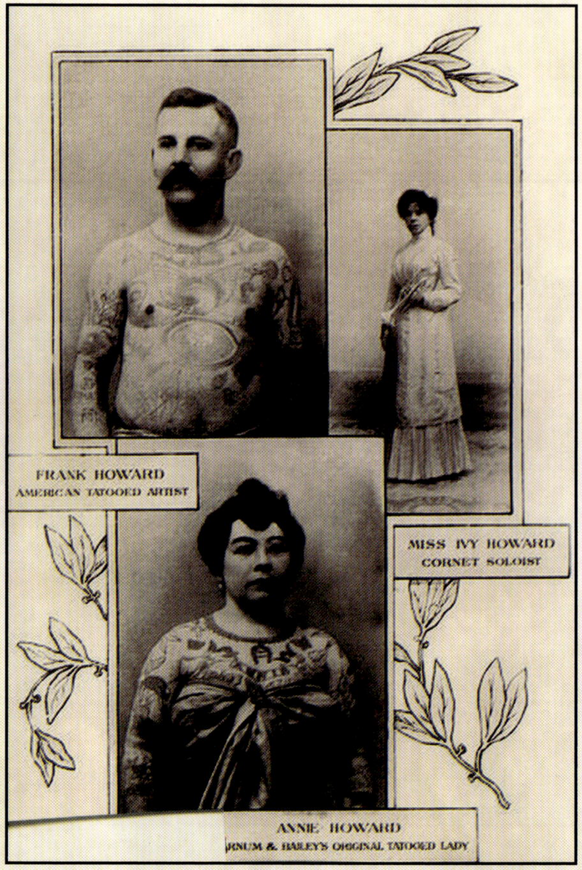

Frank and Annie had one daughter, Ivy, who traveled with them on the sideshow circuit.

In 1882, Annie made the newspapers of the day for supposedly being arrested and thrown in jail. Even though the story was most likely a publicity stunt, it quickly created a public interest in Annie Howard and increased attendance at her exhibits.

The beautiful Annie Howard photographed by Charles Eisenmann.

A MUSEUM PROPRIETOR ARRESTED

G. B. BUNNELL CHARGED WITH INSULTING A LADY ON A TRAIN.

NEW-HAVEN, Aug. 30.—Mrs. Maria McGee, a Birmingham woman, left New-York at 9 o'clock this morning on a train of the New-York, New-Haven and Hartford Railroad. She had traveled all night, and, being tired, fell asleep. According to her story, when she awakened she noticed that a well-dressed man, seated on the other side of the aisle, was smiling at her. She asked him whether the conductor had gone through, and the man, who subsequently proved to be George B. Bunnell, the proprietor of several museums in and around New-York, said that he had. Then Mr. Bunnell spoke of the volcanic eruption in Java and other things which were intended to amuse and interest Mrs. McGee. Finally Mrs. McGee ventured to look in Mr. Bunnell's direction. The first thing that attracted her attention was a huge emerald in his shirt-front, and then, casting her eyes down, she says that she noted with surprise that he was plainly exposing his person. She turned away in disgust and looked no more toward Mr. Bunnell, although she asserts he kept up his conversation and endeavored to get her to turn around. A brakeman came through the car and Mrs. McGee handed him a piece of paper on which she had written the words, "That man has insulted me." The brakeman told Officer Kennedy of this when the train arrived here, and the officer started through the cars in search of the man. When Bunnell saw him approaching he attempted to escape by leaving the car. Kennedy quickly reached his side, however, and said: "You are my prisoner, Sir." Bunnell grew red in the face and whispered nervously: "Don't arrest me; I am not guilty, and I'm a Knight Templar. This thing is all a mistake." Despite his protests, he was taken to the police station and given a hearing in the private office of Chief Webster. Mrs. McGee told her story with many blushes, but she told it in a straightforward way. Bunnell protested vehemently that the whole thing was a mistake. "I am a religious man," he said, and it would be against my conscience to commit such a crime. He was placed in a cell, where he sat for nearly half an hour in a half-dazed condition, repeating to himself over and over again: "This is a great mistake, a great mistake." Finally he sent out for Judge Blydenburgh, and that gentleman had a consultation with him in his cell. As a result, Mr. Bunnell was released on $100 collateral bond. He immediately left the city by train.

While Annie's run-in with the law was probably a publicity stunt, it is likely George B. Bunnell, owner of several Bunnell's dime museums, was not.

for their daughter than the life as a tattooed performer. In 1882, Annie made the newspapers of the day by being arrested and thrown in jail. According to the reports, Annie was on her way to George B. Bunnell's Dime Museum in New York to seek a job as an exhibitionist and was insulted by a gentleman noting her many tattoos. Annie assaulted the man, beat him badly, was arrested, charged, but then was immediately hired by Bunnell upon her release. This story, as it was meant to do, created an immediate interest in Annie Howard, guaranteeing a long line of paying customers. Promoters never let the truth stand in the way of a good story. Annie had no tattoos on her face, neck, or hands. Dressed in the custom of the day, likely no one would have guessed they had just encountered a famous tattooed lady. Oddly, George Bunnell would make the papers soon himself when he was charged with insulting a lady on a train in 1883 by "plainly exposing his person." Unlike Annie's story, this newspaper account was most likely true.

In 1887, the family traveled with P. T. Barnum to London and toured all over Europe with the troupe. They returned to America in 1903, but by 1910, Frank was married to another woman. Annie performed in Europe under the name Annie Frank, most likely after they divorced, but sadly, nothing else is known of her life or death. ♦

Annie performed in Europe under the name Annie Frank, most likely after her divorce from Frank Howard. The date of her death is unknown.

PRINCESS BEATRICE

Princess Beatrice had George Washington inked on the front of her chest, *The Last Supper* on her back, and spider webs on her shoulders. She also had a memorial to her mother and four sisters on her upper arm. (Photos courtesy of Judith Lukas, Princess Judy Historical Tattoo Art.)

Princess Beatrice was born Bertha Ritchie in 1878 in Newcastle, England. After her father died when she was young, her mother, Annie, moved the family to Galveston, Texas, where legend says they were quickly embraced by the elite high society of the town. There Beatrice met and

Bertha took the stage name Princess Beatrice after being tattooed by J. T. Clark. (Photo courtesy of Judith Lukas, Princess Judy Historical Tattoo Art.)

married her first husband and gave birth to a son. On September 8, 1900, Galveston was hit with a hurricane so intense that, to date, it is still the deadliest natural disaster ever to strike the United States, taking the lives of an estimated 6,000 to 12,000 souls in and around the area of Galveston Island. Sadly, Bertha lost most of her family in that hurricane, including her mother, four sisters, and infant son. Her child was pulled out of her arms by the rushing water, and it was said she often walked the devastated streets of Galveston, gazing into the face of each infant, hoping to find her beloved son still alive. She had been miraculously saved when a stranger dragged her out of the flood waters by her long hair. For the rest of her life, she was terrified during storms. She had another son, but her husband died soon after, in 1903, leaving her a widow and almost destitute with an infant child and no other family for support. To make matters worse, she was also reportedly now "slightly mad."

Bertha quickly became involved with John "J. T." (Thompson) Clark, a former friend of her deceased husband, either driven by need or true love. They traveled together to South Africa, eventually married, and Bertha gave birth to another son, Francis, in 1906. By all accounts, the couple was happy even

This is one of the last photographs taken of Princess Beatrice before her death. The tattoos on her arms are still visible, and it is happily noted that she did not try to hide them from view. (Photo courtesy of Judith Lukas, Princess Judy Historical Tattoo Art.)

though J. T. was a rather colorful character with a sideshow background and very different from the polite society of Beatrice's past. He claimed to be the only man in the world to have a tattooed scalp. J. T., fully tattooed himself, eventually opened a tattoo shop in South Africa and, for whatever reason, persuaded the very beautiful Bertha to allow him to tattoo her. Most likely it was to gain a source of income by displaying her for profit. She had George Washington inked on the front of her chest, *The Last Supper* on her back, and spider webs on her shoulders. She also had a memorial to her mother and four sisters on her upper arm.

In 1914, the family left Africa and moved back to the United States. J. T. and Bertha, now known as Princess Beatrice, exhibited both together and separately with Ringling Brothers and other shows. Sadly, J. T. died of pneumonia on April 14, 1918, in the Montreal General Hospital in Canada at the age of forty-seven and was buried in the Mount Royal Cemetery in Quebec. Once again, Bertha, now 40, was a widow, this time with a twelve-year-old son to support. She sent a telegram to her seventeen-year-old son, who had been placed with

MYSTERY TO SOLVE

Where is Princess Beatrice buried and when exactly did she die?

another family, saying, "*....have pity for your Mother.*" Bertha had never earned her own way in life, plus she was emotionally crippled by her life experiences. She obtained odd jobs where she could find them and made a small income by exhibiting herself and her tattoos, but shows and the paying public were mostly interested in younger tattooed ladies. Eventually she was forced to send her youngest son off to earn his own board by working on a farm. She was not able to earn enough money to properly care for the child and she was likely too emotionally fragile, as well, to provide a stable environment. In the early 1930s, Bertha requested a widow's military pension due her from J. T.'s involvement in the 1898 Spanish-American War. She listed herself as "destitute" on the application, but it is unclear why she waited so many years to pursue this avenue. It is possible that she never received the pension due to J.T.'s undisciplined actions and the serious military reprimands he received during service. Bertha died in the 1950s in Brantford, Ontario, where she had been mainly living off the charity of friends. Efforts to integrate herself into her adult sons' households over the years were unsuccessful, most likely due to her or her sons' past emotional scars. ♦

DJITA SALOME, "THE TATTOOED WOMAN," OR "SALOME, THE BLUE WOMAN" (DAS BLAUE WEIB)

Djita always claimed to be from exotic Egypt but she was actually born in Germany around 1892. She was completely covered with tattoos by the age of thirty, with the exception of her neck, face, and hands. Her sensual light brown skin made a wonderful human canvas for her well-drawn body art. She advertised on trade cards of the day

MYSTERY TO SOLVE

What happened to Djita Salome? Did she live a long and happy life or did she fall prey to the diabolical Third Reich in her homeland of Germany?

claiming to have tattoos done in fourteen colors that were created by "redskins," the Sioux Indians of Dakota. She also claimed the tattooing was done through the use of fine gold needles and that a hundred million painful punctures had been necessary to carry out the strange drawings that covered her body. She also said she had won many prizes by exhibiting herself throughout the world. Reportedly, she was an excellent businesswoman and made a very comfortable living through her stage appearances and by selling trade cards at her shows. Sadly, not much is known of her life or times since she chose to use a stage name. Her given name is not known. When The Third Reich came to power under Adolf Hitler, they considered circus people unworthy and put more than 10,000 to death. Hopefully Salome escaped her homeland of Germany before such a fate befell her. ♦

Djita always claimed to be from exotic Egypt, but she was actually born in Germany. She was completely covered with tattoos by the age of thirty, with the exception of the neck, face, and hands.

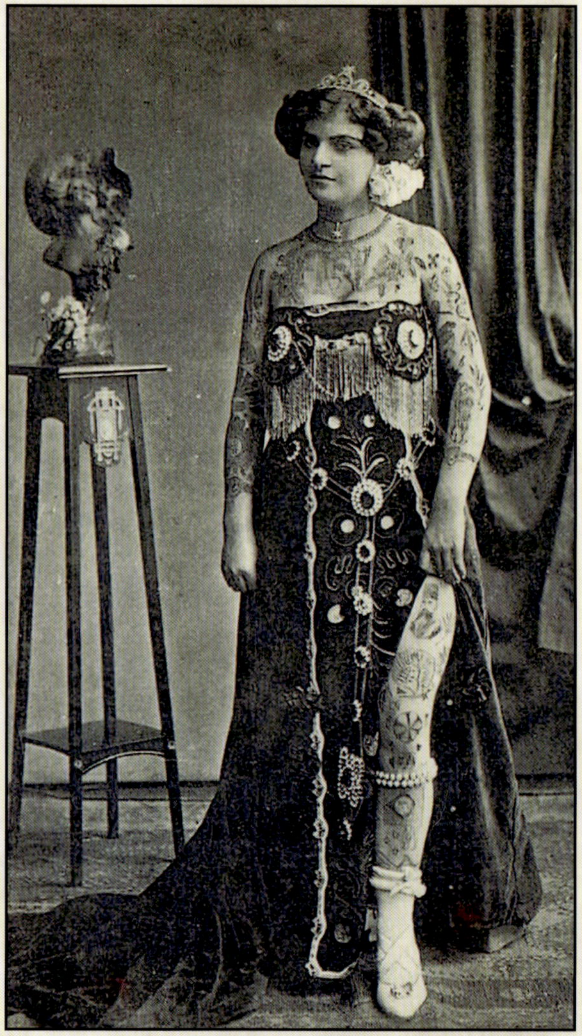

Djita Salome advertised on trade cards of the day claiming to have tattoos done in fourteen colors that were created by "redskins," the Sioux of Dakota. She also claimed the tattooing was done through the use of fine gold needles and that a hundred million painful punctures had been necessary to carry out the strange drawings that covered her body.

ANNA MAE BURLINGTON GIBBONS, "ARTORIA," OR "LADY ARTORIA"

Anna Mae Gibbons was born on July 15, 1893, in rural Wisconsin to Frank Burlington and Amma "Amie" Mabel Mason Burlington. Her father was a Norwegian immigrant who had Americanized his given name, Gunder Huseland. In 1907, the family moved to Colville, Washington. Sadly, her father died soon after the move, leaving a destitute wife with children to house, feed, and clothe. When exhibiting as a sideshow tattooed woman, Anna's lecture (the colorful, fanciful story repeated to the paying public) told of running away from home at age fourteen to join the circus for a life of excitement and travel. Anna did leave home at a young age, but it was to find odd jobs to help support herself as well as to enable her to send money home to her mother. While she was working in Spokane as a domestic she met Charles "Red" Wesley Gibbons, a tattoo artist, later referred to as "Professor Gibbons." They married on October 8, 1912. Red was thirty-two, and Anna was nineteen.

Times were hard and work scarce. The decision to ink Anna was most likely a financial one made by both Anna and Red a few years after marrying. Anna always quickly dismissed anyone who suggested that she was forced by her husband to be tattooed or that she allowed herself to be tattooed out of blind love. The uneducated and unsophisticated Anna always said that she saw this as a means to gain financial freedom, grab excitement, and to travel the world. She claimed that she never regretted her actions, saying that she had a much better life and made more money than if she had stayed home on the farm. Indeed, the money was likely

Anna Mae Gibbons was born on July 15, 1893, in rural Wisconsin. She would become one of the most famous of all sideshow tattooed ladies.

much better. Anna was one of the highest paid tattooed ladies in the industry, commanding weekly salaries of $100 to $250. Domestics at the time were earning about $5 a week. Red tattooed Anna between 1920 and 1921. He was an oil prospector by trade and did tattooing as a hobby. However,

Anna was a devout Baptist. Many of her tattoos were magnificent religious reproductions of paintings by Raphael, Michelangelo, and Leonardo da Vinci including da Vinci's *Last Supper*.

world-famous circus showman Ward Hall wrote in his book, *My Very Unusual Friends,* that Anna had the finest tattooing of anyone he had worked with on the show circuit and in the world of tattoo art. Red Gibbons is counted as one of the best of the old artists. Anna was a devout Baptist, and

Anna was popular with her peers and had a reputation in business for always being on time for performances and for always conducting herself in a professional and lady-like manner.

many of her tattoos were magnificent religious reproductions of paintings by Raphael, Michelangelo, and Leonardo da Vinci including Da Vinci's *Last Supper*. She also sported quite a few patriotic designs, including the portraits of many American presidents. Illustrations covered more than 80 percent of her body and all of her tattoos were inked by her husband, who Anna claimed "was just plain crazy about Italian masters," a fact that most likely influenced her choice of the stage name "Artoria."

Anna had a reputation in business for always being on time for performances and for always conducting herself in a professional and lady-like manner. While working with Dean Potter's show, she fell and broke her arm. She refused to go to the hospital until her performances ended several hours later.

She retired from show business initially in the 1940s, but only because Red needed her. He had gone blind from a brutal robbery in 1941 and was also badly injured in a construction accident in 1946. Anna stayed home to care for him, but returned to the circus life a few years after Red's death on June 18, 1964, at the age of eighty-four. Reportedly, she did not need the money since Red had left her oil-producing properties in Oklahoma. She returned because she missed the people and the excitement of the carnival life.

Anna's sideshow career spanned many decades and included a part in the film documentary *Being Different.*

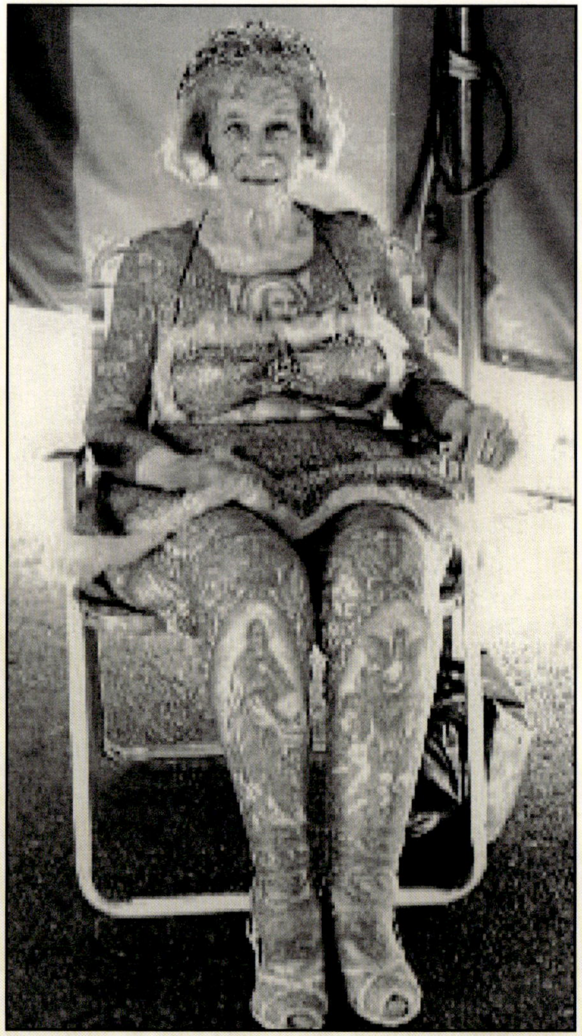

In the early 1980s, Anna retired once again and moved to Bluff City, Tennessee, to live with her only daughter, Charlene Gibbons Pickle, and her family. Her show business career had spanned many decades, including a part in the film documentary *Being Different*. Today she remains one of the most famous of all the sideshow tattooed ladies. Anna passed away on March 18, 1985, at the Bristol Nursing Home in Bristol, Tennessee. She was ninety-one. She is buried in the Shipley Cemetery in Bristol. She had changed her religious preference from Baptist to Episcopalian in later life, but she was still devoutly religious. Oddly, there was no mention of her career as a sideshow performer in her obituary. ♦

ETHEL MARTIN VANGI, ALIAS "LADY VIOLA," OR "THE MOST BEAUTIFUL TATTOOED WOMAN IN THE WORLD"

Ethel Martin Vangi used the stage name "Lady Viola." She was born on March 27, 1898, in Covington, Kentucky, to Charles Robert Martin and Flora Alice Walker Martin. She was tattooed in the early 1920s by Frank Graf and Charlie Wagner, who had shops in the Bowery and at Coney Island. Her tattoos were considered ahead of the time. They were little flower designs with the heads of popular people in them such as cowboy Tom Mix and comedian Charlie Chaplin. The United State Capitol building was on her back and the Statue of Liberty and Rock of Ages decorated her legs. She also had presidents Wilson, Washington, and Lincoln realistically drawn across her chest, among others. "Professor" Wagner, as he was often called, said in a 1933 newspaper article that he was never satisfied, "even when he was commissioned to etch the portraits of nine U. S. presidents on a considerable portion of a circus freak called Lady Viola".

Lady Viola's second husband was a giant with the sideshows. Sadly, he passed away two years after they married.

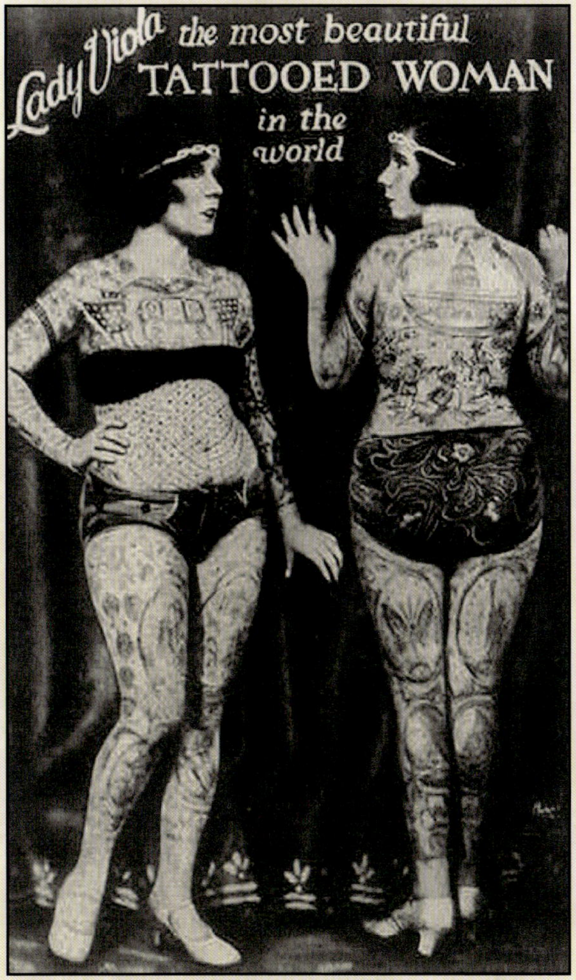

Trade card for Lady Viola, "the most beautiful tattooed woman in the world."

"Professor" Charles Wagner, the most famous tattooist of his time, said in a 1933 newspaper article that he was never satisfied, "even when he was commissioned to etch the portraits of nine US presidents on a considerable portion of a circus freak called Lady Viola."

Lady Viola worked in Coney Island and traveled with various sideshows and circuses billed as "The Most Beautiful Tattooed Woman in the World." She was also a tattoo artist in her own right.

She was married three times, divorced once, and widowed twice. Her first husband was George Michael Owenburg, whom she wed on September

Lady Viola's last engagement was with the Thomas Joyland Circus. She retired for the last time at age seventy-three.

24, 1916, when she was just eighteen. That marriage quickly ended in divorce. Her second husband was Alfred N. Ingle, a sideshow performer exhibiting as a giant, whom she married on April 2, 1928, when she was thirty. He died two years later. She married her third husband, Vincenzo Vangi, in 1932 when she was thirty-four years old. She retired soon after that, settled down to married life, and raised her three daughters and a son. However, when her husband died, she returned to exhibiting and tattooing, either needing the income or the camaraderie of the sideshow. Her last engagement was with the Thomas Joyland Circus when she was seventy-three. In 1971, she again retired. She had been, at that time, the oldest performing tattooed lady in the world. Most likely, she was also the oldest female tattoo artist, as well.

Lady Viola died on April 15, 1977, at the age of seventy-nine. She is buried in the Antioch Christian Cemetery in Fulton County, Pennsylvania. Her tombstone is inscribed "Mama." As with many of the beautiful tattooed ladies of yesteryear, neither her tombstone nor her obituary make mention of her sideshow days. ♦

Jean thoroughly enjoyed the spotlight and showing off her tattooed body, at times performing in the girlie shows.

JEAN FURELLA

Jean Furella certainly has a sideshow tale like no other tattooed lady in the business. She originally joined the circus as a bearded lady around the age of fourteen. According to Jean, she was one of the few authentic bearded ladies at that time since most of the other performing "ladies" were merely effeminate men posing as the fairer sex. As a young and beautiful bearded lady with a graceful figure, Jean had many infatuated suitors among the viewing public and circus workers. Uncle Eddie, who billed himself as "The World's Smallest Perfect Man," and later after he gained weight, "The World's Smallest Fat Man," pursued Jean for years. Even after he retired to a trailer in Florida, he would annually take a bus to the Dallas State Fair to look for his lost love, but as the story goes, or at least how the trade brochure story goes, Jean only had eyes for John Carson, a man who had been a carnival worker since his early teens. Sadly, John was appalled by Jean's beard, even refusing to kiss her. The story in the brochure claimed this went on for fifteen years, until a circus friend of the couple suggested trading the beard for tattoos. Jean

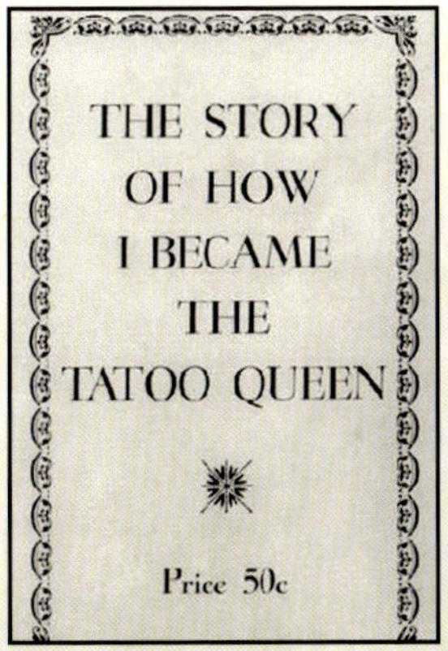

In her trade booklet, Jean claims she traded her beard for tattoos to win the heart of a man. History records her as "the woman who was tattooed for love."

MYSTERY TO SOLVE

What is the story of Jean's birth and young life and what happened to her in later life? Where is she buried?

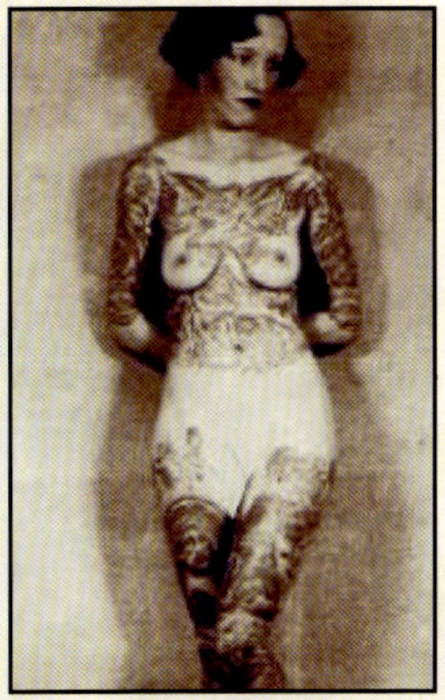

Jean's career spanned many decades before her death in 1969.

did just that. She had the beard removed with an electrolytic needle and her body covered in tattoos, thus trading her natural abnormality for a created one. The couple was quickly married and she and John remained married until his death in 1951. Pure truth, probably not, but that story will always be the one attached to Jean's name.

Jean enjoyed the spotlight and showing off her tattooed body, at times performing in the girlie shows. She later married Larry Rapp on April 30, 1953. They had met at Coney Island where he worked the sideshows as a "talker." They divorced in 1960 and Jean continued to exhibit as a tattooed lady, but her friends report that she lived in near poverty. She died in December of 1969 after an extended hospital stay, but her burial site is unknown. ♦

BETTY BROADBENT

Betty Broadbent is one of the most well-known tattooed women in the world. She was born Susan Lillian Brown on November 1, 1909, in Zellwood, Florida, but was most likely brought up in Philadelphia. Several stories have evolved to explain why she ran off to join the sideshow at the tender age of seventeen. (Some accounts say fourteen, but those accounts are mostly disputed.) A popular version claims she was a member of a socially prominent Philadelphia family who kept too tight a rein on their zealous daughter. Another version says that she impulsively got a tattoo from Jack Redcloud, a tattoo artist she encountered on the Atlantic City Boardwalk. When she returned home, her middle-class, respectable family was very displeased and she ran off after a bitter argument ensued. We will probably never know the true story, but basically she fell out with her family and ran off to join the sideshow and kept going.

In an era when women with tattoos were shunned by polite society, it is interesting to note that Betty had more than 350 tattoos all over her body. Many of her tattoos were images of famous people of the day. A likeness of Queen Victoria was inked between her breasts. Charles Wagner, the world-famous tattoo artist from the New York Bowery, did many of Betty's tattoos. He was one of the first to use the electric tattoo machine. The most heavily tattooed women of the era were usually wives of tattoo artists and basically acted as living advertising billboards for their husbands. This was not the case for Betty. She apparently just loved both the process of getting a tattoo and the joy of exhibiting her tattooed body. At one time, she even participated in a beauty pageant alongside nontattooed young women. Reportedly, she thought it

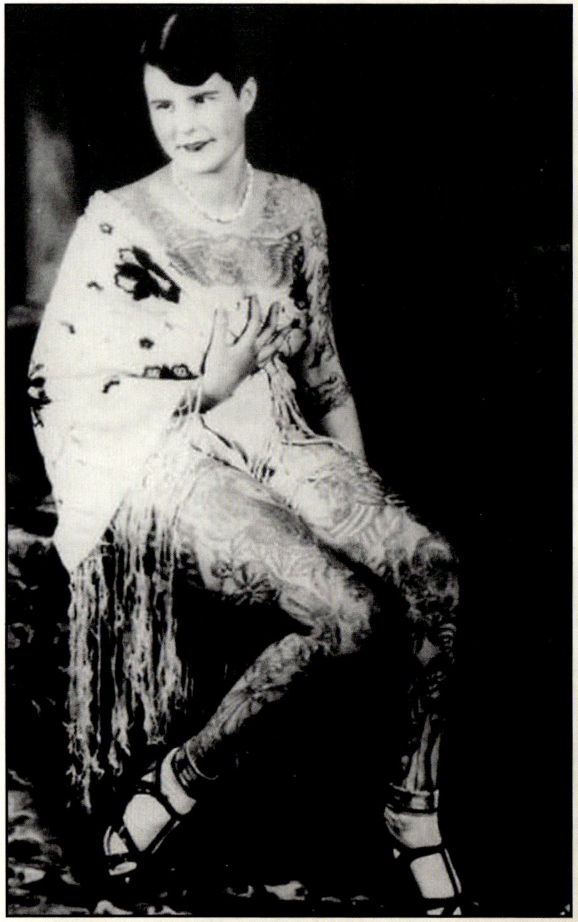

Betty Broadbent loved both the process of getting a tattoo and the joy of exhibiting her tattooed body.

At one time, Betty participated in a beauty pageant alongside non-tattooed young women. She did not win, but Betty loved the stir she created among spectators and the press.

She joined the sideshow in 1926 and her show business career spanned more than 40 years. She was very popular due to the contrast between her heavily tattooed body and sweet, child-like face.

unfair that she did not win even though she was thrilled at the stir her appearance in the pageant created among the spectators and press.

She joined the sideshow in 1926, and her show business career spanned more than forty years. She worked with every significant American circus, and she also performed in sideshows in Australia and New Zealand. She was very popular due to the contrast between her heavily tattooed body and her sweet, child-like face that she kept free of tattoos. Reportedly, she earned up to $300 a week, a very respectable salary at that time, especially for a woman.

She was married three times. Her first husband was Edwin Charles Burbank, whom she wed when she was nineteen. She married her second husband, Charles Fredrick Roark, a sideshow ventriloquist, in 1940, and they toured together for many years before divorcing. She wed her third husband, Winford Emmory Brewer, in 1969 after retiring from show business. She had an illegitimate child with a married sideshow roper, Joe (Jose) H. Carter, in the early 1930s but most likely that child was put up for adoption or simply given away. There is

Betty Broadbent was the first person to be inducted into the Tattoo Hall of Fame in 1981. She had been tattooed by the greatest tattoo artists of the day, including Charlie Wagner, Red Gibbons, Joe Van Hart, and Tony Rhineager.

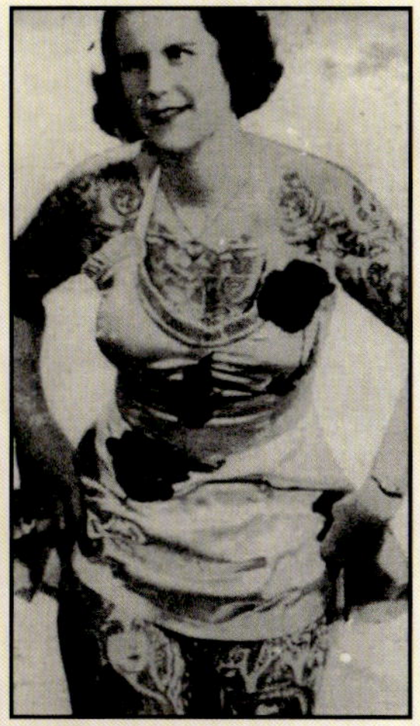

Betty earned up to $300 a week as a top performer, a very respectable salary for the day, especially for a woman. She worked with every significant American circus.

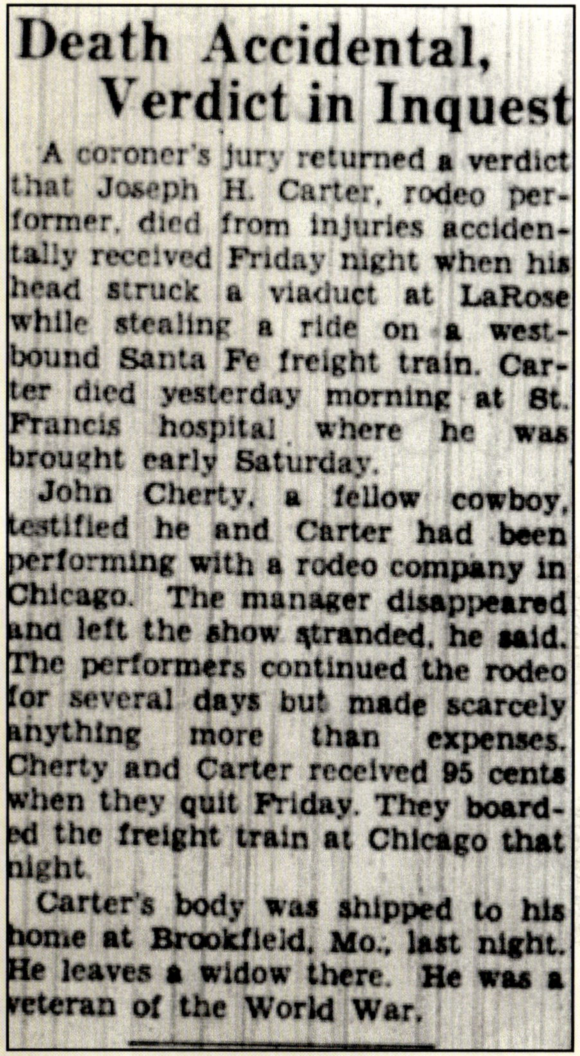

Death Accidental, Verdict in Inquest

A coroner's jury returned a verdict that Joseph H. Carter, rodeo performer, died from injuries accidentally received Friday night when his head struck a viaduct at LaRose while stealing a ride on a westbound Santa Fe freight train. Carter died yesterday morning at St. Francis hospital where he was brought early Saturday.

John Cherty, a fellow cowboy, testified he and Carter had been performing with a rodeo company in Chicago. The manager disappeared and left the show stranded, he said. The performers continued the rodeo for several days but made scarcely anything more than expenses. Cherty and Carter received 95 cents when they quit Friday. They boarded the freight train at Chicago that night.

Carter's body was shipped to his home at Brookfield, Mo., last night. He leaves a widow there. He was a veteran of the World War.

Betty had an illegitimate baby by a married sideshow roper who was killed in an accident in 1933. It is a mystery what happened to the child.

no mention of the child in the 1940 or the 1950 US census, nor in her obituary. Carter died while trying to jump a train in 1933 at the age of 41. She was an attraction at the 1939 New York World's Fair performing with the John Hix "Strange As It Seems Sideshow." Betty eventually became a tattoo artist herself when the demand for sideshow tattooed attractions drastically tapered off and the few shows seeking tattooed ladies were seeking younger, more erotic women. She was often found tattooing at one of the many arcades in San Francisco.

In 1967, she retired from the circus world and settled in Riverview, Florida, near Tampa. Her hobby was horticulture, and her gardens were said to be magnificent and over-run with her many pets. Betty died in her sleep on March 28, 1983, of natural causes. She was seventy-four years old. She is buried with her third husband in Hillsboro Memorial Cemetery in Brandon, Florida. Two years before her death she became the first person to be inducted into The San Francisco Tattoo Hall of Fame on August 5, 1981. According to Ward Hall, longtime sideshow promoter and a friend of Betty's, she once disclosed to him that she regretted having the first tattoo. ♦

Betty died at the age of seventy-four. She is buried with her third husband in Hillsboro Memorial Cemetery in Brandon, Florida.

MAE VANDERMARK

Ada Mae Vandermark obviously started in the circus as a tattooed lady at an early age judging from her pictures.

Ada Mae Vandermark obviously started in the circus as a tattooed lady at an early age judging from her picture. Not much is known about her except what can be gleaned from a 1931 newspaper article where she quipped, "When people ask me how come I'm a tattooed lady, I tell 'em it's because I love art and that's true, too, up to a certain point. I mean, I like to eat regular." It would be nice to know what became of Ada Mae and the back-story of her early entry into the sideshow. ♦

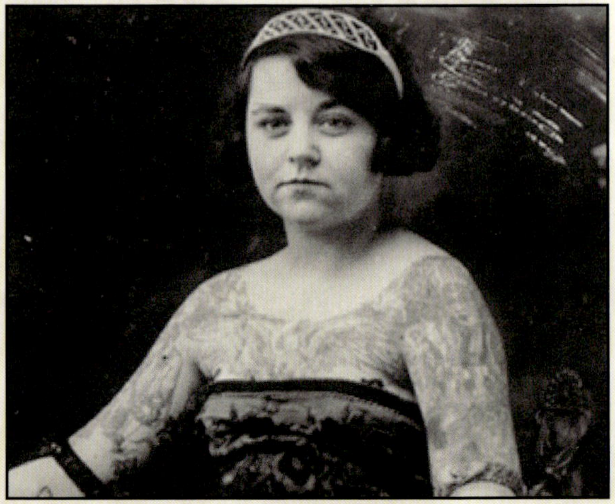

"When people ask me how come I'm a tattooed lady, I tell 'em it's because I love art and that's true, too, up to a certain point. I mean, I like to eat regular."

MYSTERY TO SOLVE

How did Mae come to join the sideshow? When and where was she born, and what became of her in her later years? When did she die, and where is she buried?

Mae is second from left on bottom row, shown with many of the famous freaks of the day.

LORETT FULKERSON, "THE LAST TATTOOED LADY"

Lorett Fulkerson was born Loretta Love on July 17, 1915. Reportedly, she started out in sideshows as a showgirl and as a cook. She always claimed that she was tattooed by Gib "Tatts" Thomas of Chicago who did most of her extensive ink for free in exchange for advertising on the trade cards she sold at shows. He was traveling as a tattoo artist with a Ringling Brothers show where Lorett was working. Lorett's career as a tattooed lady spanned over seven decades and she was still exhibiting in 2003, four years before her death on December 8, 2007, at the age of ninety-two.

She married Robert Fulkerson, a captain in the United States Air Force who served during World War II and Korea. They are buried side-by-side in the Fairview Baptist Church Cemetery in Natchitoches Parish, Louisiana. Lorett is considered the last of the great performing tattooed ladies of the sideshow. ♦

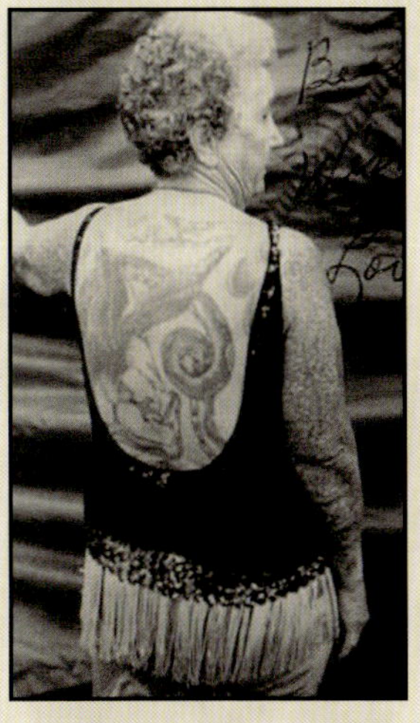

Lorett's career as a tattooed lady spanned more than seven decades and she was still exhibiting in 2003, four years before her death on December 8, 2007, at the age of ninety-two.

Lorett Fulkerson was born Loretta Love on July 17, 1915. She started out in sideshows as a showgirl and as a cook, then decided to become a tattooed lady.

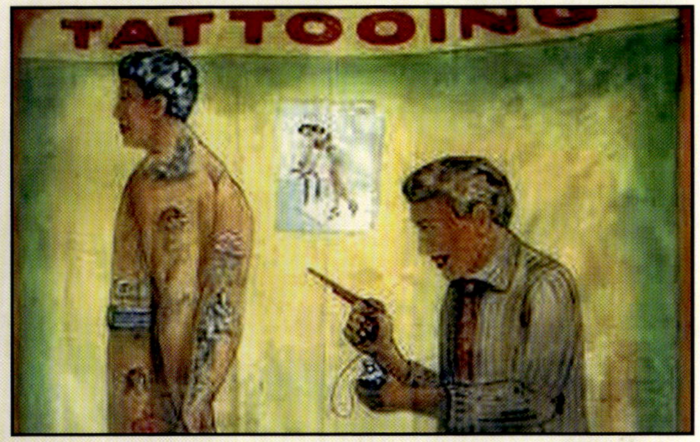

A few tattoo artists usually traveled with the sideshow and advertised their services with bright canvas circus banners.

FAT LADIES AND MEN

The visual difference between a fat man and a human skeleton always intrigued the public and sold tickets.

Many a fat person, tired of being gawked at for free, joined the circus and was paid well to be the source of visual amusement.

Poor and uneducated men and women who were tired of the ordinary means of eking out a living during harsh times, ate their way into the circus. Whole obese families joined together as fat attractions.

A sideshow would not be complete without a Fat Lady or Fat Man in the lineup. Many a fat person, tired of being gawked at for free, joined the circus and was paid well to be the source of visual amusement. Poor and uneducated men and women, who were tired of the ordinary means of eking out a living during harsh times, ate their way into the circus. Whole obese families joined together as fat attractions. It would be impossible to honor all the obese performers in one book, even all the famous ones, but this is a look at some of the more colorful ones.

While both fat women and men were wildly popular with the paying public, fat women were undoubtedly the most popular. Many of these ladies added a flirtatious dialogue to their performances and dressed in fairly risqué clothing, or at least risqué for the times. Most were not shy about lifting a skirt to reveal even more. There were literally hundreds of such performers during the heyday of the sideshow with outrageous stage names such as Jolly Ollie, Baby Ruth, Dainty Doris, Happy Val, Jolly Trixy, and Tessie Ton, to name a few. However, only a few were superstars. ♦

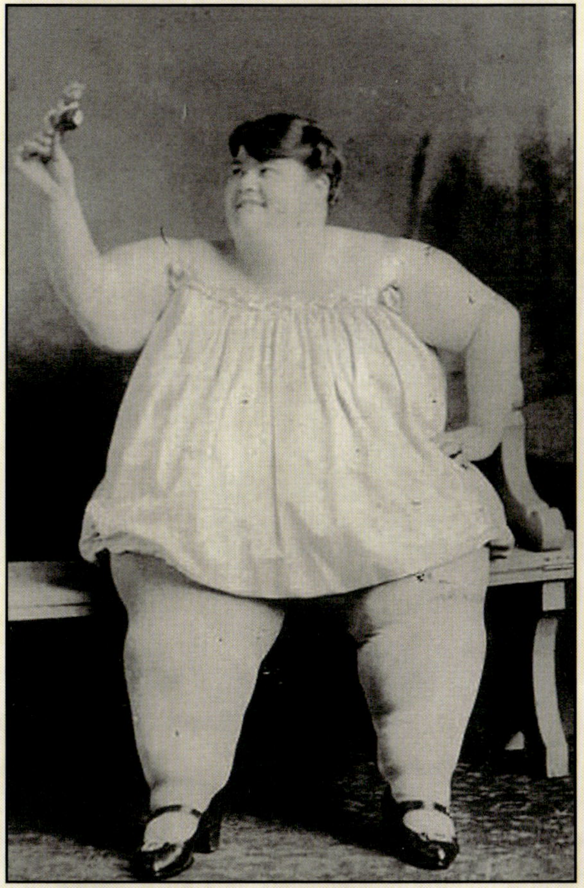

Jolly Trixy, a 685 pound Fat Lady, whose sideshow banner proclaimed "Holy smoke, she's so fat that it takes 7 men to hug her."

Unidentified fat child performer photographed with her mother. Fat children were even more of a rarity than fat adults.

While both fat women and men were wildly popular with the paying public, fat women were undoubtedly the most popular. Many times they would add a flirtatious element to their show, even lifting their skirts to show more. (Shown: Dolly Dimples)

RUTH SMITH, "IMA WADDLER," "LADY BEAUTIFUL," OR "BABY RUTH"

Ruth Smith was born in Kempton, Indiana, on February 8, 1904. She was one of the fattest women ever to appear in the circus and one of the most famous. Hype or true, most accounts record her birth weight at sixteen pounds. Reportedly, she weighed fifty pounds by the time she was a year old, and 300 pounds by the age of ten. By the end of her career, she weighed over 815 pounds, an impressive figure, but she never reached her goal of 1,000 pounds.

Ruth Smith was born fat, weighing sixteen pounds at birth and fifty pounds by the time she was one year old.

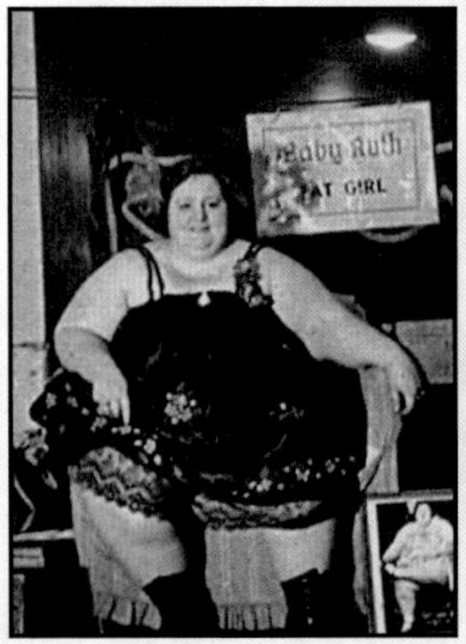

Ruth discovered many men were sexually attracted to large women. She often returned these sexual advances, and her lusty exploits were well-known and even reported in the press.

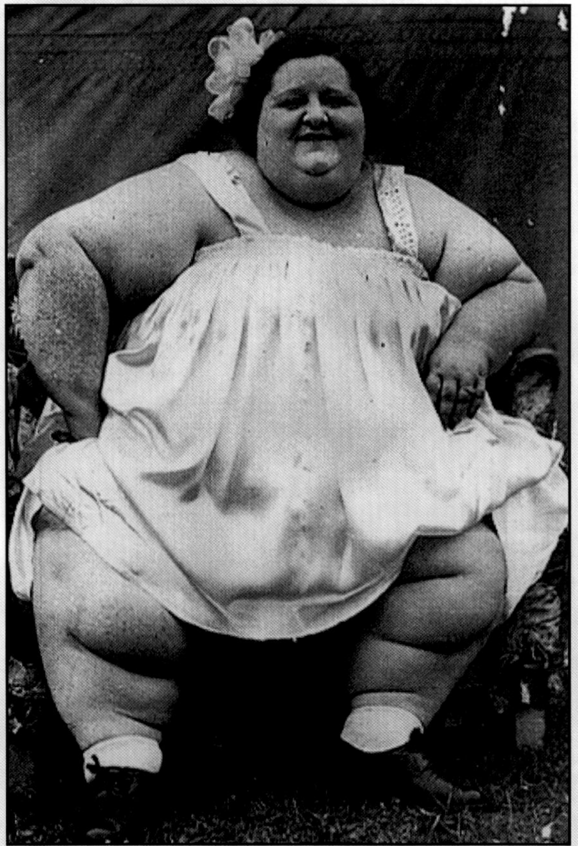

Ruth Smith Pontico died on November 29, 1941, from complications following surgery to remove fat. She is arguably the most famous of the sideshow fat ladies, but she never reached her goal of 1,000 pounds.

Ruth was very happy and comfortable with her ample proportions. She installed large three-way mirrors in her home and dressing room so she would be able to admire her body from all angles. She seemed to completely enjoy the process of gaining weight, from the eating of the foods to the appearance of new fat on her body.

She appears to have followed in her family's footsteps. Her mother had been a fat woman with the circus and weighed between 600 and 750 pounds during her career. Her stage name was "The Human Blimp." Some sources have even reported that Ruth's grandmother was also a professional fat lady. Ruth always claimed she was a light eater and her size was due to heredity. Her father was of typically developed size and her only sister was actually a fashion model. As a young girl, Ruth joined a circus. Her first professional billing was "Ima Waddler." Ruth enjoyed the entire experience of the circus from the very beginning. She had been ridiculed and stared at her whole life, but now she was actually making money from her looks. At the height of her popularity, she was making as much as $400 a day from ticket sales and sales of her photos and pitch cards. That was a fat salary in Depression-torn America.

Ruth also discovered many men were sexually attracted to large women. Reportedly, Ruth often returned these sexual advances and her lusty exploits were well-known and even reported in the press. It was during this time she changed her stage name first to "Lady Beautiful" and later to "Baby Ruth" in honor of the newly popular American candy bar. She made friends easily among the other sideshow performers and was known for her generosity and quick loans to anyone with a sob story. In 1931, she signed with Barnum & Bailey and there met Joe Pontico (1889–1953), who ran the balloon concession. They soon married and by all accounts were devoted to one another. Reports vary on Joe's size. Some newspaper articles claim that Joe only weighed 130 pounds and other stories reported that he could have been a circus fat man in his own right. (He is buried in Showman's Rest Cemetery in Tampa, Florida.) In 1931, Ruth also contracted typhoid fever while on tour in Springfield, Missouri, and for a period of time was listed in critical condition. The newspapers of the day did not look upon the situation as seriously as Ruth probably did. They gaily printed that when her husband came to take her home to Sarasota, his bride was down to a dainty 600 pounds, having lost 100 pounds during her stay in the hospital. They also reported that a baggage car on the train was needed to transport her.

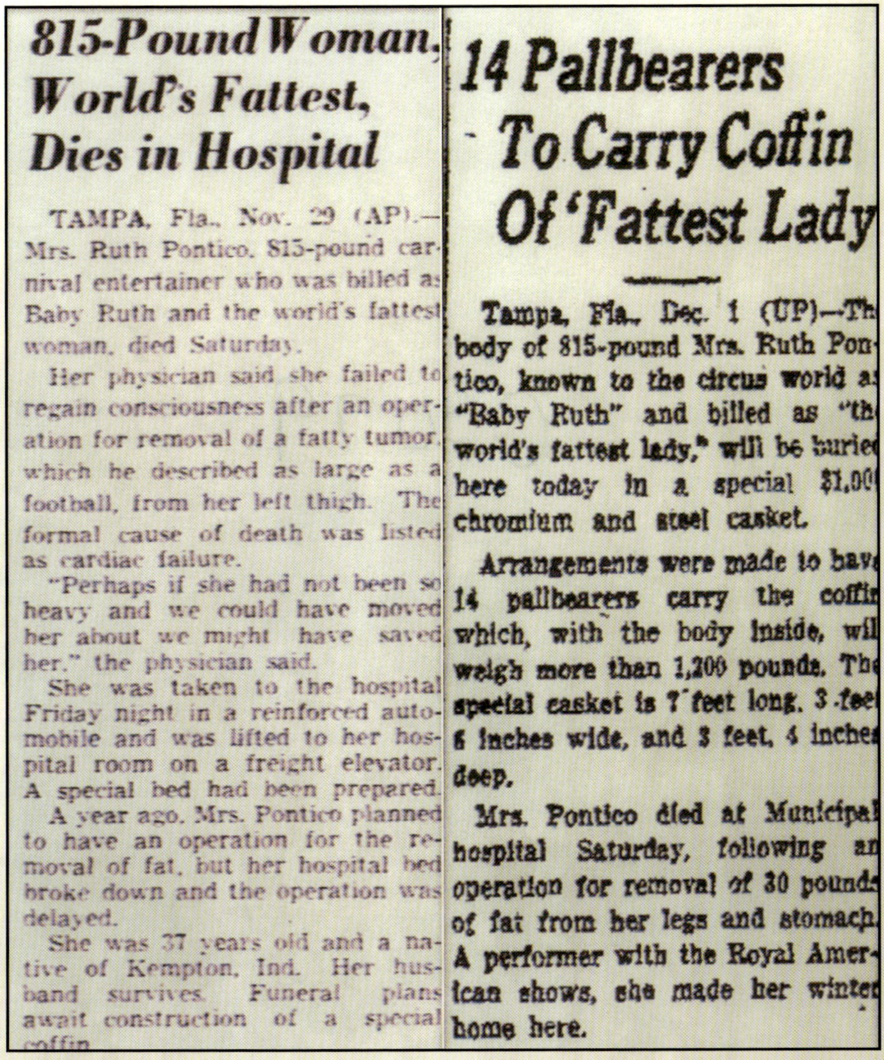
815-Pound Woman, World's Fattest, Dies in Hospital

TAMPA, Fla., Nov. 29 (AP).—Mrs. Ruth Pontico, 815-pound carnival entertainer who was billed as Baby Ruth and the world's fattest woman, died Saturday.

Her physician said she failed to regain consciousness after an operation for removal of a fatty tumor, which he described as large as a football, from her left thigh. The formal cause of death was listed as cardiac failure.

"Perhaps if she had not been so heavy and we could have moved her about we might have saved her," the physician said.

She was taken to the hospital Friday night in a reinforced automobile and was lifted to her hospital room on a freight elevator. A special bed had been prepared.

A year ago, Mrs. Pontico planned to have an operation for the removal of fat, but her hospital bed broke down and the operation was delayed.

She was 37 years old and a native of Kempton, Ind. Her husband survives. Funeral plans await construction of a special coffin

14 Pallbearers To Carry Coffin Of 'Fattest Lady

Tampa, Fla., Dec. 1 (UP)—The body of 815-pound Mrs. Ruth Pontico, known to the circus world as "Baby Ruth" and billed as "the world's fattest lady," will be buried here today in a special $1,000 chromium and steel casket.

Arrangements were made to have 14 pallbearers carry the coffin which, with the body inside, will weigh more than 1,200 pounds. The special casket is 7 feet long, 3 feet 6 inches wide, and 3 feet, 4 inches deep.

Mrs. Pontico died at Municipal hospital Saturday, following an operation for removal of 30 pounds of fat from her legs and stomach. A performer with the Royal American shows, she made her winter home here.

Ruth and Joe ran an Italian restaurant in Florida during the winter season. Joe loved to cook and Ruth loved to eat, so this was obviously a match made in hog heaven. Her usual breakfast was three eggs, eight strips of bacon, four slices of toast, a glass of orange juice, and two quarts of water—this was during the Depression when most folks were lucky to get that much food the whole day. Mobility and size were both problems for Ruth. She once visited her sister and promptly fell through the floor of the house. It took a crane and a dedicated rescue crew to hoist her out of the hole. Her own home, a hotel she and Joe purchased, sported reinforced floors and oversized sturdy furniture. She also had an oversized shower and toilet. She was famous for saying, "I once went on a starvation diet, but gained nine pounds in four days and gave it up." All problems aside, reportedly Ruth was very happy and comfortable with her ample proportions. She installed large three-way mirrors in her home and dressing room so she would be able to admire her body from all angles. She seemed to completely enjoy the process of gaining weight, from the eating of the foods to the appearance of new fat on her body.

In April of 1941, Ruth entered a hospital to have an operation to reduce her weight to allow for better mobility. She was scheduled to go on tour and her bulk was hindering her ability to do so. She was quoted in newspapers as saying, "I don't know how much the doctor is going to take away, but it probably will be from my legs and possibly my abdomen." That operation had to be postponed, however, because the hospital bed collapsed under her and a specially constructed bed had to be acquired before she could return. Ruth returned to Tampa's Municipal Hospital on November 28, but died in that hospital on November 29, 1941, from complications post-surgery. She was thirty-seven. Her physician claimed she failed to regain consciousness after the operation where he removed a fatty tumor described "as large as a football" from her left thigh, plus thirty pounds of fat from her legs and stomach. The official cause of death was listed as cardiac failure but the doctor's statement to the newspaper led way for speculation that Ruth had choked to death coming out of the anesthesia because the medical staff was unable to turn her. Later, the doctor publicly stated that if she had not been so heavy, they could have moved her and might have saved her. She had been brought to the hospital the night before in a reinforced automobile and was lifted to her hospital room in a freight elevator. Newspapers across the land carried stories about the death of the "Fattest Lady," headlining her weight at 815 to 850 pounds. It was said that fourteen pallbearers would be carrying her $1,000 chromium and steel casket that weighed 400 pounds, empty, and was seven feet long, three and half feet wide, and three feet and four inches deep. The location of her burial site remains a mystery today. ♦

MYSTERY TO SOLVE

Where is Ruth buried and was she buried in a $1,000 casket or was that just show business hype?

CELESTA GEYER, "JOLLY DOLLY," "DOLLY DIMPLES"

Celesta Herrmann Geyer was born on July 18, 1901, in Cincinnati, Ohio, the child of German-American parents who reportedly sat down a minimum of six times a day to eat. Celesta always claimed from day one she just loved all food. If she was teased at school by classmates, she would hurry home to a mother who would comfort her with special dishes. She weighed 150 pounds at age thirteen. By the time she dropped out of school, she weighed 295 pounds but only stood four feet and eleven inches tall. She said she was unable to find gainful employment due to her grand size.

She did have many suitors, however, and in 1925 she married Frank Geyer, who never weighed more than 135 pounds in his lifetime. Celesta claimed she gained 100 pounds the first year she was married. "I'd make a special pie or cake for Frank every day, he would eat a piece, and I would finish the rest off." In 1927, legend says they attended a carnival and the manager of the show offered Celesta a job at first sight. Her husband supported her decision to join the show and traveled with her and acted as her agent and performed odd jobs with the carnivals. Originally she co-starred on stage with Jolly Pearl Stanley and was billed as "Jolly Dolly." Later, she commanded the stage alone and changed her stage name to "Dolly Dimples." (Celesta had dimples an inch deep at each elbow that led to her nickname.) She kept that name for the rest of her career that spanned over twenty years. At the height of that career, Celesta weighed over 425 pounds and was making close to $300 a day. By 1950, she had topped out at 555 pounds. She once said that it took twelve yards of material to make her one dress.

Dolly Dimples sideshow banner c. 1930. Note the contrast between the very thin fair-goers of the day and The Fat Lady.

She was billed as "The World's Prettiest Fat Girl" and "The World's Most Beautiful Fat Lady." Her skin was flawless and she always maintained an hour-glass figure, albeit a very large hour-glass figure. Her measurements were reported in the news as 74.5-68-84. Eventually, she added singing and impersonation of celebrities such as Kate Smith to her act, which made her even more popular with the paying public. There was never any suggestion that Celesta's size was due to a glandular problem. Per Celesta herself, she just loved to eat and ate from the time she got up in the morning until she retired at night. Reportedly, it took a minimum of 10,000 calories a day to maintain both her happiness and size. Dolly would amaze her audience by eating large amounts of food in one sitting on stage. This proved an ideal ploy for two reasons: the crowds paid more to see these amazing feats and Celesta got to indulge in food during performances. She had formerly complained to her manager that she got too hungry during her time on stage to concentrate on her act.

Like many fat performers, Celesta was plagued by health issues. She had difficulty walking due to her girth, and her heart began to fail her. She suffered a heart attack in 1950 at the age of forty-nine and doctors told her to either lose weight or die. They put her on a menu of baby food and Celesta lost more than 400 pounds in a little more than a year. "Right before I had my heart attack I used to pray to die because I was so helpless. Now I am on the skinny side." She penned an autobiography on her amazing weight loss, *Diet or Die: The Dolly Dimples Weight Reducing Plan,* which was published in 1968 by F. Fell. She spent a good part of her last years on a lecture circuit motivating others to lose weight and get healthy. She reportedly said, "My friends told me I'd kill myself if I went on a crash

Sideshow banners for Dolly Dimples. Banner artists seldom saw the acts they were painting so they used their imagination when creating their art. Dolly sang, did celebrity impersonations, and ate on stage, but she did not dance.

Fat ladies were wildly popular during the heyday of the sideshow, and even midget fat ladies got into the act. There were literally hundreds of fat ladies exhibiting, and it would have been rare to find a sideshow anywhere that did not feature at least one.

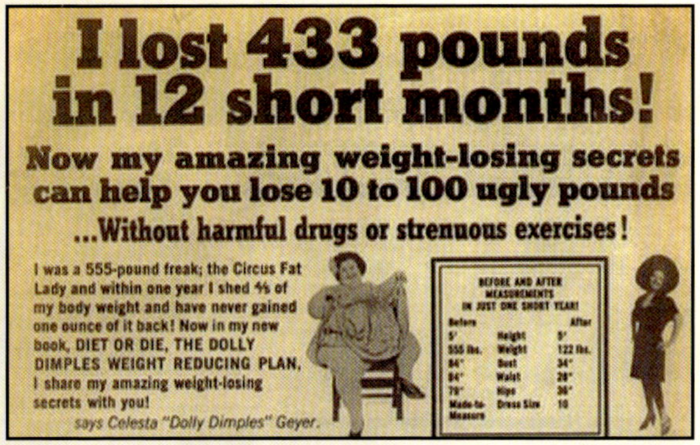

At the end of her career, Celeste had blossomed up to 555 pounds and claimed it took twelve yards of material for each of her dresses. She wrote an autobiography published in 1968 about her amazing weight loss after a heart attack in 1950.

diet. Well, if I do then they don't have to bring me (to the cemetery) on a truck. I'll fit into a hearse."

Her beloved husband, Frank, had died in 1967. As a widow, Celesta began traveling the world again, but this time on the arms of her wealthy admirers who still considered her a very beautiful woman, even though now she was slim and trim. There were several Fat Ladies who billed themselves as "Dolly Dimples," but Celesta Geyer was by far the most famous of these performers. She ran a small art gallery exhibiting amateur art in Miami, Florida, near her home in Dania, Florida, until her death on February 18, 1882, at the age of 80—and she was still thin. The location of her grave is unknown. ♦

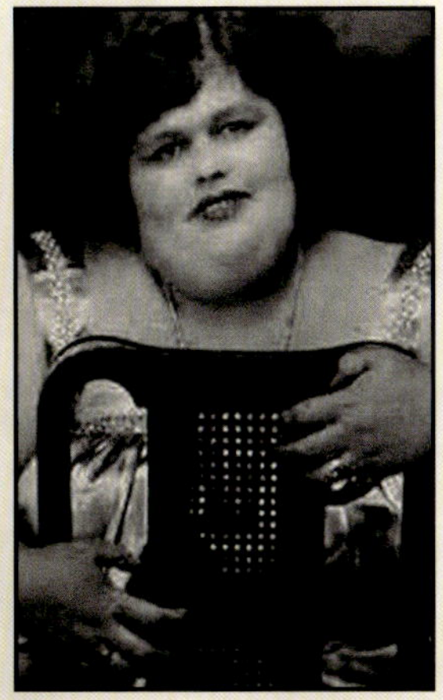

Celesta was born in Cincinnati, Ohio, in 1901. She always claimed she just loved food and had German-American parents who always rewarded and comforted her with food.

Celesta was billed as "The World's Prettiest Fat Girl" and "The World's Most Beautiful Fat Lady." Her skin was flawless, and she always maintained an hour-glass figure, albeit a very large hour-glass figure. Her measurements were reported in the news as 74.5–68–84.

HAPPY JACK ECKERT

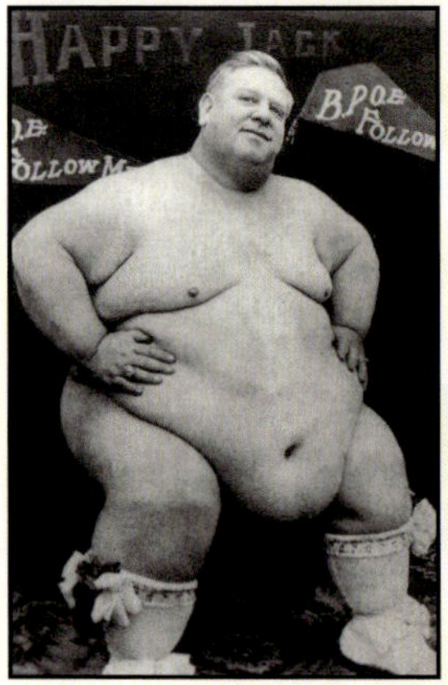

Happy Jack made a nice additional salary from selling pitch cards but the naked cards outsold the other pitch cards 3-1.

Probably the best known sideshow fat man is Jack Eckert, who was born in Lafayette, Indiana, in 1877. Reportedly, he started in show business at the early age of ten, and ate his way to a secure position with sideshows. He always claimed he would have liked to have had a more regular job, but his size prohibited him from seeking or securing employment. He was known for his outrageous costumes, many times dressing as a young toddler or in feminine attire. At any given time, he might just appear in only his birthday suit and booties. He was very proud of the beloved fraternal organizations he joined and often sported pendants on stage and in pitch cards advertising such. He billed himself as "The Largest Elk, Moose, and Woodman of the World." As outlandish as Jack was on stage, he led a somewhat typical life. He married, had two typically sized children, but was estranged from his family at the time of his death. He was not a modest man, nor was he prudish at a time in America when most citizens presented themselves as puritanical, church-going backbones of the community. Happy Jack made a nice additional salary from selling pitch cards but the naked cards outsold the other pitch cards 3 to 1. He was very proud of his girth and weighed between 739 and 789 pounds. It is said that his stomach hung to his knees and measured close to ninety inches around.

By all accounts, Happy Jack was quite healthy and void of the usual health and mobility issues that plague most morbidly obese people. Health issues did not kill him, but an unfortunate auto accident did. He was in Flomaton, Alabama, in February 1939 when his specially-constructed motor truck collided with a freight truck. It took ten men to carry him into a hospital and he was placed on two hospital beds that were lashed together. Sadly, the medical staff was not able to save him and Jack died from internal injuries and fractured ribs. He was sixty-two. His manager immediately offered Happy Jack's body to Tulane University because, according to the manager, "…Jack always wished some school be given the opportunity to study his glandular system." Jack's surviving next of kin, his sister Katharine Eckert, seventy-four, agreed, but the school refused the offer. They claimed that fat cadavers were useless for the study of anatomy, especially one of his magnitude. Instead, the body was placed in a 500-pound cypress coffin and Happy Jack was buried in Mobile, Alabama, by his beloved lodge brothers, the Elks and Woodmen of the World. ♦

ROBERT EARL HUGHES

It is probable that Robert Earl did suffer from some sort of glandular condition causing his massive weight gain. In an article in *Life* magazine, he was called a "relatively light eater."

Robert Earl Hughes was born in Fish Hook, Illinois, on June 4, 1926. He weighed eleven and a half pounds at birth, and his parents watched in amazement as their son doubled his weight more than four times from the age of six, when he weighed 203 pounds, to the age of 25, when he weighed 896 pounds. *Guinness World Records* lists Robert Earl as having the Largest Chest Measurement: ten feet, four inches. He stood just a little over six-feet tall and is usually noted as either the heaviest or one of the heaviest men in the world to be recorded by medical professionals. Robert Earl spent most of his adolescent and adult life in sideshows. He traveled in a specially constructed

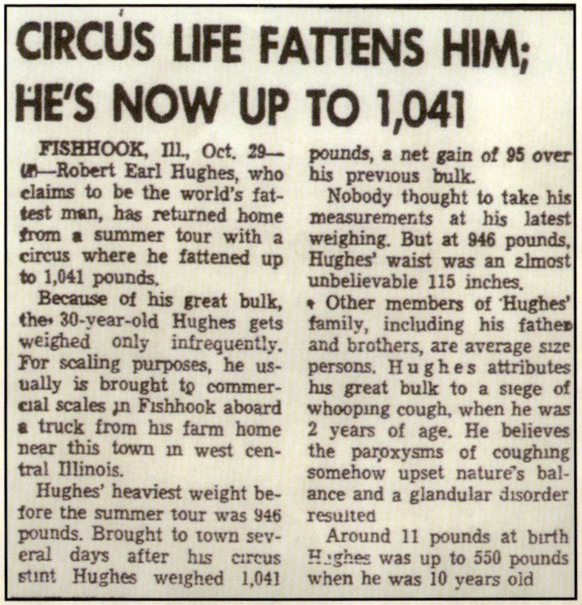
CIRCUS LIFE FATTENS HIM; HE'S NOW UP TO 1,041

FISHHOOK, Ill., Oct. 29—(AP)—Robert Earl Hughes, who claims to be the world's fattest man, has returned home from a summer tour with a circus where he fattened up to 1,041 pounds.

Because of his great bulk, the 30-year-old Hughes gets weighed only infrequently. For scaling purposes, he usually is brought to commercial scales in Fishhook aboard a truck from his farm home near this town in west central Illinois.

Hughes' heaviest weight before the summer tour was 946 pounds. Brought to town several days after his circus stint Hughes weighed 1,041 pounds, a net gain of 95 over his previous bulk.

Nobody thought to take his measurements at his latest weighing. But at 946 pounds, Hughes' waist was an almost unbelievable 115 inches.

Other members of Hughes' family, including his father and brothers, are average size persons. Hughes attributes his great bulk to a siege of whooping cough, when he was 2 years of age. He believes the paroxysms of coughing somehow upset nature's balance and a glandular disorder resulted

Around 11 pounds at birth Hughes was up to 550 pounds when he was 10 years old

Fat men and women of the circus never failed to make the newspaper. The public was always amazed by their life stories even into the 1950s. (Shown: A 1956 newspaper clipping about Robert Earl Hughes, who claimed to be the world's fattest man.)

trailer that accommodated his size, and he had to have reinforced stage areas and chairs built for all performances. He finally got so heavy that he was unable to climb onto the stage area so he was forced to exhibit himself from the ground level. His custom-sewn bib overalls that he wore every day were his trademark. It is probable that Robert Earl did suffer from some sort of glandular condition causing his massive weight gain. In an article in *Life* magazine hr was called a "relatively light eater."

Robert Earl contracted measles in 1958 while on tour in Bremen, Illinois. He was unable to fit into an ambulance. He was also too large to fit through the doors of the hospital and the beds were not strong enough to support his massive frame. Instead, he was treated in his custom trailer parked outside the hospital. Sadly, he developed uremia and died July 10, 1958. He was thirty-two. Surgeons also reported that he was also suffering from a heart condition and other medical conditions. At his death, he weighed 1,041 pounds. He is buried in Benville, Illinois, in the Benville Cemetery in a custom-made coffin the size of a piano case. Reportedly, the coffin had to be lowered into the open grave by a crane. It was said of Robert Earl at his funeral that his heart was as big as his body. ♦

BENNY AND BILLY MCCRARY

Benny and Billy McCrary are listed in the *Guinness World Records* as the largest set of twins. Benny's weight is listed at 814 pounds, Billy's at a mere 784 pounds. They boasted of having identical eighty-four inch waistlines. They often called themselves the McGuire twins because they claimed that announcers in other countries had great difficulty pronouncing their last names when they traveled the world in the 1970s as tag team wrestling partners.

The McCrary brothers were born on December 7, 1946, and grew in Hendersonville, North Carolina. They dropped out of high school to travel to Texas, where they worked branding cattle. In a 1998 interview with *Inside Wrestling* magazine, Benny said he and his brother began gaining weight when they were hospitalized as young children with a severe case of German measles that damaged their pituitary glands. The twins weighed 200 pounds each by age ten and had topped 600 pounds by the age of sixteen. It is said that the good-natured and fun-loving pair were popular and often jabbed at one another. They considered themselves ladies' men and the light arguments usually involved a young lady. The brothers enjoyed a diverse career path. They performed in sideshows and in Las Vegas. They worked for Honda Motor Company doing commercials and riding their Honda motorcycles on a promotional tour from New York to Los Angeles. They enjoyed international fame as a wrestling tag team and even appeared on *The Tonight Show* with Johnny Carson.

Billy died on July 14, 1979, from injuries sustained in a motorcycle accident in Niagara Falls when he was thrown from his bike. Reportedly, he was doing one of the many stunts he and his brother were

Benny and Billy McCrary are listed in the Guinness Book of World Records as the largest set of twins. Benny's weight is listed at 814 pounds, Billy's at a mere 784 pounds. They traveled the world in the 1970s as tag team wrestling partners.

The twins were a good-natured and fun-loving pair who often jabbed at each other. They considered themselves ladies' men, and the light arguments usually involved a young lady.

famous for. He was thirty-two. Benny continued to wrestle for a short while, teaming up with the greats such as Andre the Giant. He eventually bought a pawn shop in Hendersonville, North Carolina, and worked as an auctioneer. In 1998, he and his second wife moved to Walkerton, North Carolina, and he began working at a golf course. Benny died on March 26, 2001 of heart failure. He was fifty-four. The twins are buried together at Crab Creek Baptist Church Cemetery in Hendersonville. Their oversized tombstone is embossed with twin pictures of their mini bikes and "The World's Largest Twins." Reportedly, it is the world's largest granite gravestone, measuring thirteen feet wide and weighing three tons, a fitting tribute to the McCrary twins. ♦

HUMAN SKELETONS

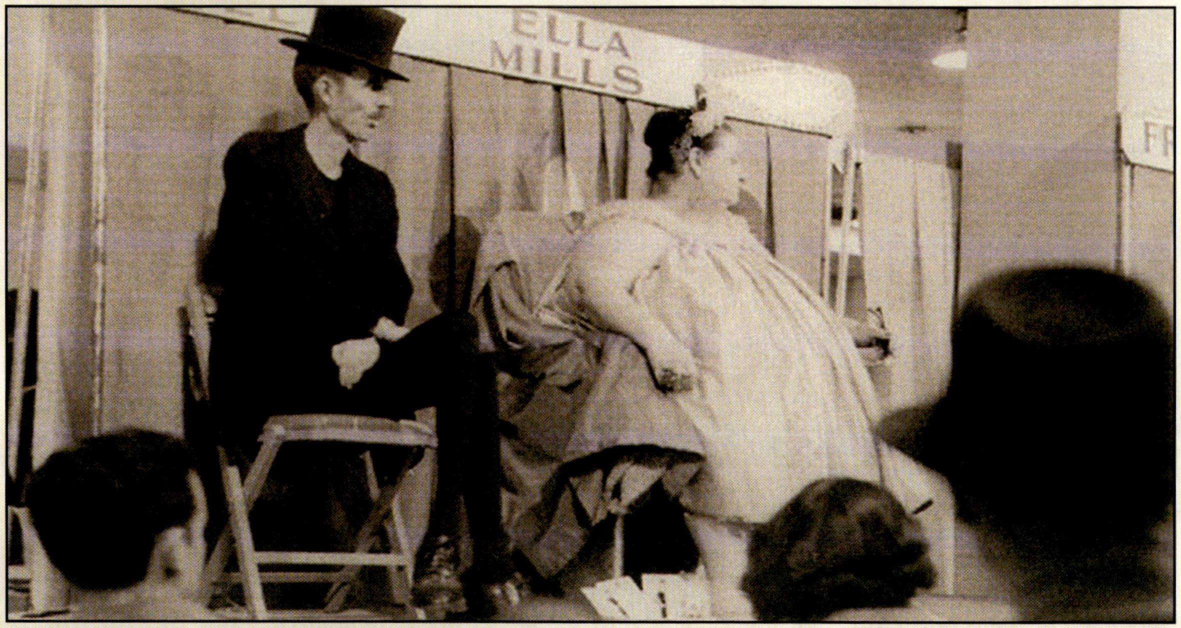

The contrast between the fat lady and the human skeleton was such a popular drawing card that many a fake marriage was staged between the two performers.

Another popular created "freak" was the human skeleton. Both men and women were exhibited as such, but the men outnumbered the lady performers by a wide margin. The human skeleton made a great contrast when exhibited beside the show's fat person, so much so that many a publicity stunt involved a fake marriage between a fat lady and a male human skeleton.

Some performers suffered from a glandular condition or from diseases such as scarlet fever or tuberculosis. Others simply starved themselves into the circus role. ♦

Some human skeletons suffered from a glandular condition or from diseases such as scarlet fever or tuberculosis. Others simply starved themselves into the circus role.

ISAAC W. SPRAGUE "THE LIVING SKELETON," OR "THE HUMAN SKELETON"

Despite his size, appearance, and physical stamina, in 1868 Isaac Sprague married a woman from Rockland, Massachusetts, and they had three sons, all of typically developed weight and size. Publicity stunts or not, newspaper stories linked him to several love interests, and he was said to have even married a few, including a female "Living Skeleton" and a beauty queen.

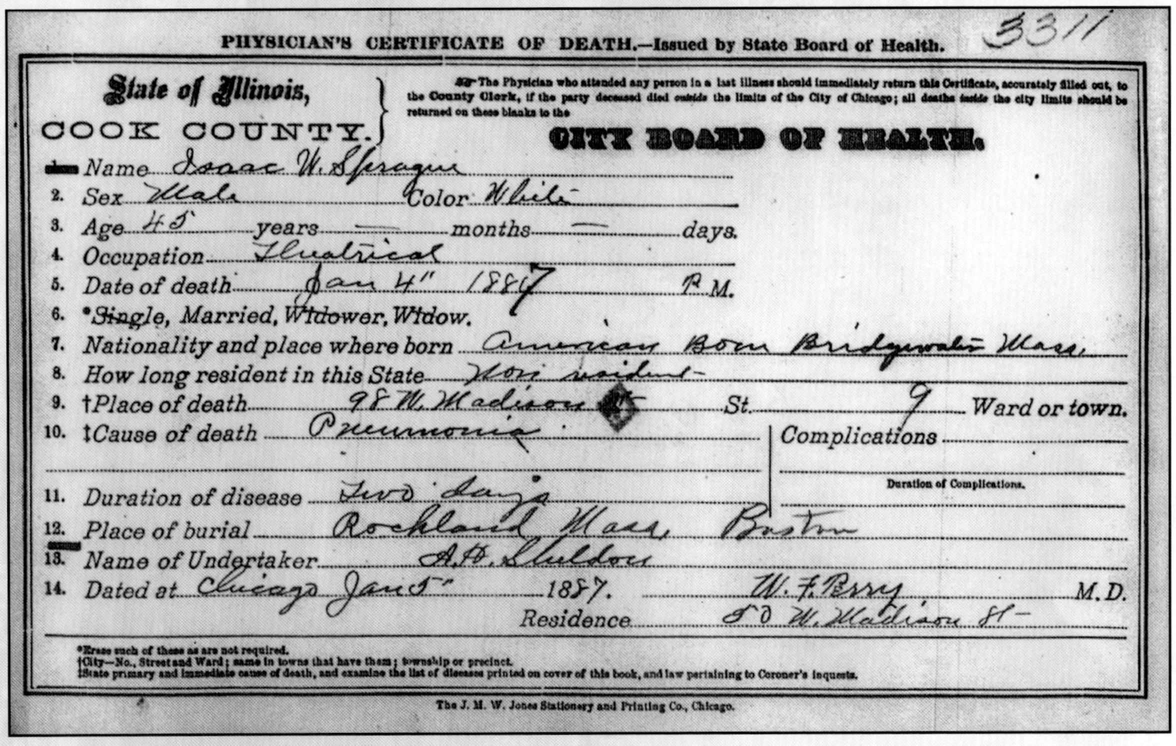

PHYSICIAN'S CERTIFICATE OF DEATH.—Issued by State Board of Health. 3311

State of Illinois, COOK COUNTY.

The Physician who attended any person in a last illness should immediately return this Certificate, accurately filled out, to the County Clerk, if the party deceased died *outside* the limits of the City of Chicago; all deaths *inside* the city limits should be returned on these blanks to the

CITY BOARD OF HEALTH.

1. Name Isaac W. Sprague
2. Sex Male Color White
3. Age 45 years — months — days.
4. Occupation Theatrical
5. Date of death Jan 4" 1887 P.M.
6. *Single, Married, Widower, Widow.
7. Nationality and place where born American Born Bridgewater Mass.
8. How long resident in this State Non resident
9. †Place of death 98 W. Madison St. 9 Ward or town.
10. ‡Cause of death Pneumonia Complications
11. Duration of disease Two days Duration of Complications.
12. Place of burial Rockland Mass. Boston
13. Name of Undertaker A.H. Sheldon
14. Dated at Chicago Jan 5" 1887. W. F. Berry M.D. Residence 80 W. Madison St.

*Erase such of these as are not required.
†City—No., Street and Ward; same in towns that have them; township or precinct.
‡State primary and immediate cause of death, and examine the list of diseases printed on cover of this book, and law pertaining to Coroner's inquests.

The J. M. W. Jones Stationery and Printing Co., Chicago.

Isaac Sprague was probably the most famous of the human skeletons, also called living skeletons. He was born in East Bridgewater, Massachusetts, in 1841 and always claimed he was a typically developed child until around age twelve. He said that he got a cramp one day after swimming, and then laid down in the shade to rest, but soon felt sick and remained sick until he was down to a mere forty pounds. He said he was never able to gain much weight after that. Isaac was afflicted with progressive muscular atrophy. This is a painless condition that comes on gradually and saps strength, causes severe fatigue, muscle wasting, and weight loss. In Isaac's case, *extreme* weight loss. Isaac had worked under his father as a cobbler apprentice and later became a grocer, but he tired easily due to his muscular wasting and was unable to keep either position. The sideshow was an alternative to literally starving to death, so in 1865 he accepted a paying position as a performer, his only requirement being to sit or stand in front of a fascinated public and tell his story. He eventually became such a popular attraction that P. T. Barnum hired Isaac to come work for him. In his publicity campaigns, he was described as being five feet, five and a half inches tall and weighing only forty-six pounds. Despite his size, appearance, and physical stamina, in 1868 he married a woman from Rockland, Massachusetts, and they had three sons, all of typically developed weight and size. Publicity stunts or not, newspaper stories linked him to several love

interests and he was said to have even married a few, including a female living skeleton and a beauty queen. No mention was ever made of a divorce from his first wife. At least one woman took the newspaper articles seriously. Minnie Johnson, the beauty queen, claimed she had married Isaac in Cleveland, Ohio, (or Jersey City) in 1883 and had lived and traveled with him for the last few years of his life. She quickly put a legal stake on his $10,000 estate when he died. The first wife and the dubious second wife were left to fight it out in court for their fair share. The scandal broke in the newspapers and headlines quipped, "Living Skeleton had Skeletons in His Closet" or simply, "The Living Skeleton Was a Bigamist."

Isaac died January 4, 1887, in Chicago, Illinois, at age forty-five. One account said he left his body to Harvard Medical College and another said he sold his body to Harvard for $1,000. He reportedly once quipped to a reporter, "…they can't have it till I get through with it." An autopsy was performed on January 15, 1887, by Dr. W. E. Whitney, curator of the Harvard Museum and a professor of pathology at Harvard College. He was assisted by various local physicians. Dr. Whitney stated the cause of death was pneumonia and the cause of his skeleton-like appearance was progressive muscular atrophy. All other organs were in a healthy condition but he noted a severe lateral curvature of the spine. Isaac's death certificate states he was to be buried in Boston or Rockland, Massachusetts, but the actual location of his gravesite, if any, is unknown.

Mystery to Solve: What was the outcome of the legal battle between wife no. 1 and wife no. 2 over Isaac's estate? Where is Isaac's gravesite located, or were his remains disposed of by Harvard in a less than traditional method? ♦

EUGENE FERALTO, "THE GIANT SKELETON," OR "THE LIVING SKELETON"

Eugene Feralto was the stage name of Orrin H. Perry, born in 1842 in Brooklyn, New York. He was 6 feet, 1 inch tall and weighed only eighty pounds. He originally started performing as a strongman. Sometime around the age of thirty-seven, he changed his act completely by starving himself down to skin and bones and began exhibiting as "The Giant Skeleton" and "The Living Skeleton," keeping the strongman element in the act by lifting heavy weights with his teeth to demonstrate his unusual strength. He was with the Forepaugh circuses for twelve years and then with Barnum and Bailey for sixteen years. While he was with the Forepaugh circuses, a false publicity stunt claimed he had married Mlle. Charcot, a beautiful woman from a good family who had become enamored by the living skeleton. It was said they married hours after meeting and her family strongly disapproved. For some reason, the public was fascinated by a living skeleton marrying, and it was

MYSTERY TO SOLVE

Where is Eugene buried? Did his few friends take up a collection to bury him? Did his estranged wife claim the body of her husband and bury him in New York? Is he in an unmarked charity plot?

Eugene Feralto is shown with his wife. He was often billed as "The Giant Skeleton," standing more than six feet tall and weighing only eighty pounds. The man on the left is Eugene at age twenty-three when he weighed 220 pounds and was a sideshow strongman.

The Crescent Park Amusement Park opened in Riverside, Rhode Island, in 1886 on the shores of the Narragansett Bay. It was called the "Coney Island of the East Coast."

a sideshow publicity stunt that never failed to deliver newspaper coverage and wanted publicity. Eugene did actually marry, however, and was the father of a son, John, and a daughter, Pearl.

Eugene made his way to Riverside, Rhode Island, to find work at Crescent Park Amusement Park sometime after it opened in 1886. It was dubbed "The Coney Island of the East Coast" and was a bustling old-time amusement park with a large midway. He had hoped to secure a position as "The Giant Skeleton" but, for whatever reason, his career never recharged at Crescent Park. He was reduced to picking up menial odd jobs and barely scratched out a living, and he became embittered. He lived for several years as a hermit in a room at Camp White, a camp inhabited largely by indigents, and shunned society except for a few friends.

Sadly, his obituary summed it up this way: Eugene died "alone and in a lonely hut he called home at Riverside, near the city of Providence, Rhode Island" in December 1907. He was sixty-five and died suddenly from a heart attack. His estranged wife and children were living in New York City at the time of Eugene's death. Reportedly, Eugene had made a great deal of money but that money was gone and he had to work small jobs after his retirement from show business. The location of Eugene's gravesite is unknown, but most likely he was buried in a charity plot nearby with no tombstone marking his final resting place. ♦

HANNAH JANE PERKINS BATTERSBY, FAT LADY, AND JOHN L. BATTERSBY, HUMAN SKELETON

Either real or a clever publicity stunt, the most popular of all the sideshow nuptials was the marriage between a fat lady and a human skeleton. The press never failed to write the story, and the public never tired of reading about such a couple. We can possibly trace this fascination back to childhood when we all recited "Jack Sprat could eat no meat and his wife could eat no lean" while gazing upon a page in our favorite storybook that was colorfully illustrated with the drawing of a very fat wife and a very thin husband; or maybe we are just impressed when the female is the one who is bigger and stronger. Hannah, 16, and John, 28, were married February 11, 1857, and by all accounts, were very happily married until the death of Hannah on April 15, 1889 at the age of forty-eight. *The New York Times* reported in Hannah's obituary that, according to her managers, she weighed 688 pounds at the time of her marriage but weighed 800 pounds at her death. Hannah's excessive weight was most likely caused by a hormonal imbalance. Unlike most sideshow fat ladies who ate their way into the limelight, it was said that Hannah was a relatively light eater.

Hannah Jane Perkins was born in Maine around 1841 and always claimed she was a typically developed infant and child until she reached the age of twelve. (It is hard to pin down birth dates on Hannah Battersby. Her death certificate and the Pennsylvania church and town records differ from the 1880 United States census. Her birth could be any year between 1835 and 1844. During this time in

Hannah died on April 15, 1889, at age forty-five. She is buried in Cedar Hill Cemetery in Philadelphia. No tombstone marks her grave.

The most popular of all the sideshow nuptials was the stunt marriage between a fat lady and a human skeleton. However, Hannah and John were actually happily married and remained so until Hannah's death in 1889.

Hannah and John shown in a lineup with other sideshow freaks.

history, birth certificates were not required and seldom obtained. Most births, marriages, and deaths were only recorded in family Bibles, at best.)

By the time she was in her late 20s, Hannah was an exhibiting fat lady with P. T. Barnum. The trade cards that she sold at her performances claimed she weighed 714 pounds, stood over six feet tall with broad shoulders measuring three feet wide, and had been pronounced the heaviest woman in the world. It was said that, at times, she was not able to fit through the door of an engagement house and special accommodations were often required due to her massive bulk.

Hannah died on April 15, 1889, in her home at 112 East Unity Street in Philadelphia. She was about forty-eight. Her death certificate cited her cause of death as "erysipelas," a bacterial skin infection that, most likely, was a result of Hannah's fall from a stage with a subsequent leg injury a few weeks prior. Her death may have been misdiagnosed, however, since while she did have erysipelas, it does not normally result in death. Her husband, overcome by grief and anguish, stood guard over his deceased wife and would not allow the many reporters and gawkers who assembled on the lawn of their home to view his wife in her oversized coffin. She was buried in the Battersby family plot at Cedar Hill Cemetery in Philadelphia. No stone marks her grave.

John was born in Lancashire, England, on Valentine's Day, 1829. He claimed his weight loss began when he was a teenager and, by the age of twenty-three, he was exhibiting at P. T. Barnum's dime museum as a human skeleton. His trade cards always gave his weight as between forty-five and fifty-two pounds, but that claim is doubtful. Sideshow performers were by no means held to a truth-in-advertising standard. Quite the contrary, entertainers were encouraged to invent any story that enhanced the performance and, thus, the ticket sales. It was while both Hannah and John were with Barnum that they met, fell in love, and married. The couple had three children, two daughters and a son who died in infancy, only twelve days old: Rachael Ellen Battersby Bantam (1858–1933), Zanobia (1859–1885), and John M (b/d 1866). Zanobia and infant John are buried in one of the Battersby family plots with their mother. No tombstone marks their graves.

In 1873, John sustained a spinal injury that required him to use a wheelchair for the rest of his life and retire from the difficult life of a touring sideshow performer. In the 1880 United States federal census, he, Hannah, and daughter Rachael were living together in Philadelphia and John's elderly widowed mother, widowed sister, and brother were living next door. Close family would have been an asset since Hannah still needed to work and was required to travel. It was said of the couple that Hannah would cradle John in her arms, much like a mother nurtures an infant, when John was sick or feeling depressed. It was also widely reported that Hannah had rescued John from a raging fire at P. T. Barnum's dime museum by throwing him over her shoulder and carrying him down a ladder to safety. While the story is very possible since Barnum's dime museum did burn down twice, most likely this was just a publicity story generated to increase public interest in this odd but loving couple. After Hannah's death, John relocated to Almena, Kansas, to live with his married daughter, Rachael Bantam. In the 1895 Kansas state census he is listed as a "cripple." He died on February 6, 1897, just a few days before his sixty-eighth birthday. His is buried in the Fairview Cemetery in Norton County, Kansas. Sadly, this strange and loving couple is separated at death. ♦

STRONGMEN

FREDERICH WILHELM MUELLER, ALIAS EUGEN SANDOW, "THE FATHER OF MODERN BODYBUILDING"

Sandow began his career as a Strong Man in the sideshow but he was soon discovered by Florenz Ziegfeld of Ziegfeld Follies. Ziegfeld realized the audience was far more interested in Eugen Sandow's magnificent body than his strength, so he coaxed Sandow into baring it all for the sake of his career. Reportedly, not much coaxing was required on Sandow's part.

Eugen Sandow was born in Prussia (present-day Konigsberg, Germany) on April 2, 1867. He became the first recognized bodybuilder in history and is referred to as "The Father of Modern Bodybuilding." Sandow began his career as a strongman in the sideshow but he was soon discovered by the famous showman of the Ziegfeld Follies, Florenz Ziegfeld Jr. Ziegfeld realized the

Sandow married the beauty Blanche Brookes and fathered two daughters with her, but his true love was Martinus Sieveking, a musician and composer. Sieveking became a bodybuilding champion in his own right due to the influence of his lover, Sandow.

audience was far more interested in Eugen's magnificent body than his strength, so he coaxed Eugen into baring it all for the sake of his career. Reportedly, not much coaxing was required on Eugen's part. Ziegfeld produced a major variety show to showcase Sandow's attributes, *Sandow's Trocadero Vaudevilles*. The show played in major theatres across the United States from 1893 to 1896 and made Sandow a very wealthy, very well-known star.

Sandow built his body to imitate the heroes of classical Greek and Roman sculptures. He even imitated their poses. He was extremely strong and was said to be able to carry a pony across the stage over his head unassisted. Despite his size and obvious strength, Sandow was actually a refined and cultured gentleman who was charming, well read, and well traveled. He also proved to be an astute businessman. On August 8, 1894, he married a woman of extraordinary beauty, Blanche Brookes, and fathered two daughters with her. However, he had difficulty in settling down to a routine married life. He had numerous affairs with other women before falling in love with a man, Martinus Sieveking (1867–1950), a musician and composer. They became inseparable. Sieveking became a bodybuilding champion in his own right due to the influence of his lover.

The most prestigious event in professional bodybuilding today is the Mr. Olympia contest. The trophy awarded the winner is a statue of Eugen Sandow and is named "The Sandow" in Eugen Sandow's honor.

Eugen Sandow's grave at Putney Vale Cemetery in London remained unmarked until 2002 when an elegant black marble marker was purchased by Sandow's biographer, Tom Manly. That marker is no longer there, having been replaced in 2009 with the current marker, a giant boulder purchased by Sandow's great-great-grandson. Sandow died in London on October 16, 1925, from complications of syphilis. He was fifty-eight years old.

Eugen Sandow died on October 16, 1925, in London from complications of syphilis. He was fifty-eight years old. His wife buried her husband in an unmarked grave at Putney Vale Cemetery, most likely the revenge of a scorned woman. The grave remained unmarked until 2002 when an elegant black marble marker was purchased by Sandow's biographer, Tom Manly, in May of that year. That marker is no longer there, having been replaced in 2009 with the current marker, a giant boulder purchased by Sandow's great-great grandson. The most prestigious event in professional bodybuilding today is the Mr. Olympia contest. The trophy awarded the winner is a statue of Eugen Sandow and is named "The Sandow" in Eugen Sandow's honor. ♦

CIRCASSIAN BEAUTIES

The moss-haired women were star attractions during these early years of the traveling sideshow and dime museums. These women were supposedly from the Circassian mountains and sold to wealthy kings and sultans as sex slaves because of their great beauty and obedience.

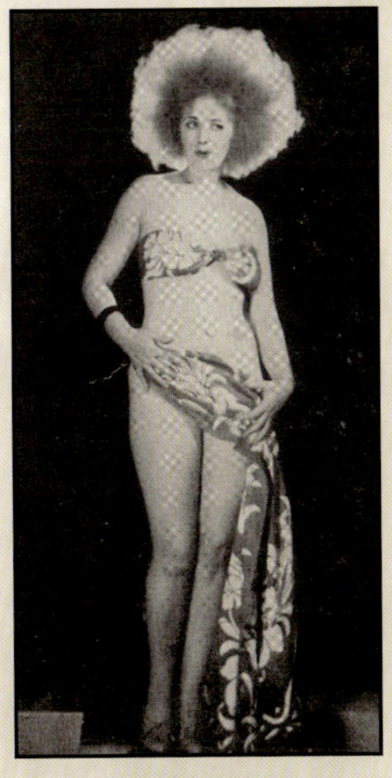

The Circassian beauties were hoaxes, but most likely few male fair-goers much cared or examined the logic of the stories too closely.

In the early years of the sideshow, people from small towns flocked to see anything unusual or out of the ordinary. The majority of these small town show-goers had probably not ventured more than a few miles from the spot where they were born. Most had limited education. It did not take much to amaze the public at this time in history, about fifty years before television, and almost 100 years before the Internet became a part of every household in America. The Circassians (also called moss-haired or sheep-haired women) were star attractions during these early years of the traveling sideshow and dime museums. Mankind is always in search of the most beautiful and exotic women on earth. Legend persisted that the women of the Circassian mountains near the Black Sea were sought after by kings and sultans because of their great beauty. This race of people was said to be very poor, so the fathers were forced to sell their desirable and obedient daughters to the highest bidder to be used as sex slaves.

The legend also played to the racial undertones of the day proclaiming these women to be females with only the purest Caucasian blood surging through their veins. The Civil War was still fresh in the collective minds of Americans and the idea of white slavery would understandably have been a shocking thought, especially the sexual slavery of a white, virginal, Victorian-era woman. The combination of oddity, beauty, sex, and the forbidden fruit was the perfect fodder for a sideshow exhibition. It is commonly believed that P. T. Barnum was the first to exhibit women whom he claimed were true Circassian beauties who had escaped from Turkish harems and kings' castles. They were typically presented as escaped victims of sexual enslavement, now free to travel all around

Oddity, beauty, sex, and the forbidden fruit were the perfect fodder for a sideshow exhibition. It is commonly believed that P. T. Barnum was the first to exhibit women whom he claimed were true Circassian beauties who had escaped from Turkish harems and kings' castles.

The most well-known of the Circassian beauties was Zoe Meleke, who first exhibited at Barnum's dime museum in New York around 1873, traveled with P. T. Barnum's Greatest Show on Earth for several seasons, and later appeared at the Tom Thumb Museum, but with canaries and conventional hair, her Circassian days behind her.

Finally even the scantiest of costumes were not enough to keep the public's interest, so most of these women added other elements to their performances, the most common being sword-swallowing and snake-handling, with the snake now most likely the star of the act.

America to recant their tantalizing tales of woe for the mere price of a ticket to their show. The Circassian beauties were, of course, hoaxes, but most likely few male fair-goers much cared or examined the logic of the stories too closely.

The most well-known of the Circassian beauties was Zoe Meleke, who first exhibited at Barnum's dime museum in New York around 1873, traveled with P. T. Barnum's Greatest Show on Earth for several seasons, and later appeared at the Tom Thumb Museum but with canaries and traditionally styled hair, her Circassian days behind her. Originally, Barnum presented Zoe as an ideally beautiful and exotic woman named Zalumma Agra, "Star of the East," who was the daughter of a prince and had just escaped a life of forced sexual slavery. For whatever reason, Zoe started to tease out her hair after pouring beer over it and letting it dry. The look worked. It set her apart from any other woman of the day, plus gave her hair an exotic look that blurred the line between a white and a black appearance, shocking the white showgoers of that time.

Barnum soon added other "Circassian women" to his array of performers, giving each one a name that started with the letter "Z" so as to sound more exotic. Soon every woman exhibiting as a Circassian adopted the same hair look of Zoe, either using beer or getting a frizzy perm. This hair style made the exhibitor immediately identifiable as an escaped Circassian sex slave. Later these women would be known as moss-haired girls or sheep-haired girls. Soon Barnum's competitors were adding Circassian women to their productions, as well. As the novelty of seeing these women wore off, the costumes first became more exotic and then later more erotic. Finally, even that was not enough to keep the public's interest, so most of these women added other elements to their performances, the most common being snake-handling, with the snake now most likely the star of the act. ♦

6

THE FAKE & THE NOT SO FAKE

Bearded Ladies, Half & Halfs, & Wild Men & Women

P. T. BARNUM, "THE FATHER OF THE SIDESHOW," MADE MILLIONS BY EXHIBITING THE EXOTIC, BE THEY REAL OR FAKE ODDITIES.

The tradition of the sideshow centered on entertainment. Most of the exhibits presented were not actual scientific human abnormalities but gaffs. The "FeeJee Mermaid" was probably the most popular created gaff and was made from the skeleton of a monkey attached to the body of a fish.

He never let truth stand in his way when it came to selling tickets to a gawking public, nor did any of his peers. The performers, themselves, also spun tales to enhance the appeal of their show and those tales often changed to accommodate the tastes of the various audiences. The tradition of the sideshow centers on entertainment, not truth. Most of the exhibits presented and a few of the categories of sideshow performers primarily tended to be fakes, or "gaffs" as they are called in the trade. ♦

BEARDED LADIES

While there were authentic bearded ladies who exhibited themselves in the sideshows, the majority of the bearded ladies were effeminate men dressed in women's clothing. Moral etiquette of the day would, of course, dictate that these "women" did not have to prove they were indeed of the female persuasion. Fake or real, the bearded lady was a popular addition to many a sideshow. This book will look at the most famous of these ladies who were authentic, honest-to-goodness bearded ladies. ♦

ANNIE (ANNA) JONES

Annie Jones was probably the most famous of the authentic bearded ladies. She was born in Marion, Virginia, on July 14, 1865, and apparently suffered from a medical condition called hypertrichosis or hirsutism. Reportedly, Annie's parents, in essence, leased her to P. T. Barnum when she was only nine months old. She was exhibited at his museum in New York at age 1. Her father died when Annie was very young, but her mother maintained a very comfortable existence since she received $150 a week for the child, a large sum at the time. She would undress the infant on stage showing off her hairy arms, legs, and shoulders. Annie was billed as the "Infant Esau." By the age of five, she had a mustache and sideburns and became known as the "Bearded Girl" and the "Child Esau." (This was a biblical reference to Esau, the hairy brother of Jacob: *And the first came out red, all over like an hairy garment; and they called his name Esau.* Genesis 25:25)

Annie shown with her mother. Annie's earnings supported her mother, father, a sister, and later a stepfather until her death.

In an incident that most likely was a publicity stunt, a New York phrenologist kidnapped Annie when she was a young child. Legend says that P. T. Barnum and the police found her exhibited at a church fair. When the man claimed the child as his, the parents had to sue to get her back. The judge had Annie separated from the others before it was her time to testify. When the child was taken to the courtroom, she went straight to her parents. The judge declared the case closed and the child was returned home. In the 1900 census, Annie's mother, Margaret Pogue is noted as giving birth to 12 children, but only 3 remained alive at that time. It also shows Annie's profession as "Show business" and living with her mother and older spinster sister, Mary. Since neither her mother nor her sister list a profession, it is most likely that Annie was the sole support of the household or her mother, listed as head of the household, was living off the money

Annie Jones dressed in mourning for her second husband.

she accumulated from exhibiting her unusual daughter since she was an infant. When Annie was 16-years-old, she married a circus barker named Richard Elliott. That union ended in divorce in 1895 after almost 15 years when she sued him for desertion. She quickly married William Donovan, a wardrobe man with the Barnum show and a long-time friend, who unfortunately died a few years after their marriage. Annie did not bear a child during either union and remained childless for

Annie Jones was often described as having the manners of a true society lady.

reasons known only to her.

As an adult, Annie became the nation's top bearded lady and acted as a spokesperson for the other performers that worked for P. T. Barnum in the 1899 protests. She hated being referred to as a "freak" and worked to have the word abolished from the industry to be replaced with "prodigies." Unfortunately, the press made light of the situation and the cause quickly died. Later in her career, Annie toured in Russia and Europe and claimed to have turned down painters who asked her to pose as Jesus.

Annie toured America, Europe, and Russia and claimed to have turned down painters who asked her to pose as Jesus. She hated being referred to as a "freak" and worked to abolish that word from the industry.

Annie Jones was probably the most famous of the authentic bearded ladies and was exhibited in P. T. Barnum's museum at the tender age of one year old as the "Infant Esau." She later became "The Bearded Girl" and "Child Esau." By the age of five, Annie had a mustache and sideburns, as well as very hairy arms, legs, and shoulders.

When Annie was sixteen-years-old, she married a circus barker named Richard Elliott. That union ended in divorce in 1895 after almost fifteen years when she sued him for desertion.

MYSTERY TO SOLVE

Why is Annie buried with Hugh H. Topne in the same grave? What is their connection?

Annie Jones was often described as having the manners of a true society lady. She educated herself, read continuously, and became an accomplished musician. She retired from show business a wealthy woman from real estate investments. Annie Jones Donovan died in her mother's home at 187 Cornelia Street in Brooklyn, New York, on October 22, 1902, from consumption (tuberculosis). She was only 37. She is buried in Evergreen Cemetery in Brooklyn, plot 1499 in the Mt. Pisgah section. Sadly, no tombstone marks her grave. Buried in the same grave is a 59-year-old man, Hugh H. Topne. The relationship between Annie and this gentleman is unknown. ♦

Annie Jones was instrumental in getting P. T. Barnum to use the word "prodigies" instead of "freaks" in advertising. However, the press and other advertisers and promoters were not as enlightened as Barnum since "freaks" better caught the attention of the reading and ticket-buying population.

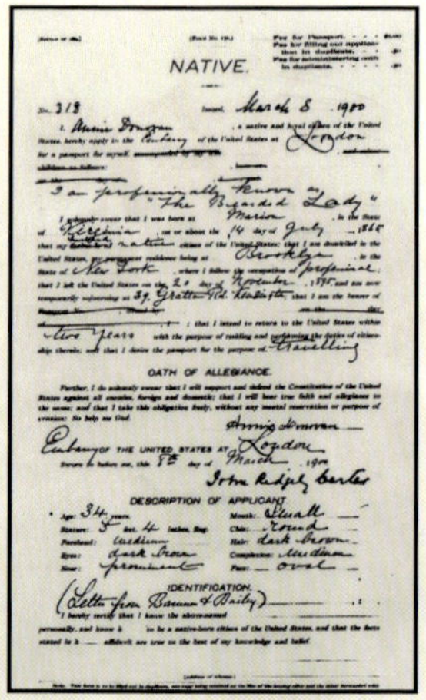

The official death certificate for Annie Jones Donovan.

JANE DEVERE, ALIAS "MADAM DEVERE," OR "THE KENTUCKY WONDER"

Jane Devere (Mary A.) was born in Brooksville, Kentucky, in 1858 of Hebrew and French parentage. She began her sideshow career when she was seventeen. She worked with many of the great circus and dime museums of her time as a bearded lady. Her beard was measured in 1884 and reported to be fourteen inches long, considered a record length for a woman. That record still holds true today.

She married a sideshow manager, Capt. J. William Devere, on October 4, 1883. According to her

The majority of the sideshow bearded ladies were small-of-stature, effeminate men dressed in women's clothing. Moral etiquette of the day would, of course, dictate that these "women" did not have to prove they were indeed of the female persuasion. (Shown: Unknown bearded "lady")

Madam Devere's beard, which reached fourteen inches at its longest hair, still holds the world record for the longest beard belonging to a woman.

She married a sideshow manager, Capt. J. William Devere, on October 4, 1883.

1912 obituary, "she was a good woman and those who knew her spoke of her in the highest terms. She was of the Christian faith, but her preference being the Methodist Episcopal Church which she always attended when convenient to do so." Very little else is known of Madam Devere, even her maiden name, which would help greatly in researching her life. She died of a heart attack at the Windsor Rooming House on South Frederick Street in Oelwein, Iowa, on June 18, 1912, while with the Patterson Carnival Company. She was fifty-four. She is buried in the Woodlawn Cemetery in Oelwein, Iowa. ♦

DELINA ROSSA, ALIAS "THE BEARDED LADY FROM PARIS"

Delina Rossa is considered the most beautiful of all the bearded ladies. Reportedly, she was from Paris, France, and always dressed in elegant gowns in the highest fashion of the day.

Little is known of Delina Rossa's life and it is very possible that Delina Rossa was only a carefully chosen stage name and that this performer never even saw Paris, much less was born there.

MYSTERY TO SOLVE

When and where was she born and is Delina Rossa her given name? What of her early years and when and where did she die? Where is Delina buried?

Delina Rossa is considered the most beautiful of all the bearded ladies. Reportedly, she was from Paris, France (not proven), and reportedly always dressed in elegant gowns in the highest fashion of the day. This undoubtedly added to her popularity. It has been said that she carried herself with style and was always the lady and the professional when performing. Not much more is known of her life. It is very possible that Delina Rossa was not her real name but merely a carefully chosen stage name. Performers often wove fanciful stories about themselves to appear more exotic and more mysterious, thus increasing interest in their act. ♦

CLEMENTINE CLATTEAUX, ALIAS "MADAME DELAIT"

Clementine Clatteaux was born on March 5, 1865, in the hamlet of Chamousey, near Lorraine, France. Her beard started growing during her teen years. She married a local baker, Jacques Delait, in 1885. They opened a café and bakery in the village of Thaon-les-Vosges. Reportedly, Madame Delait, who normally shaved every day, let her beard grow following a 500 franc bet

Clementine enjoyed bicycling but preferred to practice the sport dressed in a skirt. In 1904, a special government authorization was required to allow Clementine to wear men's clothing should she so desire.

Madam Delait grew so fond of her beard and the attention it attracted that she renamed her bakery Café de la Femme à Barbe (Café of the Bearded Woman).

Reportedly, Madame Delait, who normally shaved every day, let her beard grow following a bet with a customer of the bakery she owned with her husband.

Madame Delait died in 1939 at the age of seventy-four. She asked that her tombstone epitaph read, "Here lies Clementine Delait, the bearded lady."

with a customer. She claimed in her memoirs that everyone was fascinated with her beard and she thoroughly enjoyed the attention. She became very proud of her luxurious beard and sported it about her village without embarrassment. She even renamed her business Café de la Femme Barbee (Café of the Bearded Woman). She was known to brag, "I had a magnificent beard, curly and abundant which spread out in a double plume." She was also very proud of the fact that her beard was more magnificent than her brother's beard.
Clementine enjoyed bicycling, a fairly uncommon sport for a woman to that time, but preferred to practice her sport dressed in a skirt. In 1904, a special government authorization was required to allow Clementine to wear men's clothing should she so desire.

In 1919, she and her husband adopted a small five-year-old girl whose parents had died from the 1918 influenza. The couple, married for thirty-four years, were childless; Madame Delait was fifty-four years old.

Her fame spread and she received many requests from sideshow and circus managers to appear for profit but she would not leave her husband who was in ill health. She also said she felt it was beneath her to exhibit herself as a mere female oddity. After the death of her husband, however, she traveled to England, Paris, Ireland, and Coney Island for limited paying engagements and also sold photos of herself as was the custom of performers of the day. Madame Delait died in 1939. She asked that her tombstone epitaph read, "Here lies Clementine Delait, the bearded lady." She was seventy-four. ♦

BARONESS SIDONIA DE BARCSY

The life story of Baroness Sidonia de Barcsy (1866–1925) is truly one in which truth is stranger than fiction. Her story has it all: fame, fortune, travel, love, love lost, fortune lost. While it was very common for sideshow performers to randomly adopt a royal title to increase public interest when exhibiting, the Baroness Sidonia de Barcsy had married into Hungarian royal lineage when she wed Baron Antonio de Barcsy, a cavalry officer. She was a young and beautiful girl of nineteen. Life was most likely a series of social events, a privileged but routine existence.

While it was very common for sideshow performers to adopt a random royal title to increase public interest when exhibiting, the Baroness Sidonia de Barcsy had married into Hungarian royal lineage when she wed Baron Antonio de Barcsy, a cavalry officer.

How quickly life can change, for the better, for the worse. On February 28, 1885, their first and only child was born, a son they named Nicu. He was very small, weighing less than two pounds when born. He flourished in spite of his tiny frame and low birth weight. So did a soft, fuzzy beard that suddenly started to sprout on the baroness's beautiful face a few weeks after Nicu's birth. Unlike most true bearded ladies who grow dark beards and usually have excessive dark body hair uncommon for most females, the baroness's beard was a light brown and the remainder of her body was unchanged. About this time, the family fortune was dwindling. Some say that was due to the political and social upheaval in Hungary. Others say that most likely the baron made a series of bad investments or simply spent more than his income allowed. Whatever the reason, the family packed their bags and moved to Europe sometime in the 1890s. Sideshows were extremely popular in Europe as in America at this time. The baron luckily had a ready-made troupe in tow with a bearded lady and a midget son, both with true royal lineage. The baron, himself, also performed as a strongman and, years later, as a fat man. They were known as the "De Barcsy Troupe" and were successful performing all over Europe for more than a decade. Sometime at the turn of the century, they sailed to America.

They were very popular in the States and, by all accounts, made a handsome living. Sadly, in 1912, the baron passed away, leaving behind a wife, now forty-six, and grown son. Then, along came Frederick Valentine Tischu, a.k.a., Charles Henry Buck, "The Long-Haired Cherokee Buck Man" (1890–1951), a tall, handsome scoundrel of German heritage without a drop of Indian blood who performed with sideshows doing rope tricks. At this time, a respectable widow was required to mourn a deceased husband for two years. Remarriage and courting were scandalous acts, but Baroness de Barcsy defied social custom and quickly

The baroness passed away on October 19, 1925, at the age of fifty-nine. Many at the time said a broken heart sped up her passing when her second husband, a scoundrel named Charles Buck who was much younger than she was, ran off with another sideshow performer, Dolletta Boyle, "The World's Smallest Mother."

"married" this much younger man who had obviously swept her off her feet. (No record has ever surfaced proving a legal marriage took place, but the baroness always claimed she and Charles Buck were legally married.) The baroness and son, Nicu, earned much more money than Charles Buck did, but Charles had no problem spending all the earned proceeds. Some reports claim he had a drinking problem. Others say he was a womanizer with a very bad gambling habit. By the winter of 1914, the family found themselves in dire straits, broke, and forced to rely on credit and the kindness of others until the spring carnival season.

That spring, the three joined the Campbell Brothers troupe and exhibited in Coney Island. After the lucrative season ended, the baroness returned to Drummond, Oklahoma, and built a home on the town's main street, the first brick home built in that town. Campbell Brothers Circus wintered near Drummond in the early 1900s and the baroness always claimed she felt comfortable there due to the kindness of the town folks who accepted her and her son. Reportedly, even when not exhibiting, the baroness kept her beard in tow, but did wear a cover-up when out and about the town. Illness forced the baroness into retirement. Money again became a very big problem since she was the main draw in the family. Charles Buck must have realized that the money well was going dry for it was at this time that he ran off with another sideshow performer, Dolletta Boyle, "The World's Smallest Mother," who was a top earner in the trade.

The baroness passed away on October 19, 1925, at the age of fifty-nine. Many at the time said a broken heart sped up her passing. The baroness was cremated, and her remains were sent to New York to be placed beside her first husband.

The circus is a large part of the heritage and history of Drummond, Oklahoma. The walls of Drummond High School sport a circus-themed mural painted by a former student, Hannah Tuohy. The bearded lady of Drummond, Tuohy's favorite character, and Little Nick are painted into the mural. ♦

BARON/CAPTAIN NICU DU BARCSY, "LITTLE NICK," OR "THE SMALLEST PERFECT MAN ON EARTH"

Nicu was born on February 28, 1885, and weighed only one and three-quarter pounds at birth. He was a midget who never reached more than twenty-four pounds in his life, if his trade card is to be believed. After the death of his mother, the Baroness Sidonia de Barcsy, in 1925, Nicu continued with sideshows for a few years, exhibiting himself and performing magic tricks and a dog act. For reasons known only to him, in 1937, at fifty-two, he returned to the family home in Drummond, Oklahoma, almost destitute and relying greatly on

Nicu often dressed in military attire while performing, a tribute to his father and lineage. He preferred the title of "Captain" over "Baron." In this photograph, his father's Hungarian cavalry medal is displayed proudly on his chest.

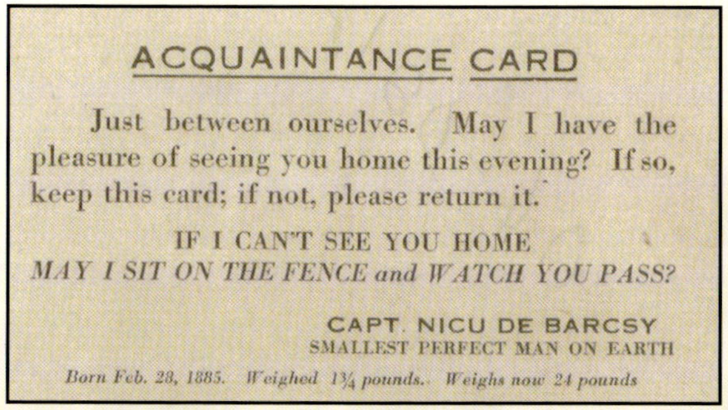

ACQUAINTANCE CARD

Just between ourselves. May I have the pleasure of seeing you home this evening? If so, keep this card; if not, please return it.

IF I CAN'T SEE YOU HOME
MAY I SIT ON THE FENCE and WATCH YOU PASS?

CAPT. NICU DE BARCSY
SMALLEST PERFECT MAN ON EARTH

Born Feb. 28, 1885. Weighed 1¾ pounds. Weighs now 24 pounds

Nicu's trade card. He was a midget who never reached over twenty-four pounds in his life, if his trade card is to be believed.

Nicu was born on February 28, 1885, and weighed only one and three-quarters pounds at birth.

the charity of friends. He eventually went on welfare. Ironically, his fortune and estate in Hungary had been lost forever when a fire destroyed the papers proving his lineage and rightful ownership.

Health reasons forced Nicu into hospitals and later a nursing home in Enid, Oklahoma. His family home was sold at auction to pay for Nicu's debts, including taxes, and because the house was condemned as a public nuisance from years of neglect, including acts of vandalism while family members were touring and away from the house. The new owner had the house torn down. Nicu passed away in an Enid hospital from kidney failure and old age on July 31, 1976, at the age of ninety-one. He is buried in the Del Norte Cemetery in Drummond, Oklahoma. His stone reads "The Smallest Perfect Man On Earth." All funeral expenses and the stone were paid for by friends and citizens of Drummond who remembered "Little Nick" as a town character. ♦

HALF AND HALFS

The half man/half woman act, a hermaphrodite, was one of the most popular acts—and probably the biggest money-maker—in the sideshow, even though most of the performers were just skilled actors who knew how to put on a good show for the intrigued public. If a thrown-together outfit had a good half and half exhibit, that outfit made money even if it had no other real draws. A half and half could, and did, carry many a carnival sideshow because the public was fascinated by such a lurid concept.

The half man/half woman act, a hermaphrodite, was one of the most popular and probably the biggest money-making act in the sideshow, even though most of these performers were just skilled actors who knew how to put on a good show for the intrigued public

Oddly, in today's world, the half and half act would probably be considered too sexually explicit for the general public.

The word "hermaphrodite" comes from the Greek legend of Hermaphroditus, the son of Hermes and Aphrodite. Hermaphroditus fell in love with a nymph and became both a man and a woman. Most sideshows' half and half exhibitors were fakes or grifters, but a few performers possessed the external sexual features of both sexes. These were either males or females who also had the developed genitals of the other sex. These performers were a rarity, however. The vast majority were male transvestites who purposefully built up the arm, chest, and leg muscles of one side of the body while leaving the other half soft and feminine. Most half and halfs showed their bodies divided literally, the right side male and the left side female, relying on the myth that the right side of any individual is the masculine strong side and the left side is the feminine, softer side. Oddly, in today's world, such an act would probably be considered too sexually explicit for the general public. ♦

BOBBY KORK

Bobby Kork was a man who skillfully portrayed himself as a half and half, mainly working in the 1940s and 1950s. He was one of the most famous of these performers in the business. Bobby was both attracted by and attractive to women and dated often. It is said he was a transvestite but still a ladies' man who broke many a heart. He exhibited himself naked and was able to pull off the scam for decades. He built up the right side of his body through exercise and a fake breast was glued to his left side. The genitals were pulled back and secured with strong flesh-colored tape. Some report he received his name because, during earlier times, he did his grift with an elastic band and a cork so it is possible that "Kork" was a clever stage name. On many an occasion, Bobby needed to rely on his built up right side to fight off the more curious spectators trying to grope him during a performance. This, of course, only added to the show's spectacle and appeal. He later became a noted photographer specializing in photos of a more scandalous nature. His collection of drag portraits and portraits of gay men (1940–1954) was acquired by Cornell University (Collection Number: 7652). Little else is known of the performer's life, except that he died of food poisoning, age unknown. ♦

MYSTERY TO SOLVE

Was Bobby Kork a stage name? When and where was he born and when did he die? Where is his final resting place?

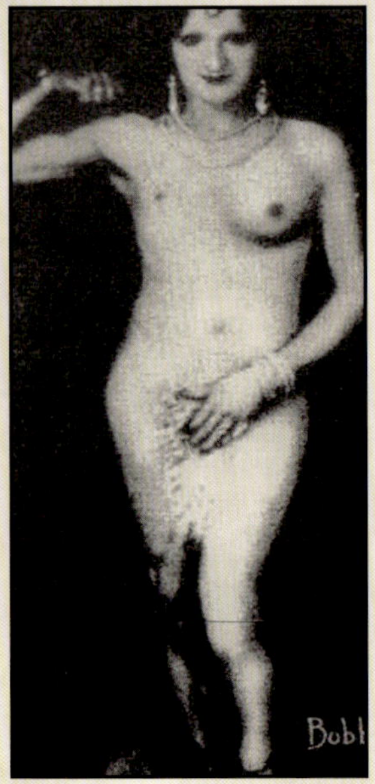

Bobby Kork was a man who skillfully portrayed himself as a half and half, mainly working in the 1940s and 1950s. He was one of the most famous of these performers in the business. It is said he was a transvestite but still a ladies' man who broke many a heart. On many an occasion, Bobby needed to rely on his built-up right side to fight off the more curious spectators trying to grope him during a performance.

FRANCIS-FRANCINE HODGKISS

MYSTERY TO SOLVE

So little is known about Francis-Francine's life, and no photos exist. Her physical condition and the moral code of the time would limit the newspaper articles written about this performer. When and where was she born and when and where did she die? Where is she buried?

Francis-Francine Hodgkiss was most likely born a female with both a vagina and penis—a very large clitoris that passed for a penis, but no scrotum. She had a very masculine face and never developed breasts. She had been put into the sideshow by her mother who traveled with the show. (Interestingly enough, the famous western woman Calamity Jane was alleged to have the same physical makeup.) When she was around twelve years old, a doctor was called in to examine her because she was experiencing so much pain. She was eventually studied by a number of doctors who were all amazed by this strange being. Her mother realized the money-making potential her daughter represented, saying later she felt like it was her duty to exhibit her in sideshows because her girl was not fake, but the real thing. She also pointed out that at home, kids and grown-ups alike cruelly ridiculed her. Truth be known, her mother most likely enjoyed the carefree, lucrative, exciting life of the traveling sideshow and did not want to return home to her husband or her old lifestyle. At the height of her career, Francis was making over $500 a week during the Depression. Her money was used to support her mother as well as a number of parasitic relatives who had jumped on the bandwagon. Reportedly, she loved children and sent much of her earnings to children's charities. She also enjoyed giving candy and gifts to kids who hung around the show. This infuriated her mother and relatives who complained that there would be nothing left for them if she continued such practices. ♦

WILD MEN AND WOMEN

An unnamed wild man from a less profitable sideshow touring America. The shoes might be a give-away.

The wild man or woman was a regular sideshow attraction, along with other stock performers such as the fat lady, tattooed people, hoochie-coochie girls, and the sword-swallower. Sideshows and circuses consistently hired people of color to portray the exotic and dangerous wild inhabitants of foreign lands or to play the part of the missing link made so popular by the evolutionary teachings of Charles Darwin.

Sideshows and circuses consistently hired people of color to portray the exotic and dangerous wild inhabitants of foreign lands or to play the part of the missing link made so popular by the evolutionary teachings of Charles Darwin. (Shown: George and Willie Muse, black albino brothers.)

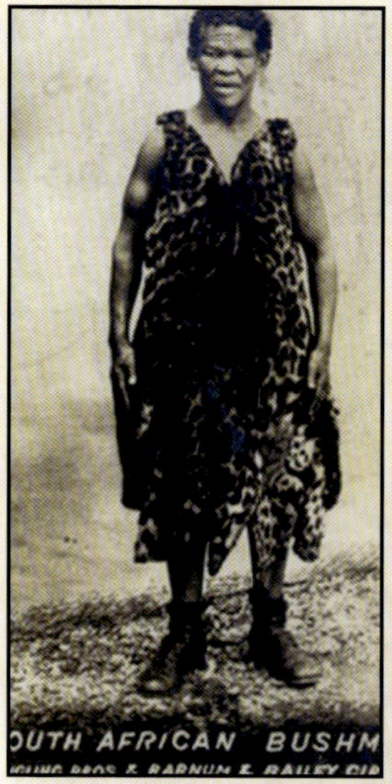

Danger was always an exciting element of the wild men and women acts. The audiences could gaze upon murderous headhunters without ever fearing the loss of their own heads. (Shown: Clico)

While a few of the so-called wild people were mentally challenged with little control over their destiny, the vast majority of the performers chose the life of the sideshow.

By adding such attractions to the show, promoters appealed to the paying audiences on two levels: first, they brought the spectator close to the dangerous without ever putting him or her in danger. The audiences could gaze upon murderous headhunters without ever fearing the loss of their own heads. Secondly, these shows addressed the pressing concerns about race that the majority of the predominantly white show-going audiences of the 1840s through 1940s harbored regarding blacks, Indians, Asians, and the waves of foreigners immigrating to America. This audience could gaze openly upon the people of color presented as savages and feel justified in their belief that the white race was indeed superior.

That said, the choice to pose as savages was a decision made by these performers or their relatives for monetary gain. While a few of the so-called "wild people" were mentally challenged with little control over their destiny, the vast majority of the performers chose the life of the sideshow. For many, the easy money or the simply-earned room and board made exhibiting themselves to a gawking public vastly preferred over the other available means of earning a living. ♦

HIRAM AND BARNEY (ELIJAB) DAVIS, ALIAS "WAINO AND PLUTANO" (PLUTANOR), OR "THE WILD MEN OF BORNEO"

The Wild Men of Borneo were actually a pair of midget brothers named Hiram and Barney Davis who were also mentally challenged . They were discovered in Connecticut by Lyman Warner in 1852 when they were around twenty-six years old. Warner, in essence, bought the brothers from their mother, Catherine Davis (Porter). Court cases as late as 1880 show that the mother tried unsuccessfully several times to regain custody of her sons, either out of guilt, love, or because she realized that her sons had a very lucrative career as sideshow performers. They stood only three feet, four inches tall and professed to weigh only forty-five pounds. Hiram was born on Long Island in 1825, and Barney was born in England in 1827.

The Wild Men of Borneo were actually a pair of midget brothers named Hiram and Barney Davis, living in Connecticut, who also suffered from intellectual disabilities. They were discovered by Lyman Warner in 1852 who, in essence, bought the brothers from their mother.

Even though the brothers had blond hair and blue eyes, Warner billed his new attraction as bloodthirsty wild men from Borneo who were captured by sailors only after a fierce fight in which many sailors were maimed or died. It was P. T. Barnum, however, who taught the brothers the show routines that would make them a star attraction. They showed with Barnum between 1852 and 1905, when Hiram died. With Barnum, they were billed as the twin sons of The Emperor of Borneo, the only wild men in captivity. (Borneo lies almost exactly south of the equator and is one of the larger islands in the great East Indian archipelago. Historically, the natives of Borneo and adjacent islands pirated European trading vessels, thus providing the basis for the lore of wild and fierce inhabitants. The returning sailors' embellished tales also strengthened the legend of Borneo.) The two brothers' natural strength was incredible. They would lift audience members with ease and wrestle any male brave enough or drunk enough to venture on stage. They would also perform acrobatics, dance, recite poems, and talk gibberish that was said to be their native language. Reportedly, the brothers were soft spoken, mild-mannered, and shy around the other performers.

When Lyman Warner died, he willed the pair to his son, Hanford. When Hanford died, the pair was then willed to his son, Henry. Thus, the "Wild Men of Borneo" remained in show business for nearly fifty years until their deaths. Reportedly, they earned in excess of $200,000 over their lifetime, a true fortune at that time. According to his death certificate, Hiram died from "old age"on March 16, 1905, at the age of eighty at 297 Crescent Street, the home of Henry Warner in Waltham, Massachusetts. Barney also died in the same house on May 31, 1912, from "anterio Sclerosis [sic]," according to his death certificate. He was eighty-five. ♦

The two brothers' natural strength was incredible. They would lift audience members with ease and wrestle any male brave enough or drunk enough to venture on stage.

WILLIAM HENRY JOHNSON, "ZIP. THE WHAT IS IT," "MAN MONKEY," "MISSING LINK"

Zip was born William Henry Johnson in Liberty Corners, New Jersey, in 1857. He was the son of William and Mahalia Johnson, former slaves, and had five siblings. Some of Johnsons' neighbors attended a circus traveling through their town and told one of the agents about the strange boy with the cone-shaped egg head, small face with a prominent jutting jaw, and long, wide nose. His parents leased or sold Zip to the agent, who then was ambitious enough to approach none other than P. T. Barnum with his new find. Barnum changed Zip's appearance by shaving his head, with the exception of a little tuft of hair on the top. Barnum fitted Zip with a furry monkey outfit that became his trademark. He was exhibited in a cage during his early years with the show and billed as eating only raw meat, nuts, and fruit. Zip would rattle the bars of the cage and growl to the total delight of the audience. The previous year, Charles Dickens had asked Barnum, *"What is it?"* when he viewed another performer. Barnum remembered his words and thought that would be the perfect name for his newly found act. Reportedly, Barnum paid him an extra dollar a day not to speak during performances, thus making him appear even more wild and mysterious. It is probable that Zip was mildly developmentally delayed but still very functional. His sister, Sarah Van Duyne, claimed in a 1926 interview with a newspaper that her brother would "converse like the average person, and with fair reasoning power" when he came to visit her.

Zip, dressed in his monkey suit, boxing "The Leopard Boy" who suffered from vitiligo.

Zip and Schlitzie were the inspiration for Bill Griffith's nationally syndicated comic strip, *Zippy.* Reprint courtesy of Bill Griffith.

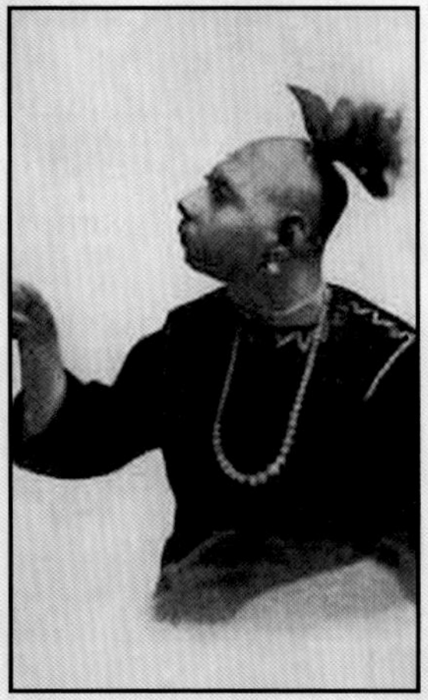

P. T. Barnum changed Zip's appearance by shaving his head, with the exception of a little tuft of hair left on the top.

Matthew Brady, the famous Civil War photographer, took tintype photos of Zip and they appeared in major newspapers in the 1920s and 1930s. Zip performed for audiences for almost seventy years and thrived on the attention of the crowds. He carried around a toy pop-gun and kept it under his seat at shows. He would threaten to shoot other acts if they were getting too much attention or infringing upon his territory. Later, he took up the violin and the public never tired of seeing Zip dance and attempt the instrument. Zip grew to love a good cigar. However, his cigars had to be the same expensive brand smoked by John Ringling North, the owner of the circus, or Zip would stubbornly refuse to perform. In his later years, he preferred to exhibit himself at Coney Island. Legend says it was there in 1925 that he saved a small child from drowning in the ocean. Zip died on April 24, 1926, in Bellevue Hospital in New York City from "stricture of urethra" and chronic kidney disease. With his sister Sarah at his side, Zip uttered his now famous dying words: "Well, we fooled 'em for a long time, didn't we?" He was sixty-nine according to his tombstone and eighty-three according to his

Barnum fitted Zip with a furry monkey outfit that became his trademark. He was exhibited in a cage during his early years with the show, and billed as eating only raw meat, nuts, and fruit. Zip would rattle the bars of the cage and growl to the total delight of the audience.

death certificate. He is buried in the Bound Brook Cemetery in New Jersey in "public ground," plots set aside for the poor or minorities. His tombstone is simple. No mention is made of his show business career, but his death certificate lists his occupation as "Showman." ♦

GEORGE AND WILLIE MUSE, ALIAS, "EKO AND IKO, SHEEPHEADED CANNIBALS FROM ECUADOR," OR "AMBASSADORS FROM MARS"

Probably one of the most fascinating sideshow life stories, among so many, is the debated tale of black albino brothers George and Willie Muse. According to family lore, in 1889, while the boys' parents were working in the fields near their home in Franklin County, Virginia, a white man named Herman "Candy" Shelton offered George, age nine, and his brother, Willie, age six, candy and a ride in his truck. Once inside the truck, the man kidnapped both children and later told the children that their mother was dead. Another version of the story, the basis of a 1927 lawsuit, states that a sideshow promoter named Stokes kidnapped the brothers from Roanoke, Virginia, and that the boys were later stolen from Stokes by another crooked sideshow manager, Herman "Candy" Shelton.

George and Willie Muse, albino blacks, claimed to have been kidnapped as young children by a white sideshow manager although that story has never been proven.

A third version of the story is very different. A 1927 newspaper reported that the boys' mother met Stokes in person and willingly contracted with the showman to let her sons join the sideshow circuit when George was twenty-two and Willie was nineteen. Most likely the true story may never be known, but it should be noted that Willie Muse never varied from his version, stating that Herman Shelton kidnapped him and his brother when they were children. It is interesting to note, however, that no sideshow photo of the brothers has ever been found showing them as performing children. Only adult photos of the brothers exist. All other exhibiting "freak" children had a photographic history in the form of trade cards. Also, as teenagers or adults, the brothers could have walked away anytime from the sideshow world and sought a life and employment elsewhere.

Another story repeated by family members claims the brothers' mother, Harriett, never gave up hope of finding her missing sons. When the circus came to Roanoke in 1927, where she lived at the time,

The Muse Brothers were musically inclined and when not performing as wild men or "Ambassadors from Mars," they often played with the sideshow band that consisted of other performers.

Kidnapping had been a favorite sideshow theme since the early days. The "girlie shows" often used the kidnapping theme "white slavery" to explain the willingness of the women to perform in lewd dress and manner and to recount their tantalizing stories to the paying audience, mostly men.

The Muse Brothers performing as "Eko and Iko," playing the xylophone. Note one brother has dyed his hair to add contrast to their appearances.

The Muse Brothers in costume as "Ambassadors from Mars."

Harriett sought the boys out. The result was a tearful reunion. In old age, Willie claimed that neither he nor George ever believed his mother was dead. However, since the mother never moved more than a few miles from the site of George and Willie's birth, a simple letter would have located her in a time when one only had to write on the envelope the name of the recipient and the town and state in which that person lived.

The brothers worked for a series of sideshows but according to them, though they received room and board, they were never paid. However, when they retired from the business in 1961, they bought a house in Roanoke and generously shared it with some relatives.

The Muse brothers traveled the world exhibiting themselves to the public. By all accounts, they

A lineup of Barnum's famous freaks including wild men, The Muse Brothers, Zip, and Clico.

enjoyed the attention and the lifestyle on the open road but when they retired, they refused interviews from curious news reporters for decades, preferring their new more quiet and private lifestyle. George died of heart failure in 1971. Willie passed away on April 5, 2001, at the ripe old age of 108. Both are buried at C. C. Williams Memorial Park in Roanoke, Virginia, but not side by side. ♦

7

THE REAL FREAKS

Giants, Midgets & Dwarfs, Body Deformities, Living Half-Ladies, Conjoined Twins, Parsitic Twins, Facial Deformities and Albinos.

THE TRUE STARS OF THE SIDESHOW SHOULD ALWAYS BE THE REAL FREAKS, THOSE INDIVIDUALS WHO WERE TRULY BORN DIFFERENT.

The true stars of the sideshow should always be the real freaks, those individuals who were truly born different. (Shown: Jo-Jo, "The Dog Faced Boy.")

These performers did not invent themselves to make money, obtain fame, or travel the world. Instead, these were the people born with body anomalies that set them apart in a crowd, and their life stories ran the full gamut. Some were loved by doting parents who felt their child was "special." Others, not so lucky, were shunned by embarrassed parents. Some found true happiness with a partner while others vainly sought to find a loving relationship in which their physical differences would be forgotten. A few made a fortune and retired to a very comfortable lifestyle. Others lost everything to crooked managers or greedy relatives and lovers. A few were murdered. Here are their very special stories. ♦

GIANTS

Mankind has always been fascinated by giants. They are usually portrayed in biblical stories and fairy tales alike as evil creatures to be feared, examples being David and Goliath and Jack and the Bean Stalk. Would Mary Shelley's Frankenstein have been as fearful if he wasn't of such imposing stature? With that said, we have always been fascinated by individuals who seem superior to the average person. We admire, even worship, those rare people who possess extraordinary physical attributes or abilities that set them apart from the masses. The average person knows more about Hollywood legends and sports figures than they do about inventors, medical geniuses, or rocket scientists. We cannot see the intelligence of a person at first glance, but we can see that coveted physical attribution.

It is a fact of human nature that we judge people at first sight. When we look upon a giant of a man, we are looking at an individual who is obviously way, way, way above the crowd. We immediately recognize this person as being of superior strength and ability. Men envy the giant's imagined physical superiority, and women are biologically driven to powerful males because we equate sexual prowess with size and strength.

The sideshow giant was always a popular addition to any ten-in-one show, and the male giant was usually portrayed as the strongman. In the controlled confines of a sideshow, there would be nothing to fear from a strong giant. Men and children could safely gawk at the giant for hours since he posed no personal threat. Women could stare without shame or embarrassment. The female giant or giantess was not so lucky. Pity the poor woman giant who outgrew every eligible male in her town. Her life is going to be very different from her male counterpart. Unlike other categories where a woman freak was more popular than her male counterpart (fat ladies, tattooed ladies, snake handlers), the male giant was far more popular with the crowds than the female giantess. ♦

ROBERT WADLOW, "THE WORLD'S TALLEST MAN"

Robert Pershing Wadlow grew to a height of eight feet eleven and a half inches, making him the tallest man to ever live to date. He was born on February 22, 1918, in Alton, Illinois, to parents of average height. He had four younger siblings who were also of average height. Robert weighed eight pounds, six ounces at birth, but by six months old, he had soared to a weight of thirty pounds. He weighed forty pounds when he took his first step, and he continued to grow at an astonishing rate. By the time he was eight, he weighed 195 pounds and was a little over six feet tall. At the age of nine, he was able to carry his father, who weighed 170 pounds, up the stairs of the family's home. At eighteen, he weighed 390 pounds and stood 8 feet, four inches tall. He wore a size 37AA

Robert is shown with his grandmother. His family tried to give him a sense of belonging and normalcy.

shoe, and his ring size was 25. It is said that Robert consumed an average of 8,000 calories a day as an adult. Robert was plagued with an overactive pituitary gland that was diagnosed when he was twelve. This gland regulates the body's growth. In the 1920s, there was no medical remedy for such a condition.

Robert lived in Alton his entire life. His family tried to give him a sense of belonging. They encouraged his hobbies of stamp and matchbook collecting and supported him in his desire to join the Boy Scouts. Robert became the world's tallest Boy Scout at thirteen. He stood seven feet, four inches and was easily head and shoulders taller than any adult scout leader. As an adult, he was dubbed "The Gentle Giant" by people who knew him because of his soft-spoken and gentle manner. He was a devout religious man and belonged to several fraternal orders. At the Franklin Masonic Lodge Temple in Alton, visitors can view the massive chair he sat in during meetings.

Robert did not travel with a sideshow, but he did appear for special performances with Ringling Bros. and Barnum & Bailey Circus in 1937. Due to the size of his feet, he was hired as a traveling spokesperson for the International Shoe Company, whose popular lines of shoes included Peters Shoes and Red Goose Shoes. As a perk of this engagement, Robert got his very expensive custom-made shoes for free. Robert's father traveled with him in the family car that had been customized to accommodate his son. He removed the front passenger seat, allowing Robert to sit in the back without being too cramped. A huge shoe of Robert's would be on display at all the store locations he visited, and it was proclaimed that he had tried on each and every one of them. They visited approximately 800 towns in forty-one states and traveled over 300,000 miles. Some stories paint an unkind picture of Robert's father who quit his job to devote his time and efforts to Robert's career. It has been suggested that the "Gentle Giant" would have preferred a more secluded life, but he was pushed into the limelight by a greedy and publicity-seeking parent.

Robert developed a fatal infection from a septic foot blister on his ankle and died in his sleep on

Robert Wadlow became the world's tallest Boy Scout at age thirteen.

The statue of Robert is life-sized and was donated by the citizens of his hometown, Alton, Illinois.

July 15, 1940, while on tour in Manistee, Michigan. He had developed the blister from a new poorly fitted brace that he first strapped on a week prior. He had almost no sensation in his feet and had not experienced any pain from the blister. The hospital was unable to accommodate Robert, so he was treated in his hotel room. All efforts, including a blood transfusion, failed. He was twenty-two years old. Reportedly, about 30,000 people attended his funeral, which was held in his hometown. All city businesses were closed for the day out of respect. His casket weighed over 1,000 pounds and required the combined efforts of a dozen pallbearers with assistance from eight more men. It measured 10 feet, nine inches long, thirty-two inches wide, and thirty inches deep. Robert is buried in Oakwood Cemetery in Alton. His gravestone simply reads, "At Rest." He was still growing at the time of his death. ♦

ANNA SWAN, "THE NOVA SCOTIA GIANTESS," "THE TALLEST GIRL IN THE WORLD," "THE TALLEST WOMAN IN THE WORLD," OR "INFANT GIANTESS" & MARTIN VAN BATES, "THE KENTUCKY GIANT"

Anna Haining Swan was born August 6, 1846, to typically developed parents. She had eleven siblings, all of typically developed height. Reportedly, she weighed eighteen pounds at birth.

Anna pictured with her parents.

P. T. Barnum paired Anna with midgets such as Commodore Nutt, who was twenty-nine inches tall and weighed only twenty-four pounds. The visual results were startling.

ANNA'S STORY

Anna Haining Swan was born August 6, 1846, at Mill Brook, Colchester County, Nova Scotia in Canada to average-sized parents. She had eleven siblings, all of average size. Reportedly, Anna, the third child, weighed eighteen pounds at birth. Anna was first exhibited in March, 1851, at the age of four. Her father took her to Halifax where she was billed as the "Infant Giantess." At that time, she was approximately four feet six inches tall and weighed close to one hundred pounds. She was almost as tall as her mother, Ann Graham Swan, who stood five feet, three inches tall. Anna's appearance caused quite a stir and was reported in the newspapers of the day. When Anna started school, her seating arrangement had to be altered to accommodate her size. At home, Anna often sat on the floor because standard-sized furniture was too uncomfortable or not sturdy enough for her large frame. She preferred the outdoors since this gave her room to move about without the physical restraints caused by being inside a building.

In 1863, P. T. Barnum persuaded seventeen-year-old Anna to come to the United States to exhibit herself at his world-famous dime museum in New York City. She was already well over seven feet tall and weighed approximately 350 pounds. He offered her a respectable salary of $23 a month in gold, plus food and lodging, a personal maid, and a complete wardrobe. Anna accepted but her parents stipulated as part of the contract that she was to have a tutor and a music coach so she could continue her education and musical training. It was Anna's dream to become a school teacher. Her mother accompanied her and remained with her for a little more than a year. Several times that first year, her father would also visit, leaving Anna's siblings in the care of relatives. She was billed as "The Tallest Girl in the World" and was an immediate success. Audiences flocked to the dime museum's lecture hall to see the only female giantess in the world and to listen to her sing, recant history lessons on giants, and act. She eventually grew to a height of seven feet, eleven and a half inches tall and weighed approximately 415 pounds. The show fliers at the time claimed that it took *"100 yards of satin, 50 yards of lace, and cost $1,000 to make each of Anna's dresses."* Barnum paired Anna with midgets such as Commodore Nutt, who was twenty-nine inches tall and weighed 24 pounds. The visual results were startling. Eventually Anna commanded a then-staggering salary of $1,000 a month, plus perks, and gave up her original plans of becoming a school teacher.

Anna appeared in Barnum's American Museum for two years until an infamous fire broke out at the museum on the night of July 13, 1865. Anna, as well as many of Barnum's performers, were housed on the top floors. If *The New York Tribune*'s account of the event is to be believed, Anna barely escaped alive and would have perished without the heroics of museum employees and bystanders who rescued her. Anna returned to her parents' home in Nova Scotia while the museum was closed. The fire was the suspected work of an arsonist.

Anna returned when Barnum reopened his new museum, dubbed "The New American Museum," in September 1865 at a new location. She worked at the museum and toured until March 3, 1868, when a second infamous fire almost completely destroyed Barnum's museum once again. He made the decision not to reopen but to take his show of oddities permanently on the road. ♦

MARTIN'S STORY

Martin Van Buren Bates was born near Whitesburg, Kentucky, on November 9, 1837, to average-sized parents. His father, John Wallis Bates (1779–1843), was a prosperous farmer and his mother was Sarah Walthrop Bates (1793–1865). He came from a large family and all siblings, with the exception of Martin, were of average size. Martin was the youngest child and, sadly, his father died when Martin was only six years old. According to his autobiography, *The Kentucky River Giant: A Historical Sketch of Capt. Martin Van Buren Bates and Mrs. Bates Formerly Anna Swan,* he claims he was an average-sized baby at birth and remained so until around the time of his father's death. He also claims it was then that he started to grow at such a rate his mother became alarmed, fearing she would lose her youngest child, as well. For the next two years she would not allow Martin outside to play and he was excused from all physical work on the farm. Finally she became convinced he was not dying and relaxed his confinement. By age thirteen, Martin was well over six feet tall and weighed close to 300 pounds, larger than most adult men in the town. In his autobiography, Martin states he received his education at the prestigious Emory and Henry College in Emory, Virginia, which was founded in 1836. However, the college has no record of Martin ever attending their school. He did go to a local school as a child, as did all his brothers. The family saw no need to educate the girls and on the 1850 US census it states that neither his mother nor his older sister, Sary

Martin Van Buren Bates ca. 1843. According to his autobiography, he was born a typically developed baby in size and remained typically developed until around the age of six when his father died. His parents and all his siblings were typically developed.

The people in Seville were very fond of Captain Bates, as he was called in later years. He had many friends, even though he had the reputation of being opinionated and easily riled.

Anna and Martin are posed with one of Martin's cousins, "Devil John" Wright.

Martin remarried a woman who only stood five foot two inches tall and was almost thirty years his junior. Reportedly, the union was not a happy one. Lavonne died in 1940 and was not buried beside her husband.

Martin reached the rank of first lieutenant during the war. Later in life, he adopted the title of captain and claimed he had risen to this rank from promotions awarded him due to his bravery on the battlefield. Truth be known, he most likely had to fight harder and smarter than most other men since he stood head and shoulders above the other soldiers on the battlefield, Confederate and Union alike.

Anna and Martin had two children. Unfortunately, both infants were unusually large and died. The Cleveland Health Museum (now closed) exhibited a plaster model of the boy baby next to that of a typically developed baby and a premature baby to show the differences in proportions.

Martin and his older brother fought side by side throughout the war. They were both captured by enemy forces and held at the Camp Chase prisoner of war facility in Ohio. Union and Confederate authorities agreed upon a prisoner exchange and a total of ten thousand prisoners were exchanged. In later life, Martin usually claimed he and his brother had escaped from the prison.

An (sic), could read or write.

It should be noted that Martin's autobiography was sold at performances later in life when he and his wife exhibited at sideshows and on stage. For that reason, one has to question much that is included within the pages. Most, if not all, sideshow performers enhanced the story of their lives to popularize themselves with the paying public.

Martin states in his autobiography that he was earning his living as a teacher when the Civil War broke out in 1861. Most likely he was instead working on the family farm. He and his older brother Robert joined Co. A, 7th Battalion, Confederate Cavalry. The two brothers fought side by side throughout the war. They were both captured on April 15, 1863, in Piketon, Kentucky, by enemy forces and held at the Camp Chase prisoner of war facility in Ohio. During the winter of 1863–1864, hundreds of prisoners there died in a smallpox epidemic. In November 1864, Union and Confederate authorities agreed upon a prisoner exchange hoping to alleviate the suffering of sick prisoners held by both sides. A total of ten thousand prisoners were exchanged. In later life, Martin usually claimed he and his brother had escaped from the prison.

Martin reached the rank of first lieutenant during the war. His older brother was a captain. Later in life, he adopted the title of captain and claimed he had risen to this rank through promotions awarded him due to his bravery on the battlefield.

Kentucky was a state divided by the war. Even though the state officially belonged to the Confederacy, there were many Union sympathizers, a fact that resulted in bloody in-state feuding. The Bates family lore, which has been maintained for generations, claims that Martin led a gang of men who hunted down and hung eight Unionists, forcing their wives and children to watch, in retaliation for their torture-killing of his brother, James, a Confederate soldier.

After the war, the South was devastated, and Martin left home. It was almost impossible to make a living, especially if one had fought on the losing side. In addition, if Martin had, indeed, hung eight Unionists, the political climate at home would have been very dangerous for him. Also, his beloved mother died in 1865, freeing him to leave home. Whatever the reason, in 1865 he joined a sideshow in Cincinnati, Ohio, and toured as "The Kentucky Giant." By this time he had reached his final height of seven feet, nine inches and weighed close to 500 pounds. His decision would prove to be an excellent one. Not only did Martin earn a very good wage as an exhibitionist, but he also met the woman who would be the love of his life, Anna Swan. ♦

THE COUPLE'S STORY

Anna married Martin Van Buren Bates on June 17, 1871. They had met in 1869 while touring. At seven feet nine inches, Martin was two inches shorter than his bride. Friends good-naturedly teased him that he needed to stand on his toes to kiss his new wife. Millie-Christine McKoy, conjoined twins who were commercially billed as "The Two-Headed Nightingale," were friends of Anna's and attended the wedding. Anna and Martin were billed as "The Tallest Couple in the World." Shortly before they married, the engaged couple gave a command performance for Queen Victoria and the Prince of Wales (later to become King Edward VII upon the death of his mother in 1901) while on a European tour. The queen presented both Anna and Martin with round, gold, giant-sized watches as wedding gifts, reportedly as big as saucers. Anna also received a six-foot gold chain for her watch, a diamond cluster ring, and an elegant wedding dress.

Anna and Martin had two children. Unfortunately, both infants were unusually large. Her daughter was born on May 19, 1972, in London and died at birth. The baby was twenty-seven inches long and weighed almost eighteen pounds. On January 19, 1879, Anna gave birth to a boy at home in Seville, Ohio. He was thirty inches long and weighed almost twenty-four pounds. He also died, just eleven hours after his birth. The 1932 Chicago World's Fair depicted the giant boy baby next to his parents in an exhibit called *The Story of Life*. The Cleveland Health Museum (now closed) exhibited a plaster model of the baby next to that of an average-sized baby and a premature baby to show the differences in proportions. *Guinness World Records* denotes this male infant of Anna's under the category, "Heaviest Birth."

After the loss of their first child, both Anna and Martin were very depressed. Anna was also physically exhausted and weakened. They were tiring of the demanding life on the road and contemplated retirement or at least, semi-retirement. They purchased a 130-acre farm in Seville, Ohio, and Martin stocked it with only the best breeds of cattle. Anna had been diagnosed with consumption (tuberculosis) and the area with a large inland lake was considered a beneficial climate for someone with her precarious health. The couple settled in a custom-made giants' home with fourteen-foot ceilings and door jams eight and a half feet tall and extra wide. Their furniture had also been custom-designed and crafted in England. All chairs, couches, and beds were reinforced and giant-sized. They kept the very back of the house in more customary proportions for the comfort and convenience of their guests and the house servants. Reportedly, a local Baptist minister presented the couple with a giant family Bible as a gift when the house was completed. Martin also purchased a custom-built carriage for himself and Anna, pulled by horses that were eighteen hands high. Those closest to the couple remarked often that this was the happiest time in their lives. Anna even purchased a pet monkey she named Buttons. Former sideshow friends would often visit the couple, who had the reputation of being entertaining hosts. Excitement always abounded at the house and Anna was a skilled cook, as well. They toured with the W. W. Cole Circus for the 1878, 1879, and 1880 seasons, but the 1879 season was cut short when Anna discovered she was pregnant. Anna was highly intelligent, well educated, and talented. She was a gifted singer, a pianist, and a Shakespearian actress. She was renowned for her charm, grace, and sunny disposition, as well as her generosity. She shared freely the rewards of her career with family members, friends, and people in her community with needs. She also achieved her original career goal by becoming a Baptist Sunday School teacher.

Anna died on August 5, 1888, at her home in Seville, Ohio, of heart failure, a complication from her thyroid irregularity. She was one day short of her forty-second birthday. Martin wired a company in Cleveland, Ohio, the measurements for Anna's coffin. The funeral was delayed when the company first sent a standard-sized coffin, believing the grand measurements cited on the wire were a mistake. Anna left an estate that was valued at $40,000. That would be approximately $1,500,000 by 2015 standards. She is buried in Mound Hill Cemetery in Seville, Ohio. Martin erected a fifteen-foot monument on her grave site, a statue in the Greek Revival style that he ordered from France. It depicts a woman wearing clothing that recalls costumes worn by Anna on stage. Most likely, Martin intended it to represent Anna in life. Inscribed on the monument is: "As for me, I will behold thy face in righteousness. I shall be satisfied when I awake with thy likeness."

More than a century after her death, Anna continues to be remembered through an annual week-long festival, "The Anna Swan Festival," held the first week in August near the town of her birth. Some of her personal items and photographs are on display at "The Anna Swan Exhibit" at the Fraser Cultural Center in Tatamagouche, Nova Scotia. ♦

MARTIN'S NEXT CHAPTER

After Anna's death, Martin continued to live in the home he'd shared with Anna until he remarried in 1901 at the age of sixty-three. His new bride, Lavonne Weatherby, was almost thirty years his junior and the daughter of a minister. She was five feet two inches and weighed 135 pounds. Lavonne refused to live in Martin's home, so the couple moved into town. Their new home was at 56 E. Main Street. Friends claimed that Martin was very uncomfortable in his new cramped living environment and despised the town house. To make matters worse, Lavonne did not approve of dancing or drinking and strictly limited their social outing and home entertainment.

The people in Seville were very fond of Captain Bates, as he was called in later years. He had many friends, even though he had the reputation of being opinionated and easily riled. He could be seen wearing his Confederate uniform around this northern town, most said just to irritate the town's people. As with most giants, he developed problems with his feet and legs and eventually needed a cane. Residents often joked that it was prudent to stay out of striking distance of that cane when the captain was angry. He was generous to those in need and loaned money freely to friends. He was especially fond of children and kept candy in his pockets for them. He would lift the excited child off the ground so he or she could fetch the treat from a jacket pocket or allow the child to climb upon his lap. Even at his advanced age, it was his hope that he and Lavonne would have a child, but they did not. After a long illness Martin died on January 19, 1919, of nephritis. He was eighty-two. He remembered the problems that had arisen trying to purchase Anna's oversized coffin, so he built his own early and kept it in a storage shed. Newspaper accounts of his funeral say it took twelve adult men to lift the casket and the doors of the hearse had to be tied shut with rope because the casket was so long. He was buried beside Anna and his infant son at Mound Hill Cemetery. Lavonne died in 1940 and was buried elsewhere. She had inherited much of Anna's jewelry, but unfortunately sold it through the years. ♦

ELLA KATE EWING

Ella Ewing was born a typically sized baby to typically developed parents, shown here. She did not show abnormal growth until shortly after her seventh birthday. By the time she was ten, she stood six feet nine inches tall.

Ella claimed she preferred the country to any city in the world and missed home when she was on tour even though a favorite cousin, Teent L. Blackwood, traveled with her as her companion after her mother's death. Note the family resemblance between the two women.

Ella Kate Ewing was born in La Grange, Missouri, on March 9, 1872, the only child of Benjamin F. and Anna E. Herring Ewing. Her father was tall, but not unusually so. Newspapers say he was six feet two inches tall. Her mother stood five feet four inches tall. When Ella was a small child, the family relocated to a farm in Gorin, Missouri. Ella was an average sized baby, weighing six and a half pounds at birth. She did not show abnormal growth until shortly after her seventh birthday. By the time she was ten, she was not only taller than the children in her class, but taller than her teacher, her parents, and all of the adult men in the area. She stood six feet nine inches in her stocking feet. Her publicity releases all claimed her to be eight feet four inches tall. Some dispute this claim, but it is at least possible since it is typical for people afflicted with pituitary gigantism to continue to grow their entire lives.

In a newspaper article, Ella said she spent a very lonely childhood. Her size made going to school difficult and her father had to build her a special desk since she could not fit in any of the desks available in the classroom. She claimed the children her age were somewhat afraid of her and "she was denied the pleasures of games other children played because her presence robbed the games of their zest," according to several news articles. The older girls avoided her because she had childish ways and childish interests. She soon became the butt of thoughtless jests and these actions often brought her to tears. Her life took a drastic turn for the better when she went with her parents to the county fair. While she was in awe of the sights at the fair, she claimed it was she that became the main attraction. A museum manager approached her father with an offer to exhibit Ella for pay. Initially, the father turned down the offer. Ella was shy and had always been hurt by her classmates' taunts and strangers' stares. However, the manager returned with a contract and a reported salary offer so large ($50 a week) that her financially

Ella's dream of owning land and her own home came true. She saved enough earnings to build a custom-sized home in Gorin, Missouri, in 1900.

strapped father finally agreed. It was arranged for her mother and sometimes both parents to travel with her. Ella was seventeen years old when she first exhibited.

Ella always claimed that being heralded as a "freak" stung her feelings at first but that she eventually learned to look upon her great height as a gift since she was able to earn such a handsome salary. Eventually, she entered a contract with P. T. Barnum and was one of his main attractions in his traveling circus touring in America and Europe. Ella was very popular and she became known as The Saintly Giantess because of her quiet and dignified manner on stage. Advertisements proclaimed her "a veritable Amazon, well proportioned, beautiful and well educated." One of the publicity stunts used to increase ticket sales was to have Ella hold a $500 bill in her hand above her head and offer the money to anyone who, standing with their feet flat on the ground, could take the bill out of her hand. Ella dressed elegantly on stage, no easy task in her case. She claimed it took thirty yards of material to make her a gown and that she wore custom-made shoes, size 24. She always wore many rings on her fingers to disguise their great length, but even her rings had to be either custom-made or a jeweler had to put pieces into the rings to make them fit. Interestingly, all of Ella's fingers were the same size, with the exception of her little finger. Another peculiarity of her growth was that above the waistline she remained almost average in size, except that her arms and hands grew in proportion to her legs. This gave her a gangly look.

Life on the road was not easy for Ella. Beds and train berths were too short, doorways and ceilings too low, plus dining accommodations always made eating a meal difficult. Even bathing in a standard tub posed its share of problems. She always said that she could seldom get comfortable on tour, even though P. T. Barnum always did his best. She also claimed she preferred the country to any city in the world and missed home when she was away even

Life on the road was not easy for Ella. She claimed that she could seldom get comfortable on tour, even though P. T. Barnum always did his best to accommodate her.

A peculiarity of Ella's growth was that above the waistline she remained almost typically developed, except that her arms and hands grew in proportion to her legs. This gave her a gangly look.

One of the most popular items sold by the giants of the sideshow was "The Giant's Ring," an inexpensive metal ring that demonstrated the enormous size of the giant's finger.

Camp, eventually complete with a bait shop, marina, boat rental, tourist trailer court, tourist cottages, a lodge, restaurant, and a TV repair shop. Legend has it that the camp was named by visiting friend Frank Lentini, "The Three-Legged Man." Many of the sideshow performers often frequented Al and Jeanie's place, which only added to the delight of other tourists.

Gibsonton, called "Gibtown" by the residents, soon became a popular winter home and retirement destination for many of the famous veterans of the sideshow industry. Al served as both police and fire chief of Gibsonton for many years and was president of the Chamber of Commerce. The town liked to boast that it had the only post office with a counter for midgets and the town residents were able to obtain a special zoning permit "for residential show business" that allowed them to keep elephants, snakes, lions, alligators, carnival rides, and other attractions in their residences and on their front lawns. A dwarf named Colonel Casper was the deputy sheriff. Al and Jeanie adopted two children.

By 1949, Al and Jeanie settled down to a quiet life in Gibsonton, Florida, and only made occasional special guest appearances. Both Al and Jeanie enjoyed camping and fishing and they opened Giant's Fishing Camp.

Their decision to do so was most likely prompted by Jeanie's experiences. Her parents had both died by the time she reached the age of thirteen, and she and her two brothers were placed in orphanages. Jeanie was adopted two years later by a sadistic woman intent only in making money off the child. Their oldest daughter, Rusty Rock, has remained active in events surrounding the sideshow world and Rusty's young grandson, Alexzander Morrow, has performed as a sideshow artist known as Alez Ander, "The Junior Torture King." He is a sword-swallower and also lies on a bed of nails.

Al died on August 30, 1962, in Gibsonton, of complications from his pituitary tumor. He was fifty. Jeanie outlived Al by thirty-seven years and continued to run the Giant's camp until her own death on August 10, 1999. She was just thirteen days shy of her eighty-fourth birthday. Both are buried in Samford Cemetery in Riverview, Florida. Giant's Camp is at 9816 US 41 in Gibsonton. At the time of publication, there was a restaurant there but not much else. The town was desolate, but this did not seem to stop the many sideshow and circus buffs who continue to flock to "Gibtown" to see the town of their past sideshow heroes. ♦

MIDGETS & DWARFS

Midgets are miniature-sized individuals who are proportionately correct. There has traditionally been a class status among midgets and dwarfs, with midgets considering dwarfs to be of a lower class.

While the terms midget and dwarf are no longer used to describe little people, historically the term midget was used to describe proportionately sized people of short stature. The term dwarf indicated individuals of short stature as well, but those with shortening of the upper limbs and thighs. As a group, these people were very popular exhibits at sideshows or circuses. In fact, it would have been unusual to find a sideshow that did not feature one of these acts.

Most likely, few other employment opportunities were open to these people in earlier times.

While there are too many to honor in this book, we will take a look at the most famous of these performers who were, in many instances, also very prosperous. Interestingly enough, there was always a perceived class status among these entertainers, with the midgets considering dwarfs to be of a lower class. It was rare to find a marriage between a midget and a dwarf or even a true friendship. Mostly, they stayed separate from one another, midgets shunning dwarfs and the dwarfs accepting the prejudices of the midgets. ♦

CHARLES SHERWOOD STRATTON, OR "GENERAL TOM THUMB," AND MERCY LAVINIA WARREN BUMP

Tom Thumb was discovered when he was only four years old by P. T. Barnum. Barnum himself undertook the training of this child and Tom Thumb is considered his biggest star and greatest find.

Many a businessman would scratch his head and wonder aloud how Barnum could make so much money with a singing and dancing midget.

Lavinia's wedding dress was described in newspaper accounts: "The design in front of the dress representing Growing Corn for America, on the right a Rose for England, encircled by buds and leaves. On the left, Laurel for France. Oak leaves for Germany, a Shamrock for Ireland, the Thistle for Scotland, and a Vine with a cluster of Grapes for Italy."

Tom and Lavinia's "Fairy Wedding" took place at New York City's Grace Church and well over 2,000 "guests" paid $75 each to attend the wedding reception that followed.

In later years, Lavinia's height increased to 40 inches and her weight to fifty pounds.

Tragically, infants were "borrowed" from local orphanages and used as props for over three years until they tragically "died" in the public spotlight.

On July 15, 1883, Tom Thumb died from a sudden stroke in his home. He was forty-six. His wife of twenty-five years was on tour and away from home when he died.

The Strattons amassed a fortune from their years of touring and built a mansion in Middleborough, Massachusetts. They traveled in a silver midget-sized carriage with two matched Shetland ponies.

Lavinia remarried Count Primo Magri, an Italian midget, on April 6, 1885. They toured together in the United States and Europe.

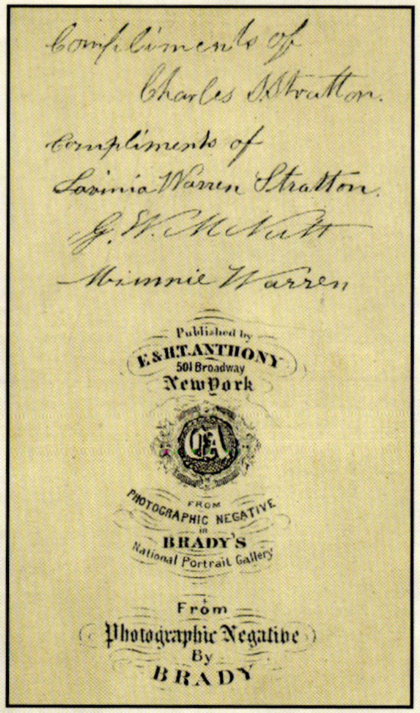

Matthew Brady, the famous Civil War photographer, was the photographer at the wedding.

TOM THUMB'S STORY

Charles Sherwood Stratton was born in Bridgeport, Connecticut, on January 4, 1838, the son of a carpenter. His parents and other siblings were all of average size. Reportedly, he weighed over nine pounds at birth, but he stopped growing around six months of age. He was twenty-five inches tall and weighed fifteen pounds. His burly father was embarrassed by his tiny son's small stature and shunned the child. P. T. Barnum discovered the child when he was four years old. He quickly made a financial arrangement with his parents to take Charles to his New York City dime museum, along with his mother, where he was introduced to the public as an eleven-year-old "General Tom Thumb," a prodigy who had just arrived from Europe. His initial salary was three dollars per week, plus room and board for both mother and child, a decent wage at the time.

Barnum himself undertook the training of the child. Charles learned high social etiquette, memorized witty sayings, and learned to sing, dance, and act. Dressed in various fancy costumes, the child would imitate a series of characters and famous people including a sailor, a Scottish highlander,

Hercules, Napoleon, and others. The public adored General Tom Thumb's show, especially the women. It was said that Tom Thumb kissed most of the women who came to the show or to whom he was introduced. He became an overnight success. Through typical Barnum showmanship and promotions, Tom Thumb soon became an international star, as well, entertaining foreign royalty and dignitaries. In 1844, at the age of six, he was commanded to appear before Queen Victoria. He also appeared before presidents Polk and Lincoln, Queen Isabella of Spain, and France's Emperor Napoleon III, whom he imitated in his act.

Tiny Tom Thumb was always considered P. T. Barnum's biggest star and greatest find. Tom remained the same size until his teens. He then grew to forty inches and, over the years, put on considerable weight for his height. ♦

LAVINIA'S STORY

Mercy Lavinia Warren Bump, called Vinnie by her family, was born on October 31, 1842, in Middleborough, Massachusetts. Her parents were of average size, as were all her siblings with the exception of a younger sister, Minnie, who was also a midget. Lavina was teaching school in her hometown when she was persuaded to join a sideshow by a distant relative, who quickly proved to be a dishonest man with no sense of honor. She loved the attention she received from the audience and enjoyed the excitement of the sideshow so she boldly wrote a letter of introduction to P. T. Barnum. Consequently, Barnum met Lavina and quickly signed her to a contract in 1862. He suggested that she use her mother's maiden name "Warren" as a stage name instead of "Bump." Lavina was a perfectly proportioned beautiful twenty-one-year-old who was thirty-two inches tall and weighed twenty-nine pounds. Very shortly after she signed with Barnum, Tom Thumb proposed to her. ♦

THE COUPLE'S STORY

They were married on February 10, 1863, in one of the most important and highly publicized social events of the New York City season. Their "Fairy Wedding" took place at New York City's Grace Church and well over 2,000 "guests" paid $75 each to attend the wedding reception that followed. Lavinia's sister, Minnie, was her attendant and Commodore Nutt stood for Tom. Matthew Brady was their photographer.

The couple received many expensive and fabulous wedding gifts, including an elegant miniature set of parlor furniture in ebony and gold, a magnificent miniature set of church service books that were mounted in a golden morocco leather case, a miniature silver horse and chariot crafted by Tiffany & Co. and ornamented with rubies and garnets, and an elegant miniature billiards table with balls, cues, and a rack to match. Drunk with the financial success of the wedding, Barnum urged the couple to start a family to keep the paying public's interest keen. However, while Tom may have been truly in love with Lavinia, Lavinia viewed the union as strictly a business proposal. Reportedly, the marriage was never consummated, and she and Tom lived as good friends only. Barnum was never one to let the true facts of life stand in the way of a good paying charade so a "newborn" was acquired for Lavinia. Tragically, an infant was "borrowed" from a local orphanage and used as a prop. The child had been proclaimed by promoters as the natural offspring of Tom and Lavinia and it was said that the child, by nature's own plan, would never grow. When the infant did grow, it was simply replaced with another new and smaller orphaned infant. The replaced child was abandoned, returned to the same or a different orphanage, or given away, never to see his "real" parents again. When they traveled abroad, it was easier to obtain a baby on location than to travel with an infant. Lavinia once explained with little feeling: "English babies in England, French babies in France, and German babies in Germany." After three years, the public's interest in the infant waned, so the child tragically "died" in the public spotlight and this cruel publicity stunt was abandoned.

In 1865, Tom and Lavinia began a tour of England and Europe that would last for three years. In 1869, they began a three-year tour of the world, appearing 1,471 times in 587 different cities. In 1881, they rejoined Barnum after the 1878 death of Lavinia's sister, Minnie, who died in childbirth. Barnum convinced the still-grieving and depressed couple to return for a final season of exhibitions as a means of coping with the loss. By now, the Strattons had amassed a fortune and were living well in a mansion in Middleborough, Massachusetts.

While on their advertised final tour in January 1883, a fire broke out in their Milwaukee hotel. Both Tom and Lavinia narrowly escaped death, as did their beloved manager, Sylvester Bleeker. However, Bleeker's wife died trying to escape the fire by jumping to her death. Tom never fully recovered from the emotional trauma of the incident. On July 15, 1883, he died from a sudden stroke in his home. He was forty-six. His wife of twenty-five years was on tour and away from home when he died.

More than 10,000 people attended the funeral of Tom Thumb. He is buried in the Mountain Grove Cemetery and Mausoleum in Bridgeport, Connecticut, 2675 North Avenue, Section 8. The granite statue at the top of the stone is said to be "life-sized" as he was at 19. After the death of her husband, Lavinia lived in retirement until she remarried Count Primo Magri, an Italian midget, on April 6, 1885, at the Church of the Holy Trinity in New York. They toured together in the United States and Europe. In later years, Lavinia's height increased to forty inches and her weight to fifty pounds. Lavinia passed away on November 25, 1919, at the age of seventy-eight. She is buried in the Mountain Grove Cemetery and Mausoleum in Bridgeport, Connecticut. Her second husband died a year later and is buried in her hometown, Middleborough, Massachusetts. He was seventy-one. ♦

HULDAH PIERCE WARREN BUMP, "MINNIE WARREN," AND EDMUND NEWELL

Minnie Warren died in childbirth on July 23, 1878, and her baby died a few hours later. She and the child were buried together in the Nemasket Hill Cemetery on Plymouth Street in Middleborough, Massachusetts. Minnie was only twenty-nine years old.

Minnie was the younger sister of Lavinia Warren. She was smaller and more beautiful but preferred to take a back seat to her older and worldlier sister.

The Illustrated London News ran an artistic depiction of the death of Minnie Warren and her child with Edmund in the forefront.

Minnie Warren was the younger sister of Lavinia Warren. She also took her mother's maiden name as her stage name. Minnie was born June 2, 1849, and, in addition to being a sideshow attraction with P. T Barnum, she performed on stage as an accomplished singer. Minnie was even smaller than her sister, as well as more beautiful, but she was shy and without the worldliness of Lavinia. Minnie was the maid of honor for her sister when Lavinia married Tom Thumb in a highly publicized P. T. Barnum wedding, dubbed "The Fairy Wedding." In July 1877, Minnie married Edmund Newell in Lock Haven, Pennsylvania. They met while touring together with P. T. Barnum. Edmund was a midget who was usually billed as "General Grant Jr." Sadly, Minnie died July 23, 1878, while giving birth to a full-sized six pound baby. The baby also died within a few hours. Minnie was twenty-nine years old and had only been married one year. She and her unnamed child were buried together in Nemasket Hill Cemetery on Plymouth Street in Middleborough, Massachusetts. A cement foundation measuring thirty-six by thirteen inches outlines their grave to indicate her approximate size.

Edmund Newell was born in Chicago, Illinois, on July 27, 1857, to average-sized parents. He toured with P. T. Barnum as well as appeared at his dime museum in New York City. After Minnie's tragic death, Edmund married an Englishwoman, Mary Ann Drake, whom he had met while touring in England with Barnum. They were married on April 5, 1888, in the St. Giles district of London, and Edmund remained in England. Mary Ann was a typically sized woman and together they had two children, a son, Edmund Charles Jefferys, born July 9, 1889, and a daughter, both of average stature. Family lore says that Edmund grew to an average adult height while in England. Edmund died on December 23, 1915, in Marylebone, London, England. He was fifty-eight. ♦

LEOPOLD "GABRIEL" KAHN, ALIAS "ADMIRAL DOT," "THE EL DORADO ELF," "THE CALIFORNIA DWARF," OR "THE SMALLEST CHARACTER IN THE WORLD," AND MABEL GLADIS "LOTTIE" SWARTWOOD

Leopold Kahn was born in 1858 in San Francisco, California, to average sized Jewish German immigrant parents. He was discovered by P. T. Barnum in 1870 while the showman was on a business vacation in the West with friends. Leopold's father approached Barnum in the hopes that the showman would be interested in exhibiting his young son. Barnum, having made a fortune with Tom Thumb, quickly accepted the offer and gave Leopold the stage names "Admiral Dot" and "The El Dorado Elf." Promoters claimed he was only twenty-five inches in height, weighed fifteen pounds, and was thirteen years old. He originally appeared on stage with his mother with whom he bore a close facial resemblance.

Admiral Dot grew taller as he aged, but his career still spanned almost two decades. Part of his success was due to Barnum's ability to market him creatively by pairing with smaller performers such as

Admiral Dot was very close to his mother. They bore a strong facial resemblance to one another.

Originally, Admiral Dot dressed in a British naval uniform and sang, danced, and played musical instruments when exhibiting.

Major Atom. Leopold also had the rare ability to keep audiences entertained throughout the years by altering his routines. Originally, he dressed in a British naval uniform and sang, danced, and played musical instruments. Later, he became widely known as "The Smallest Character in the World." Barnum had lost his American Museum in New York City twice to fire. He made a decision not to rebuild after a second fire, but instead, to take his dime museum on the road in 1871. His newest

1873 trade card for Admiral Dot who exhibited with his mother during his earlier years as a performer for P. T. Barnum.

discovery, Admiral Dot, was one of his star attractions, along with the famous conjoined twins, Chang and Eng; Annie Jones, "The Bearded Lady"; Anna Swan, a giantess; and Zip, "What Is It." Admiral Dot remained with Barnum until the late 1880s when he joined the Locke and Davis Royal Lilliputian Opera Company that featured only little people in their productions. There he met his future

Admiral Dot remained with Barnum until the late 1880s when he joined the Locke and Davis Royal Lilliputian Opera Company that featured only little people in their productions. There he met Lottie Swartwood, whom he married on August 14, 1892.

An old newspaper photo shows firemen battling the fire of February 1911 that burned to the ground the forty-eight-room Admiral Dot Hotel, dubbed the "Pee Wee Hotel" by locals. The hotel had been thought to be fireproof since it was constructed of brick with an asbestos roof. The hotel had also served as the home of Admiral Dot and his wife and their two typically developed children.

bride, Lottie Swartwood, a twenty-six inch tall midget. Lottie was born Mabel Gladis Smartwood in Van Ettenville, New York, in 1869 to a shoe-

Charles Eisenmann photograph of Admiral Dot.

maker. Her mother died when she was only six years old.

They married on August 14, 1892, at the Victoria Hall on Lexington Avenue in New York City. A *New York Times* newspaper account of their wedding noted, "That the marriage is the crowning achievement of Cupid's sly ways among the diminutive votaries there can be no doubt, for though Miss Swartwood is a Baptist she demonstrated her regard for her present lord to the extent of renouncing her religion, in order to be his helpmate and partner for the remainder of her days." She took the name "Charlotte Naomi" as her new Jewish

Admiral Dot was an astute businessman, even bottling his own brand of rye that he sold in his hotel's bar, restaurant, and bowling alley.

name. The couple honeymooned at Coney Island. Together they toured America and Europe, but eventually tired of the travel required of sideshow performers and retired to White Plains, New York. There they were proprietors of The Admiral Dot Hotel, dubbed the "Pee Wee Hotel" by locals. The large forty-eight-room hotel included a ballroom, banquet hall, restaurant, and bowling alley. Unfortunately, it burned down in a fire in February 1911,

Lottie continued to grow as an adult and reached a height of a little over four feet tall. In 1943, after having been a widow for twenty-five years, she remarried a gentleman named Edward Lappe. He was six feet tall and quite a contrast to her first husband.

even though the hotel was thought to be fire-proof since it was constructed of brick with an asbestos roof. It had also been the home of the couple and their two children, a daughter, Hazel, and a son, Gabriel, both average-sized, who had been born there. Luckily, the couple held the deeds to a large amount of city property and were financially quite comfortable even without the income from the hotel. Leopold had become a well-recognized citizen of the town and was a devout member of his synagogue. He also sang in the town choir. They moved to a beautiful home at 157 South Broadway where they remained until their deaths.

Leopold died suddenly at his home on October 26 during the great 1918 influenza epidemic that spread across America. In a matter of hours, he went from excellent health to a very ill man consumed by a fever of 105 degrees. He became delirious before he died and was difficult to restrain. According to cemetery records, he was fifty-four years, seven months, and three days old. He is buried in the Phoenix Lodge section of Mount Hope Cemetery, lot 7, a Jewish cemetery in Brooklyn, New York. His married daughter, Hazel Golden, had also died of influenza a few days prior.

Lottie continued to grow as an adult and reached a height of a little over four feet tall. In 1943, after having been a widow for twenty-five years, she married a gentleman named Edward Lappe who was six feet tall. Lottie died on December 12, 1950. She was eighty-one years old. Her new husband had preceded her in death by five years. ♦

LUCIA ZARATE, "THE MEXICAN MIDGET"

Lucia Zarate was born on January 2, 1864, in San Carlos, Mexico, to average sized parents. She was the first person in history to be identified with the very rare condition Majewski osteodysplastic primordial dwarfism type II (MOPD). Newspaper accounts of the day vary, but her mother always claimed that Lucia was extremely tiny at birth, but healthy, but she stopped growing when she was only one year old. There were several children born to this family, including a son

It was said in the press that Lucia was "beautiful, intelligent, and perfectly formed with the exception of a very prominent nose."

named Manuel, who was also a little person and who died in 1888.

Lucia was exhibited from a very young age in Mexico. In 1870, the fourteen-year-old girl (advertised as twelve) was brought to America by her parents and first exhibited at the Broadway Museum in New York City. She was extremely popular with both the public and press. Much attention was paid to her wardrobe in newspaper articles, stating that "even the smallest of baby clothes are

Lucia Zarate came to America in 1870 and first exhibited in New York City at the age of fourteen. She is pictured with her mother and father in these two photographs.

One of the most popular sideshow attractions of the day was Lucia paired with other midget men such as General Mite.

This false claim resulted in thousands flocking to view the exhibit of Lucia's death plaster.

too big for Lucia." Her feet were only two inches long, by newspaper accounts, and it was said that she was forced to pay the exorbitant price of four to sixteen dollars for each pair of custom-made shoes. The press also made much to-do over medical professionals examining and measuring Lucia. Accounts varied from 20 inches to thirty-one inches, most reported she was twenty-six inches tall. She was entered into the *Guinness World Records* as the "lightest recorded adult," weighing four and seven-tenths pounds at the age of seventeen. At twenty-six, medical doctors claimed she weighed seven and a half pounds. It was said in the press that she was "beautiful, intelligent, and perfectly formed with the exception of a very prominent nose."

One of the most popular sideshow attractions of the day was Lucia paired with General Mite. At that time, General Mite (also billed as Major Atom and Atomic Mite) was twenty-eight inches tall. Lucia traveled with her parents all over America and Europe, and she often played to royalty. She was considered a cheery, friendly professional and was said to be well loved by all. It was reported she made $200 a week and had earned her parents more than $300,000 before her untimely death in 1890.

Lucia was traveling to a scheduled performance in San Francisco aboard an ill-fated Northern Pacific train when the Great Blizzard of 1890 hit. Her snowbound train stalled in the Sierra Nevada Mountains near Truckee, California, on tracks covered with over two feet of snow. It took a large rotary snow plow working twenty-four hours a day and an army of men working for about two weeks to free the train, but it was too late. She passed away on January 28, 1890 at the age of twenty-six. Her death was officially listed as "gastric fever" but most likely she died of influenza that spread through the train, killing at least one other person, as well. Her parents took her remains back to their home in Veracruz, Mexico, for interment. A callous Mexican government delayed the process by demanding a hefty $650 duty to be paid before the parents were allowed to enter the country with their deceased daughter's body. Her Veracruz family home, Casa Grande (Big House), is open to the public as a museum. It stands as a tribute to Lucia Zarate's great sideshow career as "The Smallest Living Human Being on Earth." The newspapers of the day widely reported on Lucia's tragic death for many weeks after the incident. Wonderland capitalized on the press frenzy by announcing that they had made a plaster cast of Lucia "a few days after the recent death of this remarkable specimen of diminutive humanity" and it would be on display. Of course, the claim was false, but it was reported that thousands flocked to view the exhibit. ♦

ESPIRIDENA ALIZE CENDA, "CHIQUITA," "THE LIVING DOLL," "THE CUBAN DOLL," "LADY DOLL," OR "THE CUBAN ATOM"

Chiquita, a beautiful and perfectly proportioned midget, was born Espiridena (Esperidena) (Espiradiona) Alize Cenda in Matanzas, Cuba, on December 14, 1869. She shot to fame in November 1901 when Chiquita, thirty-one, married sixteen-year-old Anthony Charles Woeckener, a young American musician born November 25, 1885, in Erie, Pennsylvania, who had recently been employed by the sideshow where Chiquita worked.

While the polite society of that time was quite all right with an older man taking a younger wife, they were not prepared for the reverse, and a scandal ensued. Fortunately, a scandal was never a bad thing for a sideshow performer. It created a frenzy of interest in the performer and greatly increased the line of paying customers wanting to see, firsthand, the object of such shame. Fuel was added to the publicity fire when Chiquita's longtime manager, Frank Bostock, publicly claimed that Anthony had abducted Chiquita and forced her to marry him, wanting only Chiquita's money. Anthony charged back that immediately after the wedding his tiny bride was seized and held apart from him against her will by Bostock. One can only guess just how much truth is in either of these accounts, but "Chiquita, The Living Doll" quickly became a household name.

Her name shot to fame in November 1901 when Chiquita, thirty-one, married sixteen-year-old Anthony Woeckener, a young American musician born in Erie, Pennsylvania.

Chiquita always prepared for her shows by donning beautiful gowns and expensive jewelry. She often wore a diamond bracelet that she claimed was a token gift from King Edward VII. She died on April 20, 1928, at age fifty-eight after suffering health problems for years.

Chiquita was ending her set engagement at the Pan American Exposition World's Fair that ran from May 1 through November 1, 1901, attracting thousands daily, and would be going back to the sideshow with its hit-or-miss attendance. It may

Chiquita, a beautiful and perfectly formed midget, was born Espiridena (Esperidena) (Espiradiona) Alize Cenda in Cuba in 1869.

have been just a lucky coincidence, but the publicity surely guaranteed her a continued audience and profits wherever she exhibited. Chiquita's trade cards claim that she was twenty-six inches tall and only weighed eighteen and a half pounds. She always prepared for her shows by donning beautiful gowns and expensive jewelry. She often wore a diamond bracelet that she claimed was a token gift from King Edward VII. She added song and dance to her performances and fully looked the part of a living doll. Reportedly, she was educated, spoke several languages, and always carried herself with dignity and pride. At times she claimed to be Mexican and other times, of Cuban decent.

In the 1920s Chiquita retired from show business, citing health issues. She and her husband moved to Guadalajara, Mexico. She passed away on April 20, 1928, at age fifty-eight. Not much more is known of Anthony except that in 1931 he was employed on the SS *George G. Henry* that sailed from Aruba to New York City and the 1933 *U.S. City Directories* shows him living back in Erie, Pennsylvania, at 1619 Parade Street and not remarried. ♦

DOLLETTA B. DODD BOYKIN BUCK, "THE TINIEST MOTHER IN THE WORLD," OR "TINIEST MOTHER IN MEDICAL HISTORY"

Dolletta was one of ten children. Her parents, siblings, and own children were all typically sized developmentally.

Dolletta Dodd was a dwarf born on October 14, 1881 (dates vary from 1881 to 1884), in Quincy, Illinois. She was one of ten children born to average sized parents Benjamin Franklin Dodd and Anna E. Bell Dodd. Her siblings were all typically developed. There is no record of her birth weight, but one can only guess that she was a very small infant to be given the name Dolletta. Her family quickly started calling her by their nickname for her, "Dolly."

She gave birth to two typically developed children, a daughter, Luciea Boykin (1907–1978). and a son, Charles Boykin (Buck) (b. 1913), while married to her first husband, also a dwarf. The 1920 United States census shows her at age thirty-eight divorced and living with her two children in the home of a married sister and her husband.

In 1923, Dolletta took up with a married man and all-around-scoundrel who was also a sideshow performer, a tall German rope handler named Frederick "Fritz" Valentine Tischu, a.k.a. Charles Harry Buck (1890-1951), who performed as "The Long-Haired Cherokee Buck Man" even though he did not have a drop of American Indian blood in him. He was married at the time to Baroness Sidonia de Barcsy, a bearded lady also exhibiting with the sideshows. Reportedly, he was very unkind to the Baroness and her midget son, Nicu, and stole from her on his way out of town with Dolly. If he and Dolly married, the union was not legal since Charles Buck was never divorced from the Baroness. Some reports claim that he and the Baroness, in turn, were also never legally married. Charles may have fallen in love with Dolletta or in love with the money she earned. At the time, the Baroness was ill and not able to exhibit as often as she once did. Dolletta, on the other hand, was earning top dollar as "The Tiniest Mother in the World." It is said that Charles used to carry Dolly around in his arms like, well, *a doll*. Dolletta and Charles had one child, Dotella Mayo Buck.

The 1940 United States census shows Dolletta, age fifty-eight, living in Missouri in the home of her son, Charles Buck, age twenty-eight. Charles, the son, is listed as "head of the household" with a wife and his occupation is listed as "Manager of a Girls Show/ Carnival." Dolly claimed to be a widow and listed her occupation as "tiniest mother in medical history." It would appear that "The Long-Haired Cherokee Buck Man" was out of the picture, possibly due to the fact that he was now "married" to Dolletta's oldest daughter, Luciea, seventeen years his junior. Charles and his stepdaughter had three sons together. In later life, Charles became known as "The Old Indian Doctor" and practiced out of a broken-down bus. He died on February 10, 1951, in Port Arthur, Texas, at the age of sixty-one. He was cremated and his ashes given to Luciea, now forty-four. Dolletta passed away January 11, 1948, in Joplin, Missouri. She is buried in the Ozark Memorial Park Cemetery in Joplin. Dolly was sixty-six. ♦

Dolletta pictured with her family, including her daughter Luciea Boykin (1907–1978) and son Charles Boykin (b. 1913). Her husband was also a dwarf. According to the 1920 US census, they divorced. In 1923, Dolletta took up with a married sideshow performer, Charles Buck, a tall German trick roper, and they had one child.

Dolletta pictured with her daughter and her son ca. 1919. She was billed as "The Tiniest Mother in the World."

PRINCESS WEE-WEE, OR "COLORED DOLL LADY"

Princess Wee-Wee photographed with her mother, Lucy Thompson. She was born on July 15, 1901, in Pennsylvania.

Harriet Elizabeth Thompson was born on July 15, 1901, to James and Lucy Thompson in Bryn Mawr, Pennsylvania. Her parents were typically developed as were their other children. She was exhibited at a young age, but her age was always misstated to make her seem older. A twenty-something seventeen-inch grown woman is more amazing to the press and public than a seventeen-inch six-year-old child. In the course of her very long sideshow career, Princess Wee-Wee grew from seventeen inches to twenty-six inches, but she was usually billed as being twenty-one inches tall. Her weight also changed as she aged, from an initial reported seven and half pounds to fifteen pounds.

Princess Wee-Wee was first exhibited in 1906 and spent fifteen years with Barnum & Bailey. In 1911, a newspaper reported that she was their main attraction and commanded a weekly salary of $150.

MYSTERY TO SOLVE

What happened to Princess Wee-Wee after she retired? When did she die and where is her final resting place?

Early in her career, she was billed as being Jamaican or a pygmy from Africa. In 1918, Princess Wee-Wee became a central figure in a publicized movement to build, equip, and establish a place called Toyland in the Virgin Islands, which had been purchased by the United States in 1916. The idea was to populate Toyland entirely with midgets who would be in total control of their own government and country, separate from the US. They felt they would be able to sustain themselves financially through proceeds from moving picture companies paying them for their acting parts or by opening their country to tourists. The idea did not catch on. Most likely it was a publicity stunt but the press loved it and the story exploded in newspapers all across the country.

Princess Wee-Wee was a well liked professional and highly respected by all who worked with her. She stayed in great demand for numerous social events. In 1922, the press romantically linked her with Count Paacci, "The Baron," another midget performing with Barnum & Bailey, but she remained single her entire life. In the mid-1920s, she joined the famous Whitman Sisters, performing with them on stages all across America. The "Black and White Review" combined both white and black performers and the "Whitman Sisters Big Revue"

Princess Wee-Wee was exhibited at a young age, but her age was always misstated to make her seem older. In the course of her very long sideshow career, Princess Wee-Wee grew from 17 inches to 26 inches, but she was usually billed as being 21 inches tall.

Princess Wee-Wee's career spanned over three decades but after 1939, she seems to have disappeared from the performance stage altogether. Her final days are a mystery.

In a newspaper interview, Princess Wee-Wee said her favorite thing to do was go shopping and she loved to buy flowers.

PALACE THEATRE
905 E. Market St.—Greensboro
SPECIAL SHOW
For White People Only
THURSDAY NIGHT
January 28th—12:01 A. M.
"Whitman Sisters Big Revue"
30 Colored Entertainers 30
Featuring "Princess Wee-Wee"
(The smallest perfect woman in the world)
—and—
11-Piece Jazz Band
ADMISSION 50c

In the mid-1920s, Princess Wee-Wee joined the famous Whitman Sisters, performing with them on stages all across America. The "Black and White Review" combined both white and black performers.

featured thirty black entertainers performing for white audiences only. In all performances, Princess Wee-Wee was the main attraction.

In the 1930s, she performed with the Midget Village Exposition Show. One newspaper critic wrote, "Princess Wee-Wee sang 'I've Got It' with an abandon that proves that she has all the 'it' qualities. The shakes and shimmer of her white satin dress and her dexterous brown arms and legs bring down the house." After 1939, Princess Wee-Wee seems to have disappeared from the stage altogether. Possibly she retired comfortably with money earned as a top-rated attraction for over three decades. Her parents owned a home at 1520 1/2 North Mount Street in Baltimore, Maryland, so she may have returned home and lived with them, spending quiet years reviewing the many scrapbooks filled with articles and mementos of her long and illustrious career. The date of her death, location of burial, and information regarding her last years remains a mystery, but we wish her well. ♦

LYA (LIA) GRAF

Lya Graf was a half-Jewish midget born in Germany in 1910.

Lya Schwartz was born in 1910 in Reichenbach, Germany, and exhibited under the stage names Lia and Lya Graf. She was a half-Jewish midget who performed with Ringling Bros. and Barnum & Bailey Circus and in Coney Island. Very little is known of her early years or life during her sideshow career before coming to America in March of 1931, but she was involved in 1933 in the all-time most notorious publicity stunt in the annals of sideshows. J. Pierpont Morgan Jr. was the world's wealthiest man as well as the world's leading financier. He had been undergoing many days of testimony before the Senate Securities and Exchange Commission concerning his firm's responsibility in the 1920s false boom and the stock market crash that followed. He had admitted, under oath, that he and his partners had not paid any taxes during the years 1931 and 1932 at the height of the Great Depression. He also admitted guilt in some stock fraud schemes. Banks had failed and customers lost their life savings, farms fell into foreclosure, soup kitchens appeared in cities, and much of America was out of work. Morgan, rightly or wrongly, was becoming a very unpopular public figure and scapegoat.

On the morning of June 1, 1933, Morgan and his aides sat waiting for another brutal day of testimonies to begin. Lya was in town with the circus

The German wholesale slaughter of dwarfs, midgets, and "freaks" took the lives of over 10,000 people whose only offense was to be born different and to not fit into Hitler's plan for a "master race." Lya and her family were arrested in 1937 and all three were put to death in the Auschwitz gas chambers.

but she had no reason to be on Capitol Hill. However, an enterprising circus publicity man with Ringling Bros. and Barnum & Bailey Circus, Frank Braden, and Jerry Doyle, assistant editor of the *Washington Times*, orchestrated Lya being plopped onto Morgan's knee. The press immediately reacted in a frenzy of picture taking and rushed the story to print. Reporters claimed that Morgan first though Lya was a child and asked her where she lived to which she replied, "I live in a tent, sir." Other simplistic conversations were reported word for word by the press until a "flustered Morgan" finally realized Lya was a midget. In the photographs, Lya looks amused and totally in control and Morgan looks like a kindly old man. America had been given a look behind the wizard's curtain and J. P. Morgan was, indeed, only a mortal man. That photo, along with the story, had humanized him and the American public's heart was softened. The story appeared in newspapers all across the country, but not just for a few days or even a few weeks or months. The story was being referred to *decades* after the incident. Initially, Morgan was humiliated by the stories, but secretly his partners rejoiced since the heat from the Senate testimonies had been greatly reduced. Later it was said that Morgan relaxed enough to see the humor and benefit of the stunt, as well.

Into the mid-1950s, Frank Braden would always publicly claim the press got it all wrong, even down to Lya's quote about living in a tent. He claimed a reporter named Ray Tucker had completely made that quote up to sensationalize his story. According to Braden, Lya, the world's smallest woman, had simply wanted to meet the world's richest man. Braden also claimed that Morgan had been made aware of Lya and graciously agreed to meet the lady midget Braden called a miniature grande dame. In 1935, Lya and her parents returned home to Germany, but Germany under Adolf Hitler had a very different political landscape than the homeland she had left in 1931. Hitler had made the Jews hunted outcasts and the Nuremburg laws deprived Jews their German citizenship. In addition, the wholesale slaughter of little people and "freaks" took the lives of more than 10,000 whose only offense was to be born different and not fit into Hitler's plan for a master race. Lya and her mother, who was also a midget, would have been in peril. The family was arrested in 1937 and sent to a concentration camp where all three family members were put to death in the Auschwitz gas chambers. Lya had been charged under three counts: she was a midget, she was Jewish, and ironically, she had been a tool of capitalist Wall Street. ♦

The June 1, 1933, photograph that was the center of the all-time most notorious publicity stunt ever recorded in the annals of sideshows.

BODY DEFORMITIES

FANNY MILLS, "THE OHIO BIG FOOT GIRL"

Fanny Mills was born in Sussex, England, on August 30, 1859 or 1860, to average sized parents George and Sarah Mills. The family immigrated to Sandusky, Ohio, when Fannie was young. She had five siblings, all of average size. Unfortunately for Fanny, she was born with Milroy's disease, a condition that restricts the development of the lymph vessels, usually in the legs, and causes fluid build-up. Her parents first started to notice the condition in Fanny's right leg when she was a young child. The leg appeared to swell at an alarming rate. In less than two years, the left leg did the same. Her mother would claim that she had been marked during pregnancy when her husband forced her to tend to a horse with a swollen and infected leg. The family relocated to a tenant farm in Sandusky, Ohio, in the early 1860s. Fanny was a petite 115 pound woman with the exception of her legs and feet. In photos, the size of her body visually exaggerates the size of her legs and feet but still it's said that her left foot was a whopping nineteen inches long and seven inches wide, weighing twenty-six pounds and her right foot was seventeen inches long. On trade cards and in newspaper stories, it was said that Fanny wore a size thirty shoe. One account claimed that her big toe was eleven inches in circumference.

No standard-issue shoes would fit Fanny, of course, so shoes had to be specially made for her. Reportedly, each pair of shoes required three goat skins and she used pillowcases for stockings. Fanny could walk, but with great difficulty. She was in pain most of the time and even using a walking stick did not help. She spent most of her days immobile. Newspaper stories and local gossip attracted sideshow managers who were constantly scouting the countryside looking for oddities to fill the many sideshows then so popular in America. Fanny, being socially shy and awkward her entire life, turned down all offers until after the death of her father in 1885. Fanny would later claim that she started to exhibit as a last resort because her family needed money. The burden fell to her due to the many financial offers her unusual condition presented. Fanny was billed as "The Ohio Big Foot Girl" and was earning as much as $150 a week, a very respectable salary at that time, especially for a woman. Fanny was a shy and introverted woman. She found it difficult to spice her exhibit by talking and joking with spectators. To enhance the public's interest in her, Fanny's promoters came up with a publicity scheme claiming her father was offering any man that would marry his daughter a $5,000 reward and a "well-stocked farm." Never mind that the father was deceased, never mind that there was no $5,000 to offer, the stunt was amazingly successful. The catchy line on the advertising poster was "Don't let two big feet stand between you and

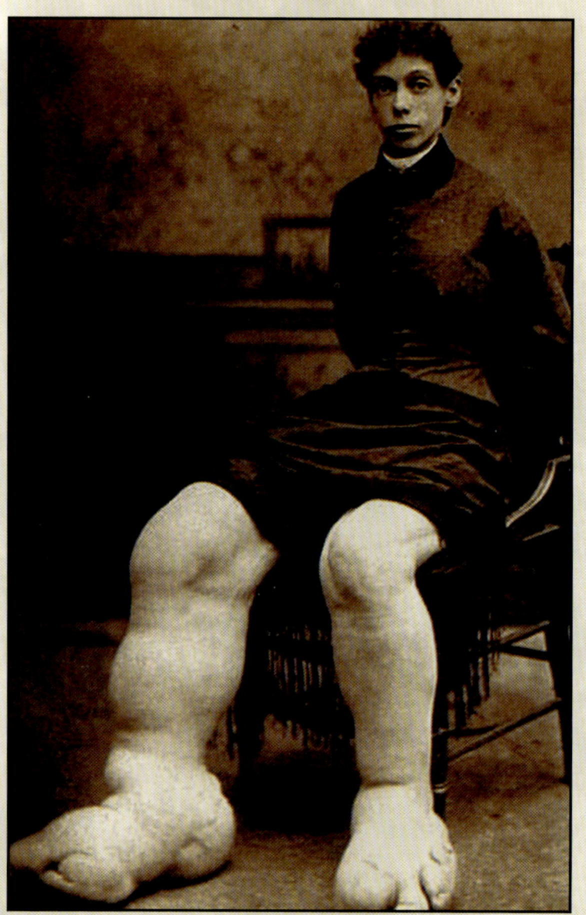

Her parents first started to notice the condition in Fanny Mill's legs when she was a young child. Her mother would claim that she had been marked during pregnancy when her husband forced her to tend to a horse with a swollen and infected leg.

On trade cards and in newspaper stories, it was said that Fanny wore a size thirty shoe. One account claimed that her big toe was eleven inches in circumference.

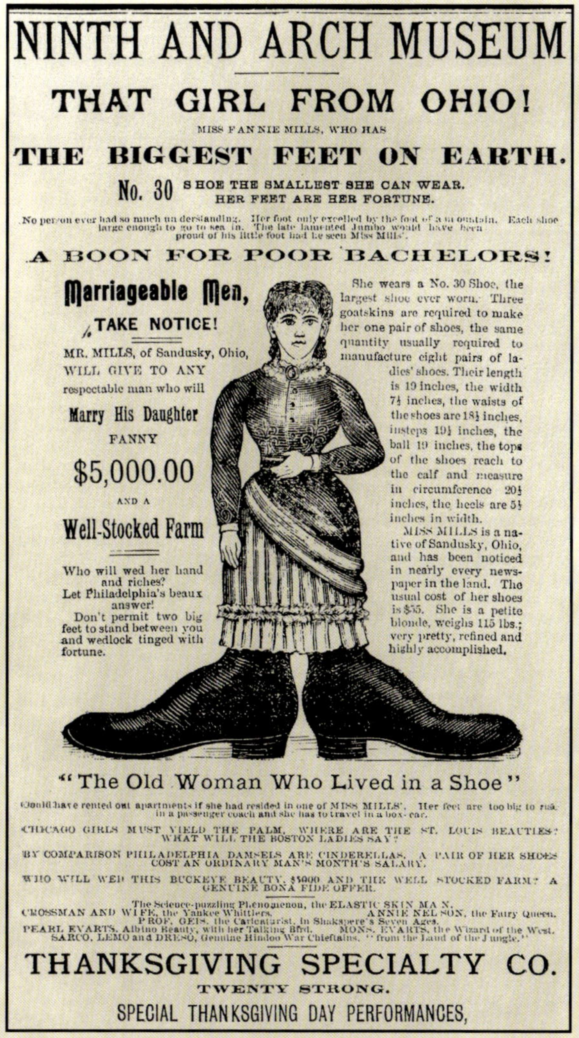

To enhance the public interest in her, Fanny's promoters came up with a publicity scheme claiming her father was offering any man that would marry his daughter a $5,000 reward and a "well-stocked farm." The catchy line on the advertising poster was "Don't let two big feet stand between you and wedlock tinged with fortune."

wedlock tinged with fortune." This spoof got many a person into the dime museum and newspaper stories continued the charade by claiming Fanny was turning down each and every prospect for one reason or another.

Fanny did marry, but the marriage was kept a secret for a long time to allow her publicity stunt to run its course. She wed William Brown (1834–1904) in 1886, a neighbor who was twenty years her senior. William was the brother of a spinster, Mary Brown, a caregiver Fannie had hired to help her at home and on the road. The Browns came from a very respectable landed family in Sandusky but, reportedly, the family fortune had dwindled away. Fanny most likely fell in love with William, the first and only man to ever show a romantic interest in her. It is possible that William had also fallen in love with Fanny, but more likely he married her to gain access to the substantial amount of money she was earning in the sideshow. A bonus, she would be touring and away from home much of the time, usually six months a year, although he did tour with Fanny on occasion. William had a reputation around the town as being a spoiled and selfish man who was too lazy to work his dairy farm hard enough to make it profitable. How much easier it would have been for a man like him to marry money than to toil for a living. This may be an unfair portrait of William, however. It would be nice to think that he loved Fanny deeply. He outlived Fanny by five years but never remarried.

In August 1887, Fanny gave birth to a child who was stillborn. Fanny blamed the death on herself, feeling her disease had somehow caused the death of the child, which is unlikely. She was not allowed the six-month's time to properly mourn the child as was the Victorian social custom of the day. Instead, needing money for her family and spouse, she went back to exhibiting at sideshows within a few months and remained a performer until health issues forced her to retire in 1892.

Fanny died in 1899 at the age of thirty-nine, basically from lymphopenia, an abnormally low level of white cells in the blood that cause the immune system to be compromised. The condition is a side effect of Milroy's disease. The cemetery records simply record the reason for death as "abscesses." She is buried in Oakland Cemetery in Sandusky, Ohio, in an unmarked grave, her husband not bothering to purchase a tombstone for his wife of thirteen years. There is a small, white stone in her plot, the engraving now illegible. This is most likely the marker for the infant child. William died in 1904 and was buried next to his wife and his infant child in the Mills family plot, Lot 6, block 76. William and Fanny's graves remain unmarked. ♦

SYLVIA PORTER, "THE ELEPHANT GIRL"

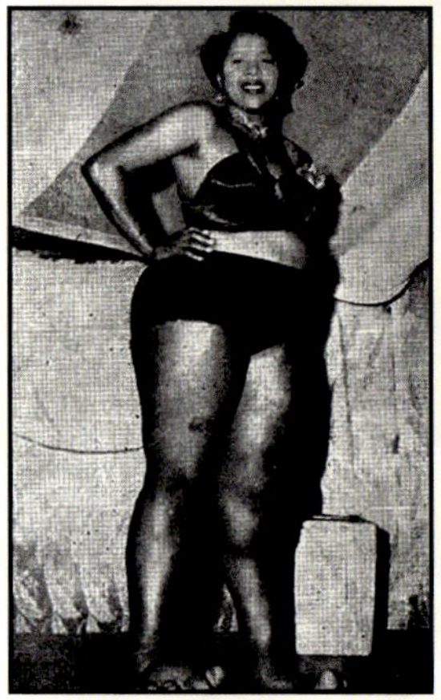

Sylvia Porter was an extremely attractive black woman, with the obvious exception of her feet and legs. She used to exhibit herself in a bathing suit to play up her appearance.

Sideshow banner for Sylvia.

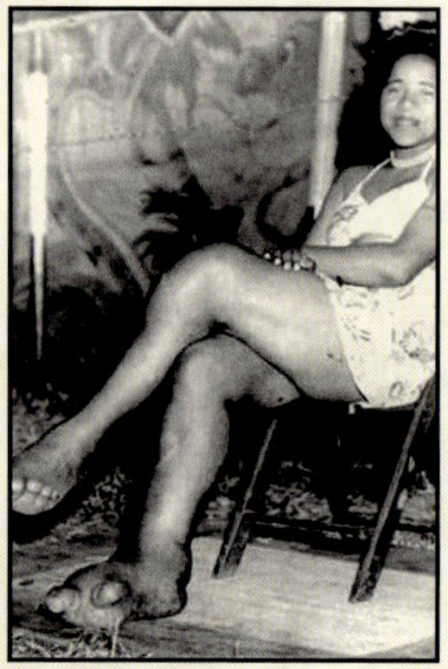

Sylvia could walk, but her steps were painful and her gait was a waddle. Sylvia hated the cold because she could not wear shoes.

Sylvia Porter was born out of wedlock and spent her early years with her mother on her grandparent's dirt farm near Mobile, Alabama. Sylvia developed a condition known as lymphedema that caused fluid to build up in her lower extremities. She had enormous legs and her feet were over two feet long. Sylvia was an extremely attractive black woman, with the obvious exception of her feet and legs. She used to exhibit herself in a bathing suit to play up her appearance and claimed she had the largest feet in the world. Legend says she was discovered in her hometown by a porter, George Jackson, who worked on a circus train. He became Sylvia's manager and husband until he ran off with another sideshow star, a fat lady named, "Baby Flo." She could walk, but her steps were somewhat painful and her gait was more of a waddle. Sylvia hated the cold because she did not wear shoes. When she was young her family could not afford specially constructed shoes and by the time she got older, she was used to going without. Even though the soles of her feet were calloused, she had to be very careful when walking to avoid glass and other hazards and she was always worried she would get frostbite in cold weather. Ward Hall tells a story in his book *My Unusual Friends* about a time in 1960 when Sylvia was booked for a few weeks with Hubert's Museum and Flea Circus on 42nd Street in New York City. Reportedly, the show manager had been trying to book Sylvia for a few years, but she was afraid to come that far north. He finally managed to get her to agree to appear by promising her it would not snow. When a blizzard came, the angry barefoot Sylvia took the first train back to Mobile. Sylvia continued to perform until her retirement in the 1970s. This was an era in our country where the young and the want-to-be-young were protesting for equal rights for all citizens. When these protestors attacked the management of sideshows and accused them of exploiting the performers, Sylvia was once quoted as saying, "Where are they going to send me? Back to the farm? No thanks, I'd rather be dead." Not much is known about Sylvia's life after her retirement, including the date of death and gravesite location. ♦

MYSTERY TO SOLVE

What happened to Sylvia after she retired? Did she return to her parents' farm? When did she die, and where is her final resting place?

BLANCHE DUMAS (DUMONT)

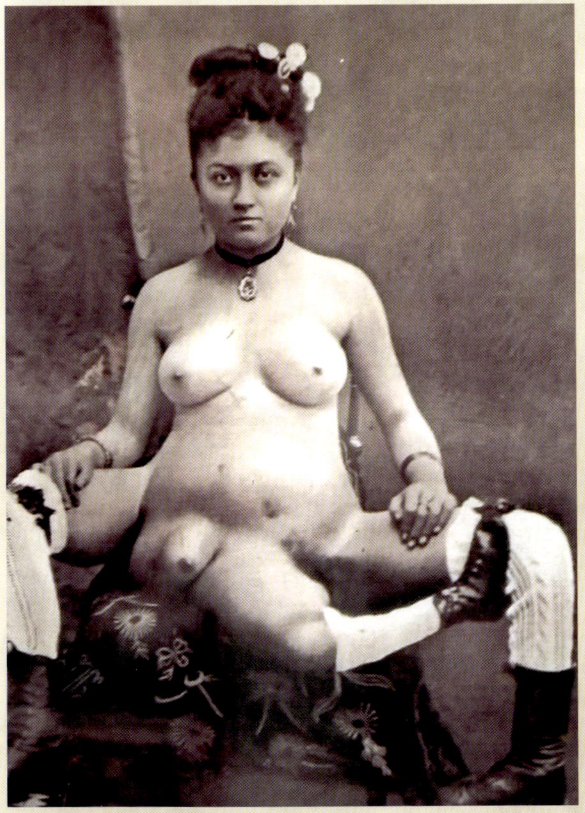

Her later photographs show painted "nipples" on her shortened appendage, obviously done to enhance the titillating sexual impact of the already explicit photo.

Blanche Dumas was raised in Issoudun, France, the daughter of a French father and a biracial mother. She was born in 1860. When she was fourteen years old, she was presented by a Dr. Balle to the Paris Facility of Medicine for examination. The findings indicated that Blanche was double-bodied from the waist down and that each body acted separately of the other. It was also noted that the two legs Blanche used for walking were the outward legs of the separate bodies and that the third leg was not sensitive to pain. No mention was made of the fourth protrusion but it was reported that the girl was in good health. A more detailed report of her deformities was documented in *Anomalies and Curiosities of Medicine* by George M. Gould and Walter L. Pyle after Blanche had been examined again in her mid-twenties. It was noted that she had a modified duplication of the lower body, plus she had a pelvis that was wider than normal with a duplication of genitalia, both having equally developed sensations, two bowels, and two bladders. Her two primary legs were reported as being abnormally formed and the third leg was missing a joint that would have aided in mobility. That third leg had a bend in it where the knee and joint should have been. Also mentioned was the undeveloped stump of another limb. Walking and standing was probably difficult. It appears from photographs that a type of leg brace was required.

The early trade photos of Blanche would indicate that she was, most likely, exhibited for profit at a young age. For whatever reason, she autographs her trade cards using the surname "Dumont." Stories abound that she eventually became a Paris courtesan with an insatiable sexual drive. This may have been merely speculation resulting from fantasies imagining a beautiful, young French woman born with two perfectly functioning vaginas or it may have been the truth. Her later photographs show painted "nipples" on her shortened appendage, obviously done to enhance the titillating sexual impact of the already explicit photo, so we can at least imagine that modesty and shyness were not a character trait of Blanche. In her defense, it was not uncommon for parents to sell their young daughters into prostitution during this time period and a girl as unusual as Blanche would have likely brought a small fortune in the trade. One erotic story that persists, truth or fiction, is the one that romantically links Blanche with Juan Baptista dos Santos, a handsome Portuguese man with two functioning penises and a lusty sexual appetite. Supposedly, Blanche openly advertised she wished for a sexual dalliance with this man and he kindly obliged. Little else is known of her life and death, nor do we know the location of her burial site. Most aging prostitutes do not face happy futures, but we can only hope Blanche was the exception to the rule and lived a long and joyous life. ♦

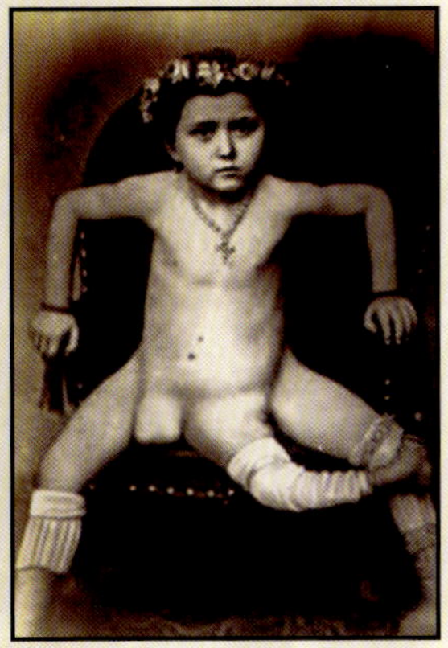

Blanche Dumas was raised in Issoudun, France, the daughter of a French father and a biracial mother. She was born in 1860.

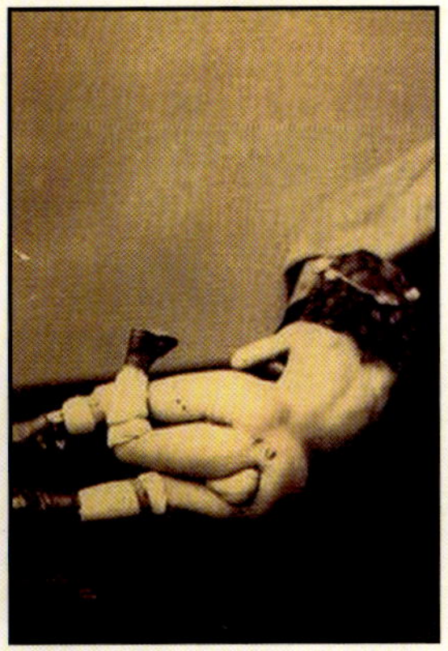

An autographed trade card for Blanche. For whatever reason, she signs her surname as "Dumont." The early trade card photos of Blanche indicate that she was exhibited for profit at a young age.

JOSEPHINE MYRTLE CORBIN BICKNELL, "THE FOUR-LEGGED GIRL FROM TEXAS"

Josephine Myrtle Corbin was born May 12, 1868, in Lincoln County, Tennessee, with two vaginas. She also had four legs and sixteen toes, five toes each on the larger, outer feet and three toes each on the smaller, inner feet. Myrtle was born with "dipygus," a severe and very rare deformity where the body is typically developed from the waist up but forks left and right below the waist. The pelvis and legs are duplicated with this condition and, in humans, the inner two of the four duplications develop much smaller than the norm. This condition has also been called teras catadidymum, or "monster twinned below." It is a type of conjoined twins deformity, but in Myrtle's case, she only had half of a sister to contend with.

Medical drawing illustrating "dipygus," a very rare congenital disability. Myrtle Corbin was born with two vaginas, four legs, and sixteen toes. Sometimes, historically, this condition was informally called "monster twinned below."

As shown in the medical drawing, Myrtle would have had two small pelvises positioned side-by-side and each of her smaller inner legs was paired with one of her outer legs. She could move the smaller legs but they were weak and too short to be used for walking. Her large right foot was a club foot that complicated her mobility even more. Myrtle could walk, but slowly and with difficulty. It was also hard for her to stand upright for any length of time.

Myrtle could move the smaller legs but they were weak and too short to be used for walking. Her large right foot was a club foot that complicated her mobility even more. She could walk, but slowly and with difficulty. It was also hard to stand upright for any length of time.

Myrtle was studied by numerous doctors and experts. George M. Gould and Walter L. Pyle, writing in *Anomalies and Curiosities of Medicine*, observed that both vaginas menstruated. This would indicate that both sides of Myrtle were able to function sexually and that it was possible to reproduce from either side. She always claimed she gave birth to her children from both sides, but this may have just been tantalizing sideshow hype to enhance her show appeal. She once confided to doctors that she almost always had sexual relations on her right side. The 1910 United States census shows that Myrtle gave birth to eight children, but only four were living at the time of the census. Obviously, there were some complications of birth with her deformity.

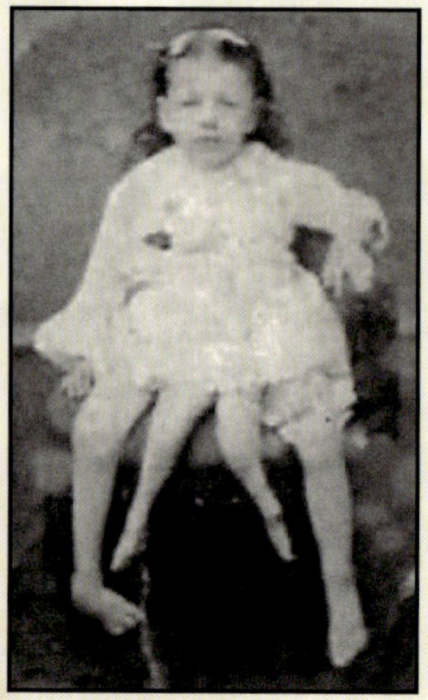

Myrtle was exhibited for profit from a very young age.

Myrtle was born to typically developed parents and all her siblings were typically developed. Her parents, William H. Corbin and Nancy Williams Sullens, were married on March 13, 1865, in Blout, Alabama. Her father had fought for the South in the Civil War in the 43rd Georgia Infantry. As with most Southern men returning home, there were not many opportunities to make a living in the devastated and war-torn South. The parents were most likely shocked when Myrtle was born, but her father quickly understood that this child was a much needed money-making opportunity for his growing family. Legend says he started charging neighbors and gawkers who showed up on his door step a small fee to look at his most unusual infant. By the time Myrtle was a young teenager, she had caught the eye of P. T. Barnum and was touring with his show in the United States and London. She was very popular, as were all "real freaks," and thus earned a very handsome salary, especially for someone so young. She would dress her tiny twin in matching socks, shoes, and bloomers. The visual effect made the tiny twin seem more "human" to the fascinated paying public. Due to her popularity, fake four-legged performers started appearing on the scene, but their show appeal never matched Myrtle's. She retired from the sideshow in 1886 at the age of eighteen. It is possible she was homesick. It is also possible that she had earned enough money to satisfy her and her family. It is more probable that she fell in love since she married a nineteen-year-old farmer, James Clinton Bicknell (1867–1946), on June 12, 1886.

Her last child, a daughter named Lillian, was born in 1909. A few years later, she returned to exhibiting at Huber's Museum in New York City and at Coney Island. She also had a contract to show with Ringling Brothers. Reportedly, she often commanded a salary up to $450 a week.

Myrtle Corbin Bicknell passed away at her home at 205 Graham Avenue in Cleburne, Texas, on May 6, 1928, just six days shy of her sixtieth birthday. The cause of death was a medical condition affecting her right leg (the big right leg) she had been suffering with for eight months. Oddly, her husband listed "house wife" on her death certificate for occupation.

She was buried in the Cleburne Memorial Cemetery in Cleburne, Texas, on May 7, 1928.

Myrtle would dress her tiny twin in matching socks, shoes, and bloomers. The visual effect made the tiny twin seem more "human" to the fascinated paying public. Due to her popularity, fake four-legged performers started to appear at sideshows, but their show appeal never matched Myrtle's.

Her father, who had lived off his daughter's earnings for years, died on March 6, 1923, in Johnson, Texas, just a few years before Myrtle's death. He was seventy-nine. Myrtle's mother quickly applied for a war pension available to widows who are in indigent circumstances. One can only wonder about the family dynamics behind these facts but since

Myrtle married and was the mother of four children. Oddly, her husband listed "housewife" on her death certificate for occupation. No mention was made of her very successful sideshow career.

Myrtle was still alive at the time of her father's passing, it would seem the money well had run dry for her parents.

Myrtle's husband outlived her by eighteen years. He remarried. James Clinton Bicknell passed away February 14, 1946, at the age of seventy-seven from cirrhosis of the liver. ♦

FRANCESCO "FRANK" A. LENTINI, "THE GREAT LENTINI," "THE THREE-LEGGED MAN, OR "THE THREE-LEGGED FOOTBALL PLAYER"

Frank Lentini was born with two sets of totally functioning genitals. Of course, he was also born with three legs, four feet (one underdeveloped foot was growing from the knee of his third leg that was attached to his spine), and sixteen toes. His excess appendages were the result of being born with a partially formed conjoined twin that projected outward from the right side of his body. As with many conjoined twins, especially those born over one hundred years ago, doctors early-on declared that to surgically remove the excess would likely result in death or paralysis since the deformed twin was attached to Frank's spinal column.

Frank was born on May 18, 1889 or 1890, in Rosolini, Sicily. He had seven sisters and four brothers, all typically developed. His family immigrated to America when Frank was a young boy.

Frank was born on May 18, 1889 or 1890, in Rosolini, Sicily, to typically developed parents. He had seven sisters and four brothers, all typically developed as well. His family immigrated to America in 1893 when Frank was a young child. He was naturalized in Philadelphia on September 22, 1919, at age twenty-nine. There are two basic accounts of Frank's upbringing. He always claimed he was born into a fairly well-to-do family that loved him dearly and afforded him comfort and security. This account appeared on his trade cards. Another popular account of his childhood persists, one not supported by Frank, claiming his parents, embarrassed by this child, rejected him and that his aunt or uncle raised him before he was eventually placed in a home for disabled children.

Most likely, Frank's parents moved to America to place their son with a sideshow for profit or were coming here anyway and Frank caught the eye of a sideshow manager. He first exhibited around the age of thirteen. An article appearing in the *Boston*

Frank Lentini was born with two sets of totally functioning genitals. He was also born with three legs, four feet (one underdeveloped foot was growing from the knee of his third leg), and sixteen toes.

Shown: Trade card for Frank Lentini.

Herald on October 28, 1906, advertising the Austin & Stone's Museum in Coney Island heralded seventeen-year-old Frank as "Frank Lentini, the three-legged Adonis, a freak unlike any other Dame Nature has yet brought into being." Frank always claimed his father insisted upon him receiving an education before joining a traveling sideshow. Census records indicate Frank had an eighth grade education, which would have been considered adequate schooling at that time. It was probably shortly after that time he went on the road. He worked with some of the biggest names in the

Frank Lentini is featured on the back cover of Alice in Chain's 1995 album. The album's front cover features Sunshine, the three-legged dog.

business as "The Great Lentini," including Ringling Brothers Circus, Barnum and Bailey, and Buffalo Bill's Wild West Show. The 1940 United States census shows Frank as a sideshow manager with the Wild West Show, age fifty, exhibiting in Tuscaloosa, Alabama. The census taker might have been quite surprised that day when he found himself taking census information from Frank and some of the show members, including several animal trainers, midgets, a human pincushion, magicians, and a pononey [sic] freak (phony freak), among others.

At times, Frank used his third leg to kick a soccer ball across theater stages, earning him the show business handle "The Three-Legged Football Player." By the time he was six, his typically developed legs were slightly different in length. The difference in lengths became even more noticeable

Reportedly, Frank good-naturedly would complain that even with three legs, he still didn't have a pair of legs. He also liked to say, "I buy two pairs [of shoes] and give the left shoe to a one-legged friend of mine who had the misfortune to lose his right leg."

when Frank was an adult. One leg was thirty-nine inches, the other thirty-eight inches, and the third leg was only thirty-six inches with a clubbed foot. Reportedly, he good-naturedly would complain that even with three legs, he still didn't have a pair and he also liked to say, "I buy two pairs (of shoes) and give the left shoe to a one-legged friend of mine who had the misfortune to lose his right leg."

Frank was Catholic. He was married twice. His first marriage was to Theresa S., from Massachusetts, who was born in 1891 or 1892 and of Irish decent. They had four children—three sons and a daughter: Josephine (born 1909 in Scotland), Natale (born December 17, 1916, in Connecticut), Frank (born September 3, 1919, in Philadelphia), and James (born July 31, 1922, in Philadelphia). They were still married when the 1930 census was conducted. The US City Directories for Hartford, Connecticut, show him working as an orderly at Hartford Hospital during 1939 and 1940. Possibly, Theresa was ill and he took the only job he could find to be near her and also pay the bills. Most likely, Theresa passed away in late 1939 or early 1940, although no record can be found. By the 1940 census he was remarried to Helen Lentini. Frank Lentini died on September 21, 1966, and is buried in the Fred Hunter's Hollywood Memorial Gardens East in Hollywood, Florida. He was seventy-seven. ♦

STANISLAUS BERENT, "SEALO, THE SEAL BOY," "SEALO"

Stanislaus Berent was born in Pittsburgh, Pennsylvania, on May 14, 1903, with a condition known as phocomelia, an extremely rare congenital disorder involving malformation of one or more of the limbs. In Stanley's case, his upper arms were not fully formed and sections of his arms were missing so that his hands were attached to the trunk. Phocomelia is usually a result of environmental influences such as the drug tha-

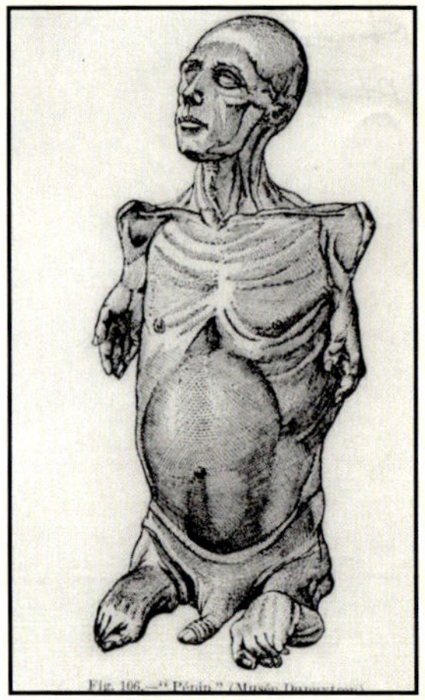

Phocomelia is a rare condition that has also been referred to as "seal limbs." It can affect any of the four limbs and, in extremely rare cases, it can also affect the face and some organs of the body. Stanley Berent was born with deformed arms.

In the mid-1970s, Stanley retired to Gibsonton, Florida. His career had spanned almost four decades.

lidomide, but it can also be inherited. The condition is commonly referred to as "seal limbs."

Very little is known about Stanley's younger days. Reportedly, he was discovered selling newspapers when he was in his thirties and went on from there to exhibit with many of the major sideshows and dime museums of the day, touring much of the United States, plus Europe and parts of South America and the Virgin Islands. By most accounts, he was one of the best liked of all performers due to his extroverted personality and keen sense of humor. His only vices were playing cards, smoking a cigar, and consuming his signature drink, a "boilermaker" that consisted of a glass of beer and a shot of whiskey. A

Stanley's act basically only consisted of him demonstrating mundane chores with his tiny arms. However, his personality and good-natured joking made him very popular with other performers, show management, and co-workers, and made his show a success.

stick with a hook on it allowed him to zip and unzip his pants unaided even when he had consumed one too many boilermakers, as was often his custom.

In January of 1942, Stanley made his TV debut on a show called *True or False*, along with a panel of five other circus performers. They challenged six young ladies dubbed "Radio Beauties."

Unlike the sideshow performers of the 1800s and the early quarter of the 1900s, it is rare to find a newspaper article about Stanley. Times and public

Sideshow banners advertising Sealo. The 1954 sideshow banner for "Sealo, The Seal Boy" smoking his trademark cigar and a 1961 sideshow banner.

attitudes about sideshow performers were changing. The exception came in 1972 when Stanley and a dwarf named Norbert P. Terhune challenged an obscure 1921 Florida state law that prohibited freak shows. Stanley and Norbert had been working with the World Fair Freaks and Attractions, Inc. when the show was closed by law enforcement officers. Their lawsuit forced the Florida Supreme Court to strike down that law as unconstitutional and rule "the state has no business telling persons they cannot earn an honest living....One who is handicapped or in an unfortunate position because of physical handicaps or deformities, not of his own choosing, must be allowed a reasonable chance within his capacities to earn a livelihood." For a brief time, Sealo became a household name as newspapers and television stations carried the story nationwide.

Stanley retired to Gibsonton, Florida, in the mid 1970s but returned to his hometown of Pittsburgh as his heath declined. He passed away in December 11, 1980, at The Mercy Hospital at the age of seventy-seven. He is buried in the Christ Our Redeemer Cemetery (originally North Side Catholic Cemetery) at 204 Cemetery Lane in Pittsburgh (Section G, Row 4, Grave No. 1) in a consummated plot. No stone marks his grave. ♦

MIGNON, "THE PENGUIN GIRL," OR "MICKEY MIGNON"

Ruth Berry Davis was born around 1910 with a variety of the congenital disorder phocomelia, sometimes called "seal limbs." Unfortunately, her left arm and both legs were affected, plus her fingers on both hands and all toes were fused together. The stunted limbs and typically-sized trunk gave Ruth the appearance of a penguin, and she waddled as she walked. The selection of the stage name "The Penguin Girl" would have been an easy choice. Where "Mickey" came from is not known, but most agree she chose "Mignon" since it means "cute" in French.

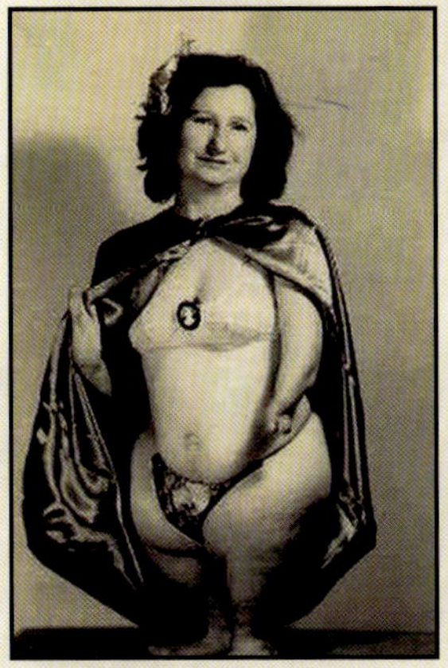

Mignon, The Penguin Girl.

As with most sideshow performers, Ruth embellished her act. Here she is shown playing a musical instrument.

MYSTERY TO SOLVE

So little is known about Ruth. Where and when was she born? What was her childhood like and what influenced her to join the sideshow? Where and when did she die, and where is her final resting place?

Little is known about Ruth, including facts about her early life, where and when she was born, and what happened to Ruth after she retired from sideshows. Most of what we know about her comes from Ward Hall, who writes in *My Very Unusual Friends* that Ruth was married to Earl Davis, who was billed in sideshows as "Hoppy the Frog." Hall claims they made a good married sideshow couple, playing in the better shows of the 1930s through the 1940s. He also says the couple retired to California in the mid-1950s to raise Ruth's son. Ward has never had a bad thing to say about anyone, and he is one of the true gentlemen of our time. Hopefully, his recollections are correct, although the timelines do not compute.

Ruth gave birth to a healthy son (around 1944) she named Tony, with the surname LaArgo reportedly from a first marriage. Little else is known about Ruth, but hopefully she and Hoppy lived a long and "hoppy" life. ♦

OTIS JORDAN, "FROG BOY," OR "THE HUMAN CIGARETTE FACTORY"

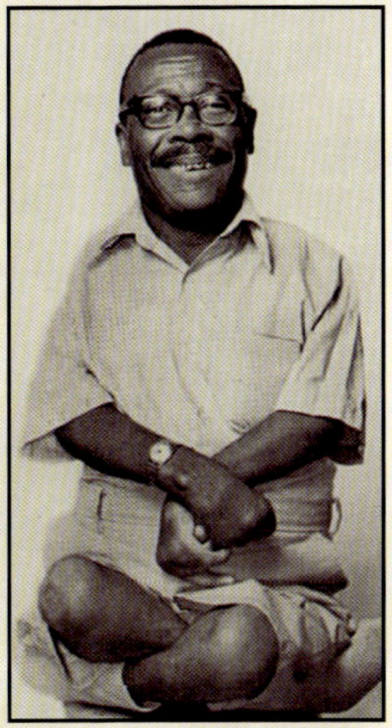

Trade card for Otis Jordan.

Otis Jordan was born in Lamar County, Georgia, on November 2, 1925, the fourth child of Curtis and Eldora Dumas Jordan. From birth, he suffered from a severe case of arthrogryposis multiplex congentia (AMC). This disease can be either inherited or result from complications occurring in the womb. Newborns with AMC have decreased flexibility of the joints affected and are unable to bend them. Both of Otis's arms and both legs were permanently locked, making it impossible for him to learn to walk or to do many tasks. According to his trade card, he had six typically developed siblings

Otis at a young age driving the goat cart he made that enabled him to get around unaided. According to his sister, "he was always on the go day and night."

and his brothers carried him everywhere until he fashioned a goat cart that allowed him independent movement. In later life, he purchased a car that was specially equipped for him and he drove that car everywhere. Otis always attributed his ability to overcome the obstacles of birth to his parents' strong determination to make him self-sufficient.

Otis started exhibiting in 1963 as "Frog Boy" when he was hired by Dick Burnett. In 1984, he was working with Whitey Sutton's sideshow during the New York State Fair when Barbara Baskin-Bogdan, disabled herself, went to court to have sideshows banned from fairs feeling they exploited the disabled. Otis Jordan and others fought back to defend their right to make an honest living and won. Shortly after that victory, however, he changed his stage name to "The Human Cigarette Factory," a more socially correct title at the time. He would roll and light a cigarette using only his lips and his tongue. His sister, Mary Baldwin, wrote, in correspondence with the author, "Otis never complained about anything and he never felt sorry for himself. He was always happy. He could tell a good joke and then laugh harder than you. His laughter would capture you. He didn't look at his condition as a deformity. His attitude was if you can do it so can I and he would always find a way. He loved the company of good people. He had a line for the women. Most of his friends were women and they loved him. He was a spiritual person and he could sing." She also fondly recalled that "if Otis asked for a glass of water, he would get mad if you tried to hold it for him. Instead, he held the glass in his teeth to drink." Otis passed away on December 1, 1991, while visiting family in Barnesville, Georgia. He was sixty-six. He is buried in the family plot at the Bethel Baptist Church Cemetery, 702 Johnstonville Road in Barnesville. ♦

ELI BOWEN, "THE LEGLESS WONDER," OR "THE LEGLESS ACROBAT"

Eli Bowen was born in Richland County, Ohio, on October 14, 1842 (although other years appear on official papers, such as 1841 on passports and 1843/1847 on various censuses). His father, Robert Bowen, a farmer, and his mother, Sarah Mursser Bowen, were both typically developed and by 1850 they had eight children, all without physical disabilities with the exception of Eli, who was born with phocomelia, or "seal limbs." He had no legs. His feet, both different sizes, jutted out from his hips. During his lifetime, he developed great upper body strength from using his arms to move around and walk.

His upper body strength served him well in his career that would span over fifty-five years. He started performing when he was in his early twenties and was billed as "The Legless Wonder" but more often as "The Legless Acrobat." He was often referred to as one of the most handsome men in show business during his early career days and newspapers and ads always praised his "Great Perch Pole Act." He was highly thought of by fellow performers and respectfully referred to as "Captain." When he was twenty-six, he wed a fifteen-year-old

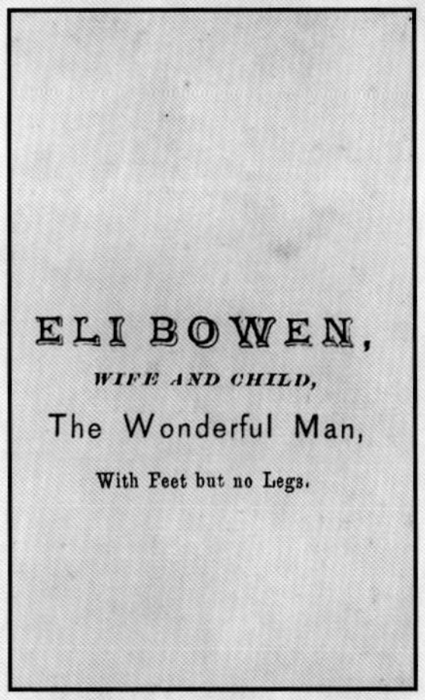

When he was twenty-six, he wed a fifteen-year-old beauty. They had four sons, all of whom were disability free. Family lore says that Eli was not very fond of children so most likely his family inclusion in posed publicity shots was to prove his ability to both maintain a happy wife and procreate.

Eli was born with phocomelia. He had no legs, and his feet, which were different sizes, jutted out from his hips. During his lifetime, he developed great upper body strength. He was often referred to as one of the most handsome men in show business.

beauty, Martha A. Haines, lovingly called "Mattie." They had four sons, all without disabilities: Frank, Robert, Adrian, and Victor. The boys would often be photographed with the parents or the father for trade cards and carte-de-visites. Family lore says that Eli was not very fond of children so most likely his family inclusion in posed publicity shots was to prove his ability to maintain a happy wife and procreate. His New York obituary says that all four sons became newspapermen, true or not. A 1907 interview claims that one son became a judge and another was a successful merchant, again true or not.

In 1903, he participated in a protest against Barnum and Bailey and the newspapers' use of the word "freak," preferring the word "prodigies." He and many fellow performers wanted the word "freaks" banned from all advertisements. Unfortunately, the press mostly made light of the protests and protesters, thus there was little change. Eli was still performing at age eighty-two when he died on May 4, 1924, in the back of the show house at Coney Island. He had worked for many dime museums and circuses, including Barnum and Bailey. He is buried in Lowell Memorial Cemetery in Lowell, Indiana. He lies in an unmarked grave. ♦

CHARLES BROTON TRIPP, "THE ARMLESS WONDER"

Charles Broton Tripp was born on July 6, 1855, without arms, but never let his condition keep him from doing almost everything anyone else could do. The one exception was putting on and taking off a coat.

Charles Broton Tripp was born on July 6, 1855, in Woodstock, Ontario, Canada, to typically developed parents, John and Jane Tripp. He was born without arms, but never let his condition keep him from doing almost everything anyone else could do. The one exception was putting on and taking off a coat.

Charles was raised in Olney, Illinois, and always said he considered Olney his home. He attended school there and participated in all school activities and sports, using his feet as others used their hands. He was known in town as an expert carpenter and handyman, able to create or fix anything with hammer, nails, and a saw. As a teenager, he supported his widowed mother and continued to do so until her death. He also provided the means for his sister to receive her education and training as a musician. According to his obituary, he never let the words "I can't" ever enter his vocabulary. In 1873, eighteen-

Charles, "The Armless Wonder," was often paired with Eli Bowen, "The Legless Wonder," and they became very good friends.

year-old Charles was hired by P. T. Barnum , who stole him away from the John Robinson Shows. He made the newspapers early while he was "teaming" to New York City in 1873. (Teaming means using a team of horses to pull a wagon.) An article claimed that Charles had to take off his boots three times to fix harnesses. It also stated that during the trip, he kept up an excellent written correspondence with Mr. Barnum because Charles wrote a good "foot." He worked for Barnum and then Barnum and Bailey for over twenty years. Later he toured with Ringling Bros. and Barnum & Bailey shows for over a decade. He was often paired with Eli Bowen, "The Legless Wonder," and they became very good friends. In 1883, he was paid forty dollars a week while Eli made sixty dollars. Both were substantial wages at that time. Both Charles and Eli Bowen publicly protested being called "freaks" and lobbied to be referred to as "prodigies" but the press did not take the protests seriously. A 1903 article pokes fun at a New York meeting where Charles was in attendance: "The human pin-cushion presided and the facile pen of the armless prodigy took down the minutes of the meeting."

Charles was always the perfect gentleman and dressed impeccably on and off stage. According to published press releases, he had many female admirers. He wed, date unknown, Mae E. Tripp. The couple never had children. His marriage was not publicly acknowledged for years to protect his image as an eligible bachelor. Charles died on January 26, 1930, in Salisbury, North Carolina, from kidney disease and complications of pneumonia. He was seventy-four. He is buried in the Haven Hill Cemetery in Olney, Illinois. After his death, friends in Olney displayed furniture that Charles had made in Bower's Drug Store, a tribute to an amazing man, a true "armless wonder." ♦

ANN ELIZA LEAK, "THE ARMLESS WOMAN"

Ann Eliza Leak was born in Griffin, Georgia, on December 23, 1842, without arms. She overcame the loss of arms by developing the dexterity of her feet and toes to the extent that she could write, sew, thread a needle, crochet, knit, braid hair, and eat with utensils. She attended a girls' school in Griffin and claims the pupils were kind to her. She had a raised platform instead of a desk and held books in her toes. She learned to write with her left foot since her right leg was shorter than the left leg.

Ann was twenty-three years old when the Civil War ended. She lost brothers in the conflict and her family, like many Southern families, was left financially devastated. In 1865, Ann first appeared at P. T. Barnum's New American Museum in Brooklyn. One newspaper reported: "Audiences never tire of watching this noble and patient woman." It must have been difficult for a somewhat sheltered Southern woman to travel to New York City so soon after the war and to work in an environment that was so very different from the one she had always known, but Ann always claimed she

Ann Eliza Leak was born in Griffin, Georgia, on December 23, 1842, without arms. She overcame the loss of arms by developing the dexterity of her feet and toes to the extent that she could write, sew, thread a needle, crochet, knit, braid hair, and eat with utensils as well as any person without disabilities.

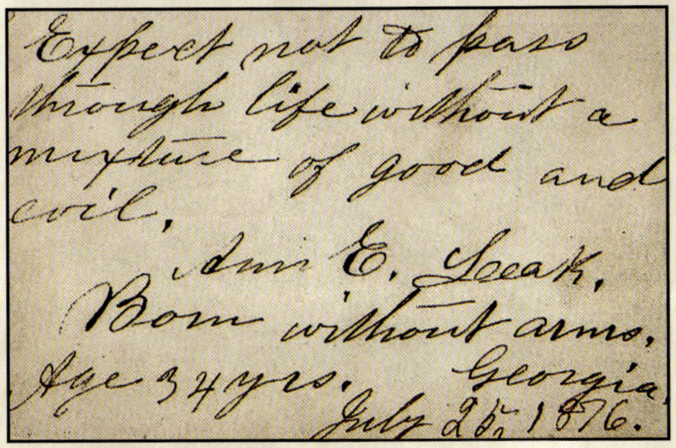
Expect not to pass
through life without a
mixture of good and
evil,
Ann E. Leak,
Born without arms,
Age 34 yrs. Georgia
July 25th 1876.

Ann continued to amaze her audience by demonstrating her skills with her feet. She would sign purchased trade cards and carte-de-visites on the back and enjoyed including simple poems or messages along with her dated signature. She was known for her fine embroidery.

In May of 1872, thirty-year-old Ann married William R. Thompson. They had one son.

accepted her role as family provider and felt no resentment. In her autobiography that was sold at shows she wrote: "Providence had assigned me, and my feet seemed to be directed in the path that I was about to tread." Newspapers often reported on Ann's beauty. As one reporter wrote, "...she is good looking, and any man in want of a wife who can't pull his hair, scratch his eyes, or thump him with a broomstick should pay his addresses to Miss Leak." It did not hurt her act to show a good portion of her legs performing stunts at a time when a show of the ankle was considered titillating by the outwardly prudish Victorian audience.

Ann did find true love, if late by Victorian customs. In May of 1872, thirty-year-old Ann married William R. Thompson of Philadelphia in Chester, Pennsylvania. He was a steamship engineer. They would have one son. After her marriage, Ann exhibited under the name Ann Leak Thompson, "The Armless Woman."

MYSTERY TO SOLVE

Did the couple go to Australia and make a great deal of money? What eventually happened to Ann after 1891, and where is she buried?

Ann was still exhibiting as late as 1891, but then seems to have disappeared from public life. Several newspapers claim the married couple went to Australia and made a great deal of money.

Ann continued to amaze her audience by demonstrating her skills with her feet. She would sign purchased trade cards and carte-de-visites on the back and enjoyed including simple poems or messages along with her dated signature, such as, "I'll write a little bit, for your especial benefit," "Expect not to pass through life without a mixture of good and evil," and "He who loans to all shows good will but little sense." Ann was still exhibiting as late as 1891, but then seems to have disappeared from public life. Several newspapers claim the married couple went to Australia and made a great deal of money. Let's hope so. Or it might have just been that a fifty-year-old woman was no longer limber enough to perform the long hours required of a sideshow performer. ♦

ELLA HARPER, "THE CAMEL GIRL"

Ella Harper was born in Tennessee in 1873. She was born with a condition known as genu recurvatum that loosely translates as "backward-bending knee." This is a rare deformity in the knee joint so that the knee only bends backwards. A person with this condition would usually experience great pain later in life.

In 1886 she was featured as the star in W. H. Harris's Nickel Plate Circus, having been with the show for four years. This is the text from Ella Harper's pitch card, an advertising flier for the sideshow:

> I am called the camel girl because my knees turn backward. I can walk best on my hands and feet as you see me in the picture. I have traveled considerably in the show business for the past four years and now, this is 1886 and I intend to quit the show business and go to school and fit myself for another occupation.

Nothing is known about her life after 1886 and only three photos of Ella are known to exist. She first exhibited at age nine. W. H. Harris's Nickel Plate Circus originated in Chicago in 1893 and operated until 1902. It was best known for the brutal story of Gypsy, the circus elephant that trampled her trainer to death in November 1902 in Valdosta, California. She was shot by the police chief of Valdosta. Reportedly, Gypsy had killed several men, one with the Cole Brothers Circus, before Harris purchased her. ♦

Nothing is known about Ella's life after 1886 and only three photos of Ella are known to exist. She first exhibited at age nine.

MYSTERY: TO SOLVE

What happened to Ella after 1886? Her life, death, and burial place remain a mystery.

Ella Harper was born in Tennessee in 1873. She was born with a condition known as genu recurvatum that loosely translates as "backward-bending knee."

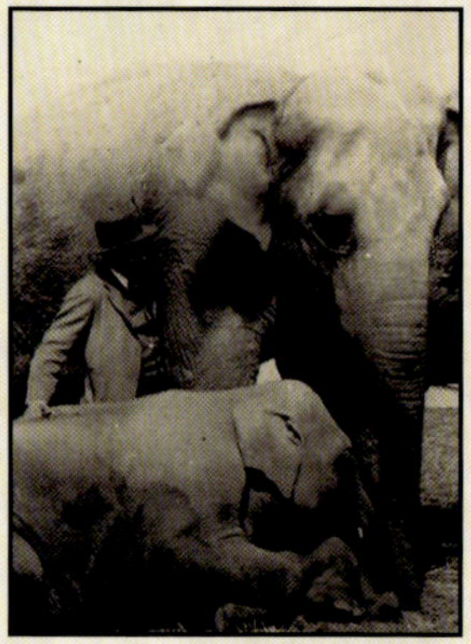

The W. H. Harper's Nickel Plate Circus is best known for the brutal story of Gypsy, the circus elephant that trampled her trainer to death in November 1902 in Valdosta, California, and was shot by the police chief.

GEORGE WILLIAMS, "TURTLE BOY," "THE ARKANSAS TURTLE BOY," OR "KING DODO"

George Williams was born in Washington, Arkansas, around 1866 with a rare bone disease known as parastremmatic dysplasia, a severe form of dwarfism that twists and deforms the limbs. His feet resembled the flippers of a turtle, hence his stage name, and his arms and legs were severely deformed. He appeared to have two knees on each leg. Another characteristic of the condition is a shortened neck.

This condition is inherited, so it is likely that another member of George's family was also afflicted with this disease; however, we know very little about his early years. The condition would have been apparent at birth. In an 1896 newspaper interview, a Mrs. Williams claims to be George's manager and foster mother. If that is the case, then "Williams" may not be the surname George was born with, and his parents, like so many of the day, may have given George to a sideshow manager either for a profit or to rid themselves of a child who was an embarrassment or too much trouble to care for. George was never able to walk and another side effect of his bone disease was incontinence.

MYSTERY TO SOLVE

When and where did George Williams die? Where is he buried?

When he was twenty-nine, he was eighteen inches tall and weighed thirty-five pounds. At seventy-eight, he claimed to be nineteen inches tall and twenty-nine pounds. His sideshow career spanned over fifty years and he was still performing at age seventy-eight, then as "King Dodo from the Fiji Islands." He added comedy and harmonica playing in his early years to his show. One reporter printed that George was "as good an entertainer as a freak." Another said he was "a most comical comedian." Some of his billings advertised him as "George Williams, The Humorous Turtle Boy." By all accounts, he was always in good humor, bright, and sharp-witted. George never married, although a publicity stunt in 1896 claimed George had entered into "an ill-fated marriage with Flossie Clark, a pretty white girl." According to the newspaper story, Flossie had "followed the dwarf from one museum to another and seemed infatuated." His manager and foster mother, Mrs. Williams, told the reporter, "How a girl in her proper senses could marry such an object as George I cannot imagine. Why, he is an imbecile. He is childish and not responsible for anything he does. He cannot read nor write and is helpless as a child." It is not clear if George was literate as many people of his time were not, but an 1894 article proclaimed him "one of the wealthiest freaks of nature in the museum business." How, when, and where George Williams died is a mystery, as is his final resting place. After the mid-1940s, the aging performer seems to have just disappeared from sight. ♦

His sideshow career spanned over fifty years and he was still performing at age seventy-eight, then as "King Dodo."

George Williams was born in Washington, Arkansas, around 1866 with a rare bone disease known as parastremmatic dysplasia, a severe form of dwarfism that twists and deforms the limbs.

GRADY FRANKLIN STILES JR., "LOBSTER BOY"

Usually we find ourselves pulling for the "freaks" of the sideshow, but not in Grady Stiles Jr.'s case. The fact that most of his family plotted and paid to have him killed somehow seems fitting. When Grady Stiles Jr. was sober, he was nice enough to convince his first wife to remarry him. When he was drunk, his action led to her divorcing him once and having him killed the second time, preferring the funeral expenses and quick widowhood to a divorce lawyer's fees, it would seem.

Grady Stiles Jr. was fifth in a direct line of male descendants born with the genetic birth condition known as "ectrodactyly" that is characterized by the congenital absence of all or part of one or more fingers or toes. It is also called "Split-Hand/Split-Foot Malformation" and "Lobster-Claw Deformity." His ancestors with ectrodactyly were William Stiles (1805–1888), Jacob Stiles (1843–1932), Elisha Stiles (1880–1935), and his father, Grady Stiles Sr. (1912–1988), who was the only other sideshow exhibitor. Most people only know of the infamous Grady Stiles Jr., however, due to the two notorious murder trials involving him.

Grady Franklin Stiles Jr. was born on July 18, 1937, in Pittsburgh, Pennsylvania. Grady's hands were split down the middle and fused to form two-digit "claws," and his feet were small flipper-like appendages at the end of shortened legs. He was never able to walk and used a wheelchair in public. He was able to get around in private by crawling, using his very strong arms and highly developed upper body strength. He performed almost all day-to-day tasks by deftly using his "claws." He was married three times, twice to Maria (Mary) Teresa Herzog and once to Barbara Browning. The genetic saga continued through the next two generations. Grady Jr. had four children. Two of the children were typically developed, Glen and Donna, but his son, Grady III, and his daughter, Cathy, were also born with ectrodactyly. Cathy married and gave birth to a daughter, Misty, who was born with the genetic disability in the 1990s. Grady III,

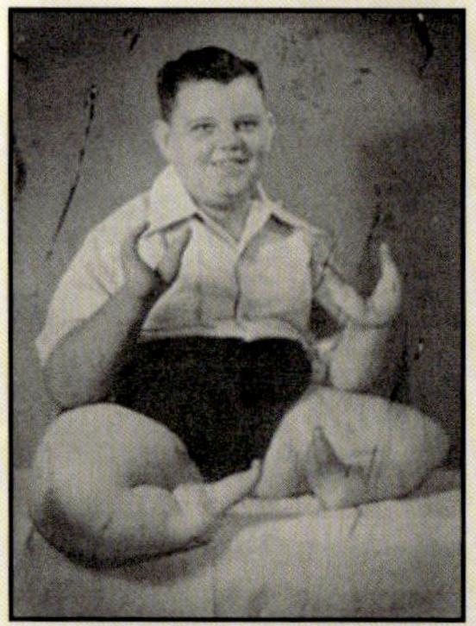

Grady Stile Jr. was the fifth generation to be born with ectrodactyly, a congenital disability often called "lobster-claw hand." His father had also been a sideshow performer.

Cathy, and Misty exhibited together. Reportedly, Grady was physically, verbally, and emotionally abusive to his wives and children when he drank, and he drank continually. He controlled his family with an iron hand, so to speak. When his eldest daughter, Donna (born typically developed), became romantically involved with a young man of whom Grady strongly disapproved, Jack Layne, Grady, forty-one, shot and killed eighteen-year-old Jack in cold blood on September 2, 1978, the day before the wedding was to take place. He was arrested, tried in court, and found guilty, but escaped prison time because his lawyer successfully argued that no prison was equipped to handle his disability. He was given the equivalency of a slap on the hand: fifteen years' probation on a third-degree murder conviction. He wheeled out of court a free man. Grady always claimed he accidently shot Jack when the boy lunged toward him and his disabilities made his aim bad. He swore in court that the shooting had nothing to do with his daughter's up-coming marriage.

Grady reconciled with and remarried his first wife, Mary Teresa, but soon after the nuptials, the physical abuse continued and, reportedly, even escalated. Grady appears to have learned at least one lesson from his trial experience, and unfortunately it was that he could get away with anything in the eyes of the law, including murder.

Some would say that the family was forced to take things into their own hands and claws, if one was to believe the testimony in court from witnesses after his wife went on trial for murder, this time Grady's. The family was living in Gibsonton, Florida, in a trailer at 11117 Inglewood Street when the shooting occurred. Mary Stiles later claimed she casually said something needed to be done about her husband's abusive behavior to her twen-

It is likely that the first person to exhibit as a "Lobster Boy" was Fred Wilson, shown here ca. 1885 as a young man. He was born in Somerville, Massachusetts, in 1866. Fred had ectrodactyly of the hands and legs, and his teeth were missing in his lower jaw. Unfortunately, little more is known of Fred's life story.

ty-year-old son by a previous marriage, Henry Glenn Newman III, "The Human Blockhead." His

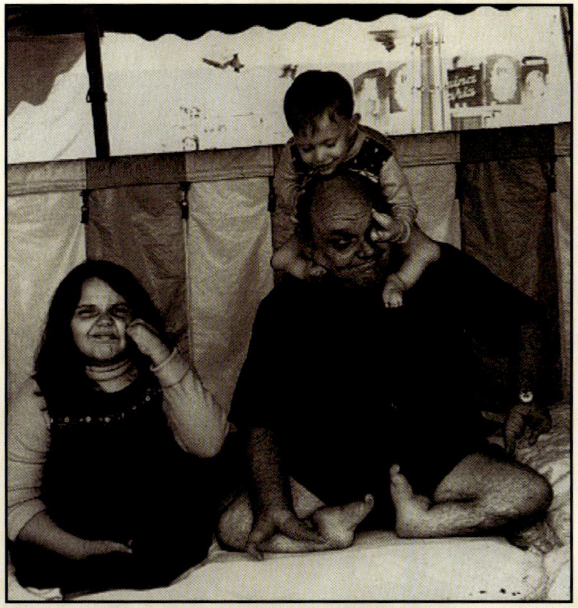

Cathy, Grady Stile III, and Grady Jr. photographed at a sideshow exhibit. They exhibited together as "The Lobster Family." Grady Jr. had four children: while Cathy and Grady Jr. both had ectrodactyly, the other two, Glen and Donna, did not have limb malformation.

father has been a midget. Henry remembered it very differently. He claimed in court that his mother pleaded with him to get someone to kill Grady for the sake of the family. On November 29, 1992, Grady was watching television in his underwear in the family trailer, drinking what would be his last beer, when nineteen-year-old Christopher Wyant, a neighbor having been paid the grand sum of $1,500, shot fifty-five-year-old Grady Franklin Stiles Jr. twice in the back of the head.

The trial was a media circus, no pun intended. The Associated Press ran headlines such as "Human Blockhead Convicted in Murder of Lobster Boy." Grady's daughter, Cathy, possibly still a little upset about her father killing her sister's fiancé, testified in court that "he was like Satan, himself." Mary Stiles tearfully testified at her sentencing hearing that "My husband was going to kill my family. I believe that from the bottom of my heart." Fortunately, or not so fortunately depending on your views, the prison system was equipped to house Mary Teresa, her son, and the hired hit-man. A sympathetic judge sentenced Mary Teresa to twelve years for manslaughter and conspiracy to commit first-degree murder. At that time, she had already spent two years behind bars. Christopher Wyant was sentenced to twenty-seven years in jail. "The Human Blockhead" received the harshest sentence. Henry Newman was convicted of first degree murder and conspiracy to commit murder. He was sentenced to life without the possibility of parole for twenty-five years.

Grady Stiles Jr. is buried in the Showman Rest Cemetery in Tampa, Florida. There was no mention of murder on Grady's official death certificate. ♦

FREDERICK WALTERS, "BLUE MAN"

Fred Walters, born in England in 1855, was not the only "Blue Man" with P. T. Barnum, nor was he the first or the last, but he was the most famous. When he died on August 20, 1923, in New York's Bellevue Hospital from heart disease, an autopsy was performed and it was discovered that not only was Fred's skin a dark indigo blue, but his organs and soft tissue were also tinted the same color, including his brain, heart, and muscles. He had been working at Dreamland in Coney Island at the time he was hospitalized.

According to his wife, Elsie Florence, in a newspaper interview after his death, Fred was heir to the title of Lord Graville had he wanted it. Instead he ran away from home, was a trooper in India and a captain in the seventeenth regiment in the Duke of Cambridge's own lancers. He was said to have turned blue after a horse fell on his body, injuring a heart valve. A few European physicians of the day supported the theory that an injury had, indeed, most likely caused the resulting blue hue. The common belief, however, was that Fred suffered from argyria, a chronic poisoning from excessive exposure to nitrate of silver. He had worked in the Australian silver mines in the 1880s and breathing the silver dust over a long period of time can cause the onset of the poisoning. There were actually a few other men and at least one woman in America who were also blue at the time and not in a sideshow. Their conditions were also attributed to silver poisoning. Almost immediately after turning blue, Fred began to pursue his career as a sideshow performer, which spanned almost forty years. He was one of P. T. Barnum's early attractions at his dime museum and traveled with his shows. In the finale of an 1892

Almost immediately after turning blue, Fred Walters began to pursue his career as a sideshow performer that spanned almost forty years. He suffered from argyria, a chronic poisoning from nitrate of silver.

Frederick Walters was sixty-eight years old when he died. He left a will in London, England, leaving all his effects to his wife, plus 212 pounds, fifteen shillings, and two pence or the equal to about $4,500 in today's market.

Barnum circus show, it was reported that "the Blue Man drove a 4-horse chariot" to the delight of the crowd. He also traveled to Europe with The Buffalo Bill Wild West Show in 1903–1905. The effects of argyria are not reversible but it is likely that Fred, not knowing this, may have ingested the chemical on a somewhat regular basis to, let's say, keep up appearances. While silver nitrate poisoning is not life threatening, it would explain why his internal organs were blue. He left behind a young widow and a six-year-old daughter when he died. His sideshow associates from Coney Island came to pay tribute to him. "The Bier of Blue Man" made a colorful newspaper piece of the day. Tears freely flowed and a midget was quoted as saying, "He was a gentleman." Frederick Walters was sixty-eight years old when he passed away. He left a will in London, England, leaving all his effects to his wife, plus 212 pounds, fifteen shillings, and two pence, the equal of about 4,500 Amercan dollars today. ♦

JOSEPH CAREY MERRICK, "THE ELEPHANT MAN"

Joseph Carey Merrick was born at 50 Lee Street in Leicester, England, on August 5, 1862, to a poor working-class family. He had two younger siblings, one with physical disabilities. His mother, Mary Jane Potterton Merrick, was also physically disabled, cited in most reports of the time as a "cripple." When Joseph was around two, his mother noticed rapidly developing disfiguring tumors on his neck, chest, and the back of his head. This condition continued to escalate until one of his arms became useless and hung at his side. At age five, he fell and injured his left hip. He developed a permanent limp when he walked. He was an above-average child in all other ways, intelligent and curious, plus a quick learner. Joseph learned to read, a rarity for members of his social class. Tragedy struck Joseph again at age ten. His mother died on May 29, 1873, of pneumonia. He had been very attached to her. Joseph's father married his landlady in 1875, but the new wife was not willing to be burdened with a child who was not hers and who required so much extra care and was unpleasant to look upon. In addition, Joseph's condition kept him from finding and keeping gainful employment in the village. She eventually forced the father to exile Joseph from the home. He went

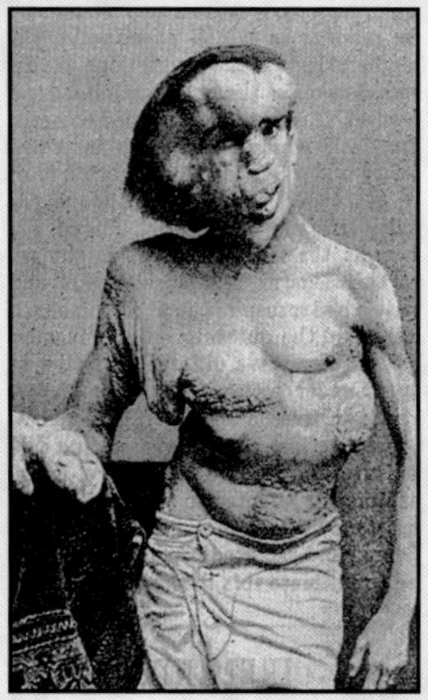
When Joseph Merrick was around two, his mother began to notice problems with her son. Joseph began rapidly developing disfiguring tumors on his neck, his chest, and the back of his head and this condition continued to escalate until one of his arms was only a useless club that hung at his side.

to live at the Leicester Union Workhouse in 1879, a dreary government establishment where homeless and destitute men, women, and children lived among the mentally ill and the infirm. The residents received a bed, a uniform, and meals, but each was required to do public work for his or her board. Joseph worked on the streets of the town selling shoe black, or shoe polish. His life was made even more miserable by the town's people, especially the children who constantly taunted him and threw rocks and rotten vegetables. By now, his face was completely distorted by the overgrown half of his head and the flesh disfigurement. He remained at the workhouse for almost four years.

Joseph willingly went to work as a sideshow freak billed as "The Elephant Man," a stage name given him because his nose resembled the trunk of an elephant. Show promoters claimed that his mother had been scared by a circus elephant while pregnant, thus "marked." London showman Tom Norman managed Joseph and was a fair and kind employer who genuinely cared for him and his well being. Joseph did very well as a performer and was able to make a good living. He moved to London and leased a home in Bedstead Square. He had been able to save 200 pounds from his earnings, a large sum at the time.

Unfortunately, Joseph was coaxed into touring Belgium with an Austrian manager who robbed him and treated him despicably, not providing enough food or adequate living arrangements. This manager left him stranded in a foreign country and destitute. He somehow managed to return to London in June of 1866. It was then that a policeman found Joseph in a train station, deathly ill, being abused by a mob of scared and shocked strangers. Joseph had a business card from Dr. Frederick Treves in his pocket. Dr. Treves had

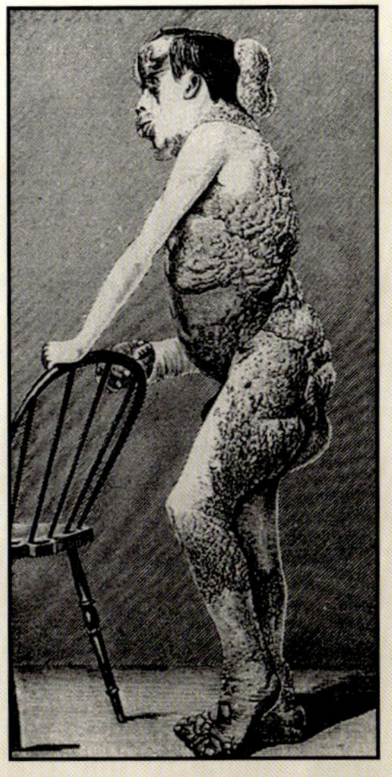

It took 100 years for doctors to correctly identify Joseph Merrick's medical condition. Proteus syndrome, an extremely rare disorder, was not identified until 1979.

previously presented Joseph before the London Pathological Society in 1844 and had been fascinated by this unusual man. Joseph was very ill, suffering from bronchitis and malnutrition. Dr. Treves brought him to the Whitechapel Hospital, nursed him back to health, and the hospital became his permanent home. Two hospital rooms were converted into his private quarters and a special chair was built for his comfort. Dr. Treves refers to Joseph in his 1922 memoirs as "John," and most attribute this to his advanced age, declining health,

Tom Norman was Joseph's first sideshow manager. He was a kind and fair man. Unfortunately, his second manager was a despicable man who robbed him and left him stranded in a foreign country.

and the poor memory of the good doctor when he wrote his studies. Joseph was relatively happy during the five years he spent at the hospital, but he was still socially isolated. He read and wrote poetry and prose. He passed time building wonderful architectural models from kits, even though that task must have been extremely difficult with the use of only one arm. The famous model he constructed of a church was built in 1888 from a German kit that Joseph most likely received as a gift. It is often erroneously reported that the model is of St. Phillips Church, which Joseph was able to see from his window. Reportedly, he built the church as a gift for a popular London stage actress of the day, Mrs. Madge Kendall, in the hopes she would come in person to pick it up. Unfortunately, she sent her husband to avoid having to visit Joseph in person. Today, that model is housed in London Hospital Medical College in a glass case, so it is probable that the actress or a member of her family donated it to the college after Joseph's death.

Joseph always longed for the freedom to walk about as an accepted human being. When going out in public, he always wore a disguise: a long, dark cloak and a black cap with an attached, loose-hanging, gray flannel drape, slit to allow vision. He also wore bag-like foot coverings. A poem often read and quoted by Joseph Merrick was this:

> 'Tis true my form is something odd, but blaming me is blaming God. Could I create myself anew, I would not fail in pleasing you. Was I so tall, could reach the pole, or grasp the ocean with a span; I would be measured by the soul. The mind's the standard of the man.
>
> —Author unknown

Joseph built his famous church model for a popular London stage actress of the day in the hopes she would come in person to pick up the gift. Unfortunately, she sent her husband. Today, the model is housed in London Hospital Medical College in a glass case.

Joseph died in his sleep on Friday, April 11, 1890. He was twenty-eight years old. As an adult, he had been forced to sleep sitting up because of the size and weight of his head. He was found lying down, suffocated, his windpipe crushed by his massive head. There has always been speculation that Joseph Merrick committed suicide. Others suggest he only wanted to lie down upon a pillow and sleep as most people can. His charge nurse had brought him his lunch but it had not been touched. He was found dead at 3:30 PM, lying prone across his bed. Joseph, a devout Christian, was not buried in a grave. Instead, Dr. Treves supervised the preservation of Joseph's body for scientific study. Plaster casts were made and samples taken but unfortunately most of those specimens were destroyed in the World War II bombing of London, through improper storage, or were stolen over the years. His skeleton is in a British museum. It took a hundred years for doctors to correctly identify his medical condition. During Joseph's lifetime, doctors claimed he suffered from elephantiasis. This is a disorder of the lymphatic system that causes parts of the body to swell. He actually suffered from Proteus syndrome, an extremely rare disorder not identified until 1979. Proteus syndrome was named for the Greek god who could change his shape. This rare genetic disease is a condition that involves atypical growth of the bones, skin, head, and a variety of other symptoms. Joseph had the most extreme case ever recorded.

In 1980, the film *The Elephant Man* was released. John Hurt played the role of Joseph Merrick and Anthony Hopkins starred as Dr. Treves. It was directed by David Lynch. The film was an immediate cult favorite and is fairly historically correct, with the exception of three major facts: first, the royal family never intervened to request the hospital give Joseph a permanent home; second, Joseph Merrick's speech was very slurred due to the condition of his mouth and jaw (only a few people close to him could comprehend what he said); and third, the portrayal of Joseph's first manager and his days as a sideshow freak were grossly misrepresented. Joseph was treated very well by Tom Norman and made a good living while Tom was his manager. In addition, one can only speculate about the riches he could have acquired and the life he could have led if he had been promoted by and toured with the legendary showman P. T. Barnum. ♦

Joseph Merrick died in his sleep on Friday, April 11, 1890. As an adult, he had been forced to sleep sitting up because of the size and weight of his head. He was found lying down, suffocated, his windpipe crushed by his massive head. There has always been speculation that Joseph Merrick committed suicide. Others suggest he only wanted to lie down upon a pillow and sleep.

LIVING HALF-LADIES

In the late 1880s and early 1900s, "Living Half-Ladies" were big draws for dime museums and circuses. They were advertised under names such as Tharnia, Thuma, Thola, Thepia, Rolo, Roila, Rhoda, Flora, Fatuna, Zanzille, Mythia, Clytie, and Vanditta. There were many others, as well. Unfortunately, the performers were mostly fakes and the exhibits were "gaffs," the sideshow term for a manufactured false oddity. These gaffs were usually poorly constructed, put together using wood, paint, chicken wire, fabric, and such. They were designed to look like a half of a woman, but most were so badly crafted they could not have passed inspection even from a nearly blind, drunk fair-goer.

The performers used magic tricks to pull off the "half- lady" act. The most popular magical illusions used a shelf, table top, or swing to carry out the trick, all using mirrors, painted screens, dark fabric, and such. Wesley Jakes is credited with being the creator of the "living half-lady." His 1900 obituary notice read: "Wesley Jakes is dead. Many a man more widely mourned has done less for his fellow beings. He invented 'The Cardiff Giant' and the living half-lady' and other harmless and interesting frauds. He was reduced to poverty, and when he died was a glass blower in a Chicago museum." One of the more tragic stories involving a "living half-lady" was the sad saga of Belle Carter (real name Estelle Doane) who was a performer at White's Museum. On July 30, 1890, the young dark-skinned beauty drank strychnine in a hotel room in Lima, Ohio, where she had traveled to meet her lover, Max Cohen. Max, it seems, had second thoughts and left town a few days before Belle arrived, leaving no forwarding address. In her trunk officials found numerous photographs of her as a "living half-lady." ♦

The majority of the "living half lady" performers were fakes. These gaffs were usually poorly constructed, put together using wood, paint, chicken wire, fabric, mirrors, and such.

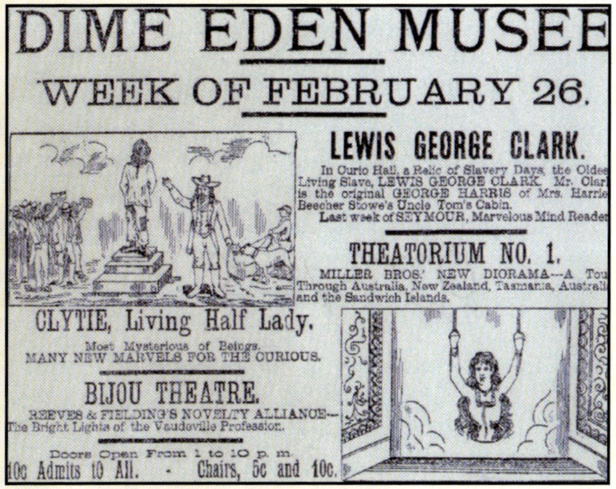

DIME EDEN MUSEE

WEEK OF FEBRUARY 26.

LEWIS GEORGE CLARK.

In Curio Hall, a Relic of Slavery Days, the Oldes Living Slave, LEWIS GEORGE CLARK. Mr. Clar is the original GEORGE HARRIS of Mrs. Harrie Beecher Stowe's Uncle Tom's Cabin.

Last week of SEYMOUR, Marvelous Mind Reader

THEATORIUM NO. 1.

MILLER BROS.' NEW DIORAMA---A Tou Through Australia, New Zealand, Tasmania, Australi and the Sandwich Islands.

CLYTIE, Living Half Lady.

Most Mysterious of Beings.
MANY NEW MARVELS FOR THE CURIOUS.

BIJOU THEATRE.

REEVES & FIELDING'S NOVELTY ALLIANCE--
The Bright Lights of the Vaudeville Profession.

Doors Open From 1 to 10 p. m.
10c Admits to All. - Chairs, 5c and 10c.

1888 dime museum advertisement for Clytie, Living Half Lady who was a gaff.

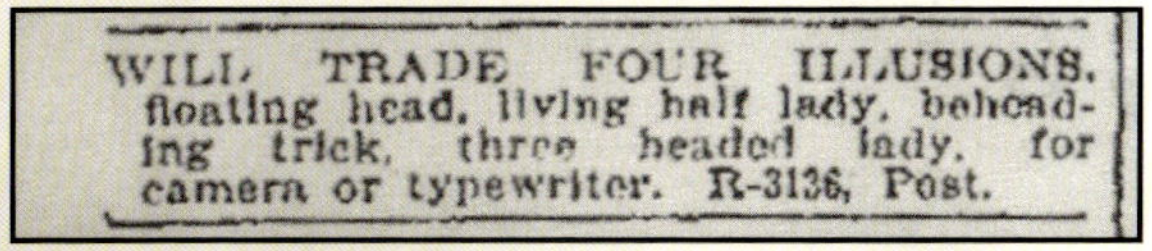

WILL TRADE FOUR ILLUSIONS, floating head, living half lady, beheading trick, three headed lady, for camera or typewriter. R-3136, Post.

1905 classified ad

MADAME GABRIELLE (GABRIEL), "THE LIVING HALF-LADY," OR "THE LIVING HALF-WOMAN"

Most of what we know about Madame Gabrielle De Fuller (born around 1884–89), we find on her trade cards. She claimed she was born in Switzerland, and we know she exhibited at Coney Island, traveled with The Ringling Bros. Circus, and that she was the real thing. While most "living half-ladies" of the day were merely magical illusions or poorly constructed gaffs, the beautiful Madame Gabrielle was only thirty-two inches in height. She was married at least once (most accounts say two or three times) since she first exhibited as a "mademoiselle," the French term for an unmarried woman. She exhibited in America around 1913–1926 and had a national reputation as a pianist and composer. ♦

MYSTERY TO SOLVE

What of her younger years? She was obviously raised in refinement. Where did she spend her last years, where and when did she die, and where is she buried?

Photos ca. 1920 of Madame Gabrielle.

So little is known of the life and times of this beautiful living half lady.

CHARLOTTE LINDA VOGEL, "SUSI, (SUSIE, SUZIE, SUZI) THE ELEPHANT-SKINNED GIRL," OR "SWAMP GIRL"

Charlotte Linda Vogel was born on February 26, 1908, in Charlottenburg, Germany, near Berlin. In newspaper interviews she would often claim to be Austrian or Swiss, but official documents stated that she was born in Germany and was a German national. Official records at the time gave her height as five feet, four inches and her weight as 124 pounds. Her passport photo shows an exotically beautiful dark-haired young woman, but unfortunately she suffered from an extreme case of ichthyosis that resulted in her entire body, except for her face, being covered with thick, rough, and discolored skin. This is an extremely painful condition. The person cannot sweat and has to soak in ice or ice water to maintain a lower body temperature. The skin cracks and infection and bleeding are a constant concern. Charlotte always claimed that her mother, Anna, would soak her skin daily in oil to aid her child. Charlotte toured Germany and parts of Europe with her manager Julius Kuehnel (later Americanizing his name to Julius Friend) and his wife, Lena (Erna), before the trio came to America in March of 1927. They often lived together in New York City and New Jersey. The 1940 census states her profession as "salary worker, private work" for the Kitchnels [sic], indicating that at that time Charlotte preferred being a domestic to being a sideshow performer. She became a naturalized American citizen on July 6, 1944, in New York City at the age of 36. She had applied for citizenship earlier in 1936 but was either denied or failed to follow through with the paperwork.

Charlotte Vogel's trade card showing her dressed in almost nothing, a lure that always sells tickets, ichthyosis or no ichthyosis.

In 1929, she was a top attraction at Coney Island. In 1933, she exhibited at the Chicago World's Fair with Ripley's Believe It Or Not Odditorium. She worked for top dime museums, circuses, and at state fairs, plus made several trips home to Germany until the pre-war climate in Germany made travel dangerous. In 1952, Charlotte was a main attraction at Hubert's Museum on 42nd Street in New York. She would first exhibit her body to an awed audience and then offer a three-part package for the price of a dime. Frank Schuerger wrote in the *Plain Dealer* newspaper: "Part 1 is an explanation of why Susie can never get married and it has nothing to do with her skin. Feature No. 2 is the story of the Swiss woman's life, and No. 3, this is the clincher, a French picture that has to be held up to the light to be appreciated." Possibly this article explains the erotic common trade photo of Charlotte dressed in almost nothing, a lure that always sold tickets, ichthyosis or no ichthyosis. In the late 1960s, an aging and always ailing Charlotte was tiring of the pressures of multiple shows per day. Her last performance was as a single

Charlotte worked for top dime museums and circuses and at state fairs. She exhibited several times a day in spite of her painful skin condition and had a reputation as a sweet and kind lady who never complained.

daily exhibit, billing herself as "The Swamp Girl." The *Omaha World Herald* reported in a 1966 article: "And crowds still flock into another freak show, Strange Cargo, featuring the swamp girl. It makes no difference that a big sign reads: 'The most unquestionable hoax of all time'". Charlotte died February 2, 1976, in New York City, just a few days short of her sixty-eighth birthday. Her burial site is unknown. ♦

CONJOINED TWINS

Conjoined twins occur when identical twins fail to separate in a developing embryo. There are many different kinds of conjoined twins including the following:

Craniopagus: Fused at the top of the head or skull; this is the rarest form of conjoined twin and the hardest to separate.

Thoraco-omphalapagus: Share a heart; this is the most common type of conjoined twin; bodies are fused from upper chest to lower chest.

Xiphopagus: Joined at the xiphod process (part of the sternum) and usually linked only by cartilage and soft tissue; often their livers are fused; these are the easiest of all conjoined twins to separate.

Pygopagus: Fused backside to backside, usually from waist to pelvis.

Ischiopagus: Fused at the backbone or tailbone with spines at an 180 degree angle to one another.

Omphalopagus: Fused from the lower breastbone to the waist.

Dicephalus: With one body but two separate heads and necks.

Cephalopagus: With conjoined necks and heads, but separate bodies; due to the malformations in the brain, these twins are never viable; in all cases, those that are not stillborn die within a few hours.

The overall survival rate of conjoined twins is only somewhere between five and twenty-five percent. Medical and historical records over the past 500 years only detail about 600 surviving sets of conjoined twins with more than seventy percent of those surviving pairs being female twins. There are no documented cases of conjoined triplets or quadruplets. ♦

CHANG AND ENG

Chang and Eng, xiphopagus twins, were born on May 11, 1811, in Siam (present-day Thailand). They are considered the original sideshow conjoined twins and the term that was long used to denote all conjoined twins, "Siamese twins," was coined from Chang and Eng (the phrase is no longer considered appropriate). Interestingly enough, the boys were three-quarters Chinese and were known in their tiny village of Mekong as "The Chinese Twins." Their mother gave birth to twelve other children, including several sets of twins. Chang and Eng were joined at birth by only a small band of cartilage at the sternum. The band was approximately an eighth of an inch thick, about six inches long, and only an inch and a half wide at adulthood. The twins, born face-to-face, stretched the flexible band over the years to allow them to stand side by side. Their livers were fused but each had a complete liver that was not dependent on the other. They could have very easily been separated, even in 1811, if anyone had chanced to do so. In America, they were constantly being examined by

Chang and Eng are considered the original sideshow conjoined twins and the term we use to denote all conjoined twins, "Siamese twins," was coined from Chang and Eng's birthplace, Siam.

The twins, born face-to-face, stretched the flexible band over the years to allow them to stand side by side.

Visitors to the Mütter Museum in Philadelphia, Pennsylvania, can view the plaster death cast of the twins.

From left to right: Sally, Eng, Chang, and Adelaide with two of the twenty-one children the two sisters had with the two brothers.

doctors in the towns where they performed, as was the custom with exhibiting freaks. Many of those doctors claimed that to separate them would mean immediate death to one or both.

The reigning monarch of Siam, King Chowpahyi, was convinced the birth of such unusual babies would cause destruction for his country and sure death for the masses. For a while, the boys' lives were in great jeopardy. A British merchant named Robert Hunter discovered the twins in 1824 and eventually persuaded both the king and the boys' now-widowed mother to allow the boys to be exhibited for profit in America. They were taken out of the country in 1829 by Captain Able Coffin aboard the ship *Sachem*. They toured in America and Europe and were a regular star attraction at P. T. Barnum's New York dime museum. They were not allowed to be exhibited in France since the French government strongly believed that to view such a sight would result in monsters (the medical term for freaks) being born to pregnant French women who would be "marked." At the age of twenty-one, they became their own managers and were quite good businessmen. Facing the brothers, Chang is on the right and Eng is on the left. Chang was an inch shorter than Eng, but he was the stronger, more dominant twin. In 1844, tired of the constant turmoil of the world of show business, they retired and settled in Mt. Airy, North Carolina. They adopted the last name of Bunker, influenced by a close friend and his family whose surname was Bunker. Chang and Eng began to enjoy a rich social life and soon courted two sisters, Adelaide (October 11, 1823–May 21, 1917) and Sarah Ann "Sally" Yates (December 18, 1822–April 19, 1892). The locals, who had befriended the two brothers previously, disapproved strongly when the couples announced their engagements, not because they were conjoined twins or even on grounds of moral decency with the obvious lack of carnal privacy, but they objected because they were of a different race.

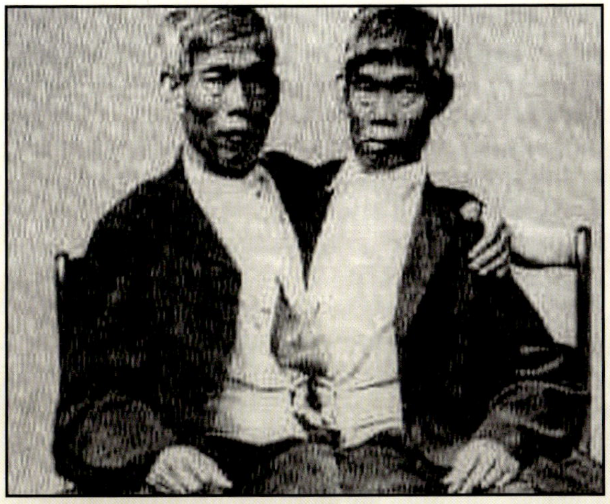

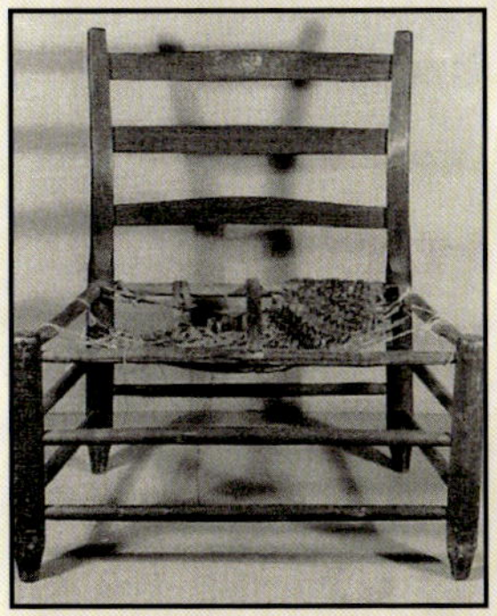

Eng and Chang sitting in their specially constructed chair.

It was during this time that the brothers secretly sought out doctors in Philadelphia to have an operation to be surgically separated. They wanted the operation to prepare themselves for marriage and the carnal duties of marriage. However, the sisters intervened. Fearing that one or both twins would die, they tearfully persuaded the brothers to cancel the procedure. They were married on April 13, 1843, in a double wedding ceremony with the good citizens of the town finally accepting the situation, if not whole-heartedly approving of such. They purchased a farm, built a home, and all lived together under one roof for nine years. It was the feuding of the two sisters that finally forced the brothers to purchase a second home in 1852, this

Chang had ten children while Eng had eleven. Also in this picture on the far right is "Aunt Grace," a slave who cared for the children for both Bunker families.

one in town. It was at this time, with the wives' urging, that they divided their finances into two separate estates. The brothers followed a strict regimen of three days at one house and three days at the other, with the "guest" brother completely submitting to his "host" brother's demands, no questions asked. They fathered twenty-one children, Chang having ten and Eng with eleven. All children were free of disabilities with the exception of two of Chang's children who were born deaf and mute. Sadly, three of Eng's children died before reaching adulthood. Initially, the youngest children would stay at the farmhouse with Sally and the school-aged children would stay at the house in town with Adelaide. In later years, some children would do sideshow appearances with their fathers. Three times during this period in their lives (1849, 1853, 1860), Chang and Eng were forced out of retirement to exhibit themselves for an extended period of time to earn additional money that was needed to feed so many mouths.

For the most part, the brothers were successful Southern gentlemen farmers who raised tobacco and prospered until the Civil War. They were slave owners, at one time owning a total of twenty-eight

slaves, and the brothers had the reputation of being hard on them. They were almost financially ruined at the end of the war when the slaves were freed. Eng was hit the hardest because he owned more slaves but less land than Chang. They once again went back on tour in 1869 to reclaim some wealth. Today, the direct relations of Eng still consider themselves the poor side of the family.

The brothers had very different personalities and, at times, fought physically. Chang drank, Eng did not, but Eng had to endure the drunken conduct and violent rages of his brother. Eng liked to stay up late and play checkers, chess, and poker, but Chang liked to go to bed early. Chang was stronger and had a temper. Eng was calmer and slow to anger. Chang had developed a spinal curvature and both brothers were partially blind in their anterior eyes, most likely from having to continuously look outward and obliquely.

In 1874, Chang died suddenly during the night of January 17. He had suffered a minor stroke a few years prior, and that stroke, combined with his heavy drinking, contributed to his deteriorating health. He had also been fighting a severe case of bronchitis and was recovering from an accident.

Eng, on the other hand, was in top health. Eng awoke to find his brother dead, and in fright, began screaming for his wife and children. Legend varies, but according to most stories, the family sent for a doctor to perform an emergency separation, but Eng had died from sheer terror by the time the doctor arrived. A more romanticized version claims that Eng refused to be separated from his dead brother. Eng died three hours after Chang. The brothers were sixty-three. Their grave is at the White Plains Baptist Church Cemetery in Surry County near their home. The land for the church and cemetery had been donated by Chang and Eng and the twins helped in the building of the church. (Sally's name is on the large, common stone, but for whatever reason, she is buried separately on Eng's farm.) Inside the church was a specially constructed two-seater pew. Today, visitors to the Mütter Museum in Philadelphia, Pennsylvania, can view the plaster death cast of the twins and see their fused livers preserved in a glass jar of formalin. ♦

MILLIE-CHRISTINE MCKOY, "THE TWO-HEADED LADY," "TWO-HEADED NIGHTINGALE," "THE CAROLINA TWINS," "THE AFRICAN TWINS," OR "THE CAROLINA NIGHTINGALE"

Since Millie and Christine referred to themselves in life in the singular, I will, out of respect, also refer to them that way in this book.

Millie-Christine McKoy was born on July 11, 1851, in the little township of Welches Creek, North Carolina, about six miles from Whiteville in Columbus County. She was a pygopagus twin, fused together from the waist down the buttocks. Her parents, Jacob and Monemia, were both typically developed and Monemia had given birth to seven other typically developed children prior to Millie-Christine. The family, including the siblings, all called the twins "sister" and thought of her as one child. In adulthood, Millie-Christine always thought of herself in the singular, as well, although she was known to have said, "Although we speak of ourselves in the plural, we feel as but one person." All family members were slaves owned by a blacksmith named Jabe McCoy. McCoy sold Millie-Christine on May 8, 1852, at the tender age of ten months, along with the infant's mother, to a showman named John C. Pervis for $1,000 plus twenty-five percent of the proceeds from her exhibitions. A provision in the contract stipulated that the mother was to remain with her infant. Pervis resold Millie-Christine or percentages of her, without the mother, until she reached her final owner, Joseph Smith. Smith located the mother and bought her back for the girl's sake. Millie-Christine's stage name was changed from "McCoy" to "McKoy" for reasons unknown. She weighed seventeen pounds at birth. She learned to walk at one year and to talk at fifteen months. The twins could not face one another, but were positioned at a 45 degree angle away from each other. She had two bladders, one pelvis, one uterus, and one rectum. Millie-Christine experienced hunger and defecated almost simultaneously, but experienced thirst and urinated sepa-

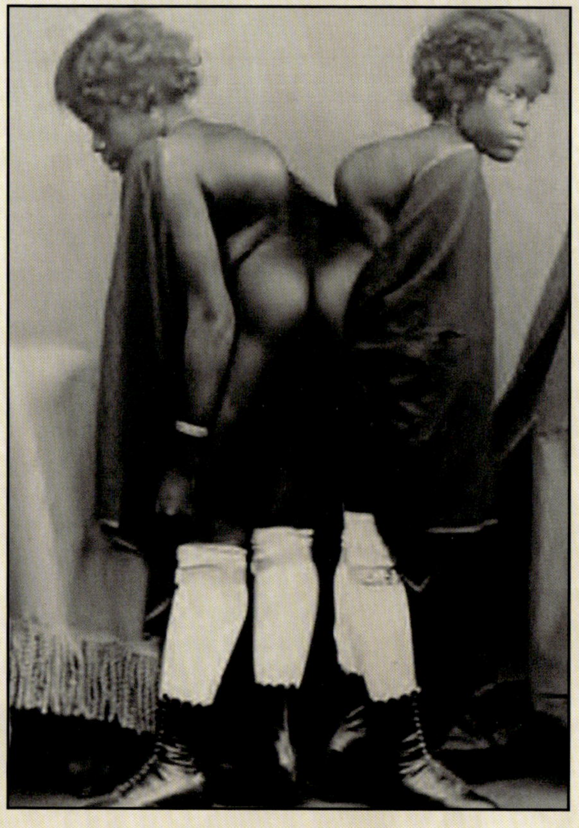

Millie-Christine's family all called the twins "sister" and thought of her as one child. In adulthood, Millie-Christine always thought of herself in the singular, as well. "Although we speak of ourselves in the plural, we feel as but one person."

CONCERT HALL

Chestnut Street, above Twelfth.

THOS. C. LOMBARD, - - LESSEE

Miss Millie Christino to be seen there and nowhere else than . . . At Concert Hall
The Eighth Wender of the World . . At Concert Hall
The 2-Headed Nightingalo . . At Concert Hall
Baron Littlefinger . . . At Concert Hall
Count Rosebud . . . At Concert Hall
One Person with Two Heads . . At Concert Hall
Singing by her in One and Two Voices . At Concert Hall
Dancing by her with Four Feet . - At Concert Hall
Pantomiming by Little Gentlemen . At Concert Hall
Dialogue by Little Gentlemen . . At Concert Hall
Fencing by Little Gentlemen . At Concert Hall
Count Rosebud's Personation of the Dutchess of Devonshire (in Character),. . . At Concert Hall

Miss Millie Christine, who is highly educated, refined and accomplished, and her Liliput Companions, the most Talented and most pleasing Dwarfs ever before the public, will be constantly in the Hall, either on Stage or promenading in the Audience.

Twice Daily this the most interesting and unique exhibition and entertainment - - At Concert Hall
To-day from 2 30 P. M. till 6 P. M. . . At Concert Hall
This Evening from 7.30 P. M. till 9.30 P. M. At Concert Hall

Admission, 25 Cts. Reserved Seats, 50 Cts. Children, 15 Cts.

Millie was a contralto and Christine was a soprano. The twins were celebrated internationally for an ability to harmonize and were often billed as "The Two-Headed Nightingale."

The custom of the day was for local doctors to examine sideshow performers and report their findings in local newspapers. Most managers considered this good free advertising. Millie-Christine was fourteen years old when she refused to be examined again. She claimed she had nothing more to prove.

rately. Reportedly, the twins could sense one another's feet being touched, but not each other's hands, arms, or face.

Christine was much stronger and larger than Millie and could easily lift both of Millie's legs off the ground and walk about with her. Also, the girls' legs facing front were far more developed than the back legs. The twins were able to lift the back legs up and walk only on the front legs, but preferred to walk on all four. Millie was said to have the stronger and more dominant personality, but fortunately the twins were in perfect accord with one another and never quarreled. While on exhibition in New Orleans, Millie-Christine, still only a very young child, was supposedly kidnapped, exhibited out of the country, and finally placed back into the arms of her mother and rightful owner after a lengthy and much-publicized court trial. This was most likely a publicity stunt, suspiciously like the publicity stunt P. T. Barnum used involving Annie Jones, the famous bearded lady, when she was also a very young child. To cast even more doubt on the kidnapping story, Millie-Christine had been on exhibit a Barnum's dime museum in New York City during the hoax. In January 1857 Professor John Lizars of the Royal Infirmary of Edinburgh wrote: "I have this day seen the African twins (girls) five and one half years old, who united by the backbones. They are sprightly and intelligent, romping with great freedom, speaking English like native children, and singing very sweetly. They are tastefully dressed and from the band of union being lower down the back, the spectator can scarcely believe they are one individual. One minute examination the band of union in between fifteen and seventeen inches in circumference, involving at the lease of the bone of the sacrum and coccyx immovable, and in all probability uniting the sacral nerves and the spinal cords, so as to constitute one individual, or two girls with one nervous system."

Millie-Christine was tutored in music and languages by Mary Smith, the wife of their manager. Song would become her preferred medium for the rest of her life. Millie was a contralto and Christine was a soprano. The twins were celebrated internationally for her ability to harmonize. She was often billed as "The Two-Headed Nightingale."

Due to Mrs. Smith's tutoring, she became an international star, learned to speak five languages fluently, and learned to play the piano (two pianos angled on stage). She also composed much of her own music and was an accomplished poet and dancer. Millie-Christine was requested several times for command performances before Queen Victoria when she toured England, and it is said the Queen found her remarkable. She presented Millie-Christine with matching exquisite brooches as a gift of appreciation on one occasion. As was the custom among sideshow performers, local doctors would insist on examining Millie-Christine when she was performing in their town to prove authenticity. Most managers considered this good free advertising for their freaks since the good doctors' results would be printed in local newspapers, causing quite a stir. Millie-Christine was fourteen years old when she refused to be examined again.

Millie-Christine earned as much as $600 a week and was one of the most recognized women in the world.

In 1969, the Columbus County Historical Society erected a historical marker on Highway 74, approximately five miles from the gravesite.

She claimed she had nothing more to prove.

When her manager, Joseph Smith, died in 1863, Millie-Christine used her earnings to care for Mrs. Smith and also to support her birth mother. She was willed to Smith's son, Joseph Jr., but the Emancipation Proclamation had ended slavery. However, she elected to stay with the family until Mrs. Smith's death. At the time, she was earning as much as $600 a week. Neither the institution of slavery nor the abolishment of that institution had much effect on Millie-Christine. She was one of the most recognized women in the world, made more money than most Americans, white or black, traveled the world, and lived a refined and cultured life both before and after the war.

In the very early 1900s, Millie-Christine retired to her hometown of Welches Creek, North Carolina. She had previously purchased the small farm where she had been born a slave. She built a large fourteen-room house on the land and moved there with her mother and many of her brothers and sisters. She had amassed a small fortune in the sideshow business that should have provided a comfortable existence for her family but for two factors: she was very generous and gave away much of her money to friends and relatives, and in 1909, fate dealt her a cruel blow. A fire consumed her home and most of her possessions, leaving her almost destitute. Also tragically lost were the many valuable gifts, photographs, letters, and souvenirs amassed from her years as a sideshow star and world traveler. Ironically, today White Marsh-Welches Creek fire station #15 is at 45 Millie-Christine Road. A small and modest six-room cottage was built to replace the lost house, but her health began to decline, possibly a result of the fire and the consequent stress and worry. Millie, always the physically weakest, contracted tuberculosis (Christine never caught the deadly disease). On the afternoon of October 8, 1912, Millie died. The attending physician, Dr. W. H. Crowell, had contacted John Hopkins Hospital when Millie took ill and inquired about separation. He was advised to give Christine massive doses of morphine upon Millie's death, indicating separation was not possible. Christine realized her sister had expired even before Dr. Crowell detected it. Reportedly, she spent the remaining hours of her life singing hymns and praying for a quick and merciful death. She died seventeen hours later on October 9. Millie-Christine was sixty-one years old. She lived longer than any female conjoined twins on record, to date, and was arguably more famous in her time than Chang and Eng, the original conjoined twins. A double coffin was constructed of cypress lumber by a neighbor and the funeral was held in a small country Baptist church near her home and the family cemetery where she was laid to rest. Her grave was originally adorned with a large grey metal marker that was placed over the grave. It consisted of two arches with a connecting slab. On that connecting slab were inscribed the words, "A soul with two thoughts. Two hearts that beat as one." Sadly, a brush fire destroyed that marker in the 1940s. Legend says that a guard was posted near the grave for almost nine months because rumors abounded in the small town that grave robbers wanted the bones to sell to a sideshow for exhibition or to a hospital for medical study. In 1969, the Columbus County Historical Society erected a historical marker on Highway 74, approximately five miles from the grave site. Millie-Christine's family graveyard had become almost completely obscured by overgrown brush and weeds. On November 22, 1969, her body was exhumed and reburied in the Welches Creek Community Cemetery. A large granite stone was erected by the historical society and engraved exactly as the original marker. A 1954 article by Rodney Council in the (North Carolina) *Our State Magazine* reported, "The twins were generous and left little property, but spent their retirement in cheerfulness, receiving thousands of visitors. Sunday was reserved exclusively for Negroes, with whom they were extremely popular, perhaps partly because of their benevolences." ♦

GIOVANNI AND GIACOMO TOCCI, "LACONA TWINS," "THE GREATEST WONDER OF NATURE," OR "THE EXTRAORDINARY TWINS"

The left twin Giovanni (often called Joseph, Jacob, John, or Juan in American newspapers) and the right twin Giacomo (often called James, Jacob, or Jacopo in American newspapers) were dicephalus conjoined twins born in Lacona, Turin, Italy, on October 4, 1877 (or July 4, 1875, as newspaper and advertising accounts differ) to nineteen-year-old Antonia Mezzano Tocci by natural childbirth. The twins were small, weighing less than eight pounds at birth. The mother eventually gave birth to nine children, all typically developed with the exception of Giovanni and Giacomo. According to a newspaper story of the day, the parents were first shocked and sought to keep the birth of the twins a secret, fearing ridicule by neighbors. Eventually, they allowed a committee of physicians to examine the boys and then quickly realized the lucrative opportunity the babies presented. The father started exhibiting his sons locally when they were only a few weeks old.

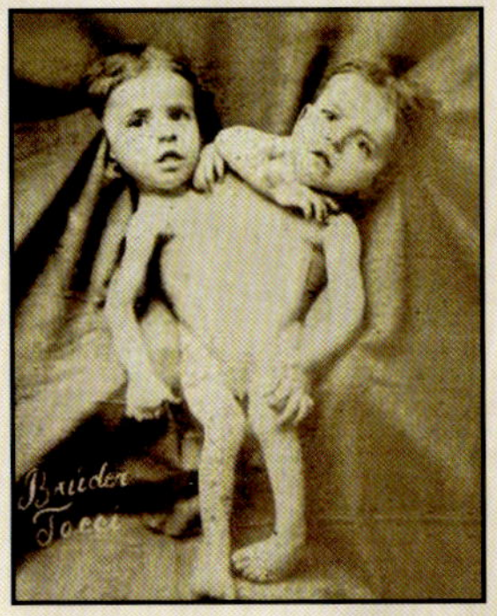

Giovanni (left twin) and Giacomo (right twin) Tocci were dicephalus conjoined twins born in Italy. Their parents quickly realized the lucrative advantage the boys offered and began to exhibit them in Italy when the twins were only a few weeks old.

The parents and family toured Italy and Europe with the twins until 1891 when they came to America. An article appeared in *Scientific American* describing the then fourteen-year-old twins as being connected from the sixth rib down, having two distinct stomachs, hearts, and a pair of lungs each. The article also reported that they had distinct arterial and respiratory systems with differing heartbeats and breathing rhythms. The American advertisements of the day proclaimed: "2 Heads, 2 Hearts, 2 Lungs, 4 Arms...All grafted upon a singular body with a single pair of legs and a single stomach."

Publicity ads of the day liked to proclaim the twins could "eat and drink separately, but all goes to one stomach." That was not true, but it was true that the boys could sleep at different times as well

The parents often exhibited their unusual twins with one of their typically developed brothers for effect. They came to America to tour in 1891 when the twins were around fourteen years old.

The twins had different personalities. Reportedly, Giovanni was the stronger twin, clever, alert, and a gifted artist. Giacomo was less bright, had no art skills, was somewhat club-footed, but was more social and conversed easily with the audiences.

The boys could sit but they could stand only with difficulty and had to balance by holding onto a chair or other stationary object for support. They never learned to walk.

as experience very different emotions at the same time. For instance, one could be sad while the other happy, one mad while the other was not.

The boys could sit but they could only stand with difficulty and had to balance by holding onto a chair or other stationary object for support. Giovanni and Giacomo would drag themselves along the floor by a cooperative effort using four hands, trailing their legs behind them, and never learned to walk. Giacomo's somewhat club-foot, most likely, also hindered the twins' ability to ever walk.

The twins also had different personalities. Reportedly, Giovanni was the stronger twin, clever, alert, and a gifted artist. Giacomo was less bright, had no art skills, was club-footed, but was more social and conversed easily with the audiences. Both boys spoke Italian and French but very limited English. They required an interpreter while in America.

MYSTERY TO SOLVE

What of the latter life of the twins? Did one or both marry? Did either father children? When did they die, and where are they buried?

In a *Boston Herald* story appearing October 19, 1893, it was reported a handsome and petite blonde was pursuing the sixteen-year-old brothers so intently that she had to be expelled from the Stone and Shaw Museum where the twins were exhibiting but "...neither Mr. Stone nor Mr. Shaw have control over the twins after the doors are closed at night." Of course, this was the type of publicity hype used and reused to create interest in performers and thus increase sales.

In 1897, the boys finished their tour of America and returned to Italy. They would have been around the age of twenty. Most accounts say they had tired of touring and, now as adults, were also tired of supporting their mercenary parents. They went home to retire, alone, and in seclusion. Some accounts even claim they married a pair of sisters, produced at least one child, and died in 1940 at the ripe old age of sixty-three. It would be nice to believe those romantic claims, even though they are highly unlikely and suspiciously mirror Eng and Chang Bunker's life, the conjoined twins they were constantly compared to in American newspapers and advertisements.

Mark Twain, fascinated by Giovanni and Giacomo's life story, wrote a short story, *Those Extraordinary Twins*, naming his conjoined twin characters Count Angelo and Count Luigi Capello. ♦

JOSEFA AND ROSA BLAZEK, "THE BOHEMIAN TWINS"

Josefa and Rosa were pygopagus conjoined twins born in Bohemia on January 20, 1878. They were the second and third child born. An older sister and a younger brother, Frank Jr., who was born in 1905, were both typically developed. The father, Frank Blazek, a farmer, was twenty years older than his wife. Newspaper stories later reported that the parents were simple people and overwhelmed by their strange infants. Reportedly, they gave the children up at age three to the French impresario Forbe. An impresario was the French equivalent of an American dime museum manager. Most likely, however, the parents first displayed Josefa and Rosa themselves locally and later allowed Forbe to basically "purchase" or "lease" the twins for profit, money trumping parenthood.

The twins were joined from above the hips to almost the knee. The backbones grew together in the region of the coccyx and they had only one pelvis but two vaginas. They could not look into the other's face, only give a sidelong glance. Josefa was taller. They got sick independently and could

Josefa and Rosa were conjoined twins born in Bohemia on January 20, 1878. They had an older sister and a younger brother, Frank Jr., who was born in 1887. The siblings were born free from physical disabilities.

not feel each other's pain. In childhood and early adulthood they were always described as delicate and frail. They also had different personalities, Rosa being the outgoing one and Josefa being reserved and quiet. In 1891, they were first exhibited in Paris, usually wearing exotic costumes to enhance their young beauty. Later they toured Europe and America. They were taught to play the violin and

Newspaper accounts say the parents were simple people and overwhelmed by their unusual infants. Reportedly, they gave the children up at age three to a French impresario, Forbe. Most likely, however, the parents first displayed Josefa and Rosa themselves and later allowed Forbe to "purchase" or "lease" the twins for profit.

In 1891, they were first exhibited in Paris, usually wearing exotic costumes to enhance their young beauty. Later they toured Europe and America. They were taught to play the violin and harp and were billed under the exotic name "The Bohemian Twins."

harp and were billed under the equally exotic name "The Bohemian Twins."

In 1906, various newspapers proclaimed that Dr. Otkar Kukula, president of the Prague College of Medicine had performed a successful surgical operation on the twins, separating them. "The operation was entirely successful and the young women are overjoyed at the separation." "The very remarkable surgical operation that has made two separate beings of the Bohemian Twins and enabled them to think and act apart." The story died down after a few months and was, of course, completely fictitious.

When asked by a reporter once about the difficulty of living attached, Rosa responded gaily, "We are very attached to each other in every respect."

On April 16, 1910, the newspapers announced that Rosa gave birth in Prague to a baby boy whom she named Franz after his alleged father, Franz Dvorak, who was a captain in the German army. The papers were buzzing with the story since it was related to the press that poor Franz was charged with bigamy and fined since by marrying Rosa he had also married Josefa. Conveniently, Captain Dvorak was "killed" in 1917 while bravely fighting for his beloved country. Rosa continued to use his

On April 16, 1910, the newspapers announced that Rosa gave birth in Prague to a disability-free baby boy whom she named Franz after his alleged father Franz Dvorak, who was a captain in the German army.

surname for the remainder of her life, respectability being a much sought after component of the time. Ironically, Rosa's manager contributed to the

Most likely, the birth of the baby was a publicity stunt and the child was obtained from an orphanage. By all accounts, however, Rosa raised her son with love and total support from Josefa.

child's upbringing for the first three years, obviously believing he was the boy's father, at least for a short period of time. This would indicate that he and Rosa had been intimate, not a far-fetched theory since they were young and spent much time together in close quarters traveling the sideshow circuit. It does not prove he was the biological father, however.

Since so much of what was publicized about the sideshow performers of the day was false or written to sensationalize their careers, the true account of young Franz's lineage will probably never be known. However, if Rosa had given birth to a baby, she would have been the only conjoined twin on record to do so. Most likely, the child was an orphan and adopted by the twins in an attempt to promote their careers. P. T. Barnum had used the same ploy years prior when it was publicized that Tom Thumb and his wife had given birth to a baby with no disabilities. The truth was they only "borrowed" a series of babies from American and European orphanages from time to time to enhance their show appeal, then dropped off each of the poor

In January of 1922, Josefa and Rosa retired to Chicago. They claimed they had amassed a large fortune from exhibiting and sought a home and rest from traveling. Most likely, their appeal had diminished as audiences of the day became more sophisticated and more was needed to entertain than two attached middle-aged women playing musical instruments and singing on stage.

infants in any convenient orphanage when the child grew too large.

To strengthen the debate, we only have to look at the location of the supposed birth of Franz: The Kukula Surgical Clinic in Prague. If the name is familiar it is because a "Dr. Kukula" is the Prague medical genius who supposedly surgically separated the twins in 1906. The media audience was very naïve at this time. Without television and the Internet, news traveled slowly and was seldom challenged. If it appeared in print, it just had to be true. No photos ever appeared of a pregnant Rosa and no news stories were written about a wedding or impending birth of a child until the child was actually "born." It was also widely reported that both twins were able to nurse the child. There is absolutely nothing to suggest that would have been even remotely physically possible considering the twin's biological makeup. A few years later, Josefa reportedly fell in love but her fiancé died before they could be wed. It was noted in one newspaper account that the child had been left in an orphanage while his mother and aunt were abroad. One could speculate that they, like Tom

Thumb, returned the child after the publicity stunt ran its course but missed the boy or the newspaper story shamed them into returning for the lad. By all accounts, Rosa raised her son with love and support from Josefa, and he is pictured in many of the later photographs used for publicity and trade cards. He was billed as "Franzel, The Son with Two Mothers" and appeared on stage with his mother and aunt. Franzel is German for "Little Franz."

In January of 1922, Josefa and Rosa retired to Chicago, a city with a large Czech population. They claimed they had amassed a large fortune from exhibiting and sought a home and rest from traveling. Most likely, their appeal had diminished as audiences of the day became more sophisticated with the advent of motion pictures. More was needed to entertain than two attached middle-aged women playing musical instruments and singing on stage. Sadly, in March of 1922, Josefa was admitted to Chicago's West End Hospital with yellow jaundice followed by pneumonia. Rosa soon developed bronchitis. Ten days later, on March 30, 1920, at 2:37 AM, Josefa passed away, followed several seconds later by Rosa. Doctors had sought permission to separate the twins upon Josefa's death when they realized she would, most likely, not recover, but the twins' brother, Frank Jr., adamantly refused, claiming he was speaking for his sisters. He was quoted in the newspapers: "No, not even if Rosa lives for hours after Josefa's death. There shall be no operation." The twins were 44. The newspapers of the day paint him as a greedy relative, only interested in inheriting his sisters' wealth, reported as "$200,000 and a large farm in Czecho-Slovakia." The twins died leaving no will. The courts postured that legally they were both the mother of young Franz and thus their intact estate should be left to their only child. Frank, the true grieving brother, ordered an autopsy to prove that only one of his sisters had given birth to strengthen his claim for at least one half of the estate. The autopsy proved that both twins were capable of bearing a child separately since each had a separate vagina. Rosa was declared the birth mother of Franz. It also proved that it would have been impossible to successfully separate the twins. Frank Jr. should have been ecstatic except that it was soon learned that his sisters' entire estate was worth only about $400. The twins were separated postmortem by surgeons on April 12, 1922, so that they could be cremated. Their ashes were intermingled in a single urn that was to be sent back to their birthplace. For whatever reason, the remains were instead buried in Chicago's Bohemian National Cemetery. When his mother and aunt died, eleven-year-old Franz was by their side in the hospital. What happened to the young child after their death remains a mystery. His maternal grandfather, aged 85, was still alive and living in Prague but his grandmother had recently passed away. He had an aunt, the older sister of his mother who had married and had grown children of her own, but she was also living abroad, plus it is doubtful Franz had met either. It is unlikely his uncle took the child in since he had immediately lodged a court case against Franz to inherit part of the estate of the two deceased sisters. Considering the times, it is likely that Franz ended up in an orphanage, full circle. ♦

LUCIO AND SIMPLICIO GODINO

Lucio John Baldelbar Godino and Simplicio Joseph Baldelbar Godino were conjoined twins born March 2, 1908, in Sulat, a province of Eastern Samar, in the Philippines Islands. They were the second and third child born to Leon Godino and his wife, Josefa. Their firstborn, a son named Jose, has no physical disabilities, nor did the parents. Lucio and Simplicio were pygopagus conjoined twins connected at the posterior. This is an extremely rare condition among male children and most pygopagus male twins are stillborn or die at birth.

Lucio and Simplicio were pygopagus conjoined twins, born connected at the posterior. This is an extremely rare condition among male children and most pygopagus male twins are stillborn or die at birth.

The parents quickly realized they had a money-making opportunity in their strange twins. On April 15, 1910, the entire family boarded the SS *Manchuria* to San Francisco. Lucio (when facing, on left) and Simplicio were two years old. Shortly after arriving in America, the parents, in essence, sold the twins to a sideshow manager, abandoned them, and sailed home with their three-year-old

The parents quickly realized they had a money-making opportunity in their twins. The boys were basically sold into the sideshow business when they were two.

They were treated very badly by early managers and in 1918 their plight caught the attention of The Brooklyn Society for the Prevention of Cruelty to Children. After a Supreme Court trial, they were rescued and awarded as "wards" of Teodoro R. Yangco, a wealthy Filipino ship owner and philanthropist, who had taken an interest in the boys after reading about their plight in the newspapers.

On July 13, 1929, the twins married their longtime sweethearts, two women from the Philippines whom they had known since childhood. The marriage ceremony was almost derailed when the Manila municipal court clerk ruled that the twins were one person, and a wedding would be an unlawful act of bigamy. The Secretary of Justice of Manila overruled the decision and two marriage licenses were quickly issued.

Jazz band of Lucio and Simplicio.

Passport photo of Teodoro Yangco from 1924.

son, much richer. There is no evidence that the parents ever saw the twins again. It is likely Lucio and Simplicio were not treated well in the Coney Island sideshow where they were eventually exhibited because in 1918 their plight caught the attention of The Brooklyn Society for the Prevention of Cruelty to Children. After a Supreme Court trial in which the twins were asked to testify, they were rescued and awarded as "wards" of Teodoro R. Yangco, a wealthy Filipino ship owner and philanthropist, who had taken an interest in the boys after reading about their plight in the newspapers. The 1920 census shows the twins, age eleven, living with Yangco in Washington, DC. The all-male household also consisted of a male secretary to Yangco, a chauffeur, a chef, a houseboy, a valet, and another twenty-year-old ward. The twins were students at Washington's St. John's School. In 1921, the twins returned to Manila to the permanent home of Yangco. They were sent to public school until 1924, then sent to Europe for two years to continue their formal education in a prestigious private boys' school. It was often noted in newspaper stories about the twins that even though Filipino was their native tongue, they spoke flawless English.

An amusing article appeared in several newspapers in 1925. The then seventeen-year-old twins learned to drive an automobile and developed a great liking for recklessly speeding within the city limits of Manila. Lucio, the twin with the more dominant personality, grazed a caribou cart and was sentenced to five days in jail. On appeal, it was successfully argued that to punish Lucio would mean that Simplicio would be illegally punished. Neither served any jail time and Lucio was released with only a stern warning.

Lucio and Simplicio were joined together in the rear by cartilage and skin. They claimed they kept the cartilaginous strip pliable through disciplined exercise. The cartilage was pliable, indeed, so much so that one could stand while the other lay in bed.

Both twins were accomplished athletes. Reportedly, they could swim, dive, run, ice skate, roller skate, play tennis, golf, and basketball, bowl, and play billiards. They were assistant Scout masters in Manila. On July 13, 1929, the twins married their longtime sweethearts, two sisters (not twins, as is often written) from the Philippines whom they had known since childhood. In an elaborate ceremony that was witnessed by over 5,000 in attendance, Lucio married Victorina Motos (born June 8, 1908) and Simplicio married Natividad Motos (born June 24, 1906) in the great Lourdes Cathedral in Intra Muros, the old Spanish city of Manila. Their guardian, Teodoro Yangco, was the twins' best man.

Lucio and Simplicio photographed with female pygopagus conjoined twins, Mary and Margaret Gibb aboard a steam ship, date unknown.

The twins and their wives toured together as dancing partners, the twins adding musical instruments to the performance. Newspaper headlines read, "Siamese Twins To Dance With Wives" and "Dancing Brides."

It was widely written in newspapers that a last-minute problem almost derailed the wedding. Manila's Municipal Court clerk ruled that the twins were one person, thus to marry two women would result in the unlawful act of bigamy. The secretary of justice of Manila overruled the decision and two marriage licenses were quickly issued. Publicity stunt or not, the public was intrigued by the story and a great deal of interest was generated for the newlyweds. This was beneficial to them when they arrived in America a few months later, touring together as dancing partners, the twins adding musical instruments to the performance. Some headlines read, "Siamese Twins To Dance With Wives."

Sadly, tragedy would come to the twins prematurely in life. Lucio contracted pneumonia while working and living in New York City. Both twins were hospitalized and Lucio appeared to be doing well when he unexpectedly passed away on November 24, 1936. Doctors rushed to separate Simplicio from his deceased brother. The operation was touted as a success and newspapers claimed "surgeons had saved the life of the survivor after he remained for nearly an hour attached to his brother's dead body." Doctors even declared that Simplicio would be allowed out of bed in a week or so, with expectations to leave the hospital soon after that. Unfortunately, Simplicio contracted meningitis and died on December 8, 1936. The twins were twenty-eight years old. Private funerals were held for each brother and their final burial site is unknown, but most likely they were laid to rest in Manila, the home of their guardian. If the twins had been born today, most likely they would have been successfully surgically separated, both children surviving the operation. Once asked by a reporter if they ever argued, Lucio responded, "Sure we argue sometimes, but only when we're playing bridge with our wives. Other times it's fifty-fifty." ♦

MARY AND MARGARET GIBB, "THE GIGLIO TWINS"

Margaret Gibb (1889–1969), the mother of pygopagus conjoined twin daughters Mary and Margaret, said in a 1930 newspaper interview, "the agony had been terrible. Then I lapsed into unconsciousness." Mrs. Gibb was referring to May 20, 1912, the day she survived the natural birth of conjoined twins. She is believed to have been one of the few women in the United States to do so at that time. She said, in the article, that for months after the birth she would not see nor talk with anyone. "I just wanted to be alone and brood over my grief and fanciful sorrow. Time heals

Mary and Margaret Gibb, conjoined pygopagus twins, were completely sheltered by their parents until the age of fifteen when they started their fifteen-year career at Coney Island and in vaudeville.

When asked once by an interested reporter how they spent their time since they never had any privacy, they responded, "When one sleeps, the other will read. When one sews, the other plays solitude. When one plays the piano, the other sings."

all wounds and in a very short time I found happiness crowding out every bit of imaginative sorrow I had. Now I find that instead of being cursed as I imagined at their births, I was really blessed because not every mother could have a more obedient pair of children than Mary and Margaret."

Mary and Margaret were joined at the base of the spine near the hips. They shared a common circulatory system, but could not feel each other's pain. Early on, doctors warned that to separate the twins would, most likely, result in the death of one or both. In later interviews, the conjoined twins would often declare, "We are perfectly happy as we are."

Mary R. and Margaret Stratton Gibb grew up in Holyoke, Massachusetts, with their father, Scottish-born John Rae Gibb (1884–1949), mother, and their younger sister, Dorothy, born ten years after the twins. At times, a paternal uncle and his wife also lived with the family. Mary and Margaret would continue to live with their parents until their deaths in 1967. Their father passed away in 1949, but their mother outlived Mary and Margaret by two years. Their sister, Mrs. Dorothy Havens, also lived in the home after the death of her husband.

The girls were completely sheltered by their parents. They never attended public school, instead receiving their education from hired private tutors. They seldom ventured far from home and had no childhood friends. Later in life, Mary and Margaret would claim they never minded being stared at, but it would certainly appear that the parents were very much opposed to the public gawking at their young daughters.

For whatever reason, all this changed when the girls reached the age of fifteen. The 1920 census shows their father's occupation as a "finisher" in a woolen mill. By the 1930 census, his occupation had changed to "manager vaudeville" and the girls were listed as "actress amusement". Most likely, the family realized the money-making opportunity available and embraced it.

The girls started their career in 1927 upon a vaudeville stage in Lowe's Theatre and at Coney Island. For over two years they performed an act that consisted of dancing and playing the piano. In 1930, the family traveled to Europe, exhibiting in France, Belgium, and Switzerland. That year the twins also debuted on the new "talking screen." They toured with the Keith circuit for four years and with Barnum and Bailey and Cole Brothers circuses from 1934 until they retired in 1941 and returned home.

By 1941, audiences were getting more sophisticated. Vaudeville was on the way out and movies were on the way in. Mary and Margaret were nice, Christian, wholesome girls from a small town, plus,

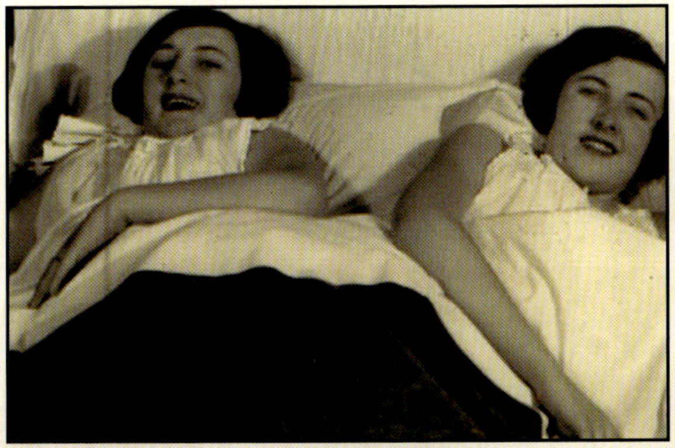

Mary and Margaret often said, "We have never had a cross word."

Mary and Margaret shared a common circulatory system, but could not feel each other's pain. Doctors warned that separating the twins would result in the death of one or both. In later interviews, the conjoined twins would declare, "We are perfectly happy as we are."

In 1929, when Margaret was seventeen, there were several newspaper stories reporting that she was seeking to be separated from Mary because she had fallen in love with Carlos Daniel Josefe of Mexico City and planned to wed.

When the twins voted on the issue of their country remaining dry, Margaret claimed she voted "dry" so "Mary could not go out and celebrate and she, Margaret, would suffer with a hangover."

truth be known, they had very little musical talent and were not great beauties. They no longer had the means to attract a wide audience base that was being wooed away by the many new and glamorous Hollywood motion picture stars and starlets with real talent.

On April 16, 1942, the twins opened "Mary-Margaret Gift Shoppe" in their home in Holyoke and the store remained in business for almost eight years, closing in 1949. The twins claimed they just wanted to live a quiet life after their fifteen-year circus and stage career and they did just that. After their gift shop closed, the twins were rarely seen around town for the next eighteen years of their life, with the exception of an occasional sighting of the girls on their way to the Presbyterian Church.

When asked once by an interested reporter how they spent their time since they never had any privacy they responded, "When one sleeps, the other will read. When one sews, the other plays solitude. When one plays the piano, the other sings." They said they both loved movies, but Mary enjoyed action movies like westerns, and Margaret preferred Mary Pickford movies. "One will nap if we don't like the movie we are watching." They both agreed on one thing, though: they each loved to cook.

Mary and Margaret remained single. In 1929, when Margaret was seventeen, there were several newspaper stories reporting that she was seeking to be separated from Mary because she had fallen in love with Carlos Daniel Josefe of Mexico City and planned to wed. On March 8, she and her parents (Mary in tow) traveled from New York to Newark, New Jersey and applied for a marriage license. The story died down within a few months and no wedding took place. Dr. Francis P. Westin, the doctor supposedly in charge of the case, was hounded by reporters. All the doctor would reportedly say was that "the proposed operation was very hazardous." Sadly, this intended marriage was, most likely, a publicity stunt meant to generate interest in the twins' early career but it would be nice to imagine that at least one twin experienced falling in love.

In 1933, they again made the newspapers in a story that circulated for several weeks. Mary and Margaret registered to vote, but commissioners were reluctant to grant them this right since voting privacy is a strict legality and the twins could not vote without each seeing the other's ballot. The twins voted for the first time in Holyoke's municipal election to decide if the district would become wet or dry. One headline read, "Siamese Twins Split Vote." Margaret claimed she voted "dry" so "Mary could not go out and celebrate and she would suffer with a hangover."

Both twins had dark hair and blue eyes but Mary was heavier and Margaret more fair. Mary was four feet, eight inches tall and Margaret was two inches taller. Their facial features also differed. Margaret suffered from health issues that Mary did not have. In 1946, Margaret had a stone removed from her bladder and in 1953, a tumor removed. They did not share each other's pain, but Mary had to be anesthetized during the operations along with Margaret and suffered with some post-operation maladies, as well, since they shared the same circulatory system.

Margaret and Mary Gibb passed away on January 8, 1967, at 12:35 PM in the Holyoke Hospital where they had been patients for eight days. They died from hypertensive heart disease. Margaret died first, quickly followed by Mary. An autopsy revealed that Margaret had bladder cancer that had spread to her lungs and to her sister's lungs. The twins were fifty-four years old and were the oldest conjoined twins in America at that time.

They are buried in Forestdale Cemetery in Holyoke, Massachusetts. In an interview, Mary once said to a reporter, "We have never had a cross word." ♦

PARASITIC TWINS

Parasitic twins are conjoined twins, one twin being small, less formed, and dependent upon the other. "Fetus in fetu" occurs when an imperfect fetus is contained completely within the body of its sibling; this condition can go undiagnosed for decades or remain undetected for life. ♦

LALOO, "THE HAPPY HINDU," OR "THE MAN AND A HALF"

Very little is known about Laloo's early life or background. What we know about Laloo is mostly taken from newspaper stories of the day. No official birth, death, or marriage certificates exist, and, most likely, his body was donated to science so no tombstone marks his final resting place.

Laloo Ramparsad Bhikaree always claimed he was born in 1872 in the village of Oovan in the Oudh region of eastern India. Supposedly he had two brothers, both dead by 1891, and an older sister, all typically developed, as were his parents. Laloo, however, was born with a parasitic twin attached to the lower right side of his sternum by a bony pedicle and attached lower by a fleshy mass. A parasitic twin differs from a conjoined twin as it is incompletely formed and wholly dependent upon the bodily functions of the complete twin. Laloo looked like a miniature person had run into his chest head first and buried his head inside. He was described in advertisements of the day as "Hindu Boy from whose breast grows a body. He has 1 head, 2 bodies, 4 arms, 4 legs, 4 feet, 20 toes, and 20 fingers". In truth, the parasitic twin's legs were shriveled and limp, and the feet were twisted. Many doctors studied Laloo and Lala, the name given the parasitic twin during Laloo's early exhibitions. Most concluded that the parasitic twin had no intelligence but did have a pulse even though the heart could not pump blood on its own. They proclaimed the parasitic twin also had intestines and functioning kidneys, plus a well-developed penis with pubic hair, but no testicles. Doctors also

MYSTERY TO BE SOLVED

Was Laloo's body donated to science and if so, which school received the cadaver? Was he buried after the body was studied, and if so, where?

Laloo was born in India in 1872 with an attached parasitic twin. Very little is known about his early life.

Laloo was described in advertisements of the day as "Hindu Boy from whose breast grows a body. He has 1 head, 2 bodies, 4 arms, 4 legs, 4 feet, 20 toes, and 20 fingers."

In February 1900, over 800 surgeons, medical students, and anatomical specialists gathered to hear Laloo speak and to see what some called "the most amazing freak in the world." The topic of the forum was the possibility of separating Laloo from his parasitic twin.

noted that the penis showed signs of erection and urine was passed through the parasite twin's penis without Laloo's pre-knowledge. Obviously, an unexpected erection or urination could pose problems for Laloo in a multitude of situations, especially in public or on stage. Laloo always claimed he felt any pain inflicted on Lala, true or not. They did both perspire and have elevated body temperatures simultaneously.

Laloo arrived in America in 1891 from England at the age of eighteen, already a seasoned sideshow performer. Most likely, he had been touring in Europe, or at the least in England, since India was a subject of the crown at the time. Many English citizens traveled to and from India so it would be probable that a sideshow manager "purchased" a young Laloo from his parents and whisked him away. Reportedly, he spoke flawless English. When he first came to America aboard the steamship *City of Berlin*, however, young Laloo traveled alone.

A ship manifest from *City of Berlin* show an eighteen-year-old male aboard, L. Ramparsad, arriving in New York on September 5, 1891. Unfortunately, the manifest is not complete and information that is generally included—such as "occupation," "reason for visit," or "who paid fare"—is not listed. It does, however, list his nationality as "English." Many possibilities for an explanation exist: this could be a different person altogether; the clerk could have assumed his nationality without asking; Laloo could have given the clerk the wrong information; Laloo could have been brought to England at such an early age that he considered himself English; or Laloo had everyone fooled and was actually born in England, his Indian Hindu roots only a ploy to create a sensationalized identity to grab headlines and increase ticket sales.

Laloo and his manager(s) were excellent showmen and they often came up with publicity stunts that made newspapers all across America. Laloo referred to his twin as a girl, more shocking to the Victorian public, and dressed it in female attire. He would often exhibit with the parasitic twin's arms encircling his neck in a show of affection. He was referred to in print as "tall, healthy, handsome, intelligent, well-portioned, very charming, a full-blooded Hindu with dark curls and sparkling eyes, and a high caste Indian who had earned $100,000 exhibiting in this country, Mexico, and abroad." Add his youth to the package and you have a ripe field for romantic speculations. Several stories appeared at various times claiming Laloo had fallen madly in love with this or that woman and was seeking to be surgically removed from his parasitic twin so as to wed. In 1893, his true love was Elsie Aimes, described by reporters as "a handsome brunette." In 1900, one headline read: "Laloo will submit to the knife to win Miss Crosby." Hopefully, Laloo experienced true love during his tour of America, although the love of money is hard competition.

At times, the press would report that Laloo would soon be undergoing surgical removal of his twin and it would be the last chance to see the amazing exhibition. Soon another story would appear in the press stating that Laloo had postponed the operation for one reason or another, but that the following week would positively be the last appearance of Laloo on public exhibition. Reportedly, "The Happy Hindu" was raking in over $1,000 a week, a small fortune at the time, enough to make anyone happy, Hindu or not. Not all reporters were enamored by Laloo. One gave a very unflattering account of his interview with the sideshow star: "He walks about, reclines, and smokes cigarettes inveterately and so great a contempt does familiarity breed that

Laloo, Noted Freak Booked in Boston, Dies in Mexico; Doctors Claim Body

LALOO, THE FAMOUS INDIAN FREAK.

Manager of Hindu at Loss to Settle Dispute Between Edinburgh and Philadelphia Professors.

In what may have been the last publicity stunt of Laloo's career, his last hoorah, his manager, George E. Gill, claimed he was at a loss to decide which doctors could claim the body of Laloo.

Laloo rolls his numerous cigarettes on his sister's back." This just proves you can't please everyone. Sadly, Laloo's career and life were cut tragically short. He was traveling with the Norris & Rowe Circus when he died in Aguascalientes, Mexico, in October of 1905 after a week's illness. He was thirty-three. Most sources say he died from injuries received in a train wreck.

In what may have been the last publicity stunt of Laloo's career, his last hoorah, his manager, George E. Gill, claimed he was at a loss to decide which doctors could claim the body of Laloo: Prof. MacDonald Brown of The Royal College of Physicians and the surgeons of Edinburgh or Barton C. Hurst, professor of obstetrics at The University of Pennsylvania. The final destination of Laloo's body is not known. ♦

JEAN-JAQUES LIBBERA, "THE DOUBLED-BODIED MAN"

Jean Libbera was born in Rome, Italy, in 1884 to parents without any physical disabilities. The siblings in the family numbered thirteen, with Jean being the fourth child. All the other children were free from physical disabilities, with the exception of the third child, who also had a parasitic twin attached. That child died at birth. Jean's parasitic diminutive twin, whom he lovingly called "Jacques," was perfectly formed with the exception of the head that was imbedded into Jean's sternum. Reportedly, doctors and surgeons in America and Europe examined both and claimed X-rays showed a fifteen centimeter head inside Jean's chest. Show advertisements and newspaper articles proclaimed the smaller twin had "arms, hands, fingers, finger nails, hips, thighs, shins, feet, toes with toe nails, and a strong bone structure." Circulation of blood and nourishment came from Jean's body to his parasitic twin, and Jean claimed they could both feel each other's pain, touch, and were equally affected by temperature changes. He was billed as the "Doubled-Body Man" and toured in Europe and America. He first performed in the US around 1907 and would continue to perform in this country at intervals until the early 1930s. Jean was married to a Belgian woman and was the father of four children. The family traveled with him, but their permanent home was in Paris. The children reportedly spoke Italian, French, a Belgian minority language, and English. Jean Libbera passed away in April 1934 in Paris. He was fifty years old. ♦

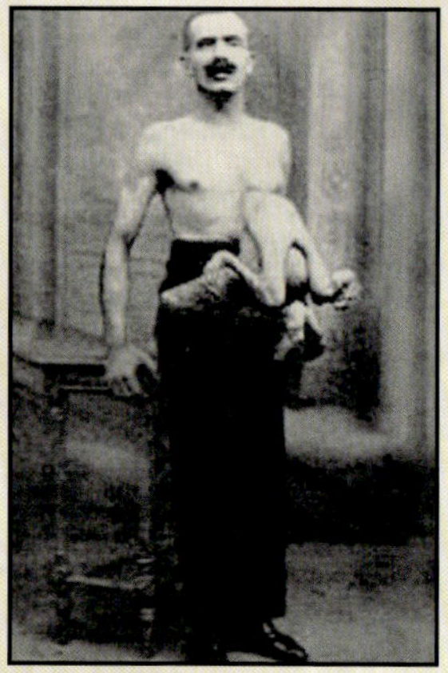

Jean's parasitic diminutive twin, whom he lovingly called "Jacques," was perfectly formed with the exception of the head that was imbedded into Jean's sternum.

Jean died in Paris in April 1934 at age fifty. He married and was the father of four children.

LILLIE B. WILLIAMS, "BETTY LOU WILLIAMS," OR "THE GIRL WITH FOUR LEGS AND THREE ARMS"

Lillie B. Williams was born on January 10, 1932, in Albany, Georgia. She was the fourth child born to dirt-poor sharecroppers who eventually had fifteen children in all. Betty Lou was born with a parasitic twin attached to the left side of her abdomen. The twin had two legs, an arm with three fingers, and a very small, second, badly deformed arm. When she was around fifteen months old, she was discovered by showman Dick Best. He gave her the stage name "Betty Lou" and put her on display at his popular dime museum in New York City that featured an all-female revue. He also hired several women to give Betty Lou twenty-four-hour care. Betty Lou caught the eye of Robert Ripley, who negotiated with Best to allow her to exhibit at The Ripley's Believe It or Not Odditorium at the 1934 Chicago World's Fair. Ripley was the first to bill her as "The Girl with Four Legs and Three Arms." To increase interest in his new-found oddity, he falsely declared that X-rays showed the perfectly developed head of her twin resting within her abdomen. Her popularity in Ripley's exhibit meant that the then two-year-old was earning approximately $250 a week for her parents. As an adult, she would earn $750 or more a week. Ward Hall, the modern showman extraordinaire, claimed "she was the highest paid human oddity of all times."

Betty Lou was a strikingly beautiful grown woman. She appeared on stage in costumes that capitalized on her good looks and perfect figure as well as displayed her "little sister," the name she gave to

Sideshow banners and signs advertising Betty Lou.

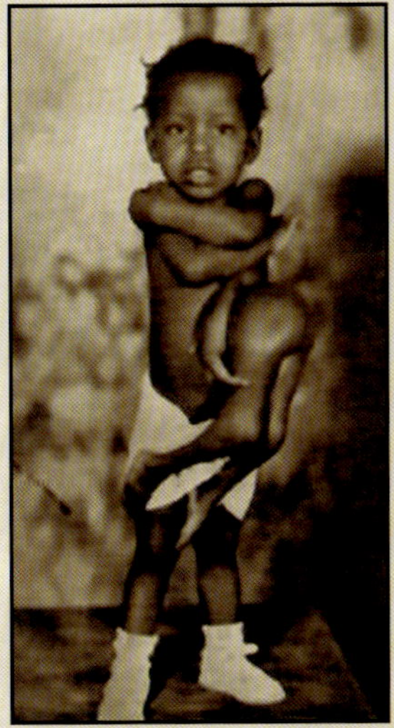

Betty Lou Williams was born with a parasitic twin attached to the left side of her abdomen.

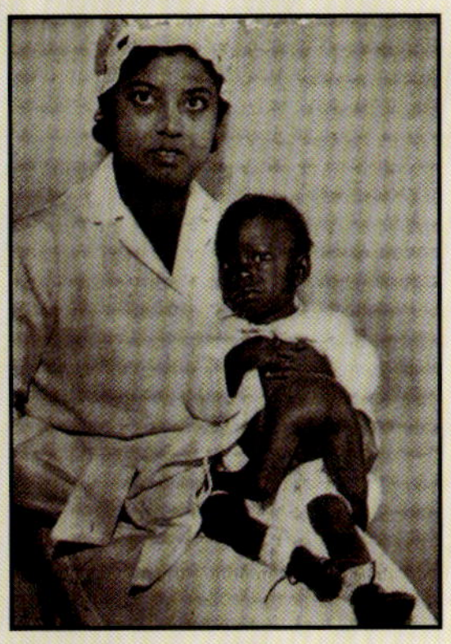

Betty Lou was discovered by showman Dick Best. He put her on display at his popular dime museum in New York City that featured an all-female revue. He also hired several women to give Betty Lou twenty-four-hour care.

She appeared on stage in costumes that capitalized on her good looks and perfect figure as well as displayed her "little sister," the name she gave to her parasitic twin.

her parasitic twin. At times, she would dress up "little sister" in specially sewn costumes to enhance her act. When not performing, Betty would wear maternity clothes to cover up her deformity. This allowed her to move freely about in public.

Even with her deformity, reportedly Betty Lou had no end to the line of suitors who pursued her. Unfortunately, she chose the wrong man to fall in love with. Close friends tried to warn her about this man, but Betty Lou flatly refused to listen. Sadly, she learned a valuable lesson the hard way. When Betty Lou pushed for a marriage commitment from this man whom she had been financially supporting and lavishing with gifts, he disappeared in the middle of the night with most of Betty Lou's savings. She died soon afterwards, in October of 1954. She had a heart attack brought on by a severe asthma attack at her home in Trenton, New Jersey. She was only twenty-two. Several thousand people gathered in Albany, Georgia, for Betty Lou's funeral. This was the largest funeral the town had ever seen. Daniel P. Mannix writes in his book, *Freaks: We Who Are Not As Others*, "Betty Lou died of a broken heart. I realize this sounds melodramatic, but three people who knew her intimately assured me that it was so." ♦

FACIAL DEFORMITIES

The most recognizable part of any human being is the face. While few close friends or even close relatives can accurately describe our hands, feet, or limbs, they would all be able to quickly describe our facial features. Now imagine a life where your face was so horribly disfigured that all who saw you stared in amazement and disbelief, at best, and more often, total strangers and small children stared at you in sheer horror. ♦

BILL DURKS ALIAS, "THE MAN WITH THREE EYES," "THE MAN WITH THREE EYES AND TWO NOSES," OR "THE MAN WITH TWO FACES"

Bill Durks's life story is the perfect example to be carefully pondered by all those do-gooders before they cry, scream, and petition to have the "freak" shows shut down because of claims they are inhumane. Please read on, you well-meaning but misguided politically correct individuals.

Bill Durks spent the first forty years of his life in abject poverty, toiling hard in the fields as a tenant farmer in the small Southern town where he was born, shunned by all including his family, and with little hope for ever having more. Then along came the sideshow and Bill found acceptance, decent wages for enjoyable work, fame, travel, and most importantly, true love. Bill Durks was born on April 17, 1913, in Jasper, Alabama. He had four siblings who were born without physical differences, but Bill suffered from frontonasal dysplasia, a very rare birth disorder characterized by abnormalities mainly affecting the head and facial region. Major

Bill's unusual face thrilled and amazed the crowd, and he was an extremely popular sideshow attraction for over two decades. He often needed "an interpreter" since his cleft palate made his speech hard to understand.

Some of Bill's earliest managers took advantage of the fact that Bill was illiterate, and they stole from him. Bill was fond of saying that he still made more from those thieves than he had made as a sharecropper and the work was a whole lot easier. He is shown with The Coleman Brothers Show in 1973 standing between Emmitt Bejano, "The Alligator-Skinned Man," and his best friend, Melvin Burkhart, "The Human Blockhead."

A rare photo of Bill Durks as a young man. Bill was born with frontonasal dysplasia, a very rare birth disorder that results in facial and head abnormalities.

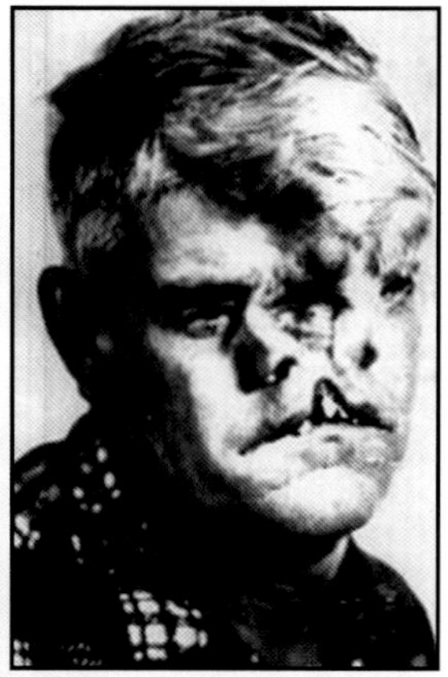

Bill's life changed drastically in the late 1950s when he joined the sideshow. He was heralded as "The Man With Three Eyes" because he would paint a third eye in the rift between his two noses.

physical characteristics include widely spaced eyes, a flat, broad nose, and a vertical groove down the middle of the face. Ward Hall, "The King of the Sideshow," wrote in his book *My Very Unusual Friends*, "(Bill) looked like he had been hit in the face with an axe." His face was, in essence, divided in half from his eyebrows to his upper lip, with a wide open gap down the middle. His eyes were spaced very far apart and he had what appeared to be two noses, one nostril on each side of the facial rift. He had a deeply cleft lip that exposed abnormally placed front teeth and his palate was so deformed that Bill had great difficulty speaking clearly. To add to his burdens, he was born with a hooded-skin film over his eyes that had to be surgically removed when he was a small child, plus he was blind in his left eye. His severely cleft palate made his speech almost impossible to understand and most mistook Bill for being mentally impaired.

If this was not enough to have going against you, factor in being born to poverty-stricken sharecroppers who were ashamed of you and saw you as a curse from God for past sins. Bill was never sent to school. The family needed him to work in the fields from a very early age, plus the family was ashamed of this "monster" and wanted to hide him away from critical eyes. Isolation, parental rejection and loathing, his inability to speak clearly, his inability to read or write (he signed his name with an "X") and the probable cruelty of others outside the family hindered Bill's social development. Reportedly, he was a painfully shy and introverted adult who kept his head bowed and wore a large-brimmed hat to attempt to hide his appearance. He once said in an interview that he never got used to the pain

Bill's life changed again drastically when he fell in love with and married Millie, "The Alligator-Skinned Woman." They remained totally devoted to one another until Millie's death in June 1968.

of seeing the shock on someone's face when they first glimpsed his.

Bill's life changed drastically in the late 1950s when he attended a local carnival near his hometown. Legend persists that once the show owners glimpsed Bill in the audience, they persuaded him to tour with their show. He was heralded as "The Man With Three Eyes" because he would paint a third eye in the rift between his two noses. Even though the third eye was less-than-believable, Bill's unusual face thrilled and amazed the crowd and he was an extremely popular sideshow attraction for over two decades. He toured with many of the big names of the day, including Ward Hall's (Hall & Chris) sideshow. Many of his earliest managers took advantage of the fact that Bill was illiterate and stole from him. Bill was fond of saying that he still made more from those thieves than he had made as a sharecropper and the work was a whole lot easier. Bill's life changed again drastically when his sideshow best friend, Melvin Burkhart, "The Anatomical Wonder"/"The Original Human Blockhead," introduced him to Millie, "The Alligator-Skinned Woman." She was also a sideshow exhibitor, her rare skin condition giving her a reptilian-like appearance. Millie was eighteen years older than Bill, but the two fell in love, got married in 1960, and remained totally devoted to one another until Millie's death in June 1968 that was brought on by a violent asthma attack. Bill was devastated by Millie's death but was eventually convinced to continue performing in sideshows to help him cope with his loss. He did so for about five more years and even played a small part as a sanatorium patient in a Hollywood movie, *Sisters,* in 1973, filmed during off-season. He retired to Gibsonton, dubbed Gibb Town by the many sideshow and circus performers who called the town home, and died there on May 7, 1975. He was sixty-six. The location of his or Millie's grave site is unknown. His best friend Melvin Burkhart lived to be ninety-four years old and passed away November 8, 2001. ♦

GRACE MCDANIELS, "MULA" AND "CLARA," OR "THE MULE-FACE WOMAN"

The life story of Grace McDaniels is probably one of the saddest stories of all sideshow performers. However, the fate of birth and not the sideshow, itself, bears the blame. The little happiness she found in life, she found during her days as an exhibitor. Very little is known about the details of Grace McDaniels's life and death. No birth certificate, marriage certificate, or death certificate exists in public records, and she cannot be located in any of the United States censuses. We have to rely on the information cited on her trade cards and from believable statements given by people who knew or worked with Grace on the sideshow circuit. Educated guesses fill in the blanks.

Grace McDaniels was born on a farm near Numa, Iowa (population 125), in 1888 with a rare disorder known as Sturge-Webber syndrome, also known as encephalotrigeminal angiomatosis. This condition caused large, wine-colored birthmarks to appear on her head and face from birth. Sturge-Webber syndrome is not inherited so her unsuspecting parents were, most likely, shocked and possibly repulsed or embarrassed by this infant. Common side effects of this medical condition are seizures, weakness on one side of the body, and learning disabilities at times so severe as to be clas-

Grace McDaniels was born with two conditions that negatively affected the appearance her face. She exhibited under the title "The Mule-Face Woman."

Legend persists that Grace joined a sideshow when she won an "Ugliest Woman Contest." More likely, a sideshow manager heard of Grace, met her, and convinced her to join his lineup, recognizing in her a money-making opportunity. Grace, always shy, is photographed in the background.

Grace was very concerned with her appearance and never got used to being called ugly. She was always clean and dressed well, styled her hair, and used makeup to cover her purple facial marks when not on stage. Sadly, no makeup in the world was able to hide her disfigurement and her admirable but futile efforts gave some heartless souls even more excuses to taunt her.

Photo of Grace with her young son and an unidentified man. It has always been speculated that this was the father of her child but most likely it is only a relative of Grace's.

Grace gave birth to a handsome son out of wedlock whom she named Elmer. Legend says an alcoholic carnival worker seduced her, then ran off.

sified as intellectual disability. Grace bore excessively more port-wine birthmarks than the vast majority of individuals with this condition, but what other symptoms of the disease she exhibited we do not know. We do know that the majority of people born with this condition have seizures (72–93 percent) and also have developmental delays or intellectual disability in varying degrees (50–75 percent). With that said, Sturge-Webber syndrome does not explain her abnormally misshapen nose, cheeks, mouth, and lower jaw.

Grace McDaniels had the misfortune to also be born with another genetic facial disorder early in life that negatively affected her appearance: neurofibromatosis, also referred to as NF, a disorder that causes the spontaneous growth of fibrous tumors in soft tissue and bone. These tumors continue to grow with age. This condition worsened to the point that it eventually made it difficult for Grace to speak or be understood. Her jaw became barely mobile, which would also have affected her solid food intake. She lost most of her teeth over time as the jaw and the roof of the mouth expanded. The few remaining teeth were discolored and jagged. Eating solid food became almost impossible in time.

It is fairly easy to imagine what life for Grace was like growing up in rural Iowa in 1888. As an adult, Grace was shy, introverted, and extremely embarrassed and hurt by people's reaction to her appearance. These personality traits were likely learned behaviors resulting from a childhood of isolation and rejection. Most likely she always lived with her aging parents, with little or no social outlets, and no means of earning a living. I have read articles that claim Grace was very popular with men and had many suitors. More likely, nothing could be further from the truth. As a poor spinster who looked as Grace did, it is doubtful that bachelors were flocking to her doorstep. Even when Grace was earning a respectable wage from exhibiting at sideshows, she still did not attract even one honorable suitor.

Legend also persists that Grace joined the F. W. Miller's Freak Show when she won an "Ugliest Woman Contest" near her home in 1935. This is probably only sideshow hype, especially considering Grace's shy and introverted personality and her reported strong aversion to being called ugly. More likely, a sideshow manager heard of Grace, met her, and convinced her to join his lineup, recognizing in her a lucrative money-making opportunity. Grace would have been forty-seven years old if one was to believe the story of the "Ugly Woman Contest" in 1935. Since Grace gave birth to an illegitimate son while on the road, logically she would have

Grace gave her son all her pent-up love and devotion. Unfortunately, she spoiled him so badly that he turned into a despicable man with a drug and alcohol addiction. There were reports of Elmer regularly beating his mother but she always forgave him.

been much younger when she ran off to join the sideshow. A better estimate would be she first exhibited sometime in the late 1920s. We know she was exhibiting with the Morris & Castle Show in July 1926 in Aberdeen, South Dakota. In 1933, Grace was managed by Cash Miller and exhibiting at Ripley's Odditorium. Also in 1933, she was a main attraction with Charlie Pyle's Chamber of Horrors at the Chicago World's Fair.

Undoubtedly, Grace's life was better on the sideshow circuit, if not ideal. She was usually billed as "The Mule-Faced Girl" but also infrequently as "Mula" and "Clara." Barkers outside the tent where she exhibited would loudly exclaim to the public that she was "grotesque and ugly beyond description" to increase ticket sales. Grace never got used to the barker's words, even if she understood the reasoning behind the pitch. At times, she was brought to tears while listening to the rehearsed and orchestrated pre-show verbal description and it was said that she would often sit with her fingers in her ears to avoid hearing the hurtful remarks.

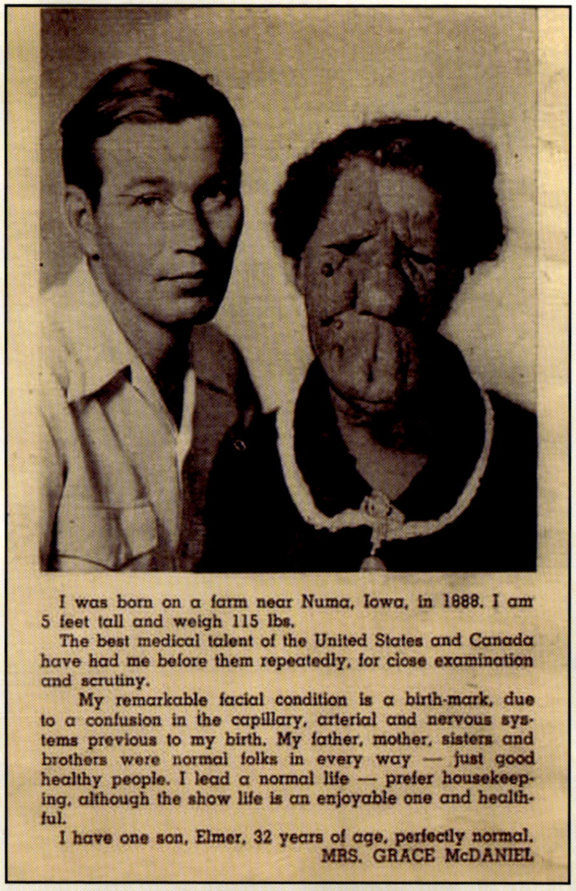

I was born on a farm near Numa, Iowa, in 1888. I am 5 feet tall and weigh 115 lbs.

The best medical talent of the United States and Canada have had me before them repeatedly, for close examination and scrutiny.

My remarkable facial condition is a birth-mark, due to a confusion in the capillary, arterial and nervous systems previous to my birth. My father, mother, sisters and brothers were normal folks in every way — just good healthy people. I lead a normal life — prefer housekeeping, although the show life is an enjoyable one and healthful.

I have one son, Elmer, 32 years of age, perfectly normal.

MRS. GRACE McDANIEL

Grace refused to work for anyone that would not also hire her son, insisting always they were a package deal. Show owners were forced to put up with Elmer stealing from them and his continual vile behavior in order to keep their star attraction.

Grace would usually be required to wear a veil covering the lower part of her face. After the paying crowd had assembled inside the tent, the barker would theatrically lift the veil for shock value. Other times, she would be seated with her back to the audience, and then turn slowly when cued to face the audience. It was said that some spectators actually fainted at the sight of her, but this claim was probably only sideshow hype even though those

A figure of Grace McDaniels is on display at the Ripley's "Believe It or Not" Odditorium in San Francisco, California.

stories actually appeared in newspapers of the day. Another hyped story reported "the shy and highly domestic mule-faced lady was constantly courted by roughish Johns with nose bags of oats at the stage door." We can truly understand how sensitive Grace was about her looks through remarks made by sideshow acquaintances that claim she took pride in her appearance. Reportedly, she was clean and took great care in dressing, styled her hair, and used makeup to cover her purple facial marks when not on stage. Sadly, no makeup in the world was able to hide her disfigurement and her admirable but futile efforts gave some heartless souls even more excuses to taunt her. When we consider all that Grace endured and had to overcome in her lifetime, it is amazing that this woman was always described by associates and friends as kind, gentle, and generous. She was a highly respected professional who was also a person who could be counted on in times of need. She loved needlework and one of her passions was cooking and sharing the food with others in the show even though eating solid food was difficult due to her condition. She also shared her money freely, giving out "loans" to anyone with a sad tale of woe.

Grace never married but did bear one son out of wedlock around 1930. Legend persists that an alcoholic carnival worker took advantage of Grace's strong desire to be loved, seduced her, took money from her, got her pregnant, and then ran off rather than do the right thing by both the mother and child. Other accounts claim he drunkenly seduced her one night to win a bet and left the show the next day because of his embarrassment from the taunting that ensued from the other sideshow workers. She signed her name as "Mrs." on her trade cards, either from the social embarrassment of having an illegitimate son, or to protect her son from public criticism. Grace's infant was a beautiful son she named Elmer. No birth record exists for the child so the date of his birth is unknown. It is known, however, that Grace poured out all her pent-up love and devotion onto this child she considered a gift from God. Unfortunately, she spoiled him rotten. No parental guidelines were set for his behavior since Grace believed this child could do no wrong. He grew into a spoiled, selfish man who turned dangerously mean when he drank or was high on drugs, which unfortunately, was most of the time.

MYSTERY TO SOLVE

Where is Grace McDaniels buried? Is there a tombstone marking her final resting place?

There were reports of him regularly beating his mother, at time so viciously that she required medical attention. He continuously disrespected her in front of other people, calling her vile names. He also stole from her and squandered much of her considerable earnings on gambling, alcohol, drugs, and an assortment of low-class women and prostitutes. Grace always forgave her son. After Elmer reached adulthood, Grace flatly refused to work for anyone that would not also hire her son, insisting always they were a package deal. She appointed Elmer as her manager and when he would steal from the shows where she performed, she would quietly pay back the money. The show owners knew that if they fired Elmer or had him arrested it would mean the loss of one of their star attractions. They learned to look the other way. Grace was still performing as late as October 1954 at the age of sixty-seven. At that time she was with Dick Best and exhibiting in Augusta, Georgia. Reportedly, Grace commanded up to $400 a week as a top attraction. Both Grace and Elmer died in 1958, Grace dying first at age seventy. Elmer died later that year from sclerosis of the liver. We logically know that Grace died first. Had she been alive when Elmer passed, there would have been a lavish funeral and a monumental grave site provided for the son she so loved. As it is, both are most likely lying somewhere in unmarked graves, possibly in a potter's field.

If we were able to ask Grace if she would still join the sideshow if she had it to do all over again, my guess is that she would not hesitate for a moment to say that, indeed, she would. ♦

JULIA PASTRANA, "WORLD'S UGLIEST WOMAN," "BEAR WOMAN," "APE WOMAN," "THE NON-DESCRIPT," "BEARDED AND HAIRY LADY," "THE MISNOMERED"

Julia Pastrana was born in Sinaloa, Mexico, in 1834 to indigent parents. Julia was born with two conditions, one not recognized during her lifetime, so the many doctors who examined her were baffled. One doctor's learned opinion was that Julia was the product of a human mating with an orangutan. In actuality, she suffered from hypertrichosis that left her face and body covered in thick, straight black hair, plus she also suffered from gingival hyperplasia, which made her lips and gums thick and gave her an exaggerated jutting jaw. In 1854, she was discovered and bought by a Mexican customs administrator, Theodore Lent, and he began exhibiting her through the US, Canada, and Europe and acted as her manager. While in New York in 1857, they married. While it is believed that Julia fell deeply in love with Lent, sadly he married her to legally control the impressive income she was earning. He taught her to sing and dance as a means to increase that revenue even more. On March 26, 1860, Julia died in Moscow from complications received while giving birth to a son who inherited his mother's hypertrichosis conditions. The child died a few days after birth. Far from being the grieving husband and father, Lent had the bodies of both his wife and child mummified and enclosed in a glass case so they could be exhibited for profit. He soon married a

Julia Pastrana was unfortunate enough to be born with two conditions that gave her an inhuman-like appearance.

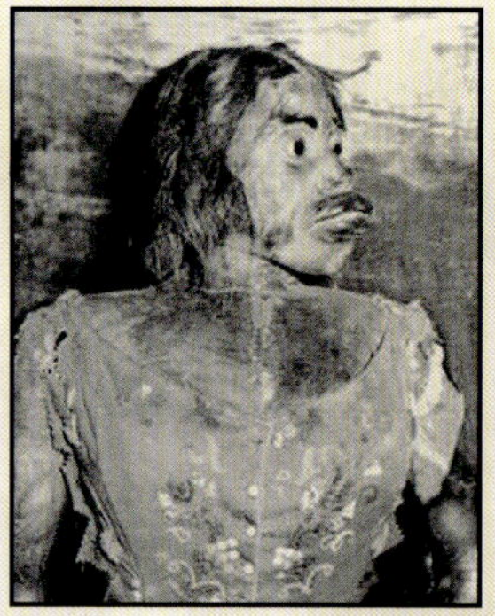

On March 26, 1860, Julia died in Moscow from complications received while giving birth to a son who inherited his mother's hypertrichosis conditions. The child died a few days after birth. Her body would remain unburied for 153 years.

bearded lady, gave her the stage name Zenora Pastrana, and proclaimed her the sister of Julia.

The bodies changed ownership many times in the decades that followed. Vandals damaged the son's remains beyond repair, but the mother's body ended up for years in a storage room at the University of Oslo in Norway where a torn arm had been repaired. On February 12, 2013, 153 years after her death, Julia's remains were finally brought back to Mexico after the New York-based visual artist Laura Anderson Barbata spent almost a decade of her life working for her return. Mario Lopez Valdez, the governor of Sinaloa state that was the birthplace of Julia, joined forces with Barbata and made a crucial monetary contribution to Julia's repatriation. After a Roman Catholic mass, Julia was buried in a cemetery in Sinaloa de Leyva, a town near her birthplace. She was laid to rest in a white coffin covered with white roses while traditional Mexican music played. Theodore Lent was committed to a Russian mental institution in 1884 and remained there until his death, date unknown. Sadly, it is not known what happened to the destroyed body of Julia's infant son. ♦

EMPL STEPHAN BIBROWSKI, "LIONEL, THE LION-FACED BOY"

Empl Stephan Bibrowski, "Lionel, The Lion-Faced Boy," was born in 1893 in Russia with the medical condition hypertrichosis. Hypertrichosis, also called Ambras syndrome and werewolf syndrome, is an abnormal amount of hair growth over the body. Lionel was described by one newspaper as "(a) boy with a soft white silky mane covering his entire face." Another paper reported in 1903, "Were he not probably the greatest living human curiosity, the lion-faced boy would earn good money as an advertisement for some hair growing remedy, for he has hair to burn. At a little distance Lionel's face seems almost an exact counterpart of a lion's covered with a long, fine hairy adornment, and there is a magnificent mane growing from his head and hanging down his back in a great silken mass." He usually exhibited in full dress, preferring long-sleeved, buttoned-up costumes with a military or regal flair. He did this to emphasize his lion-like face and disguise the fact that he also had an unusual amount of hair growth on his trunk and arms, albeit not as long as the three inches of hair all over his face.

Stephan Bibrowski, "Lionel, The Lion-Faced Boy," was born with the medical condition, hypertrichosis. Hypertrichosis, also called Ambras syndrome and werewolf syndrome, is an abnormal amount of hair growth over the body.

Lionel first arrived in New York on March 15, 1903, aboard the SS *St. Paul*. He was a boy of ten, traveling with his fifty-eight-year-old German manager and guardian Edouard Friederich. He had already been exhibiting in Europe for several years. Most likely, his parents had, in essence, sold Lionel for profit, but by all appearances, Lionel

Lionel first arrived in New York on March 15, 1903. He was a boy of ten, traveling with his fifty-eight-year-old German manager and guardian.

Lionel usually exhibited in full dress, preferring costumes with a military or regal flair.

was treated very well by his manager. Lionel had caught the eye of P. T. Barnum, then doing business as Barnum & Bailey, and Barnum quickly contracted with Friederich to bring Lionel to America. On the ship's manifest, Lionel is listed as "covered with hair freak" under occupation. His first appearance in America was at the Austin & Stone's Dime Museum, and he was an immediate success. The *Boston Herald* proclaimed, "Many strange sights have been seen at Austin & Stone's in the past twenty years, but the thousands who have visited the museum during the past week to see the lion-faced Lionel agree that he is the strangest of them all."

Lionel was, indeed, an enigma. He had the appearance of a wild and dangerous animal, yet he was of a gentle nature and dressed impeccably. He spoke German, English, French, and limited Russian and could both read and write. Likely he was more educated than the majority of the masses that thronged to see this freak. Part of any performer's

Lionel preferred Germany to other countries, even gaining citizenship sometime around 1930. Sadly, Germany, under Adolf Hitler's rise, would not have been a safe place for someone like Lionel. We might never know of Lionel's final days, his death, or his burial site, if any.

act was his or her interaction with the audience. Lionel's presentation did not disappoint. Lionel explained his congenital disability by saying that he was a victim of pre-natal influence, and that five months before he was born, his mother saw his father, who was a lion tamer, eaten alive by lions. The sight so preyed on her mind that when he was born, he was covered with lion's hair. At this point in his talk, he would present a photo of himself at three years old to show the spell-bound audience

Lionel had the appearance of a wild and dangerous animal, yet he was of a gentle nature and dressed impeccably. He spoke German, English, French, and limited Russian and could both read and write. Likely he was more educated than the majority of the masses that thronged to see this freak.

and proclaim that his skin had always been that way. He also claimed he was born in Poland, at times, and born in Germany at other times. His choice of birth places was probably best matched to the audience he was playing to. He would add more color to his rehearsed fabricated story, as well, especially on opening days of a tour to generate sales and interest, claiming such things as possessing night vision and being married to a woman without any physical abnormalities.

P. T. Barnum was not above creating media interest in his performers by completely making up fanciful stories. While Lionel was in Albany, New York, with Barnum's show in 1906, it was leaked to the press that Lionel had attracted the unwanted advances of a wealthy woman who had fallen madly in love with the boy, now only thirteen. "A well-known woman of considerable wealth fell in love with the strange young fellow and her attentions at last became so marked that interference was necessary. The woman parted from the boy with tears, and her letters, full of enduring phrases, are following the show." Even then, sex, money, and a good scandal sold tickets. Lionel toured mostly in Europe but he did do several American tours, usually with Barnum & Bailey, and one

Here we get rare glimpses of the extensive growth of hair that covered Lionel's trunk and arms. He usually wore costumes that covered his body hair.

longtime engagement with the Coney Island Dreamland Circus in New Jersey. No marriage records have been located for Lionel. His ship manifests always listed him as "single," so we can logically conclude that he had no children or, at least, any recognized offspring. The date, place, and cause of

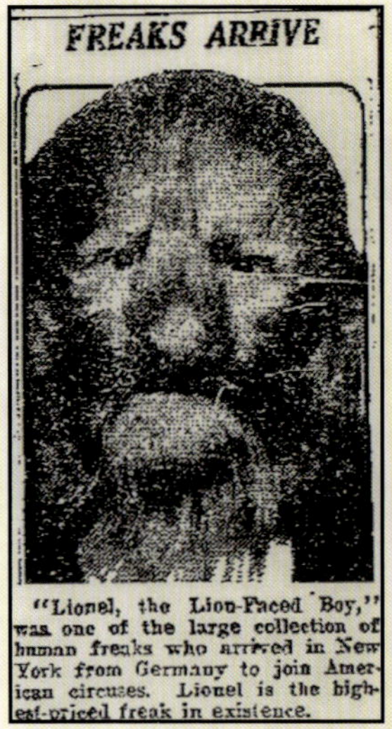

FREAKS ARRIVE

"Lionel, the Lion-Faced Boy," was one of the large collection of human freaks who arrived in New York from Germany to join American circuses. Lionel is the highest-priced freak in existence.

his death are not clear, but two accounts of his passing have survived. One states that Lionel died of a heart attack in 1932 in Italy or Germany. The second says he died in a German Nazi concentration camp. In 1932, Lionel would have only been thirty-nine years old. While it is possible to die from a heart attack at that young age, it is not likely. Also, heart problems are not a normal side effect of hypertrichosis, nor are any other health issues, for that matter, that would explain an early death.

Lionel preferred Germany to other countries, even gaining citizenship sometime around 1930. His beloved guardian was German, so most likely Lionel had spent a great deal of time in that country and was comfortable with the language, customs, geography, etc. Sadly, Germany under Adolf Hitler's rise would not have been a safe place for someone like Lionel. In Hitler's pathological attempt to create a perfect race, he not only pursued Jews and gypsies, he also sought to eradicate anyone with a physical or mental disability. Lionel was of Jewish decent as well as being a "freak," two things that would have certainly put his life in danger. We might never know of Lionel's final days, his death, or his burial site, if any, but we do know that "Lionel, The Lion-Faced Boy" was a wildly popular sideshow performer in his day and one newspaper in 1923 even proclaimed him "the highest priced freak in existence." ♦

FEDOR JEFTICHEW, "JO-JO, THE DOG-FACED BOY" (1868-1904)

Before there was "Lionel, The Lion-Faced Boy," P. T. Barnum exhibited Russian-born Fedor Jeftichew, dubbed by Barnum, "Jo-Jo, The Dog-Faced Boy." In 1884, when Jo-Jo was sixteen, Barnum brought his new find to the United States. Jo-Jo's father, Adrian Konstantinov Jeftichew, had also been a sideshow performer in Europe. Both father and son were born with hypertrichosis. Reportedly, Jo-Jo died of pneumonia at age thirty-six. ♦

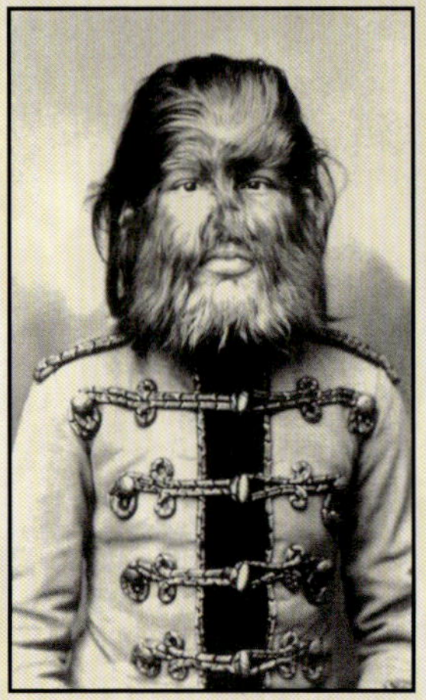

Left: Before there was "Lionel, The Lion-Faced Boy," P. T. Barnum exhibited Russian-born Fedor Jeftichew, dubbed by Barnum, "Jo-Jo, The Dog-Faced Boy."

Rigth: In 1884, when Jo-Jo was sixteen, P. T. Barnum brought his new find to the United States.

ALBINOS

Albinos were often billed as mind readers and people who could communicate with the dearly departed.

Albinos are people or animals who are born with a lack of pigmentation. The skin and hair is white or milky and the eyes have a pink or blue iris with a deep-red pupil.

The sideshow performed to an unsophisticated audience that was starved to see anything unusual and out of the ordinary. Most of America was still agricultural with a population that was born, raised, and died on a farm or in a small town. These people never saw much more than what was available within a few miles of their home. The colorful and gaudy sideshow coming to town with its human oddities on display, all just begging to be gawked at, must have been the social event of the year. Albinos were a very popular sideshow spectacle. Imagine the awe-inspiring sight that a very pale, pink-eyed person would offer the sunburned country farmer and his equally sunburned family. Albinos were often billed as mind readers and people who could communicate with the dearly departed. Their unusual and pure angelic appearance most likely added to the illusion.

Rudolph Lucasie, wife, Antonnette, and son, Joseph R., alias, "The Original Eliophobus Family"

Albinos are born with a lack of pigmentation. The skin and hair is white or milky and the eyes have a pink or blue iris with a deep-red pupil.

Joseph Lucasie was called "a famous albino" in his obituary when he died on September 24, 1909. At the time of his death, however, he was working as a cashier in a restaurant.

One of the most remarkable albino sideshow acts was Rudolph Lucasie, his wife, and his son, all of whom were albinos. It is the only known act where the entire family was afflicted by this condition. Usually the child of albino parents is born without the condition. Rudolph was born in 1833 in Madagascar, his wife was born in Italy in 1834, and the son was born in Hamburg, Germany, in 1858. The Lucasie family was discovered by P. T. Barnum while he was traveling in Amsterdam, Holland. He enticed them to come to America to exhibit in his dime museum in New York. They were a star attraction for three years. It was the original intention of the family to return home to Holland after they had made their fortune, but they ended up staying

Currier and Ives print featuring the Lucasie albino family. A second child, an albino girl, was often added to increase the appeal of the act, but she was not related.

in this country. It is most likely they realized that their earning potential in America was far greater than at home.

The Lucasies were very attractive people. Antonnette was exceptionally beautiful. They would appear together on stage and were billed as "The Wonderful albino Family/ Rudolph Lucasie, Wife, and Children, all from Madagascar. They have pure

A BARNUM ALBINO DYING.

Joseph Lucasie Imported by Showman Fifty Years Ago.

Joseph Lucasie, who was one of the Albino family which the late showman P. T. Barnum imported from Belgium to his museum in New York city, over fifty years ago, is dying of dropsy at the general hospital. It was thought last night that he could not survive through today. His hair is white as wool and his eyes are pink.

In his show bills, Barnum advertised the Lucasie family, consisting of four members, as being the last of a famous tribe of Albinos of Madagascar. They were Joseph's father, mother and sister. Joseph was 9, and his sister 12 years old. All were musicians.

Joseph was taken suddenly ill Wednesday afternoon at his home, 1117 Norton street.

Reprint of the *Kansas City Journal* story regarding Joseph Lucasie published September 25, 1909. The reported age at death is incorrect.

White Skin, Silken White Hair and Pink Eyes!!" P. T. Barnum also proclaimed the family to be of black Madagascan lineage and said that their pink eyes stayed wide open while they slept. A second child, an albino girl, was often added to increase the appeal of the act, but she was not related. Joseph Lucasie continued in show business on his own after his parents' retirement. However, he was astute enough to realize that the appeal of an albino was not enough anymore to attract large crowds. At the age of forty, he began playing the violin in a vaudeville act. He was financially successful in this endeavor, but he became increasingly resentful that the public still thought of him, in essence, as just an albino playing an instrument. At one point, he shaved his head as a means to distance himself from his condition. Joseph died in Kansas City, Kansas, on September 24, 1909, of edema. His obituary called him a "famous albino" and "great showman," but at the time of his death he was a restaurant employee. He was fifty-one. ♦

CHARLES PRICE AND ANNIE ALLEN PRICE

It was common for marriages to be performed between unlikely sideshow couples as publicity stunts. The fat lady often married the human skeleton, prompting newspaper coverage. After all, what reporter could resist that story? It was also common for show performers to meet and fall in love on the circuit, get married, and even have children. In a world where freaks had always been made to feel negative about themselves, love easily blossomed when society's misfits came together to work, play, and travel happily with one another, all overlooking the oddities of each other's conditions.

Annie Price was born Maude Pettitt in Cooktown, County in Tyrone, Ireland, in 1842–1844. She immigrated to Brooklyn, New York, with her family when she was fourteen years old and changed her name to Annie Allen. Reportedly, by the time she had reached eighteen, she weighed more than 300 pounds. At about twenty, she was hired as a sideshow attraction at the then impressive salary of eighty dollars a month, plus expenses. She was also given the services of a maid. She tired of the travel, however, and desired a more stable life so she went to work for P. T. Barnum, exhibiting herself as the fat lady at his dime museum in New York City. There she met and fell in love with fellow performer Charles Price. In the typical style of Barnum, Annie married Charles on February 24, 1884, before a paying crowd of several hundred "wedding guests" on stage at Barnum's dime museum. *The New York Times* wrote, "The Fat Woman's Choice/ Wooed And Won By The Giant From Madagascar". Each

Charles and Annie Price, the fat lady and the giant albino, were married on February 24, 1884. It was common to stage marriages between sideshow performers as publicity stunts but this was an actual marriage that lasted until Annie's death on October 25, 1889.

guest paid a dime to see the ceremony. Charles was a very tall, thin albino and the blushing bride registered 496 pounds on a hay scale the day of her wedding. Charles was about fifty and Annie was about forty-two. It is probable that this wedding

Charles's daughter from a previous marriage became a sideshow snake charmer in a Baltimore dime museum.

was not a fake ceremony. Charles had previously been married to a circus performer who left him for a sideshow fat man. Charles had been subsequently granted a divorce by the courts as well as custody of his children. Charles's daughter became a sideshow snake charmer in a Baltimore dime museum.

The New York Times spoke well of Charles when they reported on the wedding: "...The gentleman...possessing, as he does, the dual attractions of being at the same time a giant and an albino. He stands 8 feet, 4 inches on a dry goods box and often lights his cigar without effort at a street lamp. He combs his lovely hair a la Pompadour so that it stands on end like a fractured halo, and glimmers like a tin roof on a moonlight night....(His) handsome features are marred by a single defect, his left eye having suffered a total eclipse, leaving his right single to the charms of the voluptuous Miss Pettitt."

Also reported in the same article: "The reason they entered from the front of the house was that the girth of the bride prevented her ingress by the stage door. A stout pair of steps was produced and the lady was hauled and shoved over the footlights... the new Mrs. Price was attired in pink silk, en train, with cut décolleté...the only fault that the most observant critic might have found was that the bride had neglected to shave before the ceremony." Reportedly, the new bride then took her place next to Turtle Boy in the exhibition room before making a bridal tour of Harlem in a street car later that evening. About five years after their marriage, Annie took ill. She lost over a hundred pounds, going from 525 pounds to a mere 400 pounds. She died at her home at 19 Bayard Street, New York City, on October 25, 1889. She was forty-five years old. The cause of death was reported as "fatty degeneration of the heart and other trouble." Charles was by her side and had just given her a glass of brandy when she passed away. Charles also claimed she was secretly buried in Evergreen Cemetery after midnight on October 27, without a service, to avoid the expected large crowd. He also claimed she was buried in a specially built rosewood coffin that was twenty-eight inches wide, six feet long, and twenty-four inches deep. The truth was that Annie was buried in a simple pine coffin, albeit a very large pine box, and, most likely, she was buried in secrecy due to Charles' embarrassment of laying Annie to rest in a charity grave. An obituary headline read: "Death Of A Freak/ Annie Price, The Fat Woman Of A Museum, Expires Suddenly." The obituary stated that "Much difficulty was met with in getting the body down the stairs. It was wrapped in canvas and half a dozen men carried it down."

MYSTERY TO SOLVE

When did Charles die and where is he buried? Did he remarry after Annie's death?

The New York Times reported in an article dated October 27, 1889, that neither her husband nor the museum people could afford to bury her, but she was saved from a potter's field on Hart's Island because the undertaker claimed Annie was an Orangewoman. Later it was reported in the newspaper that the burial expenses had been paid by the proprietors of the museum where Annie exhibited. In truth, no one paid for Annie's burial. Annie Price was laid to rest in the Pathside section of Evergreen Cemetery, Brooklyn, in a charity grave indicating that absolutely no money was available for her burial. In the Pathside section, that is today closed, there are mostly grave sites that were untitled. This meant the plot belonged to the cemetery and it was normal for several people to be buried in the same plot, one on top of the other. Annie is buried with one other soul, Peter Lowe, who had died at Bellevue Hospital, then a psychiatric charity hospital, and was laid to rest two days after Annie. They were not related, nor even acquainted, but they share a grave together and Mr. Lowe now, so to speak, lies on top of Mrs. Price for eternity. No stone marks the site. The date and place of Charles's death or his burial site is not known. ♦

THE MARTIN SISTERS

The Martin sisters, Florence and Mary, toured with P. T. Barnum and exhibited themselves in his New York dime museum. The sisters were a favorite subject of "The Photographer of the Freaks," Charles Eisenmann. He most often photographed the sisters dressed entirely in white to enhance their angel-like, virginal appearances.

In the 1870s and 1880s, many people were becoming obsessed with the spiritual world, believing that they could communicate with the dead through séances. Mary Lincoln often paid "seers" to help her communicate with her dead husband, President

The sisters were a favorite subject of "The Photographer of the Freaks," Charles Eisenmann. He most often photographed the young sisters dressed entirely in white to enhance their angel-like, virginal appearances. Florence is on the left, Mary is on the right.

Florence married and retired from show business around 1894 but Mary continued to exhibit. She was billed in 1903 as "Mary Martin, the Bewildering Brilliant and Beautiful Albino Girl," or simply, "Mary Martin, Albino Queen."

Abraham Lincoln. There was a common belief among superstitious people that albinos could read minds, foretell the future, and communicate with the dead. P. T. Barnum played to this superstition and had the Martin Sisters "read the mind" of an audience member who was always planted there by Barnum, himself. The ploy, however, had a habit of backfiring so the fortune telling and mind reading trick was soon abandoned. The girls had no musical talent, but lucky for them beauty and sexual allure has always sold tickets to shows and the Victorian show-going, paying public was no exception. An 1886 advertisement for The Martin Sisters, at times erroneously referred to as "The Martin Twins," read: "A duo of beautiful colorless maidens… two sweet, charming lasses, framed in glorious masses of snow white hair which falls over their shoulders in graceful profusion, with features pale as sculptured marble, relieved only by their brilliant rose tinted eyes, they are strange specimens of lovely womanhood."

P. T. Barnum had the Martin Sisters "read the mind" of an audience member who was always planted there by Barnum himself.

Florence married and retired from show business around 1894, but Mary continued to exhibit. She was billed in 1903 as "Mary Martin, the Bewildering Brilliant and Beautiful Albino Girl" or simply, "Mary Martin, Albino Queen." However, around 1904, the novelty of seeing an albino, even a beautiful one, had waned with the paying public. Nothing else is known about the lives of the Martin sisters.

The girls had no musical talent, but lucky for them beauty and sexual allure has always sold tickets to shows and the Victorian show-going, paying public was no exception.

The beautiful Florence Martin.

Mystery to Solve: What happened to the Martin Sisters after they retired from show business? Did Mary also marry? When did they die, and where are they buried? ♦

8

MOVIE FREAKS

Freaks Who Appeared in Movies & Documentaries

THE LIVE FREAK SIDESHOW IN CIRCUSES, MIDWAYS, AND CARNIVALS WAS AN ACCEPTED MAINSTREAM FORM OF ENTERTAINMENT IN AMERICA AND EUROPE DURING THE EARLY DAYS OF THE SILVER SCREEN, BUT PERFORMERS WITH DISABILITIES AND WHO LOOKED DIFFERENT WERE USUALLY SHUNNED BY HOLLYWOOD AS UNDESIRABLES.

Even today, casting directors prefer to cast "normal" actors dressed in extreme costumes and makeup in the roles of abnormal beings. The early thought seemed to be that freaks were too shocking to be put into the movies. Today, shock sells. However, modern producers and directors strive to appear politically correct. Most shun social controversy, not in the script necessarily, but certainly when casting. Better to create a freak for a role than to be accused of exploiting someone with a disability. Another Hollywood misconception often portrayed in movies seemingly associates physically different bodies with a dark heart, strongly suggesting that severe physical differences are equal to evil thoughts and deeds. Those with abnormal bodies or distorted faces are often the film villains. It is also not unusual for movies to portray those with severe disabilities as also being mentally deficient. One of the rare exceptions to these hard-and-fast cinema rules is the movie *Freaks*, directed by Tod Browning and released in 1932. ♦

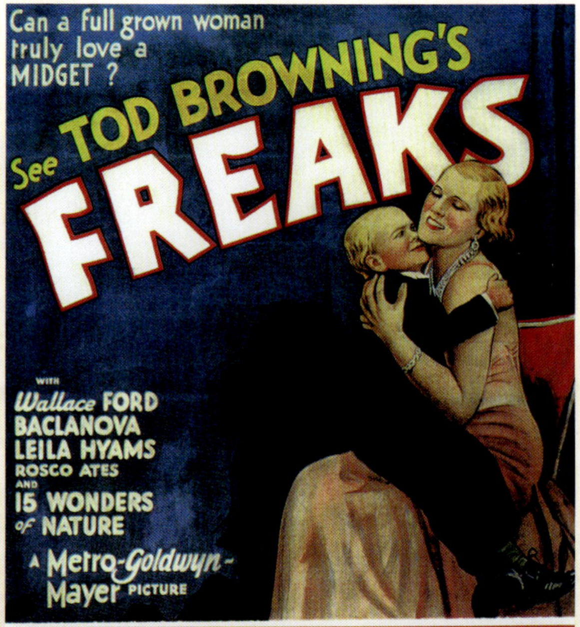

Browning had previously been heralded as an up-and-coming director. After the release of *Freaks*, he had trouble finding work and *Freaks* is considered responsible for bringing his career to an early end.

FREAKS
DIRECTED BY TOD BROWNING (1932)

Freaks was a controversial failure when it hit the movie houses of the day, but history now classifies the film as a classic. It is both a cult movie popular with young audiences and an excellent study example for students of the cinema. Censors and critics quickly forced the film to undergo extensive cuts, going from approximately ninety to sixty minutes, but the movie was still negatively received by audiences and recorded a then-staggering loss of $164,000. Sadly, the parts that were cut are considered lost today. The cut version of the film was still banned in Britain until 1963 and the Canadians called the movie "brutal and grotesque." It is still banned in Sweden to this day as well as being listed as banned in Finland and Ireland. The film was also titled *Forbidden Love* (USA informal title), *Nature's Mistakes* (USA informal title), and *The Monster Show.* Browning had previously been heralded as an up-and-coming director for his collaborations with Lon Chaney and for directing Bela Lugosi in *Dracula* (1931). After the release of *Freaks*, he had trouble finding work and *Freaks* is considered responsible for bringing his career to an early end. Browning used real professional sideshow freaks in his movie, all of

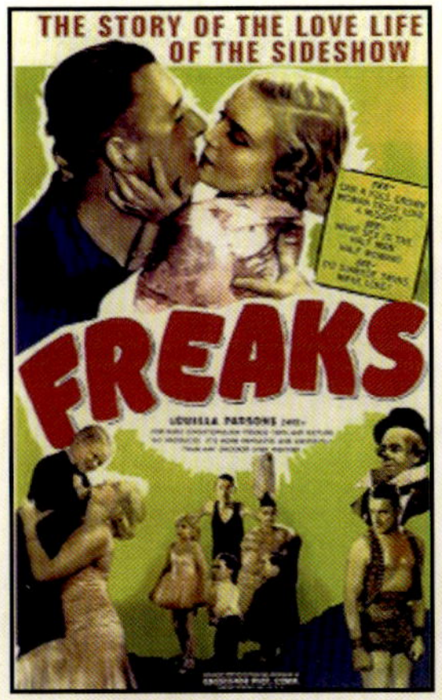

Freaks was a controversial success when it hit the movie houses of the day in 1932, and it remains a classic even now.

The cast and main crew of *Freaks*. Tod Browning is in the back row dressed in a sweater and tie.

THE CAST OF FREAKS

Wallace Ford	Phroso
Leila Hyams	Venus
Olga Baclanova	Cleopatra
Roscoe Ates	Roscoe
Harry Earles	Hans
Henry Victor	Hercules
Daisy Earles	Frieda
Rose Dione	Madame Tetrallini
Daisy Hilton	Siamese Twin
Violet Hilton	Siamese Twin
Matt McHugh	Rollo Brother
Martha Morris	Armless Girl
Randian	Himself
Olga Roderick	Bearded Lady
Angelo Rossitto	Angeleno
Schlitzie	Herself
Jennie Lee Snow	Herself
Michael Visaroff	Jean the Caretaker
Zip	Themselves
Frank O'Connor	Herself
Peter Robinson	Human Skeleton
Josephine-Joseph	Him/Herself
Tom London	
Johnny Eck	Johnny the Half Boy
Elvira Snow	Herself
Elizabeth Green	Bird Girl
Ernie S. Adams	Sideshow Patron
Louise Beavers	Maid
Edward S. Brophy	Rollo Brother
Albert Conti	Landowner

whom have since passed away. It is most likely that Browning was able to easily assemble his cast because the freaks were basically able to play themselves. They were portrayed in the movie in a dignified manner (especially by 1932 standards), they were paid well for their performances, and it probably didn't hurt that the story line of the movie called for the evil "beautiful people" to get exactly what was due them. Also, who among us can resist the rare opportunity to appear on the Big Screen?

No one has ever attempted to do a remake of Browning's masterpiece, a tribute to this creative and unique project that, quite frankly, got it right the first time. It would almost be easier to redo *Gone With The Wind* than to do a remake of *Freaks* and recapture the bold originality, core moral essence, and powerful visual shock and terror of this great masterpiece. ♦

VIOLET & DAISY HILTON, "SAN ANTONIO'S SIAMESE TWINS"

Violet and Daisy Skinner were born February 19, 1908, in Brighton, East Essex, England, to an unwed barmaid who promptly sold her two-week-old twins to Mary Hilton, the midwife who delivered them. Mary saw them as a money-making opportunity and raised them to be musical performers. The twins always claimed that they were badly mistreated by Mary Hilton and her husband, whom they called "Auntie" and "Sir." They said they were beaten, prohibited from making

Violet and Daisy Skinner were born to an unwed barmaid who promptly sold her two-week-old twins to Mary Hilton, the midwife who delivered them.

Accounts vary as to the treatment the twins received when young.

friends, isolated from human contact, and kept in a state of poverty even though they earned a substantial amount of money. In fairness to Mary Hilton, however, many who knew the twins when they were in Mary's care completely disagreed with that harsh account. Percilla Bejano, "The Monkey Girl," played with the twins when all were around the age of ten. She claimed they were never ill-treated, lived well, and that the girls were given the best education along with music lessons.

Their circus and sideshow career started at age three in England and continued in America where the twins were brought when they were around eight. They also played to American vaudeville audiences and shared billing with guests such as Harry Houdini. It is said that Houdini taught the twins self-hypnosis as a means for them to mentally obtain time alone.

As they got older, Daisy dyed her hair blond, then later red, to distinguish herself from Violet. Daisy

They came to America when they were around eight. They also played to American vaudeville audiences and shared billing with guests such as Harry Houdini. It is said that Houdini taught the twins self-hypnosis as a means for them to obtain time alone mentally.

The twins eventually successfully sued for their independence. Violet and Daisy were reportedly making as much as $5,000 a week and were most likely the highest paid freaks in the business at the time.

was said to do the most talking, Violet preferring to say little. As they faced front, Violet was on the left and Daisy was on the right. They were considered to be extremely beautiful. Violet and Daisy both hated doctors since most medical practitioners usually wanted to study the pair to see if it was possible to separate them surgically, a thought that, surprisingly enough, terrified the sisters. People around the twins were always amazed that they seemed to be able to communicate ideas to one

A 1955 photo of Violet and Daisy working in the Miami, Florida, snack bar they briefly owned.

Violet and Daisy were notorious for their loose dating practices and scandalous affairs.

another without uttering a sound. In 1931, the twenty-three-year-old twins consulted a lawyer, Martin J. Arnold, and successfully sued for their independence. Mary Hilton had died, but she had willed the girls to her husband and daughter, Edith, like property. Violet and Daisy were reportedly making as much as $5,000 a week and were most likely the highest paid freaks in the business at the time.

Violet and Daisy were notorious for their loose dating practices and scandalous affairs. Each twin vied with the other to attract the most men and there were rumors that they were not above having married suitors. Both twins married. Daisy briefly married a performer named Buddy Sawyer, but her husband moved out after ten days saying that she was a lovely girl, but he guessed he just wasn't the type of fellow that should marry a Siamese twin. Violet was married in the Cotton Bowl in Dallas, Texas, during the Texas Centennial in 1936, but it is probable that the marriage was merely a publicity stunt since the marriage was annulled shortly thereafter. Violet's left hip joined Daisy's right hip at a forty-five degree angle. In adulthood, they were four feet, ten inches tall and weighed approximately one hundred pounds each. The bones of their lower spine were joined and they shared a common blood and nervous system, resulting in shared sexual sensations. In interviews, the twins would claim that they could "blank out" what the other was doing, even read, nap, or meditate when the need arose.

In 1932, they acted in the movie *Freaks,* and in 1951, they appeared in *Chained for Life,* a biographical film about their lives. Unfortunately, *Freaks* was a box office and critical failure at the time and *Chained for Life* was poorly produced and directed, plus Violet and Daisy gave a performance in the film that even the kindest critics said was awful. As the twins aged, they were ill-equipped both professionally and emotionally to manage their own careers or financial affairs. Many romantic suitors and show business crooks took advantage of these facts and stole or bilked them out of large sums of money. Violet and Daisy earned and lost several fortunes in their lifetimes, and after 1951, they reportedly fell into abject poverty and almost total obscurity. They briefly ran a snack bar in Miami, but it folded. Their last show business stint involved making guest appearances at mostly small town drive-in movies that were showing a re-run of *Freaks.* For whatever reason, their manager abandoned the sisters shortly thereafter, leaving them stranded and destitute in Monroe, North Carolina.

On January 4, 1969, Violet and Daisy were found dead in their rental residence in Charlotte, North Carolina, huddled together on a floor heater. The apparent cause of death was influenza. They were sixty. Medical professionals determined that Daisy died first, and it was speculated that Violet lived two to four days after Daisy's death. They had been working as grocery store clerks at the time of their death. The grocery store owner remembered the day in 1962 when they walked into his store seeking employment. He claimed they were heavily made up with red toe nails, but their hair was dirty and they wore wrinkled clothing. They offered him two employees for the price of one. They worked in the store for seven years. Reportedly, they never spoke of their show business background and many of the store's customers did not realize that the two sisters working side by side were Siamese twins.

The Hilton sisters are buried under a marker inscribed, "Beloved Siamese Twins." No survivors were listed in their obituary. They were buried in a donated plot in the Forest Lawn West Cemetery in Charlotte, Section M, Lot 313. A critically acclaimed Broadway musical titled *Side Show* opened October 16, 1997. It was a musical that was loosely based on the lives of Violet and Daisy Hilton. ♦

Film Credits

Freaks . . . . (1932)

Chained for Life . . . . (1951)

THE EARLES/DOLL FAMILY OF MIDGETS: HARRY, GRACIE, DAISY, & TINY (ALL SIBLINGS)

The Earles were known as a family of midget siblings, Harry, Gracie, Daisy, and Tiny. Harry Earles was the stage name adopted by Kurt Fritz Scheider. He was born April 3, 1902, in Stolpen, Germany, and came to America from Germany around 1915 with his sister Freida (stage name, Gracie born March 12, 1899). In Germany, they had worked in sideshows as Hans and Gretel and were billed as "the smallest dancing couple on Earth." In America, they also toured in a sideshow, working for their sponsor, a man named Burt Earles, and adopted his last name to appear more Americanized. They danced, sang, and rode horses in the show. In 1925, their sister Hilda (stage name Daisy, born April 29, 1907) joined them and in 1926, their sister Elly Annie arrived (stage name, Tiny, born July 23, 1914). Daisy was often referred to as the midget Mae West. Three other siblings born into the Scheider family were of average size and structure. The four worked in the movies while simultaneously working for Ringling Bros. and Barnum & Bailey Circus. They also acted in comedies with Laurel and Hardy. Around 1939, the four left the film business, preferring the circus life, where they all worked making very lucrative salaries. Also around 1939, Burt Earles died and the family took on the new surname Doll. They claimed audiences always said they looked like "dolls" or "little dollies" so the siblings decided the new name was appropriate.

The Earles were siblings: Harry, Gracie, Daisy, and Tiny.

The Earles stayed to themselves most of the time, preferring their own company. Daisy was the only one of the siblings to marry, but she divorced her husband, who was of average size, less than a year into the marriage. When working on the movie *The Wizard of Oz*, the siblings had their own apartment and reportedly distanced themselves from the other Munchkins in the cast due to their reputed immoral behavior and bawdy antics.

In 1958, the foursome became weary of the life on the road, retired, and bought a custom-made home together in Sarasota, Florida, that had an attraction they opened to the public aptly named "The Doll's House." Grace died on November 8, 1970, at the age of eighty. Daisy died March 15, 1980, at the age of seventy-two, and Harry died May 4, 1985, at the age of eighty-three. Tiny died on September 6, 2004, at the age of ninety after a long illness. All remained in their home until their death. All four were cremated. ♦

The Earles stayed to themselves most of the time, preferring their own company. Daisy was the only one of the siblings to marry, but she later divorced.

When making the movie *The Wizard of Oz*, the Earles had their own apartment and reportedly distanced themselves from the rest of the Munchkins in the cast due to their reputed immoral behavior and bawdy antics.

Harry Earles was a lead in the 1932 movie cult classic *Freaks*.

Harry Earles' Film Credits:

The Unholy Three . . . . (1925)
That's My Baby . . . . (1926)
Baby Clothes . . . . (1926)
Baby Brother . . . . (1927)
Sailors Beware! . . . . (1927)
Three-Ring Marriage . . . . (1928)
The Unholy Three . . . . (1930)
Good New . . . . (1930, not credited)
Be Big . . . . (1931)
Freaks . . . . (1932)
The Wizard of Oz . . . . (1939)

Daisy Earles' Film Credits

Three-Ring Marriage . . . . (1928)
Freaks . . . . (1932)
The Wizard of Oz . . . . (1939)
The Greatest Show on Earth . . . .
(1952, very brief appearance)

Gracie Earles' Film Credits

Be Big! . . . . (1931)
The Wizard of Oz . . . . (1939)

Tiny Earles' Film Credits

Special Delivery . . . . (1927 uncredited)
Three-Ring Marriage . . . . (1928)
Be Big! . . . . (1931)
Freaks . . . .
(1932, brief appearance, not credited)
The Wizard of Oz . . . . (1939).

ANGELO ROSSITTO, "LITTLE MO," "ANGELINO," "LITTLE ANGELO," "ANGELO," "ANGIE," "DON BARRETT," "ANGELO ROSITO," OR "ANGELO ROSSITA"

Angelo was born Angelo Savatore Rossitto in Omaha, Nebraska, on February 18, 1908. He was a dwarf. He went to Hollywood in the 1920s to become a star, and legend says he was selling newspapers one day when John Barrymore got him a film role. He entered the movies in his teens and usually appeared in highly visible supporting roles or as an exotic extra. He stood only two feet, eleven inches tall. He was a very popular and much sought after Hollywood actor because of his talent and appearance. His dark hair and facial features made him a natural to play many of his roles. He also had the reputation in the industry for being highly professional on the set. He debuted on the Silent Screen. From 1927 through 1987, he appeared in feature films, including the 1932 movie classic *Freaks.* He acted alongside such great Hollywood legends as Lon Chaney, John Barrymore, and Bella Lugosi, and he was a stunt double for Shirley Temple until she outgrew him. He played a wide range of characters and parts such as that of a dwarf, midget, gnome, pygmy, villain monster, and alien. He acted in comedies, dramas, science fiction flicks, mysteries, fantasy films, and horror movies. He also regularly acted in the TV series *Baretta*, starring Robert Blake, and appeared in numerous TV shows. Angelo didn't become a well-known Hollywood household name even though his film and TV credits are impressive. He was in more than 200 productions, but most required only a few days or weeks of his time. Many were bit parts and not credited. He made his regular living from the 1930s through the 1960s at a newsstand in Hollywood just outside the gate of one of the studios. Reportedly, he joked that when he was needed for a film, they would simply pass the word directly to him on the street, and he would report. In 1941, he ran for mayor of Los Angeles, finishing seventh in a field of eight. In 1985, at the age of seventy-seven, Angelo co-starred as the mad "Master Blaster" in *Mad Max Beyond Thunderdome.* He was almost completely blind at the time of that performance.

He died on September 21, 1991, in Los Angeles, California, from complications during surgery. He was eighty-three. ♦

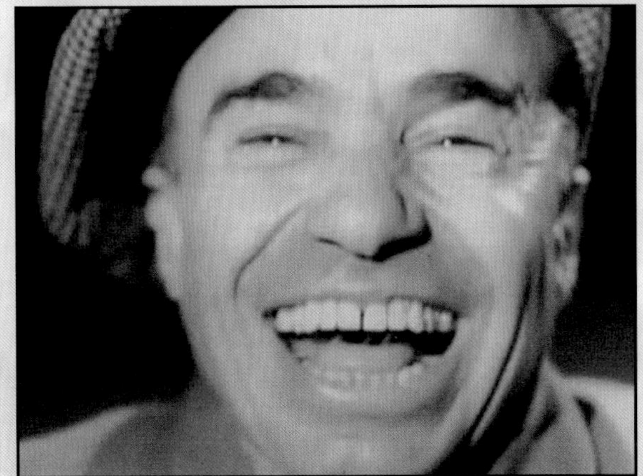

Angelo went to Hollywood in the 1920s to become a star. Legend says he was discovered by John Barrymore selling newspapers.

Angelo Rossitto Film Credits:

The Beloved Rogue . . . . . (1927, debut)
Old San Francisco . . . . . (1927)
While the City Sleeps . . . . . (1928, not credited)
Seven Footprints to Satan . . . . . (1929)
One Stolen Night . . . . . (1929)
The Mysterious Island . . . . . (1929, not credited)
The Phantom of Paris . . . . . (1931, not credited)
Freaks . . . . . (1932)
The Sign of the Cross . . . . . (1932, not credited)
The Spectacle Maker . . . . . (1934, not credited)
I Believed in You . . . . . (1934, not credited)
Babes in Toyland . . . . . (1934, not credited)
A Midsummer Night's Dream . . . (1935, not credited)
Child Bride . . . . . (1938)
Mr. Wong in Chinatown . . . . . (1939, not credited)
Doomed to Die . . . . . (1940, not credited)
Spooks Run Wild . . . . . (1941)
Hellzapoppin . . . . . (1941, not credited)
The Corpse Vanishes . . . . . (1942)
Ali Baba and the Forty Thieves (1944, not credited)
The Spider Woman . . . . . (1944, not credited)
Lady in the Dark . . . . . (1944, not credited)
Scared to Death . . . . . (1947)
The Sin of Harold Diddlebock . . . (1947, not credited)
Samson and Delilah . . . . . (1949, not credited)
The Baron of Arizona . . . . . (1950)
Jungle Jim in Pygmy Island . . . . . (1950, not credited)
The Bandit Queen . . . . . (1950)

Angelo appeared in over 200 productions. He is shown here in *Freaks*.

Mesa of Lost Women .... (1953, not credited)
Jungle Moon Men .... (1955, not credited)
Dementia .... (1955)
Carousel .... (1956, not credited)
Invasion of the Saucer .... *Men* (1957)
The Story of Mankind .... (1957, not credited)
The Adventures of Superpup .... (1958, TV)
The Wild and the Innocent ...... (1959, not credited)
The Rebel .... (1960 TV episode, "The Earl of Durango")
Pocketful of Miracles .... (1961, not credited)
Terrified .... (1962, not credited)
The Magic Sword .... (1962)
The Wonderful World of the Brothers Grimm (1962, not credited)
Circus Trick .... (1965, TV episode, not credited)
Gunsmoke .... (TV series
The Man from U.N.C.L.E. ...... (1967 TV episode: "The Hula Doll Affair")
The Trip .... (1967)
H. R. Pufnstuf .... (1969 and 1970 TV series)
Alex in Wonderland .... (1970)
Dracula vs. Frankenstein .... (1971)
Mongo's Back in Town .... (1971, TV movie)
Brain of Blood .... (1972)
Little Cigars .... (1973)
The Clones .... (1973)
Black Day for Bluebeard .... (1974, TV movie)
I Wonder Who's Killing Her Now (1975)
Baretta .... (1977, TV series, a regular on the show as Little Moe)
The Competitive Edge ...... (1978, TV episode, not credited)
The Rockford Files .... (TV series)
The Hardy Boys/Nancy Drew Mysteries (1978, TV two episodes)
Studs Lonigan .... (1979, TV mini-series)
The Dark .... (1979, not credited)
Fairy Tales .... (1979)
Adult Fairy Tales .... (1979, UK)
Jason of Star Command .... (1979, TV series)
The Incredible Hulk .... (1980, TV series)
Galaxina .... (1980)
Something Wicked This Way Comes (1983)
Mad Max Beyond Thunderdome (1985)
Amazing Stories .... (1985 TV)
The Offspring .... (1987)
Amazing Stories: Book Five .... (1992 TV, segment "Fine Tuning," postmortem release)

FRANCES O'CONNOR, "THE LIVING VENUS DE MILO"

Frances Belle O'Conner was born on September 8, 1914, in Granite City, Minnesota, without arms. She compensated for her disability by becoming extremely adept at using her feet. She was able to sew, dress herself, feed herself, and even shoot a gun without aid. Her mother took special care in rearing Frances by both showering her with love and making her self-reliant. Reportedly, those closest to her said that Frances never showed self-pity but instead constantly maintained an upbeat manner and had a very good sense of humor. Her first show-business stint was with the Al G. Barnes Circus in Sheridan, Wyoming. Her mother acted as her manager for her entire career. She also toured with the Sells-Floto Circus, Ringling Brothers, and Cole Brothers Circus. She very much enjoyed signing autographs for her fans with her feet and had excellent penmanship. She had a cameo part in the movie *Freaks,* showing her eating and drinking using her feet. Many men were attracted to Frances. She was beautiful with a sweet nature, plus it did not hurt that she was innocently able to show a lot of leg in her performances. Reportedly, she received several proposals of marriage but she never married, instead preferring to live with the mother she adored. After her

MYSTERY TO SOLVE

Where is Frances buried, and what did she die from at such a relatively young age?

mother/manager passed away, Frances went into retirement. She died in Long Beach, California, on January 30, 1982. She was sixty-seven. ♦

Frances compensated for her disability by becoming extremely adept at using her feet. She was able to sew, dress herself, feed herself, and even shoot a gun without aid.

Frances never married, preferring to live with the mother she adored. She died in Long Beach, California, at the age of sixty-seven.

Frances enjoyed signing autographs for her fans with her foot.

KOO KOO, "MINNIE HA HA," OR "THE BIRD GIRL FROM MARS"

Koo Koo was born Minnie Woolsey in New Mexico in 1880. She had a small part in the movie *Freaks*. Very little is known about her life. She was afflicted with Harper's syndrome (also called Virchow-Seckel syndrome, Seckel syndrome, bird-headed dwarfism, and nanocephaly). This is an intrauterine form of dwarfism characterized by multiple congenital anomalies such as short stature, a beak-like nose, very large ears, an absence of hair and teeth, intellectual disability, and/or joint and limb disabilities. Sadly, Koo Koo was afflicted with all anomalies and she was almost blind, as well. Koo Koo's managers capitalized on her odd appearances by dressing her in various costumes. She was billed as "Minnie Ha-Ha" and "The Bird Girl from Mars." The majority of the time, however, she performed in a bird-like costume and strutted the stage, strangely dancing, or she just sat and quietly stared out into space. She usually wore oversized glasses with very thick lenses, adding to her strange bird-like appearance. It is probable that she spent at least part or most of her life institutionalized. The date and place of her death is unknown.

Mystery to Solve: So many mysteries about Koo Koo remain unanswered. What of her early life? What happened to her in her later life? When and where did she die, and where is she buried? ♦

Koo Koo's managers capitalized on her odd appearances by dressing her in various costumes, but the majority of the time she wore a bird-like costume on stage.

Koo Koo was born Minnie Woolsey in New Mexico in 1880. Very little is known of her early life.

ELIZABETH "BETTY" GREEN, "THE OTHER KOO KOO," "BIRD GIRL," "THE STORK WOMAN," OR "MOLINA THE PINHEAD"

Betty Green's early years are a mystery. Not much is known of her background or beginnings as a sideshow freak. By most accounts, she was not a freak at all, but just an odd-looking tiny woman who capitalized upon her strange looks, accentuating it with facial gestures, a shaved head, and costumes. She had a small part in the movie *Freaks*. According to the director, Tod Browning, "Betty was a Jewish girl from Springfield, Massachusetts, who owned five apartment houses." Betty was known as "The other Koo Koo" and often fans mix up the two performers. Most likely, Betty returned home after the filming of *Freaks* and lived the remained of her life as an ordinary citizen with an extraordinary appearance. ♦

By most accounts, Betty Green was not a freak at all, but just an odd-looking woman who capitalized upon her strange looks,

MYSTERY TO SOLVE

Was Tod Browning right when he said that Betty was a nice Jewish woman who owned real estate in Massachusetts? How did she get started in show business? When and where did she die, and where is she buried?

1932 publicity shot for *Freaks* with Betty and Lady Olga.

JOSEPHINE-JOSEPH

Josephine-Joseph was born in 1913 in a village near Krakow, Poland. His father was a simple Jewish farmer. Although Josephine-Joseph claimed to be a hermaphrodite, most reports claim he was just a skillful impersonator, homosexual, or a transvestite. Although a handful of half and halfs were true hermaphrodites, most were merely "blow-off" acts. However, the sexual lure of such a possibility, plus the offered tantalizing look at parts of the human body usually clothed in public in that day, made the half and half acts very popular, so much so that they often could carry the entire show. Very little is known about Josephine-Joseph, in-

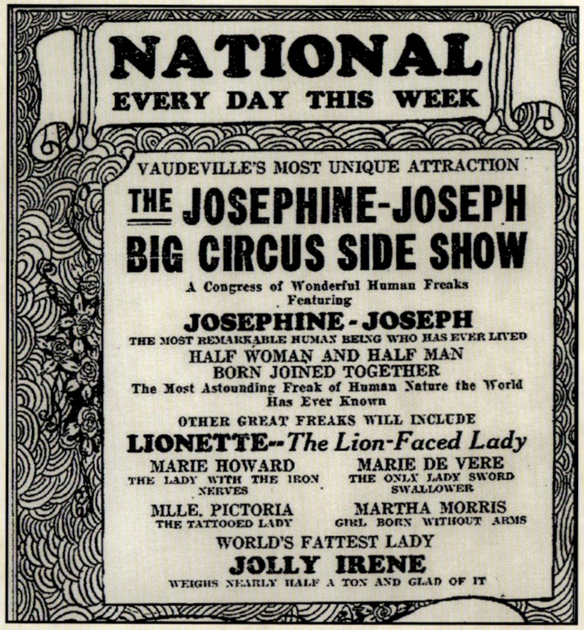

A 1928 Richmond, Virginia, ad for The National featuring The Josephine-Joseph Big Circus Side Show.

Josephine-Joseph was born in 1913 in a village near Krakow, Poland. Although Josephine-Joseph claimed to be a hermaphrodite, most reports claim he was just a skillful impersonator or a transvestite.

cluding his true name. He always claimed in newspaper interviews that he had been raised as an average boy until the age of twelve when he started to exhibit feminine traits on the left side of his body, but that story was most likely false and was just repeated as a means to gain publicity.

He built up his right side by exercising that side only, tanned that side, cut his hair short, grew a half beard, and wore jungle-style costumes to emphasize maleness. On the left side, he allowed his hair to grow and styled it, he never exercised that side nor allowed it to tan, he wore makeup, jewelry, and a false breast, plus always dressed that side in women's attire. The look was very convincing to the unsophisticated public of the day. One newspaper headline read: "Seeing is Believing. Half of her can do a stevedore's work, the other half embroidery." In 1928, The Josephine-Joseph Big Circus Side Show toured America, bringing the sideshow element and a congress of freaks to the vaudeville stage. It is not clear if Josephine-Joseph was the promoter and manager of the show or if his act merely carried the show, but he always received top billing. Since he would have only been fifteen years old, it is most likely he was not the boss. Other members of the show were Jolly Irene, a fat lady;

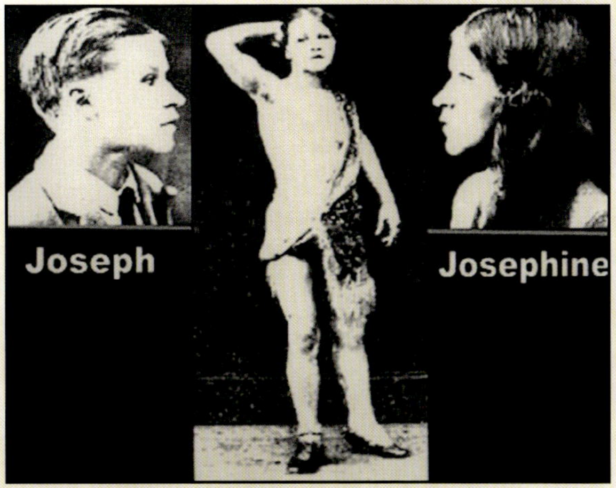

One newspaper headline read: "Seeing is Believing. Half of her can do a stevedore's work, the other half embroidery."

Martha Morris, "The Armless Wonder"; Marie De Vere, a female sword-swallower; a tattooed lady named Mademoiselle Pictoria; Lionette, "The Lion-Faced Lady"; and Marie Howard, who allowed her husband to throw knives at her without obtaining a restraining order.

In 1930, he exhibited in Coney Island. In 1932, nineteen-year-old Josephine-Joseph played himself in Tod Browning's movie *Freaks.* He had a small speaking part and portrayed a fleeting love interest in the strongman. These two clips were enough,

In 1932, nineteen-year-old Josephine-Joseph played himself in *Freaks*. He had a small speaking part and portrayed a fleeting love interest in the strongman. He remains one of the most popular cast members among the cult following of the movie.

however, to make him one of the most popular cast members among the cult following of the movie. The remainder of his life and death remain a mystery. As he aged, it is possible he could not believably pull off the feminine side of the act any longer, as was the case with many of the half and half blow-off acts. Another theory: he fell in love but his intended took exception with going out with a man who was better looking than she was or she tired of sharing her clothes, makeup, and jewelry. ♦

MARTHA MORRIS, "THE ARMLESS WONDER"

Martha Morris was born in Chicago in 1904 to David and Jennie Strumpf Morris, and the parents of eight other children. No one else in the family had physical disabilities, but Martha was born without arms, plus her legs and torso were shortened and deformed. Her feet were attached to her body just below the hips. For this reason, she could not walk nor could she dress or feed herself and required a wheelchair and care attendant at all times. She started her sideshow career in her early teens and was billed as "The Armless Wonder." Martha compensated for her disability by becoming extremely adept at using her feet. Her show and publicity shots demonstrated Martha writing by using her left foot to hold the pencil, or typing by using both feet. She could even adeptly thread a needle. She appeared at Coney Island in the 1920s and traveled with a carnival. She also appeared at the Chicago World's Fair at the Century of Progress exposition. She had a small part in *Freaks*, playing the wife of Angeleno, a dwarf. That experience must have been thrilling for Martha since in a newspaper interview, her father said that Martha's favorite thing to do was to attend the (movie) theatre. He claimed she never tired of going and could sit through the same film many times. Martha never married and passed away on April 5, 1937, in a Chicago hospital, suffering from pneumonia. She was thirty-three. ♦

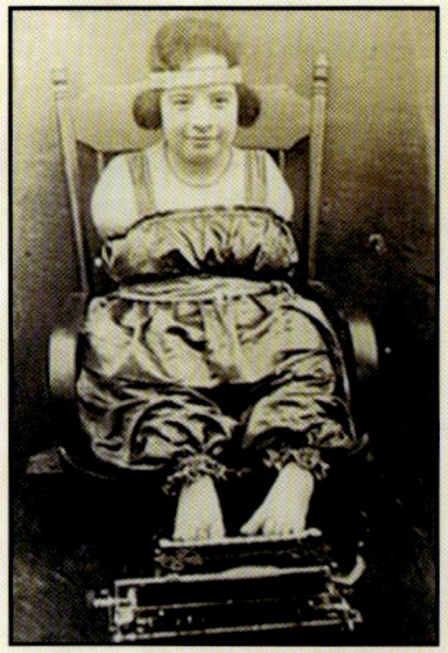

Martha Morris was born in 1904 without arms or legs. She started exhibiting in her early teens as "The Armless Wonder."

Martha shown in a lineup of other performers at Hubert's Dime Museum in 1923.

OLGA RODERICK, "LADY OLGA THE BEARDED LADY," "PRINCESS OLGA," OR "MADAME OLGA"

Lady Olga shown with Tod Browning and other members of the cast of *Freaks*. She was the only freak who publicly denounced the movie and said that she regretted being a member of the cast.

Lady Olga was born Jane Barnell on January 4, 1871, in Wilmington, North Carolina. She had two siblings but was the only one in the family with a physical abnormality. It is said her mother, in essence, sold her to a traveling circus that came through town when she was only four years old. Her father traveled a great deal and was not at home at that time. Jane ended up in Europe, fell ill, was hospitalized, and was quickly abandoned by the circus owners. Her father tracked her down to an orphanage in Berlin where she had been placed when she was released from the hospital. He took her back to her grandmother's family farm in North Carolina for safe-keeping. She worked on the farm for several years but it is probable she resented the hard work. A neighbor worked during the carnival season as a strongman. He encouraged Jane to join the sideshow again, pointing out the easy money she could make if she stopped shaving her beard. She did just that, signing on with John Robinson's Circus in the early 1890s. At that time she was billed as the bearded lady with a thirteen-inch growth.

In 1931, Lady Olga wed Thomas O'Boyle, a seasoned circus clown and barker. She was sixty years old and the groom was thirty-nine.

She toured with many of the major circuses of the day, including Ringling Bros. and Barnum & Bailey Circus in the 1930s. She performed using several stage names before finally settling on "Lady Olga." In 1932, she played a bearded lady in Tod Browning's cult classic *Freaks*. In the movie, she gives birth to a baby girl to the delight of the father, The Human Skeleton, and other sideshow freaks. Of all the cast members, she was the only one who ever publicly denounced the movie and said that she regretted being a member of the cast. In the 1930s through the 1940s, Lady Olga exhibited at Hubert's Museum in Times Square and World Circus Side Show at Coney Island. In real life, Lady

MYSTERY TO SOLVE

Were Lady Olga's two children illegitimate and did they both die before 1906? Where is Lady Olga buried?

Olga was said to have married twice and given birth to children before she was thirty. It is possible she invented the marriages to cover up two illegitimate births. Many sideshow performers did away with legal technicalities when it came to nuptials. According to family genealogy, both children died before 1906, birth dates unknown. It is also possible that one or both children were placed in orphanages instead. That was a common practice during this time if children proved too much a burden to rear for one or both parents.

In 1931, Lady Olga legally wed Thomas O'Boyle, a seasoned circus clown and barker. She was sixty years old and the groom was thirty-nine, a mere twenty-one years younger than his blushing bride. Lady Olga may have been the original cougar. The 1940 census shows the happy couple living in New York City, her occupation "bearded lady," age seventy, and still working. Thomas' occupation is listed as "ticket seller." Lady Olga passed away in Los Angles, California, on October 26, 1951, at the age of eighty. Her final resting place is unknown. Her career as a bearded lady was one of the longest in sideshow history, spanning over fifty years. ♦

JOHNNY ECK, "THE HALF MAN," "JOHNNY HALF-BOY," OR "JOHNNY ECK, THE HALF BOY"

Johnny Eck was born John Eckhardt Jr. on August 27, 1911, in Baltimore, Maryland, to John Sr. and Amelia Eckhardt. He was a second-born fraternal twin; his brother, Robert, was born without disabilities and weighed a healthy six pounds. An older sister, Carrie, born twelve years earlier, was also without disabilities. Johnny weighed only two pounds and was less than eight inches in length. He had a condition called sacral agenesis, a spinal deformity. Although he appeared to actually be a half boy, he had small, unusable legs and feet that were kept concealed under clothing that was specially created for Johnny. Even though

Johnny Eck was described in various articles as an excellent musician, well-educated, a reader of the best literature, and a fine-looking chap.

he was not expected to live at birth, Johnny thrived and was walking on his hands at age one. Johnny would say in later life that his parents were devoted to him. He was given the family name John Jr. even though he was not expected to live. This was a loving tribute by his parents that deeply moved him his entire life.

His parents made sure he had a regular childhood and his mother liked to tell everyone that her son could do anything any other child could do, and that Johnny could do a lot of things better." The 1930 census lists Johnny, age eighteen, as an actor working in a dime museum. He was actually a seasoned performer by 1930, having started in the business when he was only twelve. He was billed

A young Johnny with his twin brother Robert, who was born without physical disabilities.

Even though he was not expected to live at birth, Johnny thrived and was walking on his hands at age one. Johnny started in the sideshow business when he was only twelve. He was billed as "Johnny Eck, the Half-Boy" or simply "Johnny Half-Boy."

Johnny shown in a scene from *Freaks*. Tod Browning said of Johnny that he was an excellent actor.

as "Johnny Eck, the Half-Boy" or simply "Johnny Half-Boy" and eventually traveled with Captain John M. Sheesley's circus. By the 1940 census, his twin brother had joined Johnny and both were listed as performers in show business. Robert acted as Johnny's magician's helper and it is said that the only time the twins were separated from one another was during the filming of the 1932 movie *Freaks*. The two were famous for a magic trick in which Robert was sawed in half, producing the half-boy, Johnny.

As a child, Johnny had dreamed of becoming an employee of the railroad and traveling to exotic destinations. His mother would carry him to the railroad tracks, where Johnny would contentedly lie for hours and watch the trains. He would later in life indeed become a train conductor. In the course of his lifetime, he also succeeded as a sideshow performer, artist, window-screen painter, photographer, magician, Punch and Judy puppeteer, expert model maker, race car driver, swimmer, gymnast and movie actor. He traveled the world making a handsome salary. He was described in various articles as "an excellent musician, well-educated, a reader of the best literature, and a fine-looking chap."

Tod Browning, creator of the movie *Freaks*, said of Johnny Eck during an interview, "he has a very complete and brilliant mind." He also said that Johnny was an excellent actor and if he had been born without disabilities, he would have been a real Hollywood star. Johnny was only twenty years old when he was cast in one of the major roles in *Freaks*. Tod Browning also claimed that Johnny abhorred the sideshow life and that his true love was music.

Reportedly, Johnny climbed the stairs to the top of the Washington Monument on his hands in 1938. He was displayed in several Ripley's Believe It Or Not Odditoriums in the late 1930s. Robert Ripley was said to have called Johnny Eck "the most remarkable man alive." Johnny was very handsome and always meticulously attired. Close friends and fellow performers always said that he had an unsinkable spirit that inspired all around him. Someone asked him once if he wished he had legs and he reportedly said, "Why would I want those? Then I'd have pants to press." Unfortunately, his always-positive outlook on life and love of his fellow man came to an end in 1987 when thieves broke into Johnny and Robert's home. Not content with just robbing the seventy-six-year-old brothers, they physically attacked them, as well. Johnny never seemed to recover from the brutal physical and mental assault, and spent the remaining three years of his life in almost total seclusion. He often said that the real freaks in the world were outside his house. Johnny Eck died of a heart attack on January 5, 1991, in Baltimore, Maryland, in the house where he had been born, 622 N. Milton Avenue. He was seventy-nine. His beloved twin brother, Robert, died in 1995. Both are buried side by side for eternity in a plot at Green Mount Cemetery in Baltimore, Maryland. ♦

Johnny Eck Movie Credits

Freaks . . . . (1932)
Tarzan the Ape Man . . . . (1932, not credited)
Tarzan Escapes . . . . (1936, not credited)
Tarzan's Secret Treasure . . . . (1941, not credited)

PRINCE RANDIAN (RANDION), "THE HUMAN TORSO," "LIVING TORSO," "THE SNAKE," "PILLOW MAN," "CATERPILLAR MAN," "SAUSAGE MAN," OR "HUMAN WORM"

Very little is known about the early life of Prince Randian, including his real name. Ship manifests state his birthplace as Demerara, (British) Guyana, around the years 1870–1875. He is often photographed with a wooden box where he kept his show props and, reportedly, he constructed and painted the box himself.

Very little is known about the early life of Prince Randian, including his real name. Ship manifests state his birthplace as Demerara, (British) Guyana, around the years 1870–1875. He is also listed as an African black or East Indian and a Hindoo [sic], and it was noted that he could neither read nor write in 1917. That same year, he was traveling on the SS *Parima* with an attendant and was detained for two days in need of hospital care upon arrival in the United States from St. Thomas, his permanent address at that time. By 1923, his permanent address was in Plainfield, New Jersey. He lists his occupation as Theatrical Actor or Artist, but on the 1917 manifests, "Freak" has been imposed over that section by an inspector of the cruise line.

Prince Randian was born with tetra-amelia syndrome, an extremely rare inherited condition that results in the absence of one or more limbs. Only a few family lines worldwide are affected by this condition and most children born with tetra-amelia syndrome are stillborn or die at birth because

MYSTERY TO SOLVE

Where is Prince Randian buried? What was the cause of his sudden death in 1934?

of the other deformities that stem from this condition such as facial abnormalities, genital malformations, and heart, skeletal, and/or nervous system complications. Breathing difficulties are common because the lungs are usually deformed and not fully developed. Someone in Prince Randian's life must have decided that he would not be allowed to give in to his deformities. He learned to be self-sufficient. During his act, Randian would demonstrate his ability to shave himself, cut his hair, thread a needle, sharpen knives, roll cigarettes, and even to fill and smoke a pipe. At times, he was accompanied by a native South American orchestra that

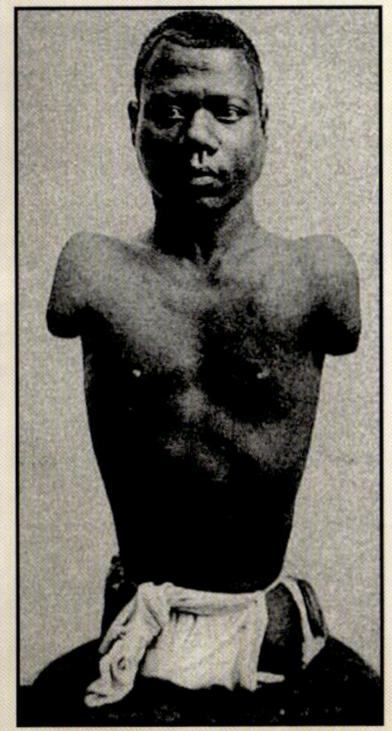

Prince Randian was born with tetra-amelia syndrome, an extremely rare inherited condition that basically results in the absence of one or more limbs. Most children born with tetra-amelia syndrome are stillborn or die at birth.

Ad for *Freaks* showing Prince Randian and other cast members. His best known show trick was rolling and lighting a cigarette using only his lips and that act was captured on film in *Freaks*.

played upbeat background music while Prince Randian went through his demonstrations in front of an amazed and dazzled paying crowd.

An older Prince Randian usually wore a knitted garment that clung to his body, visually defining his show name, "The Human Torso." Off stage he was often carried by a hired attendant, but on stage he would move by wiggling the upper and lower portions of his torso much like a snake slithers or by simply rolling to a destination. His best known show trick was rolling and lighting a cigarette using only his lips and that act was captured on film in Tod Browning's 1932 movie *Freaks*. He is often photographed with a wooden box where he kept his show props and, reportedly, he constructed and painted the box himself.

Prince Randian was a devoted family man. He married Princess Sarah, a fellow sideshow performer (year unknown), and claimed he fathered four daughters and a son. By 1932, he was the reported grandfather of eight grandchildren. Princess

Prince Randian was a devoted family man. He married a fellow sideshow performer and claimed he fathered four daughters and a son. By 1932, he was the reported grandfather of eight.

Sarah was born in St. Thomas around 1877, and played the parts of a harem girl and Native American squaw during her brief career. She remained his beloved life's partner until his death. Prince Randian semi-retired to a home in Paterson, New Jersey, in his later years, but he continued to make local dime museum and Coney Island appearances. He had tired of life on the road and long days of tedious travel. His last public appearance was an evening show at Sam Wagner's 14th Street Museum in New York City on December 19, 1934. He collapsed and died shortly after his performance. He was sixty-three. His final resting place is unknown. ♦

Prince Randian Film Credits

Freaks . . . . (1932)
I Am Not a Freak . . . . (1987, TV short documentary, posthumously).

PETER ROBINSON, "HUMAN SKELETON," OR "LIVING SKELETON"

Very little is known about the life and death of Peter Robinson. We have to rely heavily on newspaper stories and advertisements of the day that may or may not be accurate. Reportedly, he was born in Springfield, Massachusetts, in April of 1877 or 1879. He was around the age of thirteen when he inexplicably started to lose weight. As an adult, Peter never weighed more than sixty pounds and stood only five foot three inches tall. It is possible he had a medical condition that prevented him from obtaining a typical adult weight. More likely, however, he was a "created freak" and simply starved his way into the limelight. He started his career in 1899 in his early twenties and toured with P. T. Barnum and eventually with Ringling Bros. and Barnum & Bailey Circus. He was also a Coney Island sideshow favorite. Peter was said to be an accomplished harmonica player and absolutely loved to debate politics with anyone

MYSTERY TO SOLVE

Where and when did Peter Robinson die, and what caused his death? Where is he buried? Was his marriage simply a publicity stunt?

Most likely Peter's marriage to the voluptuous Bunny was merely a publicity stunt.

As an adult, Peter never weighed more than sixty pounds and stood only five feet three inches tall. He was most likely a "created freak" who starved his way into the limelight.

and everyone he could egg into a spirited debate. Beginning with Isaac Sprague, a human skeleton of fame in the mid to late 1800s, publicity stunts often played out in the newspapers regarding marriages between the sideshow fat lady and the human skeleton. It was a favorite ploy of P. T. Barnum, who once even pulled off a successful publicity stunt claiming Sprague had fallen in love with the show's female human skeleton and they were to wed. In 1924, the newspapers were buzzing over the marriage of forty-two-year old Peter Robinson and twenty-three-year-old Baby Bunny Smith, a sideshow fat lady who weighed 467 pounds. Bunny claimed to have won Peter away from Sweet Adeline, another fat lady, and quipped that her new husband had fallen in love with at least eight fat ladies in his past. Most stories about Peter and Bunny were reported in a "tongue-in-cheek" style that poked good-natured fun at the groom and his blushing bride. Bunny was quoted as saying things like, "I hope I don't roll over on him in bed." A betting person would probably wager this marriage was only a sham.

In 1932, Peter appeared in the movie *Freaks*. He basically played himself, the "Living Skeleton," who was married to the bearded lady (Lady Olga/Olga Roderick). There is a touching scene in the movie where their child is born to the glee of both parents and the other freaks. The exact date and place of Peter's death is unknown, as is his burial site. Most sources set the year of his death as 1947. He would have been sixty-eight or seventy. ♦

Peter Robinson's Film Credits

Freaks .... (1932)

Some Call Them Freaks .... (TV documentary, posthumously).

PIN HEADS

Pin head sideshow performers, such as the two in this photograph, were often hyped as Aztecs, the last of an ancient tribe. This was a play on the shape of their heads and the custom of some cultures to wrap their infant's head in a fashion so as to create the cone-shaped skull.

THE AZTEC GIRLS

AGE 18 AND 24 YEARS

SCHLITZIE, "LAST OF THE AZTECS," "THAT FUNNY LITTLE LADY," "THE PINHEAD," OR "THE WILD GIRL"

Schlitzie is probably the best known and most beloved sideshow performer we know almost nothing about.

Schlitzie is probably the best known and most beloved sideshow performer we know almost nothing about. The location and date of birth, given name, and parentage are all unknown but it is commonly accepted that what is written on his death certificate and inscribed on his tombstone is, hopefully, somewhat correct. It is all we have or will probably ever have since Schlitzie was never able to furnish any background information and anyone who could have shed light on his early years chose not to do so. An educated guess, based on the times and other child stars of the sideshow, would surmise that either Schlitzie was given or sold to a sideshow manager or that a sideshow manager found Schlitzie in an institution where his parents had abandoned him.

Schlitzie was born with microcephaly, a neuro-developmental disorder characterized by an abnormally small brain, a pointed cranium, and unusually small stature. This condition often resulted in intellectual disability and, as an adult, Schlitzie only possessed the cognitive skills of a three-year-old child. In 1911, A. W. Mills, Schlitzie's manager at the time and the proprietor of the sideshow exhibiting Schlitzie, was reportedly fined $300 by an Illinois Grand Jury for "exhibiting 'Schlitzie' the alleged idiot." In the trial, three physicians testified that Schlitzie was nothing more than an idiot and the manager and his wife, plus another manager, G. A. Johnson, should be jailed or fined for showing an idiot to the public. The good people of Bangamon County, Illinois, meant well, but Schlitzie, most likely, had a better life and future with the sideshow than the one he left behind. By all accounts, Schlitzie was loved and treated well by the members of the sideshow community.

Schlitzie was most often exhibited as a female. This was due to the fact that he could not master a zipper or buttons so a dress with elastic bloomers underneath was needed to aid him when using a toilet. Interestingly, his race is listed as "Indian" under "color or race" on his death certificate even though common knowledge concedes that Simon Metz was Schlitzie's birth name and his place of birth was the Bronx. Much information on the death certificate is marked "unknown" but the certificate information was supplied by a medical center, not by a caretaker. In 1909, in the tradition of sideshow hype, he was billed as "Schlitzie, The Wild Girl." That promotion claimed she was a Mexican girl of eighteen, found among the Aztecs, and standing only twenty-two inches tall. It also claimed she had only three ounces of brain and yet

Schlitzie's (spelled incorrectly on tombstone) background will always remain a mystery. He was buried in an unmarked grave but kind-hearted fans purchased this stone for him. The dates on the tombstone are commonly accepted, as is the information on his death certificate, but none of the facts were furnished by family.

Schlitzie was often exhibited in a cage and billed as "an untamable savage specimen of humanity." In truth, Schlitzie was always described as mild-mannered, affectionate, happy, and very sociable.

Schlitzie was born with microcephaly, a neurodevelopmental disorder characterized by an abnormally small brain and a pointed cranium. The condition often resulted in intellectual disabilities and Schlitzie, himself, only possessed the cognitive skills of a three-year-old child.

was capable of understanding and speaking broken English and Spanish. As an adult, Schlitzie only stood about four feet tall, so more likely he was closer to eight years old in 1909, not eighteen. In truth, he was never able to speak more than monosyllabic words and to form only a few simple phrases. However, it was thought he could understand what others said and he often mimicked them. He could also perform a few simple tasks but needed a constant caretaker.

WORLD'S MUSEUM

Market & Eleventh Sts.
11 A. M.—Continuous—10 P. M.

A Record-Breaking Array of Amazing Living Curiosities

FIRST TIME HERE
RANDION
No Arms! No Legs!
Just a human trunk. But, armless and legless, he achieves many marvelous feats.

FIRST TIME HERE
SCHLITZIE
Last of the Aztecs. An untamable savage specimen of humanity from an age-old race.

THE HUMAN SKYSCRAPER
CAPT. AUGER
Giant of Giants
The Tallest Man Who Ever Lived

EXTENDED ENGAGEMENT OF
KLIKKO
The Dancing Bushman

TOGETHER WITH
20 Strange Living Curiosities
ONE ADMISSION TO ALL

A 1921 newspaper ad for Schlitzie, performing with other favorites of the sideshow world.

He was often billed as "an untamable savage specimen of humanity from an age-old race" or an Aztec wild woman and sole survivor of this ancient race "who refuses to become pacified with the manners and customs of this section of the world." As late as 1921, Schlitzie was exhibited in a cage so "that she might not become ferocious at an inopportune moment," promotional material noted, also claiming "years of patient training have failed to tame (her) occasional inclination to revert to savagery and run wild in a crowd." In truth, Schlitzie was often described as mild-mannered, affectionate, happy, and very sociable. Tod Browning, director of *Freaks*, said of Schlitzie, "You forget the strange appearance of Schlitzie, the pin head, or the Snow Twins because of their personalities." Schlitzie especially loved to entertain children and to dance. According to an article in the *Greensboro Record* in 1936: "Schlitzie, the pin head, did her version of a modern dance to the enjoyment of the crowd."

Schlitzie never mastered a zipper or buttons so the dress and elastic bloomers were needed to aid him when using the toilet.

Reportedly, Schlitzie was institutionalized once again when his manager and legal guardian George Surtees died in 1965 and there was no family member who wanted to take on the responsibility of his care. He was rescued when an ex-carnival worker employed by the institution recognized him. He spent his last years in Los Angeles, at times exhibiting at various sideshows. He also became somewhat of a local celebrity in Hollywood, good-naturedly greeting and entertaining people on the streets while his caretaker sold his trade cards or in Mac Arthur Park, feeding the pigeons and socializing with people as they passed by. Schlitzie died on September 24, 1971, at Fountain View Convalescent Hospital in Los Angeles from pneumonia complicated by mudullary (cancer) and depression. He was seventy years old and then a ward of the state of California. His death certificate listed his name as "Shlitze Surtees" and his birth date as 1901. Schlitzie's body was not even embalmed. There was no funeral. He was buried in Queen of Heaven Cemetery, in Rowland Heights, California, in an unmarked grave, but in 2009, a kind-hearted fan purchased a tombstone for him from a collection

Schlitzie shown on the back row next to the bearded lady in a photo of a Clyde Beatty Circus Sideshow.

taken up to honor this most remarkable and still-beloved performer. George S. Surtees was Schlitzie's kind and caring manager and guardian from 1935 until his death in 1965. He is buried in Evergreen Cemetery in Los Angles, California. ♦

Schlitzie's Film Credits

The Sideshow .... (1928, not credited)
Freaks .... (1932, not credited)
Island of Lost Souls .... (1932)
Meet Boston Blackie .... (1941)
Tomorrow's Children .... (1943, not credited)
Freaks Uncensored .... (1999, documentary, posthumously)
Sideshow: Alive on the Inside .... (1999, TV documentary, posthumously)

THE SNOW TWINS, "ZIPPO AND FLIPPO," "ZIP & PIP," "FLIP AND PIP," "THE PIN HEAD TWINS," OR "ZIPO AND PIPO," AND POSSIBLY MORE

So very little is known about the Snow Twins. We do not know how the name "Snow Twins" came to be, since a 1940 news article in the *Augusta Chronicle* reports that they were the children of a Dr. and Mrs. Winston Trimble of Athens, Georgia, born in 1920. Worse, we do not even know if the Snow Twins are brother and sister or two sisters, as they are advertised and dressed as both. At times, it is said they are twin siblings, other times, not. We do know, however, that both individuals suffered from microcephaly. They were typically developed from the neck down, but each had a small and cone-shaped skull with a little tuff of hair on the top. They were also mentally challenged and small in stature, both conditions resulting from this disorder. The biological information about the twins differs greatly. The information on the show trade brochure is very different from other printed sources, including newspaper stories of the day. We most likely will never know the true life story of the Snow Twins. We will also probably

MYSTERY TO SOLVE

Were the Snow Twins brother and sister or two sisters? Is it possible they are not even related to one another? How did they get into the sideshow business? When and where did they die, and where are they buried?

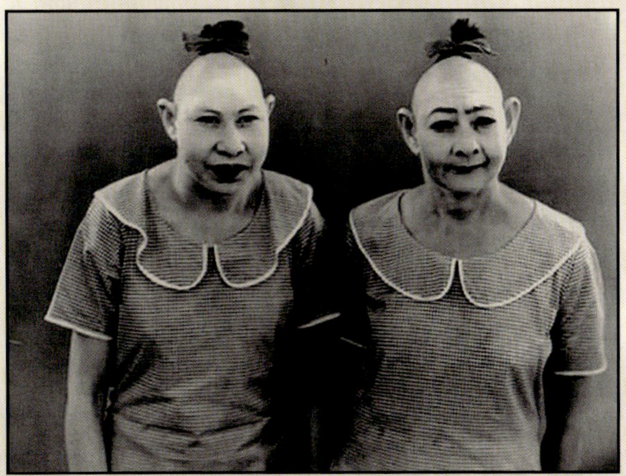

The Snow Twins were advertised as both brother and sister and as two sisters. Even today, we do not know the sex of either twin.

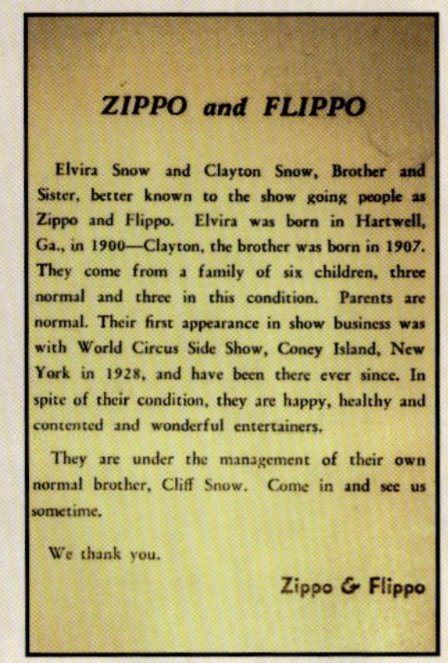

ZIPPO and FLIPPO

Elvira Snow and Clayton Snow, Brother and Sister, better known to the show going people as Zippo and Flippo. Elvira was born in Hartwell, Ga., in 1900—Clayton, the brother was born in 1907. They come from a family of six children, three normal and three in this condition. Parents are normal. Their first appearance in show business was with World Circus Side Show, Coney Island, New York in 1928, and have been there ever since. In spite of their condition, they are happy, healthy and contented and wonderful entertainers.

They are under the management of their own normal brother, Cliff Snow. Come in and see us sometime.

We thank you.

Zippo & Flippo

Trade brochure with photo of the Snow Twins. We will probably never know their true life story since so much that was written in trade brochures and on trade cards was done to sensationalize the act.

Coney Island World Circus Side Show trade card. Here the Snow Twins are advertised as "Pip and Flip."

never know if Cliff Snow, their manager, was also a biological brother.

An interview article for the 1932 movie *Freaks*, in which they appeared, reported that "Elvira and Hattie Lee Snow were born in Hartwell, Georgia, 22 years ago." That would have made them born in 1912 and twin sisters. They traded under numerous stage names at various times during their sideshow careers: Zippo and Flippo, Zip and Pip, Pip and Flip, Zipo and Pipo, The Pin Head Twins, The Snow Twins, and possibly more. The name Elvira usually remained constant, but the other Snow Twin was referred to as Clayton, Jenny Lee, Hattie Lee, Johnny Lee, or Jenny Lynn. They were both said to be social, engaging, and they loved entertaining the public, especially children. They were still performing in 1940, but not much is known about their life after that. Hopefully, a family member gave them loving care in their final days and they lived a long and happy life. It is possible, however, they were institutionalized when the sharp decline of the sideshow greatly hindered their earning capacity in the late 1940s and early 1950s. The date of their deaths and the site of their final resting place is unknown. ♦

BEING DIFFERENT

DOCUMENTARY DIRECTED BY HARRY RASKY (1981)

Being Different is a 1981 Canadian/American documentary film directed by Harry Rasky that is a look into the lives of people who were born physically different. It is an uplifting tribute to the inner courage and convictions of these people. The story unfolds through a series of interviews. The cast of characters include a bearded woman, a giant and giantess, a dwarf, a fat man, and others. The main setting of the film is Gibsonton, Florida, a town where many circus and carnival performers retire during the winter off-season. The film also takes us to other locations to view such amazing people as a grandfather with severely distorted facial features, a mechanic born with no legs, a runner who has no feet, and others who have risen above their deformities to live a full and productive life. ♦

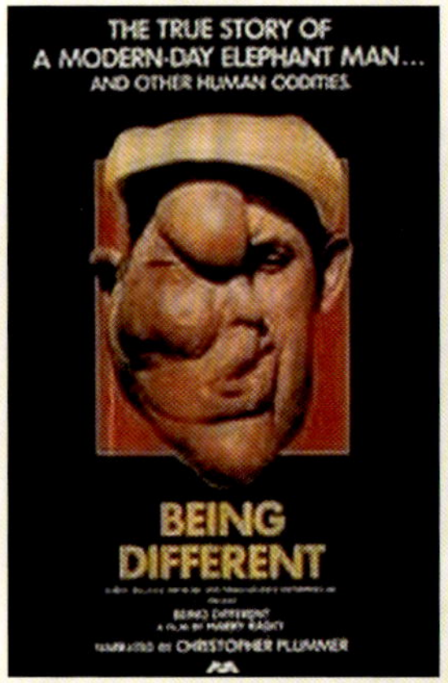

THE CAST OF CHARACTERS INCLUDES

Billy Barty	dwarf actor
Sandra Elaine Allen	"The World's Tallest Woman"
Jo-Ann Cantilla	Louise Capps (born without arms)
Paul Fishe	fat man (729 pounds)
Ronnie and Donne Galyon	conjoined twins
Bob Melvin	"The Man With Two Faces"
Dolly Regan	"The Human Doll"
Peter Strudwick	marathon runner born without feet
Christopher Plummer	narrator
Johann Petursson	"The World's Tallest Man"
Percilla Bejano	"Monkey Girl"
Emmett Bejano	"The Alligator-Skinned Man."

WILLIAM JOHN BERTANZETTI, "BILLY BARTY"

Billy Barty became the most famous twentieth-century dwarf in the world and would have rivaled Tom Thumb if he had been born sooner.

Billy began performing at the age of three when he appeared in his first Hollywood feature film, a silent comedy titled *Wedded Blisters*.

Billy's show business career spanned over seventy years, from vaudeville to films, and he played both comedy and drama equally well.

Billy died of heart failure on December 23, 2000. He was seventy-six. He was entombed in Forest Lawn Memorial Park Cemetery in Glendale, California.

Billy was presented a star on the Hollywood Walk of Fame in July 1981.

Billy Barty was born in Millsboro, Pennsylvania, on October 25, 1924, to Albert Steven Bertanzetti and Ellen Bedeker Bertanzetti, Italian-Americans. He had two sisters that he performed with on vaudeville stages as "Billy Barty and Sisters," a musical and comedy act. While his sisters were of average size, in adulthood, Billy would only reach the height of three feet, nine inches. He weighed approximately eighty pounds. He became the most famous twentieth- century dwarf in the world and would have rivaled Tom Thumb if he had been born sooner. Billy's famous quote was, "I was born with cartilage hair syndrome hypoplasia, but you can call me Billy." Billy began performing at the age of three when he appeared in his first Hollywood feature film, the silent comedy *Wedded Blisters*. According to his eulogy, Billy's parents caught the show business bug and moved the entire family to Hollywood in 1927. Billy, only three years old, had learned to stand on his head and spin around. He and his father were walking near Santa Monica Boulevard and Grower when they stopped to watch a silent film being made on the sidewalk. Billy spontaneously ran over, got Jules White, the director's attention, and performed his act. White was so impressed by this talented and vivacious diminutive child that he asked Billy's father if he could use Billy in his film.

Billy was a noted activist for the promotion of rights for others with dwarfism. He founded two organizations, The Little People of America in 1957 and later, The Billy Barty Foundation, both to aid people with dwarfism. He served on a disabilities commission for Jack Kemp when Kemp was secretary of the US Department of Housing and Urban Development. It was said that he used to joke, "Try being my size and going into a public restroom." In October 2000, he was awarded the Long Beach Film Festival's Humanitarian of the Year Award. He was presented a star on the Hollywood Walk of Fame in July 1981. For a short while during WWII, he gave up show business and attended Los Angeles City College, studying journalism, but he soon returned to the bright lights. His show-business career spanned over seventy years, from radio to vaudeville to films and he played both comedy and drama equally well. He possessed a great talent and a boyish charm that added to his immense popularity on screen and he appeared in over 200 big screen and television films. Billy became lifelong friends with Mickey Rooney after playing his little brother in the *Mickey McGuire* series. He liked to say that Mickey Rooney said they grew up together, but Billy said they almost grew up together.

His one career regret was not being in *The Wizard of Oz* but he had been too young. The MGM Studio insisted everyone be at least eighteen years old. He always claimed that one of his major pet peeves was when people would try to pick him up as though he were a child. Billy married Shirley Bolingbroke of Malad City, Idaho, on February

Billy married Shirley Bolingbroke on February 24, 1962. She had multiple epiphyseal dysplasia. They remained devoted to one another until Billy's death

24, 1962, in Los Angeles. She had multiple epiphyseal dysplasia. They remained married until Billy's death and had two children: Lori, an adopted small person born in Russia in 1963, and an average-sized son, Braden, born in 1971. Billy died of heart failure on December 23, 2000, at the Glendale Memorial Hospital after a two-week stay with lung and heart problems. He was seventy-six. He was entombed in Forest Lawn Memorial Park Cemetery in Glendale, California. In 2007, his beloved wife died and she is entombed with him. He had once written on his website, billybarty.com, "Shirley is an angel from heaven and she is the reason life is worth living for me." ♦

Billy Barty's Film Credits (partial listing)

Wedding Blisters .... (1927, debut not credited)
Mickey's Minstrels .... (1928)
Mickey the Detective .... (1928)
Mickey's Midnite Follies .... (1929)
Mickey's Champs .... (1930)
Follow the Swallow .... (1930)
Mickey's Warriors .... (1930)
Mickey the Romeo .... (1930)
Mickey's Winners .... (1930)
Alice in Wonderland .... (1933)
Gift of Gab .... (1934)
A Midsummer Night's Dream .... (1935)
Bride of Frankenstein .... (1935)
Pygmy Island .... (1950)
The James Melton Show .... (1951)
The Undead .... (1957)
Billy Rose's Jumbo .... (1962)
Roustabout .... (1964)
Harum Scarum .... (1965)
Pufnstuf .... (1970)
Godmothers .... (1973)
Six Pack Annie .... (1975)
The Day of the Locust .... (1975)
Won Ton Ton, the Dog who Saved Hollywood (1976)
W. C. Fields and Me .... (1976)
The Amazing Dobermans .... (1976)
Foul Play .... (1978)
Skatetown USA .... (1979)
Firepower .... (1979)
Under the Rainbow .... (1981)
Night Patrol .... (1984)
Legend .... (1985)
Off the Mark .... (1986)
Body Slam .... (1987)
Master of the Universe .... (1987)
Willow .... (1988)
UHF .... (1989)
Lobster Man from Mars .... (1989)
Diggin' Up Business .... (1990),
Rescuers Down Under .... (1990 voice of Bellmouse)
Life Stinks .... (1991)
Naked Truth .... (1992)
Burn Hollywood Burn .... (1997)
I/O Error .... (1998).

SANDRA ELAINE ALLEN, "THE WORLD'S TALLEST WOMAN"

Sandy Allen was born on June 18, 1955,. in Chicago, Illinois, and weighed an unremarkable six pounds five ounces. Unfortunately, she suffered from the medical condition gigantism, which quickly surfaced. At ten years of age, she was six feet three inches tall and by age sixteen, she had reached the height of seven feet one inch. On July 14, 1977, at the age of twenty-two, she had a successful operation on her pituitary gland to stop her growth. She was seven feet, seven and almost a quarter inches tall at the time. If the operation had not been successful, she would have died from her disease.

A former secretary, Sandy landed parts in several movies and documentaries and appeared on television shows including Howard Stern and Sally Jessy Raphael. She was the author of the book *Cast a Giant Shadow* and the subject of the book *World's Tallest Woman* by Rita Rose that is the story of Sandy's high-school days at Shelbyville High School. Sandy held the *Guinness World Records* for the World's Tallest Woman for sixteen years. She was officially listed at the height of seven feet seven and one-quarter inches. Sadly, she was medically required to reside in a nursing home in Shelbyville for the last years of her life. Poor circulation, spine problems, and weak leg muscles confined her to a wheelchair or her eight-foot bed. Reportedly, she spent much time indoors, fighting severe depression, and hiding from a world that was less than kind to her when she went about. She never married, nor had a serious boyfriend. Sandy died on August 13, 2008, from a blood infection. She is buried in Forest Hill Cemetery in Shelbyville, Indiana. She was fifty-three. Her tombstone reads "Gentle Giant." ♦

World's Tallest Woman by Rita Rose is the story of Sandy's high school days at Shelbyville High School.

Sandy Allen was born on June 18, 1955, in Chicago, Illinois, and weighed an unremarkable six pounds, five ounces. She is shown here with her sister.

Sandra Allen's Film Credits

Il Casanove di Federico Fellini (1976)
Being Different .... (1981, Canadian/America documentary film)
Sideshow: Alive in the Inside .... (1999, TV documentary)
Inside Extraordinary Humans: The Science of Gigantism (2007, TV documentary)
The World's Tallest Woman & Me (2008, TV series documentary),
Extraordinary People .... (2008, TV series documentary)
Extreme Bodies .... (2009, TV series documentary)

LOUISE CAPPS

In this 1955 newspaper photo, Louise was asked how old she was on her birthday and she held up three toes.

Louise learned to type, cut hair, sew, crochet, paint, write, cook, and drive both a car and truck.

One of Louise's favorite stories was when a trooper stopped her, thinking her a silly teenager showing off by driving with her feet. It was a while before he noticed she did not have arms.

Catherine Louise Capps was born on December 17, 1952, at Parkland Hospital in Dallas, Texas. Born without arms, the infant was abandoned by her Cherokee Indian mother who refused to take custody of her. For a short time, the baby was cared for by maternal grandparents, but they claimed to be too old and too poor to properly look after this special child with the dark, curly hair. She was placed in a foundling home as a ward of the state. Dallas newspapers ran a series of stories on the child's plight, dubbing her "The Waxahachie Waif." Several couples responded, all wanting to foster or adopt the baby. Eventually, Eugene and Catherine Capps, a middle-aged couple, won out. Catherine Capps, age fifty, had been a school nurse for over twenty-five years and loved children. She had previously been married and had two grown adopted children, plus five grandchildren. In 1950, Catherine remarried Eugene Capps, the owner of a prosperous ten-acre chicken farm in Seagoville, Texas. They named their new daughter Catherine Louise Capps. After over a year as the foster parents of Louise, they legally adopted her on April 26, 1954, when she was sixteen months old.

In 1955, Catherine Capps lost her adopted daughter Nola to polio. Nola, only twenty-one, had been six-months pregnant at the time of her death. This tragic loss probably made Louise even more precious to Catherine. Catherine and Eugene Capps deeply loved Louise and afforded her a remarkable life. Catherine taught her daughter to be independent and self-sufficient by using her feet in place of her arms and hands. By the age of three, Louise was riding her pony and a tricycle, dressing herself, brushing her hair and teeth, tying bows, climbing trees, swimming, and throwing rocks with better accuracy than the neighboring boys. As she got older, she learned to cut hair, sew, crochet, paint, write, type, cook, and drive both a car and truck. Basically, Louise learned to do what most anyone else could do.

MYSTERY TO SOLVE

Where is Louise Capps now, and what is her life like since she left the sideshow world behind?

Initially, she was sent to a private school, but Louise preferred to be privately tutored at home. The parents had planned to have Louise fitted for artificial arms when she turned five years old and would be strong enough to support and maneuver the heavy appendages and harness. Louise flatly refused them, claiming she did not want or need arms. Finally, when she was fifteen years old, she agreed to be fitted with a set of custom-made arms and a harness. Louise nicknamed her new contraption Rhoda and was not fond of wearing the device. Even at age twenty-two, Louise was only five foot three inches tall and weighed a mere eighty-two pounds. She always claimed the arms and harness were heavy, awkward, and slowed her down when doing many of the things she enjoyed.

Louise married and divorced twice. She joined Ward Hall's sideshow in 1979 after her first divorce, the now-single mother of two children: a son, Jeff, born in 1970, and a two-year-old daughter she named Nola Jo after her deceased foster sister. Neither child had physical disabilities. She met her second husband, Bruce Hill, while working the show at the Texas State Fair in 1984. Bruce was a human block head, nightly driving ice picks and nails into his nose. Louise's daughter later became a showgirl with Ward Hall's show when she was a teenager. Louise appeared in the 1981 film *Being Different* and is considered by most, including director Harry Rasky to be the star of the film. She was exactly what he was looking for: a spirited, upbeat person who would not let a birth deformity stand in the way of living a happy and productive life. Little is known about Louise's present-day life. It is hard to imagine that she is anything but happy and content and is still inspiring anyone lucky enough to know her. ♦

RONNIE AND DONNIE GALYON

Ronnie and Donnie Galyon were born on October 28, 1951, to Wesley Leon and Eileen Galyon at St. Ann's Maternity Hospital in Dayton, Ohio. They weighed a total of eleven pounds eleven and a half ounces. The identical twins were a surprise on two levels: they were born vaginally to a mother who was not expecting twins, and the twins were conjoined. Medical staff did not expect them to live, but the twins surprised everyone and thrived. The boys were joined face to face, from the base of the sternum to the groin with a 2- to 3-inch band of cartilage with dual sensations. They shared a naval, bladder, descending colon, and one set of male organs. They had two heads, four arms, two legs, and separate stomachs and hearts. Living conjoined twins are rare and male conjoined twins are ever rarer. In 2015, they remain the only known set of living adult male conjoined twins and the oldest living set of conjoined twins in the history of the world, male or female. They have now surpassed the life record set by the famous original Siamese twins, Eng and Chang Bunker, who died when they were sixty-two years eight months old. Ronnie (on left) and Donnie (on right) spent the first twenty months of their lives in the hospital being examined by doctors to determine if the two could be separated. The conclusion was that, most likely, one or both would die from being separated since they shared common organs. Their life became one of compromises and co-operation. Ronnie, the larger twin, and Donnie have very different personalities. Ronnie is the happy-go-lucky type and

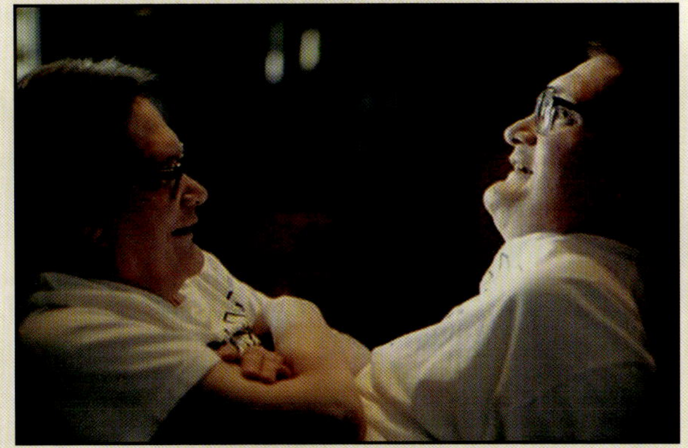

In 2014, Ronnie (left) and Donnie Galyon remain the only known set of living adult male conjoined twins and the oldest living set of conjoined twins in the history of the world, male or female. They have surpassed the life record set by the famous original "Siamese" twins, Eng and Chang Bunker, who died when they were sixty-two.

Ronnie and Donnie Galyon were born on October 28, 1951. Medical staff did not expect them to live, but the twins surprised everyone and thrived.

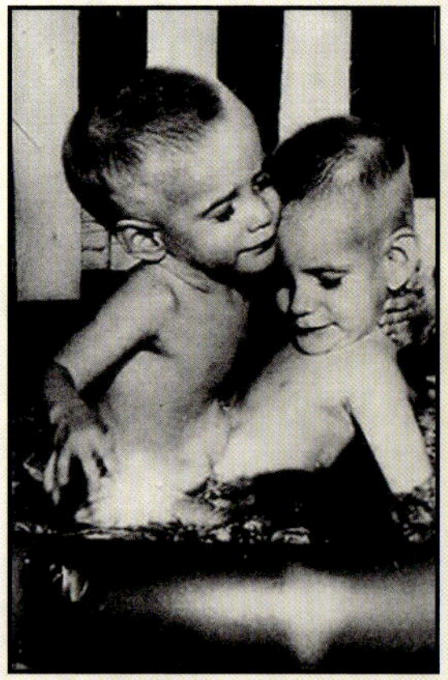

Ronnie, the larger twin, and Donnie have very different personalities. Ronnie is the happy-go-lucky type and very vocal where Donnie is quiet and serious.

very vocal where Donnie is quiet and serious. Their mother always said that Donnie was the first to do everything except talk, but while Donnie did say a word first, when Ronnie started talking, he talked in sentences. When they were twenty-nine months old, they learned to walk by methodically employing the sideward glide. Ronnie is epileptic and has to take twice as much medicine as he normally would since Donnie absorbs half. The twins can get sick at separate times. When they were children, one would resent being sent to bed when the other was ill.

They never had a typical life and they never received an education. Reportedly, neither can read nor write. Their father, a plumber's apprentice with a very fast-growing family, decided to exhibit his sons before they turned four years old. In essence, Ronnie and Donnie supported the entire family, including their seven siblings. In August 1955, their father signed a three-year contract with the Clyde Beatty Circus for a minimum of $400 a week, plus transportation and nursing care. After that, they mostly traveled as an independent exhibit. The father and the boys' grandfather would drive them around to towns in a specially designed, air-conditioned trailer and charge an admission price to see the twins. Ronnie and Donnie spent most of the time watching television while people gawked at them behind a glass window. They toured the states as well as Latin America, the West Indies, and Canada. In the 1980s, they exhibited with Ward Hall's Worlds of Wonder Show and in 1981,they appeared in the film *Being Different*.

Wesley Galyon had run-ins with the law twice while exhibiting his sons. In 1962, he was arrested in San Bernardino, California, when police evoked an 1873 statute that made it a misdemeanor to profit from exhibiting a person's deformity. It was said a complaint was lodged by a woman who claimed she had become ill after viewing the act. The father won that case in the appeals court. In 1965, Wesley Galyon was held on charges levied by the Dayton (Ohio) school system claiming he had neglected the fourteen-year-old twins' education. They alleged the twins could not read even though they could be educated. The parents testified in court that a tutor often traveled with the

The boys were exhibited before they turned four years old and, in essence, supported the entire family including their seven siblings. They never received an education. Reportedly, neither can read nor write.

boys on the road, although that claim was not proven. In May 1971, the parents of Ronnie and Donnie divorced after twenty-three years of marriage. They had married on July 31, 1948. Wesley Galyon remarried and his new wife, Mary Vaughan Galyon, aided in the care of the twins who stayed with their father. Wesley died on March 7, 1998 at the age of seventy-four. His obituary listed him as a World War II Navy vet, retired plumber, farmer, and businessman. He died from a fall. He had been taking food to a neighbor's dog when the dog knocked him down and he hit his head.

In 1991, after four decades on the road, Ronnie and Donnie retired and moved into their first independent home in Dayton, Ohio. The house was purchased with sideshow earnings. Their younger

Ronnie and Donnie Galyon's Film Credits:

The Jerry Springer Show .... (April 21, 1997, TV show)
Human Mutations-Conjoined Twins (1998, Discovery Channel TV documentary)
Being Different .... (1981, Canadian/American documentary)
The World's Oldest Conjoined Twins Move Home (2010, TLC TV documentary

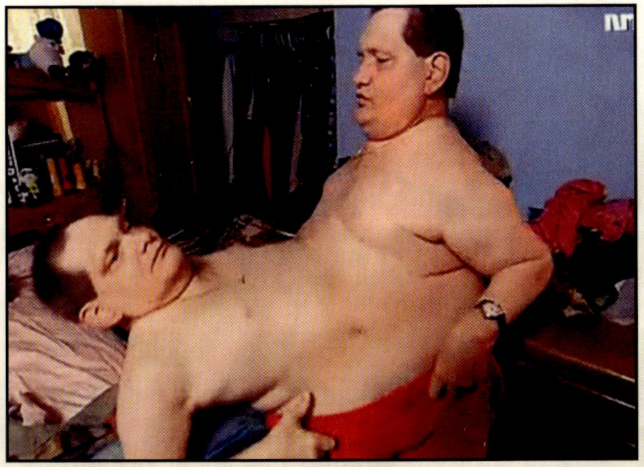

When asked if they would have ever wanted to be separated, Ronnie and Donnie always claim they would not and are happy living the way they do. They have the same haircut, wear the same clothes, eat the same foods, and at times, get drunk together.

brother, Jim, was instrumental in the twins' ability to live outside an institution. He and his wife, Mary, spend much of their time looking after them, shopping for them, doing their laundry, and taking them to doctor appointments and on social outings. In 2009, however, an infection almost killed the twins and they now require continual care. Jim and Mary, with the help of many kind-hearted people from the community, built a specially modified addition onto their home so Ronnie and Donnie would not have to be placed into a nursing home. Even after official retirement, Ronnic and Donnie still occasionally appear on TV shows and have been featured in several TV documentaries. They collect toy cars, love sports, especially the Dallas Cowboys football team, and still watch a lot of television, even though now they require two TV sets since they do not like the same programs. They say they have many fond memories of being on the road but they detest the word "freak." Their father had always referred to them as a medical exhibit. They have two social security numbers, each vote, each pays taxes, but they only require one passport. Ronnie and Donnie maintain a similar appearance. They have the same haircut, wear the same clothes, eat the same foods, and at times, get drunk together. When asked if they would have ever wanted to be separated, they always claim they would not and are happy living the way they do. Sadly, though, as with all conjoined twins, when one dies for whatever reason, the other will soon follow. Doctors say the only thing that can be done for the living twin is to sedate him and comfort him until he, too, passes. ♦

BOB MELVIN, "THE MAN WITH TWO FACES," OR "MODERN ELEPHANT MAN"

Robert Owen Melvin was born on May 9, 1920, in Lancaster, Missouri, to Fred Hern and Hazel Marie Sizemore Melvin. Bob, unfortunately, was born with a genetic condition on the right side of his face called neurofibromatosis, also referred to as NF, a disorder that causes the spontaneous growth of fibrous tumors in soft tissue and bone. It is not an inherited condition, and there is no known cure. Both parents and six other siblings were born without the condition, one son dying in infancy. His mother was very religious. The family moved briefly to Washington, Iowa, and Bob always said he had wonderful parents but they would not allow him to go to school. However, according to him, they were not ashamed of him. This was done to protect him from the anticipated cruelty of other children. He was educated at home by his mother and older siblings. At home, among his family, he was well-loved. As the tumors grew and increased, it became hard for Bob to eat solid food, to speak clearly, and he eventually lost the sight in his right eye.

Bob Melvin was born in 1920 with a genetic condition on the right side of his face called neurofibromatosis, a disorder that causes the spontaneous growth of fibrous tumors in soft tissue and bone.

In 1949, for whatever reason, twenty-nine-year-old Bob broke from home bonds and booked himself into Coney Island. He was an immediate hit. He also toured all state fairs east of Missouri, in Texas, Oklahoma, North and South Dakota, and Nebraska. He was soon making $1,000 a week. Reportedly, while working with the Royal American Shows, he sold the world's smallest Bible out of a cigar box for a quarter, walking and working the midway when he wasn't on stage. He was said to enjoy debating politics, was very left-wing, and strongly opposed the Vietnam war in the late 1960s. Like his mother, he was also very religious and had the philosophy that people have to look out for each other or were sunk in this world. He was well liked and respected by other sideshow

Bob was billed as "The Man with Two Faces." He was also billed, at times, as the "Modern Elephant Man" since many people erroneously believed Bob to be inflicted with the same medical condition as the famous original Victorian Elephant Man, Joseph Merrick.

Bob died in his hometown of Lancaster, Missouri, on November 16, 1995. He was seventy-five. He is buried in the Arni Memorial Cemetery in Lancaster.

Sideshow banner for Bob Melvin, "The Man with Two Faces" (center of banner).

employees. He moved back to Lancaster, Missouri, and became a regular fixture at the Lancaster Christian Church and about town. He was a Mason and member of Lodge of Love 259. Contrary to his parents' fears, he was fully accepted by the community. An oil portrait of him now hangs in the Schuyler County Historical Society Museum. Bob was billed as "The Man with Two Faces," which was an accurate description. He was also billed, at times, as the "Modern Elephant Man" since many people erroneously believed Bob to be inflicted with the same medical condition as the famous original Victorian Elephant Man, Joseph Merrick.

On February 18, 1952, he married his longtime girlfriend, a beautiful woman named Virginia Smyser. Many people did not expect the marriage to last, but it did. Virginia once reportedly said, "Looks are only skin-deep and he's a terrific person." They had one daughter, Teresa "Terrie" Melvin (Sandretto), who had a son, Nicholas, and daughter, Keeley, that Bob adored. He was said to have stated, "I love kids and they love me. My only regret is I didn't have two or three more." Teresa said that, as a child, she traveled with the sideshows where everyone was different. The performers seemed "normal" to her and the "normal" people were oddities. It especially bothered her when audience members would heckle her father. She did not understand this, since he always seemed perfect to her. Bob had a brief movie career and was also in several TV documentaries. The tumors made it difficult for him to speak normally, so at times it is hard to understand him. However, it is not hard to see how kind, loving, and caring this amazing man was when watching him on film. He was once asked if he blamed God for his lot in life. He said he did not and was very thankful for all the many good things he had. Bob saw his deformity as merely God's sense of humor. Bob died in his hometown of Lancaster, Missouri, on November 16, 1995. He was seventy-five. He is buried in the Arni Memorial Cemetery in Lancaster. ♦

Bob Melvin's Film Credits

The Other.......... (1972, not credited)
Sisters.......... (1973, not credited)
Being Different.......... (1981 Canadian/American documentary)
I Am Not a Freak.......... (1987, TV documentary)

DOLLY REGAN, "THE HUMAN DOLL," "JOLLY DOLLY, THE OSSIFIED GIRL," OR "HALF WOMAN/HALF BABY"

Clara Scott was born in Saskatoon, Saskatchewan, Canada, in 1919. She was born with a rare bone disease, bony ankylosis, a condition that caused her joints to fuse. After the age of eight, she stopped growing with the exception of her head. The infant-like body and the mature head gave her the look of a real living doll, hence her nickname Dolly and her stage name "The Human Doll." As an adult, Dolly was three feet tall and weighed only eighty pounds. Her legs completely atrophied and were tiny and useless appendages. Her right arm and hand were withered into a claw-like shape. Her left arm was a little better and allowed her to feed herself and operate a motorized wheelchair. She never walked and needed a wheelchair or someone to carry her to get around. Dolly used a stick with a hair clip connected to the end to smoke cigarettes, but someone had to light them for her. In fact, she was dependent on someone at all times and the shows she worked for hired round-the-clock caregivers as part of her contract.

When asked about her condition, she would always say her mother had been ill with the flu while pregnant and she had absorbed excess calcium from her mother's body in the womb in order to survive. While Dolly truly believed this, most doctors believe ankylosis is a genetic disorder that seems to run in families. Dolly also claimed that she started with the sideshow in 1942 when she was discovered at her hometown fair selling raffle tickets for the Kiwanis. A sideshow manager offered her a job on the spot and she said she jumped at the chance to join the show for a life of adventure. She received room and board, a constant caregiver, and in 1983, $200 a week. She was proud that she made her own way in the world, disabled as she was. She always said she loved the work she did, and reportedly said, "I once tried telephone soliciting and found it positively dreadful."

Dolly claimed that she started with the sideshow in 1942 when she was discovered at her hometown fair selling raffle tickets for the Kiwanis.

Once when asked by a reporter why she had chosen the circus life, she quipped, "I'd have made a lousy waitress."

Dolly never retired from show business. She claimed she liked what she did too much and that she ever made enough money to retire. Off season, she lived in her home in Gibsonton, Florida, with a caregiver. Dolly was married three times and widowed three times. One husband was Pappy Reagan, a circus juggler, magician, and knife thrower. Another husband was Percy Pape, a "living skeleton." True or not, she reportedly said of her third husband, "Later I married a ventriloquist. He had a brilliant mind but you could read his lips."

She was in the 1981 documentary *Being Different*. When covertly asked by the interviewer about the romantic side of married life, she laughed and claimed she had a very active and fulfilling sex life. Some of the best sideshow quotes of all times come from Dolly Reagan. Once when asked by a reporter why she had chosen the circus life, she quipped, "I'd have made a lousy waitress." When asked during an interview if she was ever mad about her lot in life, she said, "The deformity bothers everyone else more than if bothers me. I am very comfortable with myself. I am not mad at me." When asked that standard question, "Do you feel sorry for yourself?" she reportedly always said, "Oh, I suppose I have at times but I bet you have, too." Dolly worked for the amazing Ward Hall from 1972 until her death. She died, still performing, on April 28, 1991. She was seventy-one years old. She was cremated. ♦

JOHAAN PETURSSON, "ICELAND'S TALLEST MAN," "THE VIKING GIANT," OR "THE ICELANDIC GIANT"

Johaan Kristinn Svarfaelingur was born in Dalvik, Iceland, on February 9, 1913.

He often billed himself as standing eight foot eight inches tall, but he was actually seven feet ten inches tall at the "height" of his career.

Johann proved so popular and such a shrewd businessman that he broke away from management and went into business for himself.

Johaan was the first to sell "Giant's Rings," inexpensive metal souvenir rings.

Johaan Kristinn Svarfaelingur was born in Dalvik, Iceland, on February 9, 1913. He claimed he only weighed nine pounds at birth and was a typically developed child until the age of fifteen when he started to grow at an accelerated rate. He often billed himself as standing eight feet eight inches tall, but he was actually seven feet ten inches tall at the "height" of his career.

Originally, he dressed in a top hat, waistcoat, and tails, but soon took to wearing a Viking costume to capitalize on his exotic origins. His career started in Iceland and Europe, but in 1948 he came to America to tour with Ringling Bros. and Barnum & Bailey Circus and others such as Frank Berger's World of Mirth and Tom W. Kelly's Freak Show. In 1948, he was making a salary of $200 a week. By 1968, he commanded $350–400 a week, plus money from sales of his trade cards and photographs. Johaan, a natural businessman, sold his "Giant's Rings," inexpensive metal and plastic souvenir rings that were large enough for a silver dollar to pass through. Eventually, Johann proved so popular and such a shrewd businessman that he broke away from management and went into business for himself. He created the very successful and lucrative Single-O Show, a travelling sideshow in which he was the only attraction with few other salaries to pay.

Johaan also had a brief film career. He is most remembered for *Prehistoric Women,* a 1950 film in which he starred opposite Jayne Mansfield as the prehistoric giant Guadi. Johaan was always very popular with ladies. When asked by a reporter if he was married, he quipped, "The girls all want to know if I am married, and it happens, I'm looking for a pretty girl who likes to cook." There is no record of him ever marrying, but reportedly, he had a child that was born in Denmark. He retired from show business and the hectic life on the road in 1982 when he was sixty-nine. He had a home in Gibsonton, Florida, a favorite retirement town for sideshow performers. Unfortunately, a bad fall hospitalized him, and a brother came to take him back to his hometown in Dalvik. Johann's health declined and he passed away a short time later on November 26, 1984. He was seventy-one. Johaan's memory is honored at the Showmen's Museum of the International Independent Showmen's Association in Gibsonton, Florida, where several of his belongings are on display. The Dalvík Folk Museum (Byggðasafnið Hvoll) also has an exhibit honoring their favorite son and his grave is near the museum. ♦

Johaan originally exhibited in formal wear but changed to Viking costumes for an exotic effect.

Johaan Petursson's Film Credits

Hjertetyven .... (1943)
Lev Livet Let .... (1944)
Prehistoric Women .... (1950)
Carny .... (1980)
Being Different .... (Canadian/ American documentary)
Sideshow: Alive on the Inside .... (1999, TV documentary).

PERCILLA ROMAN LAUTHER BEJANO, "THE MONKEY-GIRL," OR "THE LITTLE HAIRY GIRL" AND EMMYTT DRIGGERS BEJANO, "LOBELLO, THE ALLIGATOR-SKINNED MAN"

There really is someone for everyone. The true lasting love story of Percilla, "The Monkey-Girl," and Emmytt Bejano, "Lobello, The Alligator-Skinned Man," proves just that. The couple met while both were performing with the Johnny J. Jones Exposition. They fell in love almost immediately and eloped in 1938. Immediately dubbed "The World's Strangest Couple," they remained together fifty-seven years until Emmytt's death in 1995. ♦

PERCILLA'S STORY

Percilla was born on April 26, 1911, in Bayamon, Puerto Rico, with a rare medical condition, hypertrichosis, the excessive growth of hair all over the body. Her entire body was covered with hair, with the exception of the skin around the eyes and the top of her feet. Extensive cases of hypertrichosis have informally been called "werewolf syndrome" and probably contributed to the ancients' belief in the existence of such a creature. Percilla had also been born with two rows of teeth, a dental condition linked to hypertrichosis. The combination of excessive hair and excessive teeth gave the child an animal-like appearance. The parents and her six siblings had none of these characteristics. Alarmed, they took her to doctors in Puerto Rico and on the mainland. Baffled doctors said her condition was "glandular" and they offered neither cure nor help.

Turning lemons into lemonade, her father decided that the public would pay to see such a child. He contacted a showman, Karl L. Lauther, who immediately recognized the money-making opportunity being offered. Percilla became known as "The Little Hairy Girl" and was almost an overnight success when she started being exhibited at age three. Her father remained in the United States with his daughter and traveled with the child right up to his untimely death when he was shot and killed during an engagement in Gainesville, Florida, three years later. Lauther petitioned to become the legally adoptive father of Percilla and, reportedly, he and his wife loved the little girl deeply and treated her well. It is not clear if the child's biological mother in Puerto Rico was notified of the adoption or if Lauther basically "bought" Percilla by paying her off. Most likely, the latter scenario played out. A woman was hired to look after the little six-year-old girl and there is no mention of the child seeing her mother again as a child.

Percilla was born with a rare medical condition, hypertrichosis, the excessive growth of hair all over the body. Extensive cases of hypertrichosis have informally been called "werewolf syndrome."

She first exhibited under the stage name of "Hairy Little Girl" at the very young age of three

As Percilla grew, the stage name "The Monkey-Girl" was adopted.

They did reconnect when Percilla was an adult and her mother often visited her grown daughter. As Percilla grew, the stage name "The Monkey-Girl" was adopted and a trained chimpanzee was added to the act, at times billing them as siblings. The chimpanzee, Josephine, rode a bicycle and smoked cigarettes. At times, the monkey was more popular with the crowd than "The Monkey-Girl."

Percilla shown with her parents. Her father toured with her up until he was shot to death in an incident in Florida. Photo courtesy of Ben Ziegler.

Percilla as a teenager.

Percilla photographed in 1971 at the Kansas State Fair by a fan that had ignored the "No Photos Taken Please" sign.

At age twenty-seven, Percilla fell in love with Emmytt Bejano, twenty-two, "The Alligator-Skinned Man," while both were sideshow attractions with the Johnny J. Jones Exhibition. They eloped in 1938, and then resumed exhibiting as "The World's Strangest Couple." Eventually in the 1950s and 1960s they would have their own show, The Bejano Family.

She added dancing and singing to her show and made additional income from people throwing coins on stage in appreciation for her performance. She always claimed that she threw pennies back. Percilla gave birth to a daughter on February 2, 1939. They named the child Francine. She had inherited her mother's condition and the parents were thrilled with their special baby, but sadly she died from pneumonia when she was only four months old. Much later in life they adopted a son, Antonio E., who was born on April 9, 1960. He worked at fairs as a ride and concession operator before joining the armed services. The Bejanos were very proud of their

son whom they affectionately called Tony, and sang his praises often.

Percilla always wore long-sleeved dresses and gloves when she went about in public, even on the show grounds. She would also hold a head scarf in front of her face so that only her eyes would show. She was reportedly fond of saying, "Clothes can cover a multitude of things." Another of her philosophical, much-repeated quotes was, "It's like a blind man or somebody without a leg or arm. You get used to it. You are never so bad that you can't be worse." She and her husband bought an acre of land in Gibsonton on the outskirts of Tampa and lived there in a trailer in the off-season, usually six months a year. They eventually retired in Zephryhills, Florida, and Percilla liked to laugh and say, "The show's over." Percilla passed away in her sleep at Westbrooke Manor in Zephyrhills on February 5, 2001. She was eighty-nine and was shaving her beard at the time of her death. She was, most likely, cremated as was her beloved husband who died in 1995. She told a reporter once that when people in the audience made fun of her she would tell them, "I can see you for nothing right here, but you had to pay to see me." ♦

EMMYTT'S STORY

Emmytt Driggers Bejano was born on August 22, 1916, in Punta Gorda, Florida, with ichthyosis, a skin condition that gives the skin a thick, dry, scaly reptile-like appearance. The word comes from the Ancient Greek word, *ichthys*, meaning "fish." Only the skin on his face, hands, and soles of his feet was unaffected. The condition is neither contagious nor inherited. He turned blue ten days after birth to the alarm of his parents. They consulted a doctor who called his condition "fish skin" and offered no cure for this strange baby. Eventually, his blue skin took on a slick look and was scored with lines like a reptile.

When Emmytt was six, his parents separated and his father put him in a sideshow. When his father died, he, too, was adopted by a sideshow manager, Johnny Bejano, who had arranged with Emmytt's mother a deal that basically constituted the sale of the child. He remained with his adopted father's show until he was a teenager and then worked for

"The World's Strangest Couple" remained together fifty-seven years until Emmytt's death in 1995. In a booklet that she sold at shows, Percilla wrote, "…fate hasn't treated me unkindly in view of my many blessings of good health, a fine husband and many friends."

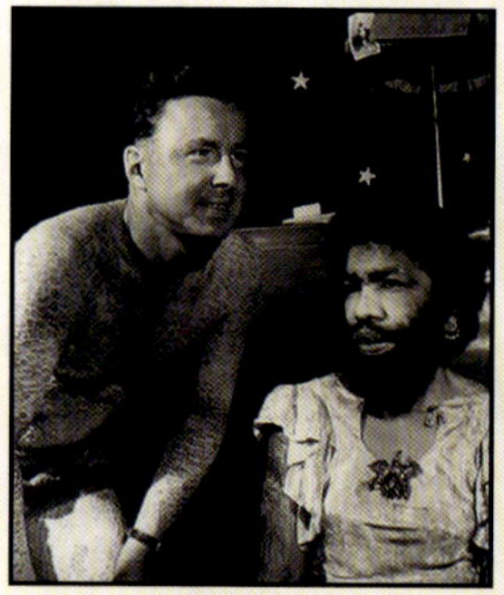

Emmytt Driggers Bejano was born on August 22, 1916, in Punta Gorda, Florida, with ichthyosis, a skin condition that gives the skin a thick, dry, scaly reptile-like appearance.

a few other sideshows until he joined Karl Luther's show. It was there that he met his future bride, Percilla Bejano, "The Monkey-Girl."

Emmytt could not sweat through his skin due to his condition. He always needed to keep a tub of ice at all times in the back of every show, even on cold days.

He wore regular street clothes, but always long-sleeved shirts. He could pass in public as a "normal" man, since his face and hands were not affected by his condition.

Emmytt passed away on May 14, 1995. He was seventy-nine. He was cremated.

Neither Emmytt nor Percilla ever regretted being placed in a sideshow as children, nor did they ever seem bitter over the circumstances of their birth. Percilla once responded to a reporter, "I felt I learned something. It kept me off the relief line. It's an honest effort and I feel more or less proud of the fact that I can earn my own living and do anything anybody else can. Nature does funny things sometimes. But I've lived a normal life." ♦

Percilla and Emmytt's Film Credits

Carney .... (1980)
Being Different .... (1981, Canadian/American documentary)
Secret Cabaret .... (1992, UK TV magic and interview show)
Sideshow-Alive on the Inside .... (1999, TV documentary, Emmytt posthumously)
E! True Hollywood Story: The Murder of Lobster Boy (TV series documentary, Percilla was in this project after Emmytt's death)
The Jerry Springer Show .... (date unknown, Percilla was in this project after Emmytt's death)

FRIEDA PUSHNIK, "ARMLESS AND LEGLESS WONDER GIRL"

Frieda C. Pushnik was born on February 10, 1923, in Johnstown, Pennsylvania, without arms or legs. Trade show cards and hype always claimed that Frieda was the result of her mother's botched appendectomy when she was pregnant with Frieda, but that story was repeated only to sell tickets. Frank and Nellie Pushnik, parents from Yugoslavia and Poland respectively, were free from disabilities, as were Frieda's older sister, Emma, and her younger brother, Frederick. Reportedly, when the doctor placed Frieda in her mother's arms, Nellie claimed he said, "This is your war baby."

Frieda only weighed thirteen pounds when she was nine years old. Her mother carried her everywhere she went, even to school daily as a young child where Frieda said she was always treated well by the other children. In a newspaper interview, Nellie Pushnik said at first she thought her infant could not cry because she was so content and happy. By all accounts, Frieda continued to exhibit those traits her entire life. She learned to write by holding a pencil in her mouth. One of her mother's proudest moments was the day Frieda won an award at school for excellent penmanship. She also learned to crochet and paint and added these elements to her sideshow act, plus a demonstration showing her using eating utensils. She was proud she could put on makeup and claimed she learned to type by watching her sister. She was known to say that everything came to her naturally.

Robert Ripley heard of Frieda and in 1933 signed up the ten-year-old for Ripley's Believe It Or Not

Frieda Pushnik was born without arms or legs. She learned to write by holding a pencil in her mouth.

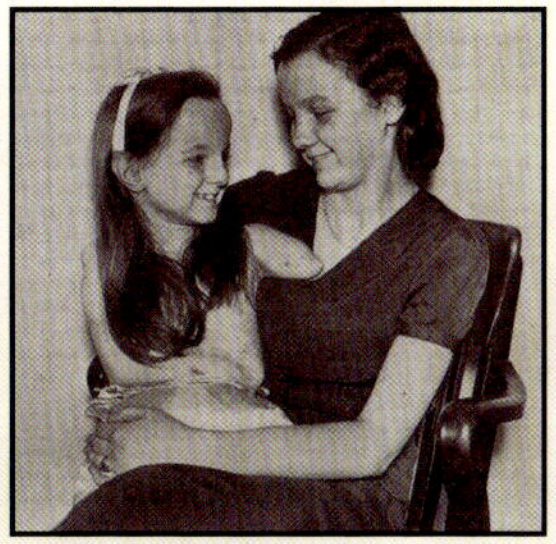

Frieda shown with her sister. (Her name was misspelled in this newspaper story.)

Frieda had a brief film career, her most noticeable performance was in *House of the Damned* where she played the legless girl.

Robert Ripley signed the ten-year-old for Ripley's "Believe It Or Not" show in 1933. She remained with Ripley until 1943, making $150 a week.

Frieda only weighed thirteen pounds when she was nine years old. Her mother carried her everywhere she went, even to school every day. After she joined the sideshow circuit, her mother always traveled with her and continued to carry her everywhere or push her in a small wheelchair.

show. She remained with Ripley until 1943, making $150 a week. She left Ripley to join the Ringling Bros. and Barnum & Bailey Circus sideshow as their principal attraction and stayed with them until 1956 when she retired at age thirty-three. Her mother always traveled with her and continued to carry her everywhere or push her in a small wheelchair that was decorated in imitation leopard skin. By this time, Frieda weighed forty pounds and stood almost three feet tall. Frieda had a brief film career, her most noticeable performance was in *House of the Damned* where she played the legless girl.

No special equipment was at their home and Frieda even used the telephone, both receiving and making calls. She was once asked by a reporter if she had minded people at sideshow performances staring at her. She replied that she did not and liked to watch people as they watched her. She added, "That's what the people were paying for."

Frieda never married and lived with her parents, then her widowed mother until her mother's death. Frieda passed away on Christmas Eve, 2000, in Costa Mesa, California. She was seventy-seven years old. She is buried in the Pacific View Memorial Park in Corona del Mar, California. ♦

Frieda Pushnik's Film Credits

House of the Damned.................... (1963)
El Costillo de los Monstrous............... (1964)
Side Show .... (1981, not credited)

BRUCE SNOWDEN, "HOWARD HUGE"

Howard Huge, considered by the industry to be the last sideshow fat man, died on November 9, 2009, alone, and in a nursing home in St. Petersburg, Florida. He was sixty-three years old. He had a career that spanned twenty-six years and although he did not reach his life goal of becoming the fattest man on record, he came very close. At his death, he was billed as weighing 712 pounds, but more likely, he was merely a slim 600 plus pounds. He always claimed he was born in Buzzards Bay, Massachusetts, but he rarely mentioned anything else about his early years. By all accounts, Bruce Snowden was a very intelligent man and well read. It is often reported that he held several degrees from prestigious universities, but that was probably just show-business hype. When asked how he got into the sideshow business, he would say he was looking for a job, just happened to read about the fat men of bygone sideshow days, and impulsively decided to take advantage of his lifelong physical tendency to gain weight. He

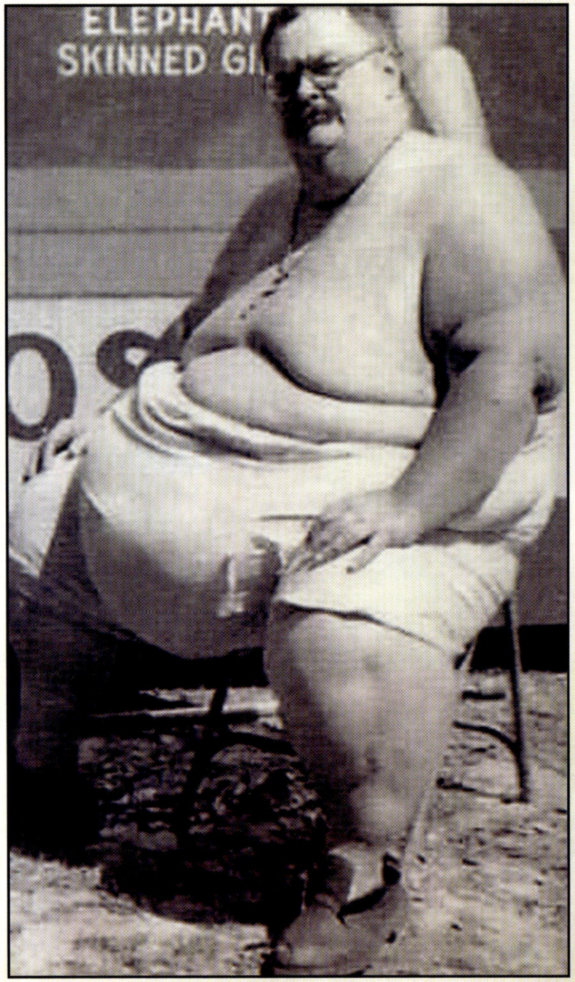

Bruce Snowden is considered by the industry to be the last sideshow fat man, the end of an era.

eventually found his way to Ward Hall, the modern-day P. T. Barnum, and joined the show in 1977 when he was thirty-one. He remained with Ward Hall's "World of Wonders Sideshow and Museum" his entire career, leaving one day in 2003 in a huff over sleeping arrangements and a mattress.

Bruce had a cameo appearance in the 2003 movie *Big Fish*, playing himself. There is a scene in the movie where he is being bathed with a long-handled

Bruce had a cameo appearance in the 2003 movie *Big Fish*, playing himself. Danny DeVito is also in the movie. There is a scene where Bruce is being bathed with a long-handled brush that was used to wash down the elephants.

brush that was used to wash down the elephants. That scene was likely inspired by truth. Bruce had a hard time staying clean due to his abundant proportions. He often had to be hosed down and preferred to air-dry since there were no towels his size. The faint of heart would most likely steer clear of his bathing area on those days.

He was often called eccentric by his friends and reportedly had a wicked sense of humor. One of his favorite sayings when asked about his enormous size was, "If there's a bitchy type of human being, it's somebody on a diet." He had always said he would like to be buried in the Sunset Memory Gardens cemetery in Tampa, Florida, in the Showman's Rest section. Sadly, there is no record of his burial there. He passed away in the nursing home where he had been bed-ridden for almost a year. Somehow the home failed to convey the sad news

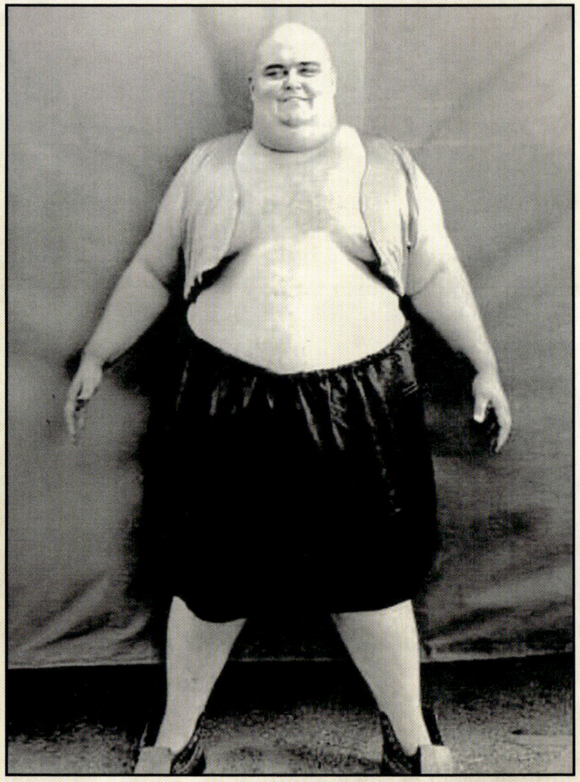

He was often called eccentric by his friends and reportedly had a wicked sense of humor. One of his favorite sayings when asked about his enormous size was, "If there's a bitchy type of human being, it's somebody on a diet."

of his death to his friends and family. He was cremated, requiring just one urn. ♦

ANDRE RENE ROUSSIMOFF, "JEAN FERRE," "ANDRE THE GIANT," OR "THE 8TH WONDER OF THE WORLD

Andre used his size, combined with a strong drive and athletic talent, to become a legendary wrestler and later, a film star.

Andre was not an actual sideshow performer, but he is included in this book because he took his abnormal condition and made a living by performing live for audiences, albeit performing in a wrestling ring and not on a sideshow stage. Andre was born in Grenoble, France, on May 19, 1946, to average-sized parents. He had four siblings who were also of average size. His body grew his entire life because of his disease, acromegaly, which is caused by an overabundance of growth hormones. At seventeen, he was six feet seven inches. He was seven feet four inches tall and weighed 500 pounds by the time of his death at age forty-seven.

He used his size, combined with a strong drive and athletic talent to become a legendary wrestler, and later, a film star. He was given the nicknames "The 8th Wonder of the World" and "Andre the Giant." He became one of the most recognizable names in the wrestling world. In 1993, Andre was the inaugural inductee into the WWF Hall of Fame. He was mentioned in the 1974 *Guinness World Records* as the highest paid wrestler in history, earning $400,000 in one year. Close friends always claimed that Andre was kind and generous to a fault. As with most stricken with acromegaly, Andre's heart gave out. He died in his sleep in a hotel room in Paris, France, on January 27, 1993. He was in Paris to attend the funeral of his father. His ashes were spread over his Ellerbe, North Carolina, ranch. He was forty-six. ♦

As with most stricken with acromegaly, Andre's heart gave out. He died in his sleep in a hotel room in Paris, France, on January 27, 1993. He was forty-six.

Andre Roussimoff's Film Credits

Six Million Dollar Man . . . . (1976, TV series)
B. J. and the Bear. . . . . (1979, TV series)
The Fall Guy . . . . (1982, TV series)
The Greatest American Hero . . . . . . (1983, TV series)
Conan The Destroyer . . . . (1984, not credited)
Micki + Maude . . . . (1984)
Saturday Night's Main Event. . . . . (1985, TV series)
WWF: The Big Event . . . . (1986, video)
Princess Bride . . . . (1987)
Zorro . . . . (1990, TV series)
Trading Mom . . . . (1994, released posthumously)

9

PHOTOGRAPHERS OF THE FREAKS

Charles Eisenmann & Matthew Brady

WE ARE VERY FORTUNATE TODAY THAT WE HAVE SO MANY PHOTOGRAPHS AVAILABLE OF THE FAMOUS PAST PERFORMERS OF THE SIDESHOW.

Two main factors contributed to this phenomenon. First, photography became wildly popular and very affordable with the introduction of the carte-de-vistes in 1859 and later, the larger parlor cards. Absolutely everyone from the famous to the poor was having their portraits done. Second, the sideshow performers had photographs done to be used in promotional advertising and to sell to the public at shows to increase their income. There were many photographers who took pictures of the freaks, but the three most noted are Charles Eisenmann, his business partner and son-in-law Charles Frank Wendt, and Matthew Brady, also known as "the Photographer of the Civil War." ♦

CHARLES EISENMANN & FRANK W. WENDT

By far, Charles Willard Eisenmann was the most prolific and important photographer of the freaks. Other photographers soon realized the money to be made photographing sideshow performers, but Eisenmann is noted in history as the first and the best of such professionals. He was often referred to by people in the industry as "P. T. Barnum's Photographer." Barnum's dime museum was at 221 Bowery and Eisenmann's studio was situated at 229 Bowery. Reportedly, Barnum encouraged Eisenmann to open his studio in that location. They had met during Charles's years playing aboard river boats. The studio opened in 1876, and eventually Charles owned two studios and a factory. The second branch gallery was at 18 West 14th Street and the factory was at 537–543 East 15th Street (rear of building).

Charles Willard Eisenmann was the most prolific and important photographer of the sideshow, often call "the Photographer of the Freaks."

Charles Eisenmann's photographs are coveted today due to his great artistic talent and the highly honed technical skill that he used to create his images. His photographs have the profound effect of making us wonder about his subjects and the lives they led. Who can gaze upon a portrait done by Eisenmann and not want to know everything about the life of the intriguing person he captured on film? He also used beautiful settings and backgrounds when photographing the freaks, giving each a respect that was not always afforded them.

Charles was born in Stuttgart, Germany, on June 9, 1849, and immigrated to America in 1865 with his family. They settled very briefly in the Bowery, then a mostly German neighborhood in New York City. The family changed the spelling of their surname from "Eisemann" to "Eisenmann" to Americanize the pronunciation. His disenchanted family soon returned to Germany, but Charles so loved America that he quickly boarded a freighter and sailed back alone. He was sixteen years old. For a time, he played various musical instruments aboard river boats to earn a living. There, family lore says, he was befriended by Mark Twain and married Twain's sister, but that is only lore. His first wife was Emelia Gastauer, a native of New Orleans. Mark Twain was, however, a family friend and remained so throughout the years. Emelia's father did not approve of the marriage, and the couple moved to New York City to flee the father's

Eisenmann used beautiful settings and backgrounds when photographing the freaks, giving each a respect that was not always afforded them.

wrath. Sadly, Emelia soon died in childbirth, along with the infant. Charles was so distraught over the loss of his young wife and child that he disappeared from history for about seven years. The family believes he went to China although there is no concrete proof to support that fact. However, as an adult, Charles

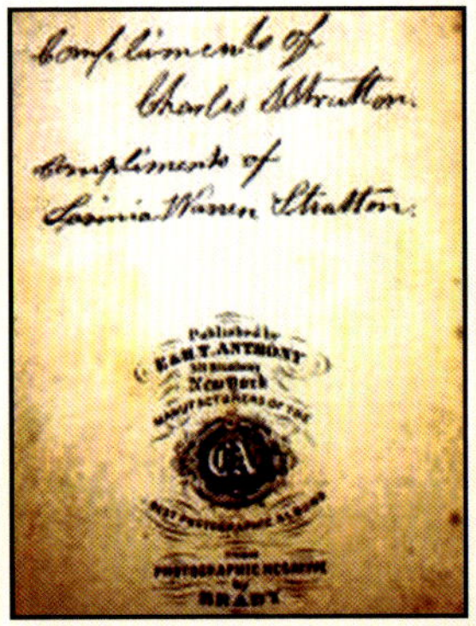

The much-publicized Tom Thumb wedding on February 10, 1863, was photographed by Matthew Brady. These photos he did as a personal favor to P. T. Barnum.

In 1850 or 1851, Brady married Julia Handy, pictured on the left with Brady and another woman, believed to be a relative.

Portrait of Brady taken shortly before his death. Brady died a destitute alcoholic in the charity ward of a New York hospital. He lost everything when he was unable to sell his Civil War photographs after the war ended.

Matthew Brady, "the Photographer of the Civil War."

win the election. Matthew Brady is often referred to as "the Photographer of the Civil War." However, Brady did not actually shoot most of the Civil War photographs attributed to him, with the exception of the Battle of Bull Run.

He was one of the first to realize the role photography could play in chronicling national events. It was his intent to document the war as a historical record and to make money from his venture. He used a group of about twenty photographers who actually followed the troops into the fields, outfitted with traveling darkrooms that allowed them to process their shots immediately. Brady acted as the supervisor of these battlefield photographers from his studio in Washington. He spent his money equipping and financing these photographers and his time and energy organizing the finished photographs and preserving their negatives. He also used his own money to purchase war photographs from independent sources. "Photograph by Brady" was the tag line on all of these Civil War photographs later published, although the vast majority were actually the work of others. In 1862, Brady shocked Victorian America by displaying photographs of battlefield corpses in his New York gallery. Most Americans had never witnessed the horrors of war. *The New York Times* said that Brady had brought "home to us the terrible reality and earnestness of war." After the Civil War, Brady found that no one was interested in purchasing war photographs, preferring instead to put the conflict behind them. This included Washington. During the war, Brady spent over $100,000 of his own money to obtain approximately 10,000 prints. He believed the government would buy his historical collection of war photographs when the conflict ended. When the government refused to do so, he was forced to sell his Washington gallery in 1868 and later, his New York City gallery. He filed for bankruptcy in 1873.

Congress granted Brady $25,000 in 1875 when they purchased his entire collection, but the amount was less than he needed to clear his debts. He opened and closed several studios but was unable to regain his success. He began to drink heavily. Matthew Brady died a destitute alcoholic in the charity ward of Presbyterian Hospital in New York City on January 15, 1896. The official cause of death was listed as pneumonia, a complication from a streetcar accident. He is buried in Congressional Cemetery, Washington, DC, and his funeral was paid for by the veterans of the 7th New York Infantry, thus saving Brady from a pauper's plot. He was around seventy-three. In his final years, Brady reportedly said, "No one will ever know what I went through to secure those negatives. The world can never appreciate it. It changed the whole course of my life." Sadly, Brady died not knowing the extent of his contribution to history and his lasting effect on the art of photography and photo journalism. ♦

10

SIDESHOW BANNER ART & THE ARTISTS

Fred G. Johnson
& David C. "Snap" Wyatt

EVERYTHING ABOUT THE SIDESHOW WAS DESIGNED TO SELL TICKETS TO THE USUALLY POOR BUT HIGHLY INTRIGUED LOCALS WHO CAME OUT EVERY TIME A SHOW HIT THEIR SMALL TOWN.

These "tips" might have believed they were only going to mosey on over just to see what the excitement was all about, but the owners and managers of the show had other plans. They were intent on milking the good town's folks out of every dime they could get, as well as enticing them to return to the show before the troupe pulled up stakes and moved on down the line.

The sideshow banners were the first thing at a show to sink that hook into the unsuspecting. Even before the crowds could hear the barker or see the selected performers on the bally stage, even before they could smell the smells of the show, they could see the huge, brightly-colored canvas art portraying the most lurid, sexual, and fascinating pictures most had ever seen. Who among them would not rush to pay a dime to glimpse the visual delights promised behind those canvas curtains?

Relatively few sideshow banners exist today. The life expectancy of these banners left out in the sun, wind, rain, and dust was about two years. The carnies breaking down or setting up a show would not think of the banner as anything special so the banners would not have been handled with care. If a performer left a show or was fired, his or her canvas banner would be cut down and typically used to repair the circus tents or just left behind in the dust when the show left town.

How differently we view these banners today. We are still mesmerized by their bold, distinct, and almost primitive look, just as the original viewers were, but

Even before the crowds could hear the barker or see the selected performers on the stage, even before they could smell the smells of the show, they could see the huge, brightly colored canvas art portraying the most lurid, sexual, and fascinating pictures most had ever seen.

modern eyes view these canvases as pure works of art. Most of the artists who produced the banners did not sign their work and were probably just trying to make a few bucks at the time. They would be pleasantly surprised at the prices many of these banners command today and the respect paid their artwork. Snap Wyatt and Fred Johnson are arguably the best of the best when we talk about sideshow banner artists. There were other good ones, even great ones, in the business such as Jack Cripe, Jack C. Sigler, Chad Hill, G. M. Caldwell, Neiman Eisman of Neiman Studios, Danny Casella who worked almost exclusively for Coney Island, August Wolfinger, Millard & Bulsterbaum, and the last of the line, the amazing Johnny Meah, but the masters of the trade were Wyatt and Johnson. ♦

Shown is "Armless Wonder" by Danny Casella. He was a banner artist who worked almost exclusively for Coney Island.

DAVID C. "SNAP" WYATT

David Clarence Wyatt was born in Ashville, North Carolina ,on October 21, 1905, to William H. and Clara M. Wyatt. From a very early age, he showed an interest in and a talent for drawing. After serving in the US Army during World War II, Snap atteded a few art classes at Cooper Union for the Advancement of Science and Art School in New York City, an old and prestigious school. He started out his art career creating three-dimensional displays for department stores and traveling shows. While living in Florida, Ringling Bros. and Barnum & Bailey Circus gave him an early start in banner painting when they commissioned him to do ninety banners for their sideshow. Snap used a bold and almost cartoon-like style to produce his late 1940s to 1970s banners. He also was known for working very quickly. Legend says the nickname Snap was earned by his reputatuion for aggressively seeking work or "snapping signs," an industry insider term. Others claim it was given to him for his ability to paint a banner in a snap. He was one of the most prolific banner painters of all times. Snap would have probably been the first to tell you he was not aiming for fine art when he turned out his banners. His style is totally in your face and shocking. He was hired to get both the paying public's attention and ticket money, and he was not worried about composition, shading, line, or style. He was just doing a job.

Snap started each banner by first stretching a canvas on a frame and standing the frame up. He would secure a piece of drawing charcoal to a long stick and sketch his design. He then used an oil-based paint mixed with water and casein to fill in the drawing. He usually drew a dark line around the key figure in the composition to make it stand out and shadowed blue lettering with green. He destroyed a few brushes on every job, and could finish a typical ten by ten foot banner in under eight hours. Snap was paid an hourly wage, plus material costs, or he probably could have done each banner in less time. He averaged about eighty-five dollars for each banner. Like most banner painters, Snap usually worked from imagination and had never seen the subject he was painting. Many times, the show performers complained that it was impossible for them to make their performances as exciting as the banner advertising their acts. He also had a reputation for heavy drinking, which may or may not have affected his art. Today, his banners can command thousand of dollars, a fact that would more than likely amaze him.

Today, a Snap Wyatt banner can command thousands of dollars, a fact that would most likely amaze him.

Snap continued to accept jobs in the 1960s and 1970s even after he retired to a nursing home in Florida. He died on December 26, 1983, in Pinellas, Florida, at the age of seventy-eight. He is buried at Showman's Rest Cemetery in Tampa, Florida. He was briefly married in his youth but had no children. ♦

FRED G. JOHNSON

Fred George Johnson was born in Chicago, Illinois, on January 25, 1892, to Louis and Delia Part Johnson. Not much is known about his life before he became a banner painter for the O. Henry Tent & Awning Co. in Chicago except that he married Anna M. Wiese on February 14, 1914, and they had one son, Elsworth Johnson, born in 1920. On his 1917 World War I draft card registration, he lists his occupation as "artist."

His career as a banner painter spanned from 1934 to 1974 when he passed away at the age of eighty-two. He often called his creations "flash," a term he used to describe the very quick way in which he worked and his abundant use of bold colors and unusual color combinations. His trademark, however, was his ability to wow the viewer with his unique eye-catching compositions. Some modern critics claim he overworked his banners, cramming too much into each picture. Others praise his work as more painting style than banner style. Today, his original banners command prices into the thousands of dollars and are highly sought after by the more serious collectors. A few very serious collectors will only purchase a Fred Johnson banner.

Fred worked at the O. Henry Tent & Awning Shop on Clark Street, occupying a studio in the attic of the building. Downstairs, the company

MYSTERY TO SOLVE

Where is Fred Johnson buried? What did he do before 1934 when he became a banner painter?

made, as expected by the name, tents and awnings. Upstairs, Fred made show banners using the same canvas. He was paid by the piece. In a newspaper article, Fred was quoted as saying, "The secret of the banner art is the color and never mind if you exaggerate the subject matter. The idea is to attract attention." He always used lead-based oil paints. He started with white lead paint and mixed it with benzene, linseed oil, and other things as eccentric as ground crayons until the mixture had the consistency of paste. In a good season, he said he'd use about 500 pounds of white lead. To economize, he'd wet the canvas before painting so the paint would not bleed through to the backside. Fred had a reputation for being a heavy drinker and he always claimed alcohol improved his work, freeing him to be more creative. ♦

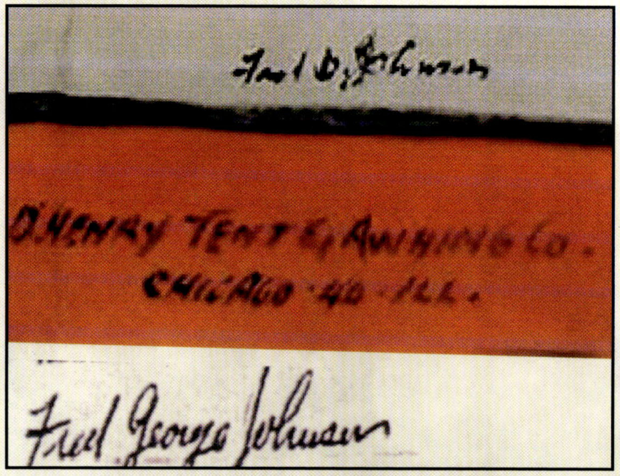

Fred Johnson's signature on a sideshow banner and his written signature on his World War I draft registration card in 1917.

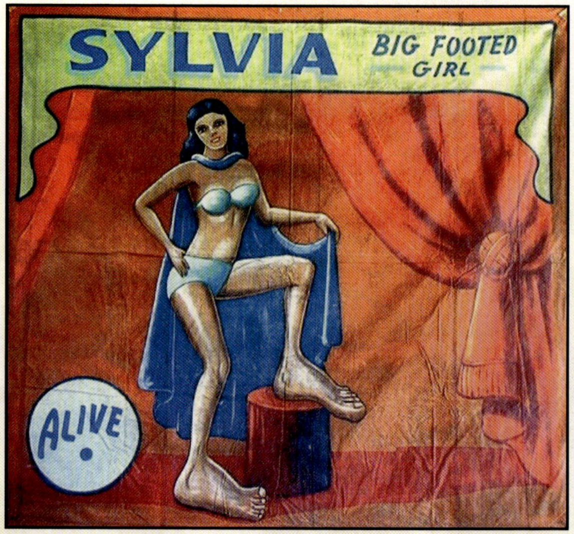

Fred was often quoted as saying, "The secret of the banner art is the color and never mind if you exaggerate the subject matter. The idea is to attract attention."

11

GAFFS

Homer Tate

"King of the Gaffs"

WITHOUT A DOUBT, THE MOST FAMOUS OF ALL OLD SIDESHOW GAFF CREATORS IS HOMER MARTIN TATE, THE UNDISPUTED "KING OF THE GAFFS."

Homer started making his gaffs in the 1940s, and even eventually published a sale catalog of his wares. Today, an intact Homer Tate catalogue sells for top dollar on Internet auction sites such as eBay and in antique stores.

He displayed his creations in a storefront in Apache Junction, Arizona, that he dubbed Sideshow World, a type of personal museum he opened mostly for the amusement of his friends and the curious. His most prolific creations were shrunken heads but he also made a variety of other oddities from found objects such as bone, feathers, and twigs. He would add these found pieces from nature to mud, canvas, chicken wire, human hair, and pretty much anything else he could scrounge up to create his oddities. This was a simpler time in life where the gaff did not have to be sophisticated or finely crafted to amaze and frighten the viewing public. Homer's creations become sideshow wonders, amazing and frightening generations of viewers.

Homer was born in Turners Point, Texas, on September 7, 1884, to a devout Mormon family. Around 1892, the family moved to Indian Territory, Oklahoma, and then again westward several more times. As an adult, Homer worked several conventional jobs—farmer, miner, and even served as the publicly elected sheriff of Graham County, Arizona, from 1925 to 1928. He was also a businessman, owning a motel and gas station. He married Emma Tate and was the father of two sons and two daughters.

No one has been able to explain why Homer, mid-life, started creating his special type of bizarre and macabre art, but it is speculated that his new hobby/business upset some members of his Mormon family, especially an adult son. Homer unfortunately spent a few months behind bars on a moonshine charge. In his absence, his son removed all of Homer's creations and most likely destroyed them. They have never resurfaced. He did go on to create more gaffs, but unfortunately so many of his best works were forever lost. Homer died on February 21, 1975, at the ripe old age of ninety, and he lives on through his creations. His gaffs are legendary within the sideshow world. When collecting, however, beware of modern reproductions of Homer's pieces. He never signed any of his work so make sure it is a true Homer Tate gaff before spending the $200 to $300 or more that his amazing pieces are currently commanding. ♦

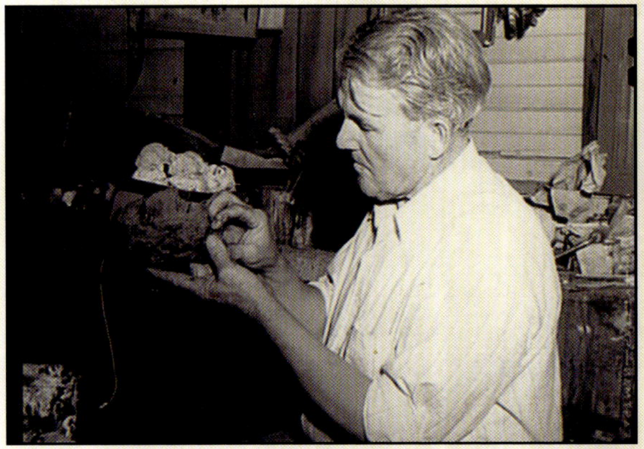

Without a doubt, the most famous of all old sideshow gaff creators is Homer Martin Tate, the undisputed "King of the Gaffs."

Some of the more bizarre and macabre creations of Homer's on display in his personal museum. His motel is visible from the window.

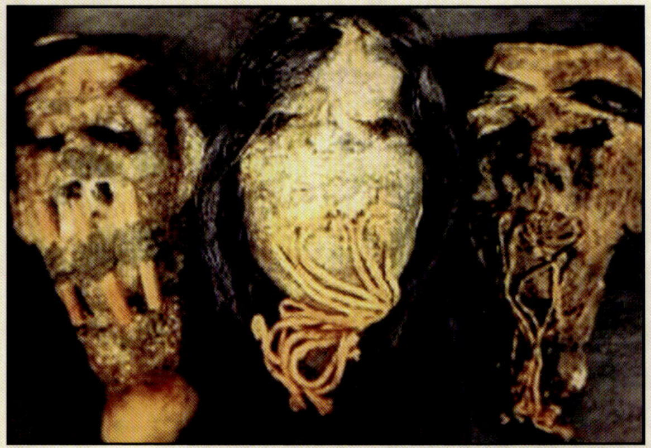

Examples of Homer Tate's shrunken heads, probably his most prolific gaff. They were created from mud, chicken wire, human hair, wood, bone, feathers and any other found object that was handy.

12

TODAY'S FREAK SHOWS

The Amazing Ward Hall, Coney Island, & Cyberspace Freaks

DURING THE HEYDAY OF THE SIDESHOW, THERE WERE OVER A HUNDRED OF THESE SHOWS ROAMING THE LAND ON ANY GIVEN SUMMER DAY. TODAY, THERE IS NOT EVEN ONE SIDESHOW LEFT THAT TOURS.

Ward Hall's World of Wonders closed in November 2003, thus ending an institution as American as apple pie, if not as traditional.

Ward was asked on a radio interview in 2003 why he was leaving the business after almost six decades. He said his fat man, Howard Huge, and his dwarf, Poobah, were tired of traveling and getting old as was he. Besides, he added, "There just aren't any real freaks left and it's almost impossible to shock anyone these days. Who can compete with television? You don't have to pay to see TV." ♦

WARD HALL, "KING OF THE SIDESHOW"

Ward Hall grew up during the Depression. He signed on with his first circus in 1946 when he was only fifteen, partly to get away from an abusive father and because he felt that the circus was in his blood. He claimed he had always wanted to be a circus performer but could never explain why. As a teenager, he read *The Billboard*, a weekly newspaper about show business that included the routes the circuses traveled. When he learned a circus was to appear in nearby Boulder, Colorado, he scraped together the money for a bus ticket and went to see his first show. He was hooked. That summer he practiced a variety of acts, trying to find his niche. He checked out any and all books from the public library on circuses and worked to perfect acts such as fire-eating, juggling, magic tricks, and puppet manipulation. In March of that year, Ward read that the Daily Brothers Circus was looking for sideshow acts. He applied for and got a shot at his dream, with a message back that pretty much said: "winter quarters at Gonzales, Texas. Show opens April 1. Get here the best way you can." According to Ward in his book, *My Very Unusual Friends,* "I arrived in winter quarters with two dollars to my name… (they) put me to work helping to refurbish the equipment for which I received meals, sleeper, and $4.00 a week. I had never been happier." He remained with this show for four years, working as a clown magician while he learned and perfected other sideshow acts, as well.

Ward Hall, the undisputed modern-day "King of the Sideshow."

Ward Hall with his business and life partner Chris Christ.

Ward started his own sideshow in 1951 and began a business and life partnership with Chris Christ in the mid-1960s. They always traveled with at least ten human oddities, plus a dozen working acts such as the fire-eater, human block head, and the knife thrower. At his prime, Ward was the front talker and worked thirty shows a day, twelve hours a day, seven days a week, seven months a year. The other five months were spent in winter quarters.

The last of the old-time sideshows, Ward Hall's "World of Wonders" closed in November 2003. It was the end an institution as American as apple pie, if not as traditional.

In the final years of the World of Wonders show, it became mostly a museum displaying about fifty dilapidated wax figures and mannequins of former freaks. His usual admission price was two dollars and many a show attendee complained he had been suckered. His only live acts were his fire-eating

Ward started his own sideshow in 1951. His career spanned almost six decades.

dwarf who sported a hearing aid and his fat man who kept getting sick and losing weight. Ward even opted for a taped carnival barker, saying he was just too tired to keep up the pace anymore. Ward never felt guilty. He liked to say, "If you came to see these freaks alive, you came forty years too late." Ward Hall had worked with many of the best freaks of all time, but unfortunately these performers got older, got sick, and died. The statues in his show, even in their current poor condition, are a tribute to the greatest sideshow performers from our country's past. To Ward, they are a tribute to close friends who have come and gone.

When Ward looks back on the years when the freaks were alive and on stage, he makes no apologies. He doesn't think he exploited them. He explains that the impulse to get up close to the freaks then was no different than the desire to get close to a rock star or Hollywood idol now. He adds, "Many of the top ones were paid every bit as well as today's stars." Today, Ward resides in a trailer in Gibsonton, Florida. A sun-faded statue of a sad-faced clown marks the entrance to the home. Numerous yellowed newspaper clippings adorn his walls, a tribute to himself, his career, and his lasting legacy. His show is for sale. He is retired but he quickly suggests that he will speak at dinners or go on a lecture tour, addressing anyone still interested in the lost American sideshow. Who could do it better than the undisputed "King of the Sideshow"? ♦

CONEY ISLAND

Sideshows by the Seashore is a chance to still see a real traditional sideshow. The show is at the corner of Surf Avenue and West 12th Street in the heart of the Coney Island amusement park, just a few steps from the ocean. The show is housed in an historic building, ca. 1917, and is where such sideshow greats as Sealo "the Seal Boy" and Jo-Jo "the Dog-Faced Boy" played to amazed audiences. As the current owners like to tout, this historical building can be rented for parties, business meetings, bar mitzvahs, or weddings, with or without the performers, when the show is not in progress. They also proudly added a freak bar that sells beer and a gift shop. If you've ever dreamed of being in a circus or think you have what it takes to become a sideshow star, they even have a school to help you become the freak you and your mom always knew you could be.

Sideshows by the Seashore opened in 1985 as a not-for-profit arts group, and it was the first of its kind in sideshow history. Today's performers consist of a lineup of mostly "created freaks," such as tattooed people, and working acts, such as the sword-swallower, fire-eater, or human block heads. There are no human oddities or real freaks currently in the show.

Dick D. Zigun, a graduate of Yale and called "The Mayor of Coney Island" by most, is working to keep Coney Island's past alive and its future bright. He came to Coney Island in 1979 and the following year founded "Coney Island, USA." He has stuck by his dream through some lean financial times as well as boom times. As Dick was quoted as saying, "It is the one place left in America where you can see a traditional circus sideshow done the way they used to be with all of the traditional ballyhoo, the free demonstrations outside, gathering

a crowd, getting people in, turning them over, running eleven hours a day without a break." Admission cost to the Sideshow by the Seashore show has risen to ten dollars, a big difference from the early days of the dime museums and their admission prices, but this could easily be the most fun you ever had for ten bucks. ♦

VENICE BEACH

The Venice Beach Sideshow let's you experience the thrill of the old time sideshow but with a modern flair.

The Venice Beach Sideshow is another chance to glimpse a bygone tradition with a modern spin. Located at 909 Ocean Front Walk in Venice, California, this family-owned show offers an amazing variety of performers. For the admission price of five dollars, you will see Little People and giants, as well as "created freaks," such as the performer with so many facial piercings and body tattoos that he literally stops traffic wherever he goes. Added to the show's strong appeal are the working acts: sword swallowing, fire breathing, and freaks who suspend themselves in the air from hooks. Also on display are live, two-headed animals plus amazing oddities. In 2013, the show owner, Todd Ray, turned his sideshow into an unscripted reality documentary television series on the AMC network, aptly titled *Freakshow*. It is truly one unique program that will keep you glued to your television set. In 2014, production started on the second season, and currently Todd Ray and his family are making plans to open a second sideshow in Las Vegas, Nevada. ♦

CYBERSPACE SIDESHOWS

Today, we can see the freaks of modern times as well as explore the performers of past fame without leaving home. One of the best sites for experiencing all the thrills and chills from the comfort of your own computer chair is by visiting www.sideshowworld.com. There are many other sites that a little bit of research will help you locate, but none is better than this one. The graphics are amazing, the information is mostly accurate, and the site is easily maneuvered. A bonus: the site is updated on a regular basis. ♦

POINTS *of* INTEREST

ALBUQUERQUE MUSEUM, 2000 Mountain Road NW, Albuquerque, New Mexico, 505-243-7255, www.albuquerquemuseum.org. Sideshow banners; not all are on display, call in advance to check availability.

THE BARNUM MUSEUM, 820 Main Street, Bridgeport, Connecticut, 203-331-1104, www.barnum-museum.org, info@barnum-museum.org. A museum dedicated to master showman P. T. Barnum. Changing exhibits keep the museum interesting. The museum was closed for repairs at the book's publication time; check online before planning your visit.

CIRCUS CITY MUSEUM, 154 N. Broadway, Peru, Indiana, 765-472-3918, wwwperuamateurcircus.com, This museum is filled with photos, miniatures, displays, and costumes from circuses past. Varying hours and activities depending on dates. Call or go online before visiting.

CIRCUS HISTORICAL SOCIETY: www.circushistory.org. Online site dedicated to preserving, promoting, and sharing though education, the history and cultural significance of the circus and allied arts, past and present.

THE CIRCUS MUSEUM, 5401 Bay Shore Rd., Sarasota, Florida, 941-359-5700, www.ringling.org/circus-museum. See costumes, posters, photographs, and a wide variety of circus memorabilia. Of special interest is a permanent exhibit honoring famed circus performers.

CIRCUS WORLD MUSEUM, Baraboo, Wisconsin, 550 Water Street, Hwy. 113, Baraboo, Wisconsin, 608-356-8341, www.circusworldbaraboo.org. Great museum for all circus lovers. Changing exhibits and live shows at various times of the year. Check site for best time to visit depending on your interests.

CONEY ISLAND, Brooklyn, New York, 1208 Surf Avenue, Brooklyn, New York, www.coneyisland.com, info@coneyisland.com. Freak shows still abound at Coney Island. Not the Coney Island of days gone by, but still a fun place to visit. Experience the rides and Nathan's hot dogs. Don't miss the Coney Island Museum at 1208 Surf Avenue (between 12th Street & Henderson Walk).

GIBSONTON, FLORIDA, "Gibtown," "Showtown U.S.A.," twenty minutes south of Tampa, Florida, on US Highway 41: This town has been the winter home for a large population of circus and carnival sideshow performers for nearly seventy years. Few performers remain, but it is fun to walk the streets of a still-colorful town that was once the home of some of the most famous "freaks" in the world.

INTERNATIONAL CIRCUS HALL OF FAME: Big Top Circus & Circus Hall of Fame Museum, 3076 East Circus Lane, Peru, IN, 800-771-0241, www.circushalloffame.com. The "Circus Greats" enshrined in the Circus Hall of Fame, along with the colorful posters, wagons, models, and exhibits, bring the circus to life. Changing exhibits and dates so check website before going.

INTERNATIONAL MUSEUM OF FOLK ART, Santa Fe, New Mexico, 706 Camino Lejo, Santa Fe, New Mexico, 505-476-1200, www.internationalfolkart.org. Sideshow banners; not all on display, call in advance to check availability.

SCHUYLER COUNTY HISTORICAL SOCIETY MUSEUM, the corner of Washington and Lynn streets, Lancaster, MO 63548, no phone. The museum, open only in the summer, has dozens of circus-related photos, posters, and items on display that remind the visitor what an important part of American history circuses played before TV and the Internet. Also on display is an oil portrait of Robert "Bob" Melvin, "The Man with Two Faces," a former resident of Lancaster. If visiting this small town, you might want to travel to Arni Memorial Cemetery in Lancaster where Bob is buried.

SHOWMEN'S REST CEMETERY, 3541 N. North Blvd., Tampa, Florida (Section 12, Township 29, south Range 18, east NW corner of North Boulevard and Indiana Avenues). Final resting place for many of the sideshow and circus performers. Site has list of persons buried in the cemetery.

SHOWMEN'S REST, Woodlawn Cemetery, 7750 W. Cermak Road, Forest Park, Illinois, 847-691-1545. This is a 750 plot section of Woodlawn Cemetery where a mass grave of fifty-six to sixty-one employees of the Hagenbeck-Wallace Circus were interred. They were killed in the Hammond circus train wreck on June 22, 1918, at Ivanhoe, Indiana.

SYRACUSE UNIVERSITY LIBRARY /RONALD G. BECKER COLLECTION OF CHARLES EISENMANN PHOTOGRAPHS (1840–1930), Special Collections Research Center, Syracuse University Library, 222 Waverly Avenue, Syracuse, NY, http://scrc.syr.edu. More than one thousand photographs of nineteenth-century sideshows and circuses, most by photographer Charles Eisenmann or his successor Frank Wendt, the remainder by unknown photographers. Most of the photographs depict the physical abnormalities of humans and animals featured at these shows. Subjects include P. T. Barnum, the P. T. Barnum Firm (Barnum and Bailey Circus), and Tom Thumb. Also included are Becker's research notes, an 1865–1868 run of *The New York Clipper* (forerunner of *Billboard Magazine*), and various print (broadsides and posters) and nonprint circus memorabilia.

SOURCES

"A Banner Pick." *American Pickers*. The History Channel. 2013 Season.

Aberdeen (TX) Daily News. July 2, 1926, July 17, 1929, October 12, 1972.

Abilene (TX) Reporter. February 23, 1995.

Americansideshow.blog.com. "American Sideshow Blow-Off." Marc Hartzman, March 11, 2007.

Amusement Business Magazine. Various photographs. May 31, 2006.

Anderson (IN) Daily Bulletin. October, 28, 1959.

Anderson, Polly. "A Final Tribute to Those Who Left a Mark." *Seattle Times*. January 1, 2006.

Augusta (VA) Chronicle. November 14, 1923. October 30, 1940. October 28, 1954.

Alton Museum of History and Art, The. Alton, Illinois.

Anniston (AL) Star, The. February 8, 1937.

Arkansas Gazette. November 28, 1886. July 15, 1895.

Atlanta Constitution, The. November 14, 1901.

Bailey, Brad. "Carney Freaks Content with Life." October 11, 1981. "View From a Sideshow: A Vanishing Breed." October, 12, 1983.

Barnum Museum, The. Bridgeport, CT.

Barskey, Harry. *Being Different*. Canadian-American TV documentary. 1981.

Bates, Martin Van Buren. *The Kentucky River Giant: A Historical Sketch of Capt. Martin Van Buren Bates and Mrs. Bates Formerly Anna Swan*. (Trade booklet sold at performances.)

Benton, Joel. *How Barnum Made His Millions*. Chicago, IL. M. A. Donohue & Company. 1905.

Bismarck (ND) Tribune. April 4, 1890.

Boston Herald. December 20, 1903. November 29, 1905. October 28, 1906. June 20, 1906. September 16, 1906. December 30, 1907. March 3, 1920. June 2, 1933. September 13, 1935. May 21, 1943.

Boston Journal. January 31, 1887. February 7, 1887.

Boston Record American. December 16, 1967.

Brasscastlearts.blogspot.com. "General Tom Thumb." (Author unknown.) January 5, 2011.

Brannan, Dan. *Boy Giant*. Alton, IL. Alton Museum of History and Art. 2003.

Bridgeport (CT) Post. May 20, 1964. July 6, 1973.

Bridgeport (CT) Telegram. November 29, 1954.

Bridgeport, CT Public Library. Historical Collection.

Bristol Herald Courier, Virginia–Tennessean. Obituaries. March 19, 1985.

Brooklyn Daily Eagle. April 2, 1928.

Brownsville (TX) Herald. September 12, 1942.

Chambliss, Nina. Ancestry.com. "Hiram and Barney Davis, the Wild Men of Borneo."

Charleston Daily Mail, The. December 1, 1933.

Cincinnati Post. January 4, 1883. November 16, 1893.

Circus World Museum, www.circusworldbaraboo.org.

Columbus Ledger. August 5, 1903.

Council, Rodney. "Twins Stranger than the Siamese." *Our State (NC) Magazine*. November, 1954.

Crusader (Chicago). October 22, 1954.

Cumberland (MD) Evening Times. May4, 1977.

Daily Constitutional Union (Philadelphia). April 4, 1866.

Daily Illinois State Register. May 7, 1899. October 7, 1911. October 8, 1911.

Daily Inter Ocean (Chicago). August 1, 1890.

Daily News, The. (New York). May 31. 1957
Daily Register Gazette (Rockford, IL). May 26, 1930.
Dallas Morning News. March 4, 1899. July 15, 1929. March 29, 1932. December 1, 1941. April 9, 1955. July 18, 1955. January 19, 1963. October 17, 1967. October 12, 1972. August 19, 1973. October 18, 1975. September 27, 1981.
DeGenaro, Stephen A., "Fanny Mills, the Ohio Big Foot Girl." *Timeline Magazine.* September/October 1998 (Vol 15).
Denver Post. August 4, 1903. December 10, 1905. January 28, 1906.
Rocky Mountain News (CO). May 22, 1883.
Drummond Historical Society. Drummond, OK.
Eastern Arizona Courier News. August 22, 2012.
Eastern State Journal (White Plains, NY). February 25, 1911.
Encyclopedia of American Biographies. New York, NY. HarperCollins. 2nd edition. October 3, 1996.
Evansville (IN) Courier and Press. October 15, 1891. April 17, 1906. April 8, 1934.
Evening News (London). October 17, 1900. January 10, 1908.
Evening Post (Bristol, TN). June 8, 1903. January 27, 1913. .
Evening Star (Washington, DC). March 24, 1900. April 28, 1907.
Evening Tribune (Hornell, NY). April 11, 1905. January 25, 1932.
Fadner, Frederick. *The Gentle Giant: The Biography of Robert Pershing Wadlow.* Roswell, GA. Wipporwill Publication. 1981.
Fitchburg (MA) Sentinel. January 4, 1967.
Flint (MI) Journal. January 11, 1923.
Fort Wayne (IN) News and Sentinel. March 22, 1919.
GeneologyBank.com
Gettysburg Times, The. February 23, 1978.
Geyer, Celesta and Samuel Roen. *Diet or Die the Dolly Dimples Weight Reducing Plan.* New York, NY. Frederick Fell Publishers. 1968.
Globe, The. February 16, 1837.
Gould, George M, MD and Walter L. Pyle, MD. *Anomalies and Curiosities of Medicine,* reprint of Saunders, W. B. 1856.
Greensboro (NC) Daily News. March 31, 1922. May 4, 1978.
Griffith, Bill. *Zippy* (cartoon strip). May 2 (year unknown).
Guinness World Records. Guinness World Records Limited. 2006.
Hall, Ward. *My Very Unusual Friends.* Self-published. 1991.
Hix, John. "Strange As It Seems." *Greensboro (NC) Record.* October 13, 1920. September 15, 1923. January 27, 1932. September 17, 1936.
Hoffman, Renoda. *It Happened in Old White Plains.* Efficiency Printing Co. 1989.
Holtman, Jerry. *Freak Show Man, the Autobiography of Harry Lewiston as Told to Jerry Holtman.* Holloway House Publishing Co. 1968.
Horan, James D. *Matthew Brady: Historian with a Camera.* New York, NY. Crown Publishers, Inc. 1955.
Howell, James D. and Peter Ford. *The True Story of the Elephant Man.* London. Allison & Busby. 1955.
Illustrated London News, The. July 31, 1878.
Independent Press-Telegram (Long Beach, CA). December 13, 1964.
Indiana Evening Gazette, The. November 26, 1924.
Jewish Chronicle (UK). September 19, 1930.
Johnson, Forrest. "Lessons from Bob Melvin, the Two-Faced Man." *The Reader.* August 23. 2002.
Kansas City Journal, The. September 24, 1909.
Kansas City Star. February 6, 1885.
Kansas State Census. 1885.
Kingsport Times News (TN). June 24, 1951.
Klem, Amelia. "A Life of Her Own Choosing Anna Gibbons' Fifty Years as a Tattooed lady." *Wisconsin Magazine of History.* Spring, 2006.
Kokomo Tribune (IN). February 27, 1930.
Kunhardt, Phillip B., Jr., Phillip B. Kunhardt, III, and Peter W. Kunhardt. *P. T. Barnum: America's Greatest Showman.* Westminister, Maryland. Alfred A. Knopf. 1995.
Lancaster Eagle Gazette (PA). August 11, 1928.
Lebanon Daily News (PA). June 2, 1971.
Library of Congress. Prints and Photographs Online Catalog Collection. "Life Goes to a County Fair." *Life Magazine.* September, 1937.
Lukas, Judith. "Princess Judy Historical Tattoo Art." Facebook access.
Macy, Beth and Jeff McCaffery. "Performing…And Profitable" *Roanoke Times (VA).* July 9, 2001. "Out of the Spotlight." July 12, 2001.
Macon Telegraph (GA). March 25, 1882. January 29, 1885.
Macon Weekly (GA). May 14, 1872.
Martell, Joanne. *Millie-Christine: Fearfully and Wonderfully Made.* Winston-Salem, NC. John F. Blair, Publisher. 2000.
Mannix, Daniel P. *Freaks We Who Are Not As Others.* Juno Books/Juno Publishing. 1999.
Mansfield News Journal (OH). March 13, 1937.
Marietta Journal (GA). August 30, 1994.
Melone, Mary Jo. "Without a Sideshow A Clown Eyes His Next Stage." *St. Petersburg Times (FL).* January 25, 2004.
Mifflin, Margot. *Bodies of Subversion: A Secret History of Women and Tattoo.* Brooklyn, NY. powerHouse Books. 2013.
Monte, Mitchell. "Home with Unique History Hits Market." *Charlotte Observer (NC), Winton-Salem Journal.* April 30, 2003.
Morning Herald (PA). April 15, 1930. July 24, 1944.
Mourning Star (NC). November 30, 1921.
Mountain Democrat (CA). August 27, 1892.
Nevada State Journal. November 28, 1936. March 12, 1937.
New Hampshire Patriot and State Gazette. January 27, 1881.
New Haven Register (CT). January 15, 1887.
News and Courier, The (SC). November 11, 1905.
New York Passenger Lists, 1820–1957.
New York Post, April 7, 1931.
New York Times, The. August 31, 1883. February 25, 1885. October 27-28, 1889. April 16, 1889. August 15, 1891. May 5, 1924. November 18, 2001.
North Adams Transcript (MA). March 8, 1929. May 23, 1957.
Oakland Tribune. October 29, 1956. January 9, 1967.
Oelwein Daily Register (IA). June 19-20, 1912.
Ogden Standard Examiner, The (Ontario). November 30, 1936.
Ohio. Bureau of Vital Statistics. Birth, Death, and Marriage Official Records.
Omaha World Herald. January 20, 1895. February 25, 1888. August 24, 1923. January 15, 1932. June 2, 1933. April 6, 1937. August 9, 1955. April 8, 1970. October 12, 1972.
Oregonian. September 10, 1922. August 15, 1937.
Petersen, Brent. *Parade Magazine.* March 1, 1981.
Patriot (NY). March 3, 1893. February 26, 1895.
Peoria Evening Star. May 23, 1933.
Philadelphia Inquirer. November 23, 1890. September 24, 1891. October 18, 1891. October 23, 1891. January 9, 1892. December 2, 1894. February 10–11, 1900. February 18-19, 1900. February 25, 1900. January 9, 1921. January 11, 1921.
Plain Dealer (OH). May 3, 1866. February 1, 1891. January 3, 1893. August 21, 1923. November 17/19, 1933. November 30, 1941. June 26, 1977.
Portland New Age (OR). March 24, 1900.
Reno Evening Gazette (NV). March 22, 1962.
Repository (OH). January 23, 1884. April 30, 1884. July 21, 1895. July 30, 1933.
Richmond Times Dispatch (VA). April 13, 1922. February 19, 1928. June 23, 1952. August 25, 1934.
Riverside Independent Enterprise (CA). April 30, 1903.
Rockford Republic (IL). April 22, 1922.
Saginaw News (MI). April 28, 1883.
Salina Journal (KS). June 24, 1951.
Salt Lake Telegram (UT). April 11, 1903.
San Antonio Express (TX). October 28, 1905
San Diego Union. March 29, 1925. JANUARY 26-28/31, 1932. February 1, 1932. April 6, 1941.
Sandusky Register (OH). February 1, 1919.
Sandusky Star-Journal, The (OH). November 23,1918.
Saxton, A. H. (edited by). *Selected Letters of P. T. Barnum.* Columbia University Press. 1983.
Shank, Ann A. "Promotor Brought Talents to Sarasota". Sarasota County History Center. Journals of Yesteryear, www.sarasotahistoryalive.com. 2007.
Shapiro, Stephanie. "The Second Life of Johnny Eck A Decade after His Death." *Baltimore Sun,* The. April 4, 2001.
Shelby County, OH. Official Archives and Records for Sidney, Ohio.
Sloan, Mark, Roger Manley, and Michelle Van Parys. *Dear Mr. Ripley A Compendium of Curioddities from the Believe It or Not! Archives.* Ripley Entertainment, Inc. 1993.
Sniqurowicz, Diana. "Sex, Simians, and Spectacles in Nineteenth-Century France." *Canadian Journal of History.* April, 1999.
Springfield Republican (IL). February 3, 1928.
Springfield Union (IL). August 2, 1954. November 1, 1968.
State (SC). April 22, 1897.
State Times Advocate (LA). February 23, 1938. April 27, 1954. November 6, 1956. March 1, 1981.
St. Albans Daily Messenger (VT). July 23, 1994.
St. Louis Republic (MO). January 31, 1890. October 10, 1891.
St. Petersburg Times (FL). Obituaries. February 7, 2001.
Sun (NY). April 9, 1896. September 19, 1915. December 12, 1920.
Syracuse Herald (NY). January 24, 1930.
The Learning Channel TLC. *The World's Oldest Conjoined Twins Move Home.* (TV documentary.) 2010.
Thomas, Rosemary Garland (edited by). *Freakery.* New York and London. New York University Press. 1996.
Times Bulletin (OH). August 20, 1955.
Tomlinson, Tommy. "A Story of Two Sisters, Together, Always." *Charlotte Observer, The (NC).* December 7, 1997.
Trenton Evening News (NJ). April 6, 1913. February 15, 1938. March 3, 1975.
Troy Record (NY). January 9, 1967.
Truth (CA). March 20, 1882.
Tucson Daily Citizen (AZ). August 17, 1976.
United States Census. 1850. 1900. 1920. 1930. 1940.
US City Directories. 1933.
United States World War I Draft Registration Cards. 1917–1918.
Valley Independent, The (PA). May 2, 1979.
Virginia. Bureau of Vital Statistics. Birth, Death, and Marriage Official Records.
Vita, Tricia. "Step Right Up!" *Art & Antiques.* April 4, 1997.
Viagas, Robert. "The Admirable Admiral Dot A Short History Lesson." *Suburbia Today (White Plains, NY).* January 26, 1986.
Winston Salem Journal (NC). December 7, 1924.
Wisconsin Rapids Daily Tribune. September 17, 1929.
Xenia Daily Gazette (OH). December 10, 1965.
Yuma Daily Sun (AZ). April 6, 1962

PHOTO SOURCES

MOST OF THE PHOTOGRAPHS USED IN THIS BOOK ARE IN THE PUBLIC DOMAIN.

www.1stdib.com
www.2.lieu.edu/cwis
www.365thingslearnedblogspot.com
www.5.plala.or.jp.com
www.aglimpse.com
www.altonmuseum.com
www.ancestry.com
www.andrethegiant.com
www.anima.x51.org
www.answers.com
www.anyten.blogspot.com
www.apocatastasisblog.blog
www.art.com
www.artnet.com
www.artsandmusicpa.com
www.barnstablepatriot.com
www.bastabalkane.com
www.bbc.co.uk
www.bestabalkana.com
www.billybarty.com
www.bizarremag.com
www.blueridgecountry.com
www.bodybuilding.com
www.bookpatrol.net
www.buzzfeed.com
www.captcook-ne.co.uk
www.casagrande-museo.blogspot.com
www.celebgreat.com
www.chickenopolis.com
www.chnm.gmu.edu
www.circushistory.org
www.circusnospin.blogspot.com
www.classichorror.free-online.co.uk
www.cnn.com
www.coneyisland.com
www.corbis.com
www.cuantomide.net
www.cultofweird.com
www.curiosity-killed-the-cat.com
www.czarofbizarre.com (Johnny Meah)
www.delcampe.net
www.demagogue.com
www.demensionmagazine.com
www.disabilitymuseum.org
www.docsmidwaycookhouse.com
www.dreadloki.com
www.dulltooldimbulb.blogspot.com
wwww.eBay.com
www.ephemeralnewyork.wordpress.com
www.etsy.com
www.enidnew.com,
www.entertainmentdesign.com
www.eventful.com
www.examiner.com
www.fansshare.com
www.fiercefatties.com
www.findagrave.com
www.flicker.com
www.forensicgenealogy.info
www.freaks.monsters.com
www.fringepop.blogspot.com
www.from-bedroom-to-study.blogspot.com
www.frontierhistory.blogspot,com
www.genesisbgiants.com
www.getbig.com
www.grand-bazaar.tumblr.com
www.guinnessworldrecords.com
www.haaretz.com
www.history.amusement-parks.com
www.ibtimes.co.uk
www.imdb.com/biographies
www.jenaichinnews.blogspot.com
www.jonmwessel.wordpress.com
www.johnstownhistory.blogspot.com
www.jsitton.pwp.blueyonder.co.uk/elephan
man/dates.htm
www.kohlerfoundation.org
www.kootation.com
www.Lafemmeabarbe.blogspot.com
www.library.umass.edu
www.lostmuseum.cuny.edu
www.members.optusnet.com.au
www.memory.loc.gov
www.miista.com (Laura Villasenin)
www.millarca-millarcu.blogspot.com
www.missinglinkclassichorror.co.uk
www.missioncreep.com
www.movies2.nytimes.com
www.myspace.com/tifgroves
www.naid.sppsr.ucla.edu
www.nat-n-bio.santotomas.edu
www.noticiastribo.blogspot.com
www.nytimes.com
www.nygeschichte.blogspot.com
www.online.no/innhold.com
www.ohiohistorycentral.org
www.pacificislandtravel.com
www.patkelly.com
www.pbs.org
www.phreeque.com
www.phsc.ca
www.pintgerest.com
www.princessjudy.com
www.postkarten-archive.de/taet.com
www.quasi-modo.net
www.rarediseases.about.com
www.rootsweb.com
www.sandowmuseum.com
www.sandowplus.co.uk
www.showhistory.com
www.sideshowworld.com
www.sideshow-art.com
www.skinillustrations.cardpress.com
www.skyrunner.com
www.slamcanoe.ca
www.snarkout.org
www.societypages.org
www.stevenbolin.com
www.stevequayle.com
www.stunninginterestingfacts.blogspot.
com
www.sugarchurch.tumblr.com
www.tatliaskim.org
www.tattooarchive.com
www.thetallestman.com
www.tintanapple.com
www.travsd.wordpress.com
www.thehumanmarvels.com
www.themafucage2.tumblr.com
www.theremainsoftheweb.com
www.thesocietypages.org
www.thescotsman.com
www.time.com
www.tintanapele.com
www.toplessrobot.com
www.twinstuff.com
www.docsouth.unc.edu
www.unknown-history.tumblr.com
www.virginiacaputo.com
www.vintagevandalizm.com
www.viola.bz/hairy-men-and-then-fake.
com
www.uwm.edu
www.washingtonpost.com; "The Road
Less Traveled"; Kurlantzkk, Joshua;
9/19/2004
www.webmd.com
www.welcometobaltimore.com
www.westland.net
www.weirdnj.com
www.wildbeautyworld.com
www.worthpoint.com
www.yelp.com/biz_photos
www.youtube.com
www.zagria.blogspot.com
www.zazzle.com

INDEX

SPECIAL FREAKS INCLUDED IN THIS BOOK (IN ALPHABETICAL ORDER)

THE AUTHORS

MARY BRETT was born into a family of antique dealers and claims she loves the olden days much more than modern times. This is her third book. She holds a BFA from Virginia Commonwealth University and lives in Richmond, Virginia. She became interested in sideshow performers after seeing the 1932 cult classic *Freaks*. Mary spent over three years researching the lives of the 152 performers presented in this book.

STEVAN GOULD was born in San Francisco. He has traveled extensively, including two years spent riding freight trains across America. The circus is in his blood. He is related to William C. Coup, P. T. Barnum's business partner, and he worked for a summer with Stanley Shows of Hot Springs, Arkansas, where he experienced carnival life first-hand. Today he lives a much quieter life in Richmond, Virginia, but is still inclined to occasionally give in to wanderlust and hit the road.